Date Loaned

Fe 13 39 M			
Apr 7 '41			
My 4 '43 H			
My 14 7 W			
May 0 50 NC			
My 3 52 MP			
My 8 52 B			
MY 10 '63			
AP 22 '66			
MY 6 '66			
MY 1 '70			
SEP 1 4 198			

PRENTICE-HALL POLITICAL SCIENCE SERIES
Schuyler C. Wallace, Ph.D., Editor

PRESSURE POLITICS
IN
NEW YORK

PRENTICE-HALL
POLITICAL SCIENCE SERIES

Schuyler C. Wallace, Ph.D., Editor

CHINESE POLITICAL THOUGHT, *by* Elbert Duncan
Thomas, United States Senator from Utah.

A SYLLABUS IN AMERICAN GOVERNMENTAL ORGAN-
IZATION, *by* A. Gordon Dewey, Ph.D., Brooklyn College, New York.

POLITICS, PRESSURES, AND THE TARIFF, *by* Elmer E.
Schattschneider, Ph.D., Wesleyan University.

PRESSURE POLITICS IN NEW YORK, *by* Belle Zeller,
Ph.D., Brooklyn College, New York.

THE CARIBBEAN SINCE 1900, *by* Chester Lloyd
Jones, Ph.D., University of Wisconsin.

HISTORY OF POLITICAL PHILOSOPHY, *by* Thomas I.
Cook, B.Sc., University of California at Los
Angeles.

Other titles in course of preparation

PRESSURE POLITICS
IN
NEW YORK

*A Study of Group Representation
Before the Legislature*

by
BELLE ZELLER
*Assistant Professor of Government
Brooklyn College, New York*

New York
PRENTICE-HALL, INC.
1937

TO THE MEMORY OF

MY MOTHER
AND
MY FATHER

Preface

T ENURE in public office was never more dependent upon the "consent of the governed" than it is today. As never before, popular support, whether passive or active, is secured and maintained through the clever and skillful manipulation of the forces of public opinion. This is inevitable in a society where revolutionary technological developments in the channels of communication and transportation facilities are taking place on a wide scale. The mass contacts of the radio, the newspaper, and the school particularly, and the "streamlined" transportation progress on land, on sea, and in the air have made intellectual and physical isolation more difficult.

Rugged individualism in the interrelated fields of economics and politics may eventually meet the fate of annihilation. The complexity of a machine society makes the economic struggle for the survival of the individual more difficult and necessitates greater governmental intervention and supervision. In the course of these significant changes, the process of government has become a group process in which organized minorities have today become so closely identified with the formal governmental structure itself as to constitute the real center of political and economic power.

Students of politics have only in recent years turned their attention to a practical analysis of this problem. While a splendid beginning has been made with significant studies, these studies are of a fragmentary nature, confined largely to the national arena.[1] The very character of the American constitutional system compels an examination of pressure

---

[1] See especially E. P. Herring, *Group Representation Before Congress,* Baltimore, John Hopkins Press, 1929, and *Public Administration and the Public Interest,* New York, McGraw-Hill, 1936; H. L. Childs, *Labor and Capital in National Politics,* Columbus, The Ohio State University Press, 1930; P. H. Odegard, *Pressure Politics,* New York, Columbia University Press, 1928; E. E. Schattschneider, *Politics, Pressures and the Tariff,* New York, Prentice-Hall, 1935. See also, H. D. Lasswell, R. D. Casey, and B. L. Smith, *Propaganda and Promotional Activities—An Annotated Bibliography,* Minneapolis, The University of Minnesota Press, 1935; H. L. Childs, *A Reference Guide to the Study of Public Opinion,* Princeton, Princeton University Press, 1934.

group activity before a state legislature if the rôle of organized groups is to be realistically understood. Although the totality of interests represented at a state Capitol is indeed enormous, it has hitherto escaped extensive study.

The purpose of this book, then, is to present a picture of the interplay of statewide pressure groups as they come into contact with the legislature of the Empire State, and by so doing to indicate their power and influence in the process of government itself.[2]

In a study of this character very little material could be gained from secondary sources. The author was therefore forced to lean heavily upon the information secured through correspondence and interviews with those who had intimate knowledge of the organizations under investigation. Much valuable information was secured from the files of those organizations that were good enough to open them to the author, as well as from their annual reports and bulletins. During the five-year period that this study has been in preparation, the author has traveled over a good portion of the State of New York and interviewed well over one hundred persons. Chief among these have been the legislative agents and officers of the associations, the legislative leaders, clerks, and other members of the New York Senate and Assembly, members of the state administrative departments, newspaper correspondents, and students in the field of political science.

To acknowledge here all who have graciously helped in making this book possible, would be difficult indeed, although a number of them have been mentioned in footnotes. The author feels, however, that she must take this opportunity to acknowledge her deep gratitude to Professor Schuyler C. Wallace of Columbia University for suggesting that this study be undertaken and for his advice and counsel which were of inestimable value in the preparation of the manuscript; to Professors Arthur W. Macmahon and Joseph P. Chamberlain of Columbia University for their kindly criticism; and to Pro-

---

[2] The relations of pressure groups with the state administrative and judicial branches of the government are not within the scope of this study. However, the author realizes that it is no more possible to completely divorce the activities of pressure groups in the three branches of government than it is to divorce the activities of the divisions of government themselves under our system of separation of powers. See *infra*, pp. 240–242.

fessor Charles E. Merriam of the University of Chicago for
his friendly counsel.

The writer is also indebted to the following who have given
generously of their time in interviews or in reading parts of
the manuscript: Mr. John M. O'Hanlon of the New York
State Federation of Labor; Mr. Mark A. Daly of Associated
Industries, Inc.; Mr. E. S. Foster of the New York State Farm
Bureau Federation; Mr. L. R. Simons, Director of Extension
of the New York State Colleges of. Agriculture and Home
Economics, Cornell University; Mr. H. E. Babcock of Co-
operative G. L. F. Exchange, Inc.; Mr. E. R. Eastman, editor
of *American Agriculturist*; Misses Elsie M. Bond and H. Ida
Curry of the State Charities Aid Association; and Mr. W. E.
Hannan, librarian of the Legislative Reference Section of the
New York State Library.

Finally, to the members of her family, particularly her sisters, Florence Silverman and Harriet Zeller, and her brother,
Edward W. Zeller, the author's obligation is beyond measure
and recompense for the many hours they placed at her disposal in the performance of tasks too numerous to mention.

BELLE ZELLER

New York City,
February, 1937.

Contents

CHAPTER I

Introduction

IN spite of the ever growing sphere of federal activity, the state governments still possess a tremendous sweep of legislative and executive power, which is directed toward many more variegated and diverse objectives than is the power of the central government itself. In no state is this fact more fully illustrated than in the State of New York. For the most part the specific application of this power is the resultant of the play of political, social, and economic forces, sometimes organized in the form of political parties; more often, in the form of pressure groups.

Nowhere, in consequence, is it more appropriate to study the conflict of these groups which dominate so large a part of our legislative development than it is in the Empire State.

These interest groups take their rise from a variety of elements which make the complex of forces in New York State typical of those at play in the larger industrial states of the Union, even though in certain particulars they may be unique to New York. The most significant grow out of the sharp cleavages in the state itself. In broad outline these cleavages are based on certain fundamental divisions; most influential among these are the differences between the rural and urban parts of the state; between capital and labor; and between the various nationalities, races, and religions which go to make up the heterogeneous population both of the metropolitan area and of the state itself.

Despite the fact that ten and one half of the twelve and one half million individuals who constitute New York's population are concentrated in seven great metropolitan areas,[1] the state possesses large open stretches of agricultural

---

[1] In fact 84 per cent of the state's population is found in the belt formed by the Mohawk and Hudson Valleys, an area 500 miles long covering only 16 per cent of the land area of the state. Six of the seven metropolitan areas of the state—Buffalo, Rochester, Syracuse, Utica, Albany, New York City—

country which support a population of more than two
million people.[2] In point of agricultural income New York
ranks fifth among all the states in the Union, and in several
agricultural products it leads the nation. In dairying, for
example, it contends vigorously for first place with Wisconsin.[3]
Consequently, despite the preponderantly industrial and commercial character of the state, its agricultural interests
are a factor of no small importance. Nor is their influence
in any way diminished by the fact that, due to certain
peculiarities of New York's political system—peculiarities
which will be discussed later [4]—this agricultural bloc possesses political power out of all proportion to its numerical
strength.

The natural resources of the state, moreover, have contributed to the development of a highly diversified industrial
and commercial organization. In this connection its water
power and mineral resources should, perhaps, be mentioned
first. The water power resources of the state are among the
most important in the country.[5] With the largest sources of

are included in this area. Binghamton is the seventh area. The urban population of the state is 83.6 per cent of the total and 66 per cent of the urban
population lives in New York City. During the past 30 years, 99.5 per cent
of the total increase in population in the state has taken place in the seven
metropolitan areas. *Cf. Report of the New York State Planning Board,*
Jan. 14, 1935, pp. 22, 23. See Alexander C. Flick, ed., *History of the State
of New York,* 8 vols., New York, Columbia University Press, 1933–1935.

[2] In 1930 only 267,373 individuals, 10 years of age or older were gainfully
employed in agriculture in New York State. This represents two per cent of
those so employed in the United States.

[3] Yet the New York State Commission for the Revision of the Tax Laws
reported that from 1925–1930, the New York farmer faced an average annual
deficit of $288 per farm. See *Second Report* of this commission, 1933, p. 132.
Farm land in New York State has been continuously abandoned since 1880.
From 1880 to 1930, the area of farm land had been reduced by an average of
100,000 acres a year until, in 1930, there remained only 17,980,000 acres including approximately 160,000 farms. Farm acreage in New York State is less than
two per cent of the farm acreage of the country. It has been estimated
that the rugged hill sections of New York contain about 5.8 million acres
of submarginal farm and idle land. The New York State Planning Board
recommended recently that at least 4.5 million acres of these submarginal
lands, constituting the "problem" area in New York, be gradually acquired
by the state in a 20 year program to be used for timber production, game and
wild life protection, water protection, and public recreation. *Report of the
New York State Planning Board, op. cit.,* pp. 29, 32.

[4] *Infra,* ch. IV, IX.

[5] New York has the largest market for power of any state. *Cf. Report of
the New York State Planning Board, op. cit.,* p. 55.

water power, actual and potential, concentrated in the
Niagara and St. Lawrence Rivers, it has been estimated that
about three and a half million horsepower could be produced
from the streams of the state.[6] At the moment central power
plants, capable of producing five and a quarter million kilo-
watts are operating within the state's borders. With these
tremendous sources of power available, it is little wonder that
the Empire State has long since become predominantly
industrial in character. Nor has the existence of mineral
deposits—limestone, clay, gypsum, sand, gravel, salt, natural
gas, petroleum, and iron ore—in any way retarded this development. Moreover, New York enjoys unique advantages
of water transportation including the greatest port in the
country: New York Harbor. In consequence, there is little
cause for surprise in the fact that New York leads all other
states in the number of persons employed in all categories of
commerce and industry.[7] The largest number of these is to be
found in manufacturing, trade, transportation, communication,
and the clerical occupations.[8] In 1929, for example, more than
one million wage earners were engaged in manufacturing
alone, producing goods valued at almost ten billion dollars
and earning in wages one and a half billion dollars.[9]

---

[6] A total generating capacity of 1,451,000 horsepower has been developed,
based on powers procurable 60 per cent of the time. Approximately half of
the state's two million undeveloped horsepower can be obtained from the
proposed St. Lawrence project. So tremendous is this potential water power
that in recognition of it the Power Authority of the State of New York has
been created. *Ibid.*, p. 57; *New York Legislative Manual*, 1935, p. 503.

[7] In 1930, when New York State's inhabitants constituted 10.2 per cent of
the nation's total population, they also constituted 11.1 per cent of the total
number of persons in the United States, 10 years of age or older, gainfully
employed.

[8] Between 1910 and 1930 there was a shift in occupational employment from
manual to "white collar" workers. In these years there was a decrease from
49.6 per cent to 38.9 per cent in the number of persons engaged in productive
occupations, such as manufacturing, agriculture, and forestry. On the other
hand, the number of clerical workers increased markedly from 35.6 per cent
to 43.2 per cent. See *Report of the New York State Planning Board, op. cit.*,
p. 81.

[9] In New York City there were 51 per cent of these wage earners who
received 55.3 per cent of the wages and the goods produced equalled 60.4
per cent of the state's total. When the economic depression had greatly
decreased the actual number of these workmen, New York City led all other
cities by an even higher proportion. In 1933, New York City's wage earners
equalled 53.3 per cent of the state's total, and earned 58.1 per cent of the
wages and the value of goods produced equalled 62.2 per cent. The actual

Very significant is the fundamental conflict between the owners and managers, and the employees. The latter may or may not be organized in labor unions or benevolent associations. The former usually have some sort of professional associations or more informal organizations through which they can iron out their differences, and whenever it is necessary present a united front to the public.

Needless to say, there is no such thing as solidarity of point of view at all times within these two basic groups. Among the business groups such unity is difficult, indeed. As has already been indicated, the business world falls into a number of distinct categories: manufacturing, mining, banking, insurance, real estate, transportation, and commerce. Within each of these groups are subordinate interests which are sometimes allied and sometimes in conflict. Thus, within the field of transportation are the railroads, the street cars, the automotive concerns, and the shipping lines. And even within these sub categories, individual corporations pursue their independent policies, as frequently motivated by the desire for individual profits as by the common interests of the industry as a whole.

Partly as a result of the industrial development of the state, and partly as a result of our historic immigration policy, there has settled in New York such a diversity of nationalities, races, and religions that the population of the Empire State today is one of the most heterogeneous in the nation—as heterogeneous as any similar geographic area anywhere in the world.

------

numbers in the state in 1933 were: 733,452 workers; $754,366,881 in wages earned; and $4,596,257,962 value of the goods produced. *Cf. U. S. Biennial Census of Manufactures,* 1933, U. S. Department of Commerce, Bureau of the Census. The inspection of factories engaged in manufacturing conducted by the New York State Department of Labor in 1932 disclosed that only 63 factories out of the total of 42,338 in the state each employed 1,000 or more workers, aggregating 120,678 employees or 13.3 per cent of the total for the state. Thirty-nine of these 63 factories are found outside of the metropolitan area with 82,640 employees, whereas most of the small factories were found in the metropolitan area (comprising New York City, Long Island, Rockland and Westchester counties). Of factories employing 24 persons or less, 28,831 with 193,917 employees were in the metropolitan area and 6,792 factories with 40,149 employees were in the remainder of the state. *Cf. Directory of New York State Manufacturers,* 1932, Vol. II, p. 5, published by the New York State Department of Labor.

Thus 61 per cent of the total population of the state is of foreign origin; [10] 66 per cent of these reside in New York City; 25 per cent are scattered throughout the other urban centers of the state; whereas, only 9 per cent have become an integral part of the countryside. One of every three in New York City's population, consequently, is foreign born; approximately eight of every ten are of foreign origin. Although the percentage of those of foreign origin in other urban centers of the state is somewhat lower—one out of every two—it is nevertheless sufficiently high to affect the cultural tone of each individual city.[11]

Thus, if there were no economic differences between the city and the countryside, this one factor in and of itself might explain to a considerable degree the differences between the urban and rural points of view.

No less important, moreover, are certain religious factors. Curious though it may seem to the uninformed, there are more church members in New York State in proportion to its population than there are in any other large state east of the Mississippi River. Of every hundred persons, resident in New York, sixty-one are affiliated with some religious organization or other.[12] These religious organizations for the most part fall into three categories: Jewish, Roman Catholic, and Protestant. Once again, however, the geographic distribution is uneven. The 1,765,000 Jewish congregants in New York City constitute 92 per cent of the Jewish congregation throughout the state. Similarly the 1,733,954 Roman Catholics in New York City constitute 55.6 per cent of the total number of that denomination in the state. On the other hand the 500,000 Protestants in New York City comprise only about 30 per cent of the adherents of various Protestant denominations in the state.[13] Still another factor, conse-

---

[10] Of these 25.4 per cent are foreign born and 35.6 per cent are natives of foreign or mixed parentage. Figures are based on the white stock in the state. The non-white population is 437,773.

[11] The foreign white stock in New York State embraces 7,676,347 persons. All except 719,699 are found in the urban areas.

[12] The total number for the state is 6,796,142. It is interesting to note that though New York State contains only 10.2 per cent of the nation's population, it possesses 12.4 per cent of the nation's church members.

[13] U. S. Department of Commerce, Bureau of Census, *Religious Bodies*, 1926, Vol. I. See also pamphlet issued by the Chamber of Commerce of the

quently, contributes to the difference between the rural and urban centers of New York.

Furthermore, due consideration must be given to the unique position occupied by New York City in relation to the rest of the state. Within the boundaries of Greater New York is a majority of the total population of the state. In contrast to upstate New York, this population is composed chiefly of foreign born or the children of foreign born. In other words the metropolitan area is dominated by the newer immigration which has come from a non-English speaking background bringing with it religious beliefs and customs alien to those of the so-called native born American or the children of the older immigration.[14] In addition, the politics of the City of New York has long been dominated by a political machine which, rightly or wrongly, has in the opinion of the residents of upstate New York symbolized the worst in American politics.

The total consequence of all these factors is that there is a very distinct difference between the point of view of the metropolitan area and the point of view of upstate New York.[15]

Thus there is in New York State a diversity of interests indeed. On the one hand, there is a powerful agricultural interest which is itself capable of subdivision into significant segments: the dairying, the fruit growing, and the truck gardening interests. On the other hand, there is an industrial interest which can also be subdivided into its various elements. Most significant among these are the categories already indicated. No less important is the division in the industrial field between capital and labor.

State of New York, *Items of Interest Concerning New York State Products, Manufactures, Finances, and Government,* 1928–1929.

[14] The countries represented in the largest number among the 2,293,400 foreign born whites of New York City are Russia, Italy, Poland, Germany, and the Irish Free State. Significantly, 27.1 per cent of these arrived between 1920 and 1930.

[15] In fact, this cleavage has actually been expressed in the suggestion that New York City and the surrounding counties be erected into a separate state. Before the home rule amendment to the state constitution was accepted in 1923, the "hardy perennial" State of Manhattan bill was annually introduced into the State Legislature for many years. See *New York Times,* Jan. 12, 1923, and *New York American,* Apr. 4, 1921.

Finally, there are certain geographic and sociological factors which have been productive of a surprising degree of sectionalism even within the confines of a single state. Chief among the latter, are the factors of nationality, race, and religion. The geographic factors which characterize the state have led to the growth not only of the great metropolitan area around New York City but also to the development of prosperous agricultural regions along the Mohawk and elsewhere; and also to the rise of important manufacturing towns at strategic places throughout the state.

It is because of this heterogeneity, making as it does for conflicts in interest and in points of view, that New York State presents such an absorbing study.

Inevitably, these conflicting forces organize into various and sundry associations devoted to the defense of their common interests. These are the organizations; these are the conflicts which in a very real sense constitute the most vital aspect of New York politics—an aspect which has heretofore been, to a surprising degree, overlooked by our local political commentators. Moreover, this is the field of politics in which there still exist many of the most serious problems of democratic government, problems to which little attention has as yet been given.

To an analysis of the activities of the more important of these pressure groups, as they attempt to influence the course of legislative policy; and to a solution of some of the more pressing problems created by their activities, the pages which follow are devoted.

CHAPTER II

Organized Labor and Its Allies

THE most vigorous pressure at Albany proceeds from those groups that exist to advance labor legislation. Of these, three merit particular attention: the New York State Federation of Labor, the Women's Trade Union League of New York, and the Consumers' League of New York.

New York State Federation of Labor

Most powerful of such organizations is the New York State Federation of Labor. Its organization, in April, 1864, was precipitated [1] by the favorable consideration given to the "Folger Anti-Trades Union Strike Bill" by the Senate committee to which it had been referred. As a result of mass meetings of representatives of labor unions held in New York and Albany, a Joint Committee presented to both houses of the legislature petitions bearing the names of thousands of workmen, and the bill was consequently killed.

The success of this opposition to the Folger bill led to the formation in Albany, in February and September, 1865, of a statewide association known as the Workingmen's Assembly of the State of New York. The purpose of the new organization, carrying on the work of the Joint Committee, was to act as a watchdog in the interests of labor. In 1898 the state branch of the American Federation of Labor was fused with the Workingmen's Assembly, and the resulting combination was named the Workingmen's Federation of the State of New York. In 1910, the name was changed to the New York State Federation of Labor, which now purported to represent all organized labor, both men and women, in the

---

[1] The writer is indebted for these facts to the historical pamphlet issued by the New York State Federation of Labor: *When and Where and by Whom the New York State Labor Movement Was Given Life, 1864–1923*, 1923, pp. 3, 4; and to the *Official Yearbook of the New York State Federation of Labor*, 1933, p. 43.

state, exclusive of the four railroad brotherhoods. Though its name has changed, its purpose has remained, and still remains, the same: agitation to secure the enactment of measures beneficial to workers and the repeal of all laws inimical to their interests.[2]

The New York State Federation of Labor represents the largest constituency of any state federation of labor in the United States. With it are directly affiliated almost 800 unions, the central labor bodies of the various cities, many district trade councils, and state organizations of various crafts and occupations. The Federation thus represents, directly and indirectly, approximately 850,000 of the state's wage earners.[3] Approximately 55 per cent of these wage earners live in the City of New York.

The income of the Federation is derived chiefly from dues, initiation fees, and paid advertisements in its *Official Year-book*. Dues are based on the payment of a per capita tax of 1½ cents per member per month by affiliated unions, and are paid into the Federation's treasury quarterly; but no local group may pay dues of less than three dollars per year. The central labor bodies and the trade councils are required to pay $15 per year.[4] In addition, local and central bodies pay an initiation fee of $5. The chief items of expenditure are the salaries of the president, the secretary-treasurer, and clerks, and the operating expenses of the Federation office, the annual conventions, and the executive council meetings. A picture of the financial operations of the Federation over a period of fifteen years is to be found in the following table.

---

[2] Historical pamphlet, *op. cit.* See also *Bulletin of the New York State Federation of Labor*, Oct., 1931. In the *Declaration of the Purposes of the New York State Federation of Labor*, adopted Aug., 1929, the Federation expresses its faith in the democratic form of government existing in the United States and in the State of New York.

[3] This does not include the membership of the four railroad brotherhoods in the state. *Cf.* letter of John M. O'Hanlon, Secretary-Treasurer of the New York State Federation of Labor, Oct. 7, 1935.

[4] *Constitution of the New York State Federation of Labor*, Art. X, Sec. 1.

FINANCES OF THE NEW YORK STATE FEDERATION OF LABOR

(Fiscal Year August 1 through July 31)

Year Ending July 31	Total Receipts Incl. Cash Balances On Hand	Income From per Capita Tax & Initiation Fee	Income From Advertisements	Total Expenditures	Amount On Hand in Cash & Investments
1921....	$40,984.29	$21,457.74	$11,799.86	$37,916.49	$4,630.90
1922....	39,537.72	22,589.21	8,701.63	37,281.74	2,321.62
1923....	32,689.90	22,919.90	6,561.50	29,901.18	2,856.98
1924....	36,219.34	21,694.20	11,494.25	30,676.90	5,742.44
1925....	48,859.98	22,848.97	20,297.77	34,957.07	18,102.91
1926....	54,651.07	25,556.80	14,937.39	34,268.94	24,918.68
1927....	62,578.39	26,027.33	21,750.15	38,579.92	35,041.08
1928....	54,803.58	26,513.09	9,243.50	35,047.12	36,780.50
1929....	51,681.35	27,701.74	9,747.88	40,048.33	35,392.88
1930....	46,487.50	27,485.19	8,190.00	38,281.96	34,002.39
1931....	41,383.68	25,344.89	7,684.25	38,090.17	30,113.60
1932....	36,002.29	21,733.28	5,940.00	32,482.63	25,586.95
1933....	32,717.60	17,359.79	4,825.65	29,211.75	18,752.03
1934....	26,971.36	18,269.48	5,182.53	22,116.50	20,297.54
1935....	34,831.89	21,567.73	4,903.30	29,896.70	20,539.27
Totals		$349,069.34	$151,259.66	$508,757.40	
Averages		23,271.29	10,083.97	33,917.16	

Total resources, July 31, 1935................................. $20,539.27

The annual convention and the executive council are the agencies that determine the Federation's policies. The first, composed of some 400 delegates of the various affiliated bodies, meets in an upstate city for three days late in August of each year. The business of the convention is to elect the officers from a list submitted by a nominating committee,[5] to act on reports presented by the previous year's officers [6] and by the chairman of the Legislative Committee, and to act on such other matters as may come before the meeting. At the conclusion of this business, the delegates from the local unions are asked to submit resolutions. These resolutions are posted for reference by the delegates and are assigned to two of the convention's 15 committees,[7] the Committee on

---

[5] Officers are nominated at a conference held for this specific purpose during the annual convention, and all delegates may attend this conference. The chairman and secretary of the conference are appointed by the president of the Federation.

[6] This includes even the reading of a diary of the president's daily activities. See the *Official Yearbook, Proceedings of the 69th Annual Convention*, 1932, p. 51.

[7] *Ibid.*, p. 33.

Resolutions and the Committee on Education, for study and report before the convention adjourns. Resolutions requiring legislative action are referred to the Executive Council of the Federation.[8]

The Executive Council of the Federation, composed of the Federation's president, 13 vice-presidents, one of whom must be a woman, and the secretary-treasurer, is the second policy-determining agency. It prepares the legislative program of the Federation, edits the *Official Yearbook,* names the legal adviser, chooses the next convention city, and acts for the Federation between conventions.[9] One month before the regular opening of the legislature, a two-day meeting of the Executive Council is held for the purpose of preparing a legislative program. To this meeting come delegates from the affiliated bodies, particularly those who have introduced legislative resolutions during the previous convention, to explain their measures.[10] On the second day, after due consideration of the measures thus proposed, the council in executive session completes its legislative program. Although most of these proposals are incorporated in the Federation's legislative program, the Executive Council may reject any or all of them to which there is internal opposition.[11] There may, in addition, be included in the program a plank or planks originally sponsored not by any local organization but by the American Federation of Labor. Under such circumstances the national plank is usually adapted to meet local needs.[12]

The importance of this legislative program is reflected in the stipulation in the constitution of the Federation that

---

[8] The convention of 1935 referred to the Executive Council about 30 resolutions calling for new labor legislation. See the *New York Times,* Aug. 23, 1935, and *Official Yearbook,* 1935, pp. 134–154.

[9] *Constitution of the New York State Federation of Labor,* Art. V, Sec. 4, 5, and Art. VI, Sec. 5.

[10] Ninety-nine members participated in this way in the preparation of the 1935 legislative program. See *Bulletin of the New York State Federation of Labor,* Dec. 12, 1934.

[11] *Official Yearbook,* 1931, pp. 49, 53.

[12] The Unemployment Insurance bill drafted by the New York State Federation of Labor, introduced for the first time in the 1933 session of the State Legislature by Senator W. T. Byrne and Assemblyman W. F. Condon, followed closely the standards laid down by the American Federation of Labor at its 1932 convention. A somewhat modified measure was enacted in 1935, after a vigorous campaign during three sessions of the legislature.

any individual who, or any organization which, opposes a legislative bill recommended by the Federation or espouses a bill opposed by the Federation, shall not be entitled to a seat in the Convention, and the Executive Council is empowered to expel such individual or organization from the New York State Federation of Labor.[13]

The actual execution of the legislative program rests with the Legislative Committee, composed of the secretary-treasurer, the chairman, and five associate members elected annually by the convention.[14] This committee is, in one sense at least, the most important in the Federation.[15] During the 1935 session the Legislative Committee studied, followed, and reported on 132 labor bills introduced into the Senate and Assembly.

The Federation maintains permanent headquarters in Albany, a half block from the Capitol. There, under the supervision of the secretary-treasurer, its records are kept and its publications are prepared and distributed. The most voluminous of the publications, the *Official Yearbook,* contains about 150 closely printed pages of proceedings of the annual convention and a multitude of paid advertisements. Occasionally special pamphlets describing certain phases of the activities of the Federation are issued. Detailed accounts of the current affairs, however, appear in the *Bulletin,* a leaflet of from four to six pages. On the back page of each bulletin appears a condensed calendar of all labor legislation, including the number, subject, and introducer of each bill, the committee to which it has been assigned, its position on the legislature's calendar, and other pertinent information. During legislative sessions bulletins may appear as often as once a week, although usually they are published monthly. Federation publications all bear Labor's seal and motto, *Labor Omnia Vincit.* Many of them exert a wide influence in labor circles.

As is already self-evident, the influence of the Federation in Albany is chiefly dependent upon the efforts of two persons, the president and the secretary-treasurer. To official

---

[13] Art. III, Sec. 5.

[14] Art. VI, Sec. 1, and *Official Yearbook,* 1934, p. 126.

[15] In the *Official Yearbook,* 1934, the legislative chairman's report occupied 29 closely printed pages.

Albany the symbol of organized labor is John M. O'Hanlon, Secretary-Treasurer of the Federation. His intimacy with the state Capitol dates from 1893, when, at the age of 24, he began his long association with the organized labor movement. In 1905, while editing the *Legislative Labor News,* a weekly news report of labor legislation during sessions of the State Legislature, which was utilized by both labor publications and the regular newspapers in the state, he became the first president of the Labor Press Association. He served as a member of the Legislative Committee of the State Federation from 1898 to 1916, and as its chairman from 1921 on. In 1924, when he was elected secretary-treasurer of the Federation, he established the monthly *Bulletin.*[16]

Although, in maneuvering bills through the legislature, the Federation employs methods that do not differ radically from those employed by other pressure groups at Albany, a number of such techniques are peculiarly adapted to the needs of organized labor, and have, consequently, been developed by the Federation.

Bills are usually drafted by the Legislative Committee of the Federation, with the assistance of the legal adviser. They are then introduced into the legislature by a senator or assemblyman friendly to labor. Public hearings before legislative committees are frequently requested by the Federation, but whether requested or not, representatives of the Federation are present and are heard in all public hearings that have under consideration bills in which labor has an interest. In connection with these hearings, plans are worked out with great care so that the Federation may exert the greatest possible influence.[17]

In addition, the Federation not infrequently urges representatives from unaffiliated organizations to register their attitude toward a particular bill either by appearing at the hearing in person or by writing to the legislative committee

[16] Interviews, Aug. 9, 1933 and May 5, 1936. Biographical sketch in files of the Federation. *Cf. Who's Who in American Labor,* New York, Hanford Press, 1925. In 1924 the offices of chairman of the Legislative Committee and secretary-treasurer were amalgamated. George Meany has become a familiar figure during legislative sessions at Albany since his election to the presidency of the State Federation in 1934.

[17] A schedule of speakers is prepared in advance.

that has it in charge. Thus, the four railroad brotherhoods, customarily make a joint appearance with the Federation in regard to many items of legislation. And not infrequently the Women's Trade Union League of New York, the Consumers' League of New York, and other women's and welfare organizations similarly participate in the public hearings.[18]

Not only are briefs succinctly stating labor's views read to the committees at these hearings, but lengthy memoranda are also often left with the chairmen for the committees' further perusal. Moreover, at almost any time during a session, committee chairmen and legislative leaders may be deluged with letters and telegrams from members of the Federation—the "folks back home" have been requested to let their local legislators know their sentiments.

The Federation's official stand on a particular bill is frequently set forth in letters to the legislative leaders, signed by the president and secretary-treasurer of the Federation or by all members of the Executive Council.[19] Frequently, however, many of these officers find it more effective to make personal visits to the leaders. Nor is the Governor neglected. A delegation of labor leaders is almost certain to call at the gubernatorial offices if there is the slightest chance that the Governor can be persuaded to include the Federation's recommendations in his annual message to the legislature,[20] if his help is needed in putting pressure upon recalcitrant legislators, or if veto of a bill is desired.[21] No less close is the personal contact maintained with the State Department of Labor; indeed, the advice and support of the Industrial Commissioner is often sought before pressure is brought to bear upon the legislature.

A concrete illustration of the procedure followed by the State Federation in opposing legislation which it considers detrimental to its interests may be found in the defeat, in 1932, of four amendments to the Workmen's Compensation Law, prepared and sponsored by Associated Industries, Inc.,

---

18 See *infra*, pp. 32, 39, 174.
19 *Official Yearbook*, 1931, p. 59.
20 At this time copies of the program are mailed to the homes of all members of the new legislature. See *Bulletin*, Dec. and Jan., of each year.
21 *Official Yearbook*, 1931, p. 81.

a rival pressure group.[22] Although Governor Roosevelt had
promised the president of the Federation that he would veto
the measures if they reached him,[23] organized labor waged a
vigorous battle against their passage in the legislature. The
story can best be told, perhaps, in the words of the chairman
of the Legislative Committee of the Federation.

Letters were at once sent from our office to the chairmen
of Senate and Assembly committees to which the bills had
been referred, declaring our uncompromising opposition to
each of them, and requesting that public hearings be held,
so that we might present our opposition. Accordingly, a
joint hearing was held before the Senate and Assembly
Committees on Labor and Industry, on Feb. 17, commenc-
ing at 2 p.m., when representatives of organized labor from
all sections of the State appeared in opposition to the four
bills, as did also State Industrial Commissioner Frances
Perkins . . . Following the hearing, letters were sent by
this Federation and its affiliations throughout the State to
all members of the Legislature, urging them to vote to
defeat the Gates-Thompson bills. Responding to our request, central labor bodies and local unions in various
localities also sent committees to the members of the Senate and Assembly residing therein, to ask for their cooperation in defeating the bills.

Notwithstanding this general and pronounced opposition,
the Senate and Assembly committees, on Feb. 24, voted
to report the bills favorably in both houses, the minority
members voting in opposition and the majority members in
favor of the bills. This information was telegraphed to
central labor bodies and district councils and affiliated
state organizations at once, requesting that all members
of the Legislature be telegraphed, urging defeat of the bills.
The response was state-wide and immediate. A conference was sought by your President and Secretary-Treasurer with the leaders of the Legislature, and, on February
25, we interviewed Senator Fearon, temporary president
and majority leader of the Senate, and Speaker McGinnies
of the Assembly in the Speaker's office by appointment.
We presented labor's opposition to the Gates-Thompson

---

[22] See *infra*, p. 49.

[23] Interview with Mr. John Sullivan, former President of the Federation,
Jan. 10, 1933.

bills and informed them of the hearing held the previous week, when all organized labor of the state joined in opposition. At the same time we presented labor's legislative program in the shape of files of the introduced bills, explained their purpose, and asked for their favorable consideration. On the same day we also called on Senator Dunnigan, the Senate minority leader, and Assemblyman Steingut, the Assembly minority leader, and presented the same matters to them. Senator Fearon and Speaker McGinnies promised to give full consideration to our legislative proposals and to our opposition to the Gates-Thompson bills, saying they were going to New York City together that afternoon and would fully discuss the situation en route. Senator Dunnigan and Assemblyman Steingut assured us of their support of our position on all of the measures presented to them.

On Monday night, February 29, following the session, the 27 majority members of the Senate held a conference and at that conference made the four Gates bills party measures by an overwhelming vote, despite the objections of majority senators who were opposed to the bills.

When the Gates bills were reached on the Senate calendar about noon on the following day, Majority Leader Fearon had them laid aside temporarily and ordered a "close call" of the Senate to bring all Senators in and keep them in the chamber until the four bills were voted on. Senator Fearon then moved the bills to final passage and opened the debate and voting, which continued until 4:20 p.m., when the fourth bill was passed by the same vote as the others—27 ayes to 24 noes, including the full membership of the Senate. All of the arguments in favor of the emasculating amendments during the three-hour debate were made solely by Senator Fearon, majority leader. He said the amendments would reduce the cost of compensation to industries of this state, quoting Associated Industries, Inc. figures . . . No other Senator said a word in defense of the bills, which were acknowledged to have been drafted by Associated Industries, Inc.

Minority Leader Dunnigan led the attack on the bills, placing on the record the fact that the State Department of Labor, the New York State Federation, the Railroad Brotherhoods and numerous groups of organized citizens were emphatically opposed to the amendments as destructive of the Workmen's Compensation Law . . .

On March 7, the four Gates bills, scheduled for a final vote in the Assembly on March 8, were laid aside until March 9. In the meantime, letters and thousands of telegrams were sent by the Federation and by labor unions from all localities of the state to their district Senators and Assemblymen, protesting against the enactment of the Associated Industries' amendments to the Compensation Law. The legislators were not left in any doubt as to the attitude of their wage-earning constituents on the four Gates bills, and the information received by them certainly had its effect in turning a number of the Assemblymen away from support of the bills or any one of them. By unanimous vote three of the bills were recommitted to the Committee on Labor and Industry and there died. The fourth bill came to a vote in the Assembly and was defeated. Unlike the situation in the Senate, these measures were not made party measures.[24]

The Federation has also found it necessary to exert influence on amendments to the state constitution, including those proposed in the legislature as well as those proposed in constitutional conventions,[25] for even after a progressive labor law has been passed, the state courts may declare it unconstitutional. Such, for example, was the case in 1903, after passage of a law prescribing for public works an eight-hour day at the prevailing rate of wages. On this occasion the Federation prepared an amendment to the constitution that, having been passed by two legislatures, became a part of the constitution in 1905, after a strenuous campaign for its ratification. Similarly, in 1894, as a result of long, protracted agitation by the State Federation, a constitutional convention inserted in the constitution a section abolishing the contract system of convict labor.[26] More recently, in 1915, the Federation's planned opposition undoubtedly contributed to the defeat of the proposed constitution, which was, in its opinion,

[24] *Official Yearbook*, 1932, pp. 74, 75.
[25] *Cf. Constitution of the State of New York*, Art. XIV.
[26] *Official Yearbook*, 1933, p. 45. *Cf.* Historical pamphlet: *When and Where and by Whom the New York State Labor Movement Was Given Life, 1864-1923*, pp. 20, 21.

"the product of aristocrats who were seeking to chain the will of the people and substitute caste government for democracy." [27]

To facilitate the passage of its legislative program, the New York State Federation, unlike most other pressure groups in the state, openly participates in political campaigns and attempts to secure the nomination and election to office [28] of those friendly to labor and the defeat of those who are hostile. To this end it maintains a State Non-Partisan Campaign Committee, composed of the president, the first vice-president, and the secretary-treasurer. [29] This committee generally submits to the state conventions of the major political parties legislative proposals adopted by the Federation at its annual convention, with the request that these proposals be included in the platforms of the parties. After the close of the party conventions, the platforms and the records of such candidates for office as have been nominated are studied by the committee. Statements endorsing only that party platform which is more responsive to labor's proposals and those candidates whose records disclose them to be friendly to labor are transmitted to all labor organizations in the state. [30] Frequently the action of the committee in this direction is foreshadowed by the resolutions of the annual convention. Such action by the convention, however, is usually confined to those holding high office. [31]

---

[27] Historical pamphlet, *op. cit.*, p. 11.

[28] This influence is extended to include the chairmen and members of such legislative committees as those on Labor and Industries, persuasion being often exerted to induce particularly desirable legislators to seek these posts. Interview, Mr. George Meany, Sept. 16, 1935.

[29] This committee cooperates with the National Non-Partisan Political Campaign Committee of the A. F. of L. in the election of the President of the United States and members of Congress from New York State. See H. L. Childs, *Labor and Capital in National Politics*, Columbus, Ohio State University Press, 1930, p. 192.

[30] See *Bulletin*, Oct. 15, 1932 and Oct. 10, 1934. It should be noted that only candidates for Governor, Lieut.-Governor, Attorney-General, Comptroller, and U. S. Senators are nominated by party conventions in New York State. Candidates for the State Legislature are nominated in the primary.

[31] The convention of 1932 endorsed Governor F. D. Roosevelt for the Presidency and Lieutenant-Governor Herbert H. Lehman for the Governorship. In Mr. Lehman's case, the Federation, probably anticipating factional struggles in the Democratic convention of 1932, stated rather equivocally that "the interests of the people of this great state will be securely conserved in

Organized Labor and Its Allies 19

Even more elaborate are the efforts to influence the nomination and election of members of the State Legislature.[32] For the purpose of guiding the labor forces, there is prepared and widely publicized—annually for the Assembly and biennially for the Senate [33]—a careful record of the votes cast by each legislator on labor bills in each session of the legislature. Soon after the close of the regular legislative session, a specially prepared issue of the *Bulletin,* containing a condensed tabulation of this record, is distributed to all affiliated labor organizations in the state, together with a statement calling to the attention of all organized workers the necessity of studying the record and voting in the September primary accordingly. The record is also reprinted in the *Official Yearbook,* which reaches the local labor organizations shortly before the November elections, and in about 20 labor newspapers in the state.[34] In addition, general newspaper correspondents in Albany are regularly supplied with Federation releases.

Based upon this record, about the middle of September letters of appreciation are sent to assemblymen and senators of both major parties who have cast no adverse votes on major bills endorsed by the Federation.[35] A typical letter was that sent from Albany on September 11, 1935:

---

the future conduct of their state government if Hon. Herbert H. Lehman can be induced to continue *as one of their high public servants."* (Italics are the writer's.) *Official Yearbook,* 1932, p. 127. William Green, President of the A. F. of L., at the convention of the State Federation in 1935, eulogized Governor Lehman as a friend of labor who will receive the solid support of organized labor "when he will be called to serve the country in a bigger and broader way." *New York Times,* Aug. 21, 1935. *Cf. Official Yearbook,* 1935, p. 17. Again in 1936, the Federation endorsed President Roosevelt and Governor Lehman for reelection. *Cf. Bulletin of the New York State Federation of Labor,* Sept. 8, 1936.

[32] The first organized effort by the Federation in this direction was undertaken in 1882, when a State Political Branch was established to influence the election of legislators in favor of the abolition of contract-convict labor. The branch existed until 1888. See *Official Yearbook,* 1933, p. 45.

[33] Because of the importance of the labor legislation enacted at the 1935 session, a record of votes was compiled for both the Senate and the Assembly. See *Bulletin,* June 15, 1935.

[34] These have greater circulations in upstate cities than they have in New York City. Interview, Mr. George Meany, President of the Federation, Sept. 16, 1935.

[35] Again, in 1935, because of the importance of the labor legislation enacted, these letters were sent to senators as well as assemblymen, although the former were not seeking reelection in that year.

THE NEW YORK STATE FEDERATION OF LABOR

Albany, N. Y., September 11, 1935.

Dear Assemblyman:

Our 72nd Annual Convention, at its session in Albany on August 22nd, adopted a resolution instructing the undersigned officer of the New York State Federation of Labor to extend to you the appreciation and thanks of Organized Labor of the State of New York for your splendid support of the very important labor legislation enacted by the 1935 session of the Legislature. I am enclosing a copy of our Official Record of Votes cast on twelve of the most important labor bills enacted in that session, and you will note that you are recorded as voting for these bills which are now labor laws of the State of New York.

I take personal pleasure in communicating to you the appreciation of the New York State Federation of Labor for your excellent public service in supporting these and other important labor measures in the Legislature of 1935, and I hope that you will be returned to the State Legislature of 1936 to continue your good work.

Sincerely yours,

(Signed) JAMES M. O'HANLON

Secretary-Treasurer and
Chairman Legislative Committee of
NEW YORK STATE FEDERATION OF LABOR

In addition, the Political Campaign Committee sponsors labor rallies in almost every city of the state during the even numbered years, when an entire state ticket is to be elected. It often concentrates its efforts upon some particular district in which an unusually desirable or undesirable legislator is seeking reelection. In off years these rallies are held in conjunction with those of the central labor bodies for city and county elections. Moreover, at times, the committee prepares a questionnaire for local committees to use in determining the views of candidates on labor legislation,[36] and, on occasion, actively sponsors members of particular labor organizations

---

[36] *Bulletin,* Sept. 3, 1932.

for nomination and election.[37]   While it is not customary for
either local unions or the State Federation to contribute
directly to the campaign funds of candidates, there are no
organization rules that specifically forbid such a practice.

It is impossible, of course, to determine definitely the extent
of the Federation's influence in the election or defeat of a
candidate for state office, since peculiar local conditions often
dominate such elections; it is, nevertheless, not surprising to
find the Federation, in its various publications, often claiming
its endorsement to be indispensable to the success of a candidate.   Labor's opposition to the candidacy of Senator Folger
for the Governorship certainly contributed to his defeat in
1882.   And between 1882 and 1888 it is certainly true that at
least eight members were elected to the State Legislature
largely because of their support of the Federation's campaign
to abolish contract-convict labor.[38]   More significant, however, is the fact that since 1921, when the Federation entered
politics "more widely and intensely than ever before," many
Republican strongholds in the state—Albany, Erie, Monroe,
Westchester, and Oneida counties—have yielded, wholly or in
part, to the Democrats and have supported a continuous succession of Democratic Governors, all of them endorsed by the
State Federation of Labor.   It is no mere coincidence that
upstate cities with a large number of wage earners are to be
found in several of these counties.   For example, Rochester,
third among the cities of the state in both size and in number
of wage earners, constituting as it does a major segment of the
46th Senatorial district, was consistently Republican for 46
years until 1934.   In that year labor-sponsored Senator Nor-
man A. O'Brien, partner in a law firm representing organized
labor in legal actions, was elected to the legislature on the
Democratic ticket.[39]   Moreover, although it does not neces-
sarily indicate solely the influence of organized labor, the fact
is that New York City, containing half the wage earners of the
state, has consistently sent its large delegations of Democratic

---

[37] *Bulletin,* Dec. 12, 1934.

[38] *Official Yearbook,* 1933, p. 45.   *Cf. supra,* pp. 8, 19, note 32.

[39] Letter of John J. Scully, Senator O'Brien's law partner, to the writer,
Sept. 20, 1935. It should, however, be noted that, in 1935, two Democratic
assemblymen from districts in Rochester failed of reelection though they
possessed good labor records. See *New York Times,* Nov. 6, 1935.

legislators to Albany, except for the temporary reaction arising
from the election of Republican-Fusion Mayor La Guardia in
1933.[40]   Buffalo, containing the second largest number of wage
earners in the state, though formerly a Republican stronghold,
sent to Albany, in November, 1934, a delegation of nine legislators, of whom seven were Democrats.[41]   During the fifteen
years between 1921 and 1935, Democratic majorities controlled
the Senate five times [42] and both houses once.[43]

With such instances of its growing influence, it is not to be
wondered at that the State Federation's friendship is courted
and its opposition feared.   Its letters of appreciation, regarded
as highly valuable endorsements, are anxiously awaited by
legislators seeking reelection and are thoroughly exploited during campaigns, particularly in labor constituencies. Moreover,
candidates for higher state offices, including the governorship,
encourage and eagerly accept invitations to address the annual
conventions and rallies of organized labor.

The criticism has been leveled at the State Federation that
it is "an adjunct of the Democratic party" [44] and that it "seldom, if ever, gives the Republican party any credit for . . .
its efforts in passing labor bills." [45]   Thus, although favorable
records in labor legislation have been made by legislatures controlled, in one house at least, by Republican majorities since
1919,[46] labor leaders have in these same years endorsed, both
for reelection and promotion, an unbroken succession of Democratic Governors.   In 1930, for example (according to Melvin
C. Eaton, Republican State Chairman), when Republicans

---

[40] New York City elected 13 Republican-Fusion and 49 Democratic assemblymen at this time. Of the Republicans only two cast no adverse votes on
the ten major bills endorsed by the New York State Federation of Labor in
1934. Of the Democrats all but one cast no adverse votes on these bills.
Official Yearbook, 1934, p. 81.

[41] Of these, the two Republicans, Senator N. W. Cheney and Assemblyman
H. B. Ehrlich, voted against some of the twelve major bills endorsed by the
New York State Federation of Labor in the 1935 session of the State Legisla-
ture. Not one of the seven Democrats, however, opposed any of these bills.
Official Yearbook, 1935, p. 93.

[42] 1923, 1924, 1933, 1934, 1935.

[43] 1935.

[44] Interview, Senator George R. Fearon, Aug. 8, 1933.

[45] *New York Times,* Aug. 25, 1935.

[46] Except in 1935, during the first year of Gov. Lehman's second term, when
both houses had Democratic majorities.

were in control of both houses of the legislature, as well as of the committees which were considering labor bills, William Green, President of the A. F. of L., congratulated Governor F. D. Roosevelt specifically on "his wonderful record in the matter of labor bills enacted into law during the session of that year and urged that he be a candidate to succeed himself." [47]

Though founded on facts, as the study of any recent annual report of the Federation's Legislative Committee will show, such criticism of the Republicans is not entirely justifiable. In 1930, the year mentioned by Chairman Eaton, the Federation indeed records:

> We were successful this year in defeating in the Legislature all bills opposed to the interests of Labor, which included measures defeated in former years and several new proposals . . . In 1930 we secured the enactment of our chief labor bill to abolish ex-parte injunctions in this state. [48]

In fact, of the nine major labor bills endorsed by the Federation in 1930, all but one were passed by both houses of the legislature without a single adverse vote from either Democrat or Republican. [49] But the Federation's repeated support of Democratic candidates has its foundation in the realization that such Republican friendliness to the Federation's labor program is most unusual. A study of the votes cast on important labor bills in the Senate and Assembly since 1921 clearly indicates this fact. On 284 major bills endorsed by the Federation and introduced into both houses between 1921 and 1935, 87.6 per cent of those legislators who recorded no adverse

---

[47] Excerpt from letter of William Green to Governor F. D. Roosevelt, Aug. 22, 1930, to which Chairman Eaton undoubtedly refers: "I share with the working people and their friends in the great State of New York their feelings of satisfaction and gratification over the humane, practical social-justice legislation enacted at the last session (1930) of the Legislature of New York and for which you were largely responsible. I commend you highly for the service you rendered. You deserve the support of labor and of all classes of people who seek to perpetuate our free institutions and who are engaged in preserving our principle of free government through the advancement of the highest and best interest of the masses of the people."

[48] *Official Yearbook*, 1933, pp. 51, 53.

[49] See accompanying chart and the Federation's *Bulletin*, June 1, 1930. *Cf. Official Yearbook*, 1930, p. 103.

SUMMARY OF THE VOTES IN THE NEW YORK SENATE AND
ASSEMBLY ON MAJOR LABOR BILLS ENDORSED BY THE
NEW YORK STATE FEDERATION OF LABOR

	SENATE						ASSEMBLY				
Year	Party Representation in Senate	Number of Major Labor Bills Endorsed	Number of Senators who supported all the Endorsed Bills	Number of Senators who cast only one adverse vote	Number of Senators who cast more than one adverse vote[b]	Year	Party Representation in Assembly	Number of Major Labor Bills Endorsed	Number of Assemblymen who supported all the Endorsed Bills	Number of Assemblymen who cast only one adverse vote	Number of Assemblymen who cast more than one adverse vote[b]
1921	Rep- 39 Dem-11 Soc- 1	11	Rep- 0 Dem- 3 Soc- 1	Rep- 0 Dem- 3	Rep- 39 Dem- 5	1921	Rep-119 Dem-28 Soc- 3	10	Rep- 0 Dem-18 Soc- 3	Rep- 0 Dem- 9	Rep-115 Dem- 1
1922	Rep- 39 Dem-11 Soc- 1	12	Rep- 0 Dem- 8 Soc- 1	Rep- 0 Dem- 2	Rep- 38 Dem- 1	1922	Rep- 96 Dem-53 Soc- 1	13	Rep- 0 Dem-46 Soc- 1	Rep- 0 Dem- 7	Rep- 95 Dem- 0
1923	Rep- 25 Dem-26	22	Rep- 0 Dem-21	Rep- 0 Dem- 4	Rep- 25 Dem- 1	1923	Rep- 81 Dem-69	21	Rep- 0 Dem-33	Rep- 0 Dem-26	Rep- 80 Dem-10
1924	Rep- 25 Dem-26	10	Rep- 0 Dem-21	Rep- 0 Dem- 5	Rep- 25 Dem- 0	1924	Rep- 87 Dem-63	11	Rep- 0 Dem-58	Rep- 1 Dem- 5	Rep- 84 Dem- 0
1925	Rep- 29 Dem-22	7	Rep- 0 Dem-22	Rep- 0 Dem- 0	Rep- 29 Dem- 0	1925	Rep- 96 Dem-54	10	Rep- 0 Dem-54		Rep- 94 Dem- 0
1926	Rep- 29 Dem-22	7	Rep- 0 Dem-16	Rep- 0 Dem- 6	Rep- 29 Dem- 0	1926	Rep- 91 Dem-59	9	Rep- 2 Dem-59		Rep- 88 Dem- 0
1927	Rep- 27 Dem-24	9	Rep- 5 Dem- 5	Rep- 17 Dem-18	Rep- 5 Dem- 0	1927	Rep- 84 Dem-66	11	Rep- 3 Dem-66		Rep- 79 Dem- 0
1928	Rep- 27 Dem-24	3	Rep- 0 Dem-24	Rep- 1 Dem- 0	Rep- 26 Dem- 0	1928	Rep- 88 Dem-62	5	Rep- 0 Dem-62	Rep- 1 Dem- 0	Rep- 85 Dem- 0
1929[a]						1929	Rep- 89 Dem-61	9	Rep- 0 Dem-60		Rep- 88 Dem- 0
1930	Rep- 27 Dem-24	9	Rep- 25 Dem-24	Rep- 2 Dem- 0		1930	Rep- 86 Dem-64	9	Rep- 83 Dem-64		
1931[a]						1931	Rep- 80 Dem-70	10	Rep- 2 Dem-17	Rep- 4 Dem-52	Rep- 72 Dem- 1
1932	Rep- 27 Dem-24	10	Rep- 0 Dem-24		Rep- 27 Dem- 0	1932	Rep- 80 Dem-70	10	Rep- 4 Dem-67	Rep- 0 Dem- 1	Rep- 73 Dem- 0
1933[a]						1933	Rep- 77 Dem-73	11	Rep- 3 Dem-41	Rep- 1 Dem-32	Rep- 72 Dem- 0
1934	Rep- 25 Dem-26	11	Rep- 0 Dem- 4	Rep- 1 Dem-21	Rep- 20 Dem- 1	1934	Rep- 85 Dem-64 Ind- 1	10	Rep- 3 Dem-62	Rep- 3 Dem- 2	Rep- 77 Dem- 0 Ind- 1
1935	Rep- 22 Dem-29	12	Rep- 1 Dem-26	Rep- 2 Dem- 1	Rep- 19 Dem- 1	1935	Rep- 73 Dem-77	12	Rep- 1 Dem-70	Rep- 3 Dem- 6	Rep- 69 Dem- 1
Total		123	Rep- 31 Dem- 198 Soc- 2	Rep- 23 Dem-60	Rep-282 Dem- 9			161	Rep- 101 Dem- 777 Soc- 4	Rep- 13 Dem- 140	Rep- 1171 Dem-13 Ind- 1

[a] No official summary of Senate votes on major bills was compiled by the Federation during this year. Only the members of the Assembly are elected annually, the Senators are elected biennially in the even numbered years.

[b] An aggregate of 171 Senators (all Republican) and 840 Assemblymen (all Republican) cast adverse votes on **more than half** of the bills for each of the years (1921–1935) under review.

In the Assembly the presiding officer is the Speaker who seldom votes on bills. Between 1921 and 1935 inclusive, a Democratic Speaker presided over the Assembly only in 1935.

votes were Democrats, while only 11.8 per cent were Republicans.[50] Of the adverse votes cast in these same years against one or more such labor bills, 86.9 per cent were Republican, 12.9 per cent Democratic.[51] In many cases Democratic Governors responding to the request of the Federation vetoed certain undesirable bills passed by the legislature.[52] Moreover, it was often necessary for the Federation to exert the utmost pressure on the Republican legislators who finally did vote for labor legislation to line them up on labor's side at the various roll calls.[53]

An examination of two recent regular sessions of the legislature, in which Democrats controlled the Senate while Republicans controlled the Assembly, further reveals a difference in attitude on labor legislation between the two parties:

> Whereas 25 labor bills endorsed by the Federation in 1933 were passed by the Democratic Senate, all 25 were defeated in the Republican Assembly. Only 2 endorsed labor bills that were passed by the Assembly, however, were defeated in the Senate.[54]

> Whereas 21 labor bills endorsed by the Federation in 1934 were passed by the Democratic Senate, all 21 were defeated in the Republican Assembly. Once again only 4 endorsed labor bills that were passed by the Assembly were defeated in the Senate.[55]

Finally, it should be noted that many more of the Federation's legislative proposals have received favorable consideration in Democratic than in Republican state conventions. In 1934, for example, although six of the eight proposals submitted by the Federation to the two parties were incorporated in the Democratic state platform, only two were included in that of the Republicans.[56]

---

[50] In the Senate 85.7 per cent of such members were Democrats and 13.4 per cent were Republicans; in the Assembly 88.1 per cent were Democrats and 11.4 per cent were Republicans.

[51] In the Senate 81.5 per cent of these votes were Republican and 18.4 per cent were Democratic; in the Assembly 88.4 per cent were Republican and 11.4 per cent were Democratic.

[52] See *Official Yearbook*, 1932, p. 73.

[53] Interview, President George Meany, Sept. 16, 1935.

[54] *Bulletin*, May 12, 1933.

[55] *Official Yearbook*, 1934, p. 60.

[56] Though the Federation, for practical reasons, does not concern itself with Socialist candidates, it publishes the labor planks in the state platform of the

In view of these facts, it is not surprising that the Federation has favored the election of Democratic rather than Republican administrations. That the Federation is not thoroughly partisan, however, is indicated by the transmission of its letters of appreciation to all legislators deserving of them, Republicans and Democrats alike.[57]

The New York State Federation of Labor is the most powerful of the three principal groups organized by and for the wage earners of the state. Backed by the combined power of hundreds of thousands of individuals, it is, like other mass groups in the state, feared and respected largely because of its potential influence at the ballot box. It is unquestionably the largest pressure group in the state that systematically and openly strives to direct a solid labor vote to "reward the friends and defeat the foes of labor legislation in the State of New York."

Women's Trade Union League of New York and the Consumers' League of New York

The two other organizations of statewide influence which are effectual in advancing labor legislation, the Women's Trade Union League of New York and the Consumers' League of New York, may be considered together, because, while cooperating with the New York State Federation of Labor in supporting general progressive labor legislation, they both concern themselves especially with such legislation for women and children.

The Women's Trade Union League of New York, the office of which is located in New York City, was founded in 1903 for the purpose of stimulating and promoting the formation of trade unions among women.[58] Affiliated with the National

---

Socialist party, and usually lists the names of the Socialist candidates on the state ticket, in the same bulletin that carries the analyses of the labor planks in the Democratic and Republican platforms. See *Bulletin*, Oct. 15, 1932.

[57] It might also be added that Democrats do not always adhere to the Federation's endorsements. The Child Labor Amendment, for example, voted upon in 1935 in the Assembly only, was here defeated despite the Democratic majority in the Assembly. The roll call on this amendment was not incorporated with those of the major bills endorsed by the Federation, although it was featured in the Federation's labor program for 1935. See *Bulletin*, Dec. 12, 1934.

[58] *Constitution of the W.T.U.L. of N. Y.*, Art. II.

Women's Trade Union League, the American Federation of Labor, and the New York State Federation of Labor, its members elect annually five officers: a president, two vice-presidents, a secretary, and a treasurer. These, together with twelve additional members of the League, make up an Executive Board, which conducts the business of the organization, subject to such laws and resolutions as may be passed for its guidance.[59]

The membership of the Women's Trade Union League is composed of such local unions in New York State as have women members and are affiliated with the American Federation of Labor.[60] The dues paid by its membership, however, are not sufficient to support the activities of the Women's Trade Union League. For this reason the League's finances depend upon voluntary contributions in addition to dues and are supplemented by receipts from an annual concert conducted for the benefit of its Educational Department.

The membership of the League is composed of three classes. In the first class are local unions, which pay $10 annually, and auxiliaries, which pay $6. In the second class are individual members of the American Federation of Labor and workers in unorganized industries, who pay $2 annually. The third class is made up of contributing members and civic-minded individuals who believe in the work of the League. The contributing members pay from $10 to $25 annually, while the others pay $5.[61]

For the detailed execution of the activities of the League, its constitution provides for five standing committees and such special committees as the Executive Board of the League may by resolution deem necessary. Members of these committees are selected by the president of the League, with the approval, in the case of the standing committees, of the Executive Board.[62] The work of the committees is given publicity in the League's monthly *Bulletin* and *Annual Report*.

The first of the two functions of the League, that of pro-

---

[59] *Ibid.,* Art. V, Sec. 1, 2.

[60] The membership numbers approximately 100,000.

[61] From an undated leaflet published by the League, entitled, *The New York Women's Trade Union League.*

[62] *Constitution,* Art. IX, Sec. 1, and Art. XI.

moting the unionization of women wage earners, is delegated
to the Educational Committee, which conducts a program
including forums, lectures by prominent speakers, and courses
of instruction to both members and nonmembers of the League.
Although most of these courses, since their inception in 1923,
have dealt with problems of interest to women in industry,
some of them, such as those in effective English or hand-built
pottery, are only indirectly influential in the unionization of
women.[63] Of more direct importance, in this respect, is the
special assignment of a so-called Organizer to facilitate the
formation of trade unions for women, although in recent years
the Organizer has been chiefly concerned with the problems
arising from strikes in the various locals of the International
Ladies' Garment Workers Union.[64]

The second function of the League, that of securing the
passage of labor laws favorable to women in industry, necessitates its close cooperation with other organizations that seek
the same legislative objective. The State Federation of Labor,
the Consumers' League of New York, the League of Women
Voters, the Child Labor Committee, and the Women's City
Club are the most prominent among these. To facilitate effective action in this direction, the League's Legislative Committee was formed in 1910. Many of its members are connected
with the aforementioned organizations.[65] Close contact is

---

[63] During the academic year, 1932–1933, of 20 weeks, 8 courses were offered,
attended by 100 students. In the past 30 years about 2,000 workers, some of
them now leaders in their unions, have attended the League's classes.

[64] During the depression the League has concerned itself, in cooperation with
the emergency unemployment agencies, chiefly with the relief of the unem-
ployed woman worker, sometimes through small, noninterest bearing loans,
and sometimes through scholarship subsidies at continuation schools. See
Annual Report, 1931–1932, p. 2. *Cf. Bulletin*, Jan. 9, 1933.   The depression
also compelled the League, in 1932, to discontinue its Compensation Advisory
Service, founded in 1922, to advise women injured in industry of the provisions
of the Workmen's Compensation Law of the state. See *Annual Report,* 1931–
1932, p. 5.

[65] Miss Rose Schneiderman, President of the W.T.U.L., is also a member of
the Legislative Committee of the League of Women Voters and the Women's
City Club. Miss Maud Schwartz, Vice-President of the W.T.U.L., is also a
member of the Legislative Committee of the New York State Federation of
Labor and was secretary of the New York State Department of Labor until
Jan., 1931. Mention, too, should be made of Mrs. F. D. Roosevelt's active
interest in the work of the W.T.U.L.

thus maintained between the League and these other groups, for the advancement of their common legislative programs.

The chief of these groups, and the third statewide organization with which this chapter is concerned, is the Consumers' League of New York. The genesis of this organization was the Working Women's Society, formed in 1888 for the purpose of promoting trade unions.[66] The work of the Society focussed the spotlight of publicity on the intolerable working conditions then prevalent among women workers in the retail stores of New York City, and, as a consequence, a public meeting was held in Chickering Hall, New York City, on May 6, 1890. At this mass meeting, held under the auspices of the Working Women's Society and certain liberal clergymen,[67] a set of resolutions was adopted. One of these read as follows:

> Resolved that a committee be appointed to assist the Working Women's Society in making a list which shall keep shoppers informed of such stores as deal justly with their employees, and so bring public opinion and public action to bear in favour of just employers, and also in favour of such employers as desire to be just, but are prevented by the stress of the competition, from following their own sense of duty.[68]

It was clear to this committee that only by enlisting the sympathy and interest of the women patrons of retail stores could the working conditions of women employees be ameliorated. On January 21, 1891, therefore, there was organized, under the presidency of Josephine Shaw Lowell, the Consumers' League of the City of New York, on the plan of a prototype organization founded in London a few months earlier.[69] Very shortly similar local leagues were formed throughout the state, each taking the name of its home city. In 1898 these local groups were merged together to form the Consumers'

---

[66] The writer is indebted for various facts in this discussion of the Consumers' League to L. L. Irvin, *The Consumers' League of New York as a Pressure Group,* Columbia University Master's Essay, 1935.

[67] U. S. Department of Labor, *History of Labor Legislation for Women,* Bulletin of the Women's Bureau, 1929, No. 66, p. 69.

[68] Maud Nathan, *The Story of an Epoch-Making Movement,* Garden City, N. Y., Doubleday, Page, 1926, p. 22.

[69] See *ibid.,* p. 130, for a statement of the principles of this London organization.

League of New York. A year later, various state leagues united to form the National Consumers' League.[70]

The constitution of the Consumers' League of New York provides at present for officers and a Board of Governors. The Board of Governors is composed of forty members, including the officers. They determine the policies and direct the work of the League. This Board of Governors elects an Advisory Board, of not more than 25 members, and an Executive Committee, composed of the officers of the League and the chairmen of the standing committees, which exercises the powers of the Board of Governors between meetings of the latter.[71] Annual dues range from $1 to $5, but the payment of $200 for life membership is accepted in lieu of annual dues. An auxiliary to the League, subject to the approval of the Board of Governors, may be formed by 25 persons; but 50 per cent of the annual dues of such an auxiliary must be paid to the general treasury of the League.[72] The constitution, moreover, clearly states the object of the Consumers' League "to be to ameliorate the condition of women and children employed in the retail merchandise houses of New York City, by patronizing, so far as practicable, only such houses as approach in their conditions to the 'Standard of a Fair House,' as adopted by the League, and by other methods." [73]

Accordingly, the first task of the League, soon after its organization, was the establishment of the *White List,* a modification of the Working Women's Society's *Standard of a Fair House.* The list was drawn up only after consultation with the officers of the leading retail stores of the city.[74] As a result of the League's investigations, the first *White List* contained only eight names. The list was published as an advertisement in leading city newspapers and was circulated among the League's members. Within two years the *White List*

---

[70] The New York State League and the New York City League were merged in 1922. See *ibid.,* p. 191.

[71] *Constitution of the Consumers' League of New York,* Art. IV.

[72] *Ibid.,* Art. II.

[73] Maud Nathan, *op. cit.,* p. 25.

[74] Fourteen hundred letters, with copies of the *Standard of a Fair House,* were sent to retail dry goods stores in the city, followed by requests for permission to investigate. Even if the store refused, its name might appear on the *White List* as a result of information obtained by the Working Women's Society, or from employees.

carried the names of 24 stores, but it was never to grow very large. Instead, influential stores whose names did not appear on the list brought pressure to bear on newspapers in which the *White List* had been advertised, with the consequence that the columns of almost all the leading newspapers, with the exception of the *New York Evening Post,* were closed to the League's list. As a result, the publication of a *White List* was abandoned in 1912 and not revived until 1928. Nevertheless, the League has continued its efforts "to acquaint the consuming public with the conditions under which the things they eat, wear, and use are made and sold." [75]

As a result of its experience with *White Lists,* the League has more and more come to the realization that legislation is the only certain method of improving industrial conditions. [76] Therefore, its activities have since then been directed increasingly to the enactment and enforcement of labor laws, especially for women. Thus, since the early part of the century, the Consumers' League has worked actively, in cooperation with the Women's Trade Union League and the New York State Federation of Labor, for such laws as those prohibiting night work and reducing working hours for women in mercantile establishments, factories, and restaurants, [77] as well as for the first minimum wage law in New York, passed in 1933.

Indeed, the most vigorous battle conducted by these organizations was that which was waged for the 48-hour week and the minimum wage law. Bills providing for an 8-hour day and 48-hour week for women and minors were introduced into the New York Legislature in 1914. These measures were sponsored by the Women's Trade Union League. [78] In 1915

---

[75] Frances Perkins, in the report of investigation of candy factories, *Behind the Scenes in Candy Factories,* published by the Consumers' League of New York, 1928. See also Maud Nathan, *op. cit.,* pp. 32, 46.

[76] *Cf.* pamphlet, *The Conference on the Breakdown of Industrial Standards,* National Consumers' League, Dec. 12, 1932.

[77] U. S. Department of Labor, Bulletin of the Women's Bureau, *op. cit.,* pp. 75–103. For the description of a bill, approved by the State Federation, but, nevertheless, opposed by the Consumers' League and the W.T.U.L., see *ibid.,* p. 87. This bill to exempt employees in the canning industry from the 60-hour law applicable to factories, was vetoed by the Governor in 1916.

[78] See S. P. Breckenridge, *Women in the Twentieth Century,* New York, McGraw-Hill, 1933, ch. 16.

they were followed by a minimum wage bill, sponsored chiefly by the Consumers' League.   But, though introduced year after year, the bills were always defeated.

Gradually the realization dawned that only more effective coordination of the efforts of the several organizations striving for this legislation could result in success.   As a result, the Women's Joint Legislative Conference, composed of representatives of various women's welfare, church, and civic organizations, was formed under the leadership of the Women's Trade Union League of New York, the Consumers' League of New York and the New York State League of Women Voters. By 1918 this body represented some 16 organizations and 300,-000 people.[79]   Although there were other items on its program, the 48-hour week and minimum wage bills constituted the crux of the conference's agenda.   Yet, although by 1920 bills regulating working hours for women engaged in transportation and elevator service had been passed, the major objective of the conference, the passage of the 48-hour week and minimum wage bills, remained unachieved.

The chief weapon in the battle thus far had been the accumulation and dissemination, by the Joint Legislative Conference, of factual material gathered with the aid of the Women's Bureaus of the New York State Department of Labor, the United States Department of Labor, and friendly Governors and legislators.   Under the auspices of the Joint Legislative Conference or of the more important of the organizations represented in the conference, this material was organized into pamphlets, leaflets, bulletins, briefs, and news dispatches, and was presented to the public.

On January 1, 1923, Alfred E. Smith was returned to the Governorship, and in September, 1924, the Joint Legislative Conference was able, through such key Republican women as Sarah Schuyler Butler, Mrs. Charles H. Sabin, and Jeanie W.

---

[79] These 16 organizations were: Women's Trade Union League of New York, Consumers' League of New York, New York State League of Women Voters, Vocational Service for Juniors, Girls' Friendly Society, New York Child Labor Committee, St. Catherine's Welfare Association, United Neighborhood Houses, Women's Christian Temperance Union, New York League of Girls' Clubs, Women's City Club, American Association for Labor Legislation, National Consumers' League, Young Women's Hebrew Association, Carroll Club, New York Council of Jewish Women.

Miner, to effect the inclusion of the 48-hour week bill in the Republican as well as the Democratic, state platforms. It was, therefore, with a good deal of hope that the Joint Conference looked forward to the legislative session opening in January, 1925. The result, however, was failure. A substitute bill, called the Joiner bill, was passed by both houses, but was so unacceptable to the Joint Conference that Governor Smith promptly vetoed it.[80]

The session had been a very stormy one. It was during the debate on hours legislation for women that the majority leader in the Senate found it necessary to take an appeal from a decision of a presiding officer of his own party. "To the utter amazement of Republican and Democratic Senators, this occurred at the close of the debate on the 48-hour bill, when, on a point of order raised by Senator Knight to retard the progress of the measure, Lieutenant-Governor Lowman delivered an adverse ruling from the Chair . . . Lowman and Knight glared at each other, then Knight called for an appeal on the ruling." [81] Senator Mastick, the Republican senator who had been asked by the Republican leaders to introduce the bill, called the Republicans' attention to the fact that this legislation had been endorsed in the state platforms of both parties. A senator charged that "the women interested in the measure have come up year after year, not to be honestly beaten, but to be tricked." A letter from the Women's Joint Legislative Conference was read, threatening retaliation against Republicans, who were charged with deception and fraud, as having "played with stacked cards and letting us play believing the game clean"; and "the insidious influence of the most notorious lobbyist in this state" was held as the explanation of the Republicans' broken pledge. During the session, reminding him symbolically of party and individual pledges, a bright-hued card was placed on each legislator's desk.[82]

---

[80] For objections to the Joiner bill prepared by the Women's Joint Legislative Conference, see U. S. Department of Labor, Bulletin of the Women's Bureau, *op. cit.*, p. 99. Twenty organizations appeared before the Governor in opposition to the bill.

[81] *New York Times*, Mar. 28, 1925.

[82] *Report of the Women's Trade Union League of New York*, 1924–1926, p. 15.

The session was hardly over when the drive began again. The Women's Trade Union League published a four-page leaflet entitled *How Broken Pledges Defeated the 48-Hour Week in New York State*. The Republican and Democratic pledges, word for word, were printed on the cover of the leaflet, below which, in bold type, appeared the Webster's Dictionary definition of the word, "pledge." After reciting the course of events in the 1925 legislature, the leaflet concluded with:

> DEMAND GOOD FAITH OF YOUR REPRESENTATIVES. This is the truthful story of a broken party pledge. A pledge, the meaning of which is understood in the English language to mean a *guarantee* for the *performance of an act*. The Republicans were bound to the voters of this state by a promise which should have been sacred. Their candidates were elected on the principles contained in the party platform. WE ASK YOUR COOPERATION to the end that those men who forgot their principles, rode roughshod over their pledges, ignored their *guarantee for the performance of an act* shall understand that a basic principle of our democracy is that of good faith between the people's representatives and the people whom they represent. PULL WITH US FOR A REAL 48-HOUR LAW.

Although the bill was defeated again in 1926 in the closing hours of the session, the legislature did provide for a Joint Committee, consisting of three senators, to be appointed by the Temporary President of the Senate, and five assemblymen, appointed by the Speaker. It was "to investigate as speedily as possible the existing conditions under which the manufacturing and mercantile business of the state is carried on . . . to the end, among other things, that such remedial legislation, to the extent necessary, may be enacted, as will advance the prosperity, health and safety of the working people, the prosperity and safety of the industry, and the prosperity of the people of the State of New York as a whole." The committee was further authorized to select three additional persons, one representative of the working people, one of the manufacturing and mercantile interests, and one of the public, to sit with it in its deliberations, to furnish it with information and suggestions, and otherwise to assist it in its investigations. The expenses of the committee were not to exceed $25,000, from which the salaries of counsel, assistants, etc., were to be paid.

The committee was to report to the legislature on or before February 15, 1927.

The most important problem before this committee—the New York Industrial Survey Commission—was the 48-hour week bill. The opponents and proponents of the measure were given full opportunity to present their cases, and much testimony was laid before the commission, the most pertinent of which were studies which had been made by the Women's Bureaus of the New York State Department of Labor, the United States Department of Labor, and the Consumers' League of New York. The study by the Consumers' League indicated clearly that "the working women wanted the 48-hour legislation, even if a reduction in hours meant less money." [83] In addition, an argument was presented on behalf of the Women's Joint Legislative Conference as to what would be the actual effect of the 48-hour week in industries in New York. The testimony of the proponents had as much weight as that of the opponents. The commission, consequently, recommended a measure which, though not wholly satisfactory to both sides, was accepted by the supporters of the original bill because it upheld the principle, at least, of the 48-hour week bill.[84]

It is, of course, obvious that the opposition to these bills was both strong and influential. Consequently, it is not surprising that a large portion of the program of the sponsors of the legislation was devoted to counter-attacks—answers to, and "exposés" of, the three chief opponents of the measures: Associated Industries, Inc.,[85] the National Woman's Party, and the Women's League for Equal Opportunity. Thus, in 1920, a special pamphlet was prepared by the New York State League of Women Voters—one of the organizations represented in the Women's Joint Legislative Conference—addressed "to the Governor, the Legislature, and the People of the State of New York." It accused Associated Industries,

---

[83] Pamphlet by the Consumers' League of New York, *The 48 Hour Law: Do Working Women Want It?* New York, 1927.

[84] *New York Session Law,* 1927, ch. 453, provided for an 8-hour day where women worked 6 full days a week; 9-hour day or 49½ hours a week where women were allowed a full half holiday in addition to their regular full day of rest; in addition, not more than 78 hours of overtime work a year.

[85] *Cf. infra,* p. 49.

Inc., of conducting a lobby—through its secretary, Mark Daly —which, by virtue of the methods it used to defeat social legislation was, in the opinion of the League, a menace to popular government.[86] Various reports both of the Consumers' League and the Women's Trade Union League stated that "the insidious way in which the influence of this numerically small group of organized employers is made to outweigh the expressed demand of the vast majority of people for relief of women workers"[87] is through the "control of upstate members of the legislature who constitute a majority of all the members."[88]

Even more vigorously did the Joint Legislative Conference repel the propaganda of the National Woman's Party. Formed in 1913 as the successor to the Congressional Union, which had been highly active in the cause of woman suffrage, the National Woman's Party has focussed its attention chiefly upon legal discriminations against women, and upon the passage by Congress of a constitutional amendment to grant equal rights to men and women throughout the United States.[89]

---

[86] *Cf. infra*, p. 52.

[87] *Bulletin of the Consumers' League*, May, 1923, *Legislative Sidelights of the Minimum Wage and 48 Hour Week Bills*, by Mary E. Drier and Clara Beyer.

[88] *Report of the Women's Trade Union League of New York*, 1924–1926, p. 16. In asserting such to be the case, the Consumers' League and the Women's Trade Union League were, one might remark parenthetically, calling attention to one of the fundamental problems of the lobby.

[89] In the course of this campaign, its Legal Research Department has distributed to the state branches of the National Woman's Party a summary of legal discriminations in each state, so that its separate state legislative programs might be intelligently prepared. Some of the proposals for the correction of such discriminations in New York are:

1. *The Guardianship Law*, to give mothers equal rights with fathers to the services and earnings of minor children, and to sue for certain injuries to minor children.

2. *The Illegitimacy Law*, to give mothers of children born out of wedlock the right to demand from the father equal responsibility for care and custody.

3. *The Domestic Relations Law*, to give married women the right to earnings secured by their labor in the home or in the business of their husbands.

4. *The Jury Service Law*, to give women the right to serve on juries on the same terms as men.

5. *The Education Law*, to give women teachers equal pay, equal promotion, and equal opportunity with men teachers. The Woman's Party actively helped in securing passage of an equal pay law in 1924, which was invalidated in 1927 by Court of Appeals decision.

The National Woman's Party opposed the 48-hour week and minimum wage legislation for women on the basis of its conviction that special legislation for women is a discrimination against them and can serve only as a handicap for women in competition with men.[90] It was, however, energetically refuted by the Joint Legislative Conference:

> A lesser, but by no means less virulent opposition is that of the Woman's Party. They pursue as a general practice, the method (if anything so slip-shod may be called method) of issuing statements, printed and verbal, with an utter disregard of facts. They are the most ardent supporters of the employers' "opposition," although their antagonism is always disguised under the pretense that they are working for equality. If one-quarter of the energy given to supporting the manufacturers' lobby were to be devoted to constructive legislation for the Woman's Party leisure class membership, the Party might make a slight contribution to social progress.[91]

Though less influential than that of Associated Industries, the opposition of the National Woman's Party, obviously, weakened the united front presented by organized women, so that members of the Joint Legislative Conference—particularly the Women's Trade Union League—engaged in speaking tours throughout the state to build up women's support, were present in Albany every week of the most stormy sessions,[92]

---

6. *The Labor Law,* to give working women the right to sell their labor on the same terms as men, unhampered by restrictive legislation applying to them but not to men.

7. *The Prostitution Law,* to make it apply equally to both sexes.

With the recent trend toward interstate industrial conferences, the state branches of the National Woman's Party, including that for New York, instead of introducing their legislative proposals into the state legislatures, have preferred to submit such proposals to these interstate conferences. It should be noted, however, that in its campaigns for industrial equality for men and women, the National Woman's Party has met with militant opposition from almost all other organized women's groups in New York State, with the exception of Business and Professional Women's organizations. See *Equal Rights,* Feb. 4, 1933, pp. 4, 5. *Cf. infra,* p. 219.

[90] U. S. Department of Labor, Bulletin of the Women's Bureau, *op. cit.,* p. 100. *Cf. New York Times,* Jan. 13, 1927.

[91] *Report of the Women's Trade Union League of New York,* 1924–1926, p. 16.

[92] Especially 1925 and 1926.

and publicized the problem widely in the press. At hearings before the Governor and legislative committees there were present large delegations of working girls, victims of reactionary legislation, to arouse human interest. Both members and nonmembers of the Joint Legislative Conference were prevailed upon to write or see their local representatives. Reports of how legislators voted on the 48-hour bill were circulated, the legislators being threatened with dire results at the polls if they failed to support progressive legislation. Legislators who voted favorably, on the other hand, were warmly thanked and even celebrated in song.[93]   In the end, as we have already seen, victory perched on the shoulders of the Joint Conference.

The battle, however, did not cease with the passage of the unsatisfactory compromise measure of 1927,[94] for in 1931, after the dissolution of the Joint Legislative Conference, the Women's Trade Union League, with the assistance of the League of Women Voters, the Consumers' League, and the Women's City Club, succeeded in securing an amendment to the law, making compulsory a weekly half holiday in addition to the weekly day of rest.

Achieved despite the vigorous opposition not only of Associated Industries and the National Woman's Party, but of the department stores as well,[95] the passage of this measure was due in no small part to the close scrutiny maintained by the Misses Mabel Leslie and Mary Hutt [96] over the maneuvers of Senator Knight, Republican leader, who was said to be overfriendly to the opposing side. In addition, the fact that representatives of both the merchants and the women's

---

[93] *Cf.* Song to Assemblyman Shonk at the W.T.U.L. luncheon, June 25, 1925.

[94] The law permitted a 49½ hour week for a five or five and a half day week, and an additional 78 hours of overtime during the year. The proponents of the law had believed that employers would be compelled to give their women employees a weekly half holiday in order that they might utilize the 78 hours overtime. A decision of the court invalidated this interpretation. See Women's Trade Union League, *Annual Report,* 1929–1930, p. 12. Though the 49½ hour schedule was adopted almost universally by the factories, the law was very difficult to enforce.

[95] *New York World,* May 4, 1930. *Cf.* detailed notes in the files of the New York State League of Women Voters.

[96] Legislative representatives of the Women's Trade Union League and the New York State League of Women Voters, respectively.

groups met with the Commissioner of Labor in order to arrive at some agreement *before* the introduction of bills into the legislature facilitated the enactment of a more satisfactory amendment.[97]

With the breakdown of industrial standards in depression years, the campaign for minimum wage legislation was even more vigorously renewed.[98] Under the auspices of the National Consumers' League, a conference of representatives of 50 organizations from 12 states met in New York City, on December 12, 1932. At this conference a committee of six was appointed to draft mandatory minimum legislation for women and minors, to be introduced into the various state legislatures.[99] As a consequence, on January 9, 1933, the Consumers' League of New York called a conference, attended by representatives of 76 civic, welfare, and religious organizations, to proceed with plans for a campaign in New York. Out of this conference, with the realization that voluntary cooperation from sympathetic employers was insufficient to counteract the breakdown of industrial standards, there was created the Labor Standards Committee, which was charged with the working out of a legislative program including mandatory minimum wage legislation and a 44-hour bill for women and minors.[100] Since membership in this Labor Standards Committee was open to organizations and individuals without financial obligation, more than 70 organizations, with an aggregate membership of over two million individuals, soon joined. Among the latter were several experts on labor legislation.

After careful preliminary arrangements, bills to attain the objectives of the Labor Standards Committee were introduced into the legislature early in the legislative session.[101] The

---

[97] See Consumers' League leaflet, *The 1931 Amendment to the Mercantile Hours Law.*

[98] The decision of the Supreme Court in the Adkins Case in 1923, which held the minimum wage law for women in the District of Columbia unconstitutional, gave this campaign a severe setback, though 15 states, as well as Puerto Rico, had already adopted minimum wage laws for women.

[99] *Cf.* pamphlet, *The Conference on the Breakdown of Industrial Standards,* National Consumers' League, Dec. 12, 1932.

[100] Unpublished minutes of *The Conference on the Breakdown of Industrial Standards* in files of Consumers' League of New York. *Cf. New York Times,* Jan. 10, 1933.

[101] Interview with Mrs. Elinore Herrick, Executive Secretary of the Con-

campaign for a minimum wage for women was short, heated, and effective.[102] Its success was due to three reasons. In the first place, the economic situation was unusually favorable to the enactment of such legislation. In the second place, passage of the bill was facilitated by the influential political connections of the leading sponsors.[103] Finally, the Labor Standards Committee, in and of itself, proved to be exceedingly astute in directing the pressure of the 70 organizations it represented.

Summary

In conclusion, it is seen that the chief pressure group at Albany for general labor interests is the New York State Federation of Labor. While railroad legislation falls more fittingly within the domain of the four railroad brotherhoods, their representatives look to the Federation for leadership and cooperation, seldom relying solely on their own efforts in promoting their legislative campaigns. In the special sphere of labor legislation for women, the Women's Trade Union League of New York and the Consumers' League of New York are all-important. While both have found it effective to work through some centralized agency dominated largely by organized local women's associations—like the Joint Legislative Conference in the 48-hour week campaign or the Labor Standards Committee in the minimum wage battle—they lean heavily upon the support and advice of their more experienced, protective big brother, the New York State Federation of Labor.

---

sumers' League of New York, in charge of most of the legislative work at this time, Feb., 1933.

[102] In 1936, however, the law was declared unconstitutional by the Court of Appeals (270 N. Y. 233), and the Supreme Court (298 U. S. 587).

[103] For example, Miss Mary Dewson, the president of the Consumers' League of New York, was, at this time, also president of the National Women's Democratic Organization. The vice-president was Mrs. F. D. Roosevelt. Women active in Republican circles, such as Mrs. Allen Moore, former legislative chairman of the State Federation of Women's Clubs, likewise did their part.

CHAPTER III

The Business Interests

A T the forefront of the forces engaged in a continuous battle for legislative influence at Albany are found a score or more of lobby groups representing the interests controlling money and industry. In the wealthiest and most highly industrialized state in the Union, it is no accident that those who dominate the fields of investment and production of consumers' goods should thus exercise tremendous pressure.

It is not feasible—nor would it be profitable here—to examine the efforts of all such aggregations; but, on the other hand, it is possible to arrive at a general understanding of the nature and extent of this pressure by studying a selected few of the most influential agents of the five basic fields of economic activity in New York: real estate, banking, insurance, manufacturing, and public utilities.[1]

The most intense activity of these organizations, like that of other groups, springs from the necessity for counteracting the demands of opposing bodies—a struggle that has been sharpened in the depression years. Though devoted to the theory of rugged individualism, capitalistic groups have found it expedient to cooperate with each other—when their individual group interests do not diverge [2]—in the presentation of a united front in support of concerted campaigns for protective legislation. Such campaigns have recently been waged toward two ends: (1) reduction of governmental expenditures and taxation, and (2) retardation of governmental regulation of business. Almost all organized groups in the basic fields of economic activity have joined hands, therefore, for the attainment of these two aims.

---

[1] For national trade associations see *Trade Association Activities,* 1927, published by the U. S. Department of Commerce in its *Domestic Commerce Series.*

[2] *Supra,* p. 4; *infra,* pp. 264, 265.

Real Estate

The first of these fields, real estate, has in recent sessions been one of the chief concerns of the legislature. As many as a thousand bills in a single session, representing nearly one-fourth of the total number of bills introduced, have had direct or indirect bearing on real estate.[3] Pressure has come primarily from two organizations among a host of local real estate boards: the Real Estate Association of the State of New York, and the Real Estate Board of New York, Inc. The first of these, founded in 1905 by a small group of real estate business men in various parts of the state, had grown by 1935 to a membership of some 34 real estate boards and 6,500 individuals.[4] The second was organized in 1896 and is concerned primarily with the real estate needs of the Borough of Manhattan in New York City, where most of its members reside.[5] In both associations the membership is composed chiefly of real estate brokers, owners, and managers. The services rendered by these organizations are informational as well as legislative; their most active committees are those on Taxation, Arbitration, Appraisal, Ethics, Education, Mortgage and Finance, and Legislation.[6]

The Committee on Legislation and Taxation of the Real Estate Association of the State of New York, composed of representatives from the legislative subcommittees of the six territorial districts of the state, presents the legislative program of the Association at the annual convention of the membership in the fall. By resolution the program is referred to

---

[3] *New York Times,* Mar. 10, 1935.

[4] The State Association has its own building in Albany near the state Capitol. Its annual budget has fluctuated between $12,000 and $23,000. It should be noted that in addition to the two most influential real estate groups, the Brooklyn Real Estate Board has its own legislative agent in Albany.

[5] The Board has a membership of 2,600 companies and individuals, its own building being in Manhattan. Its annual budget is in excess of $100,000. Its membership is not restricted to New York City.

[6] See the following publications of the Real Estate Association of the State of New York: (1) *Constitution and By-Laws;* (2) *Real Property,* a quarterly periodical; (3) *Annual Blue List Directory of the Real Estate Profession of the State of New York* (recently combined with the quarterly magazine).

See also the following publications of the Real Estate Board of New York: (1) *The Diary and Manual of the Real Estate Board of New York,* published annually; (2) *Real Estate and Building Management Digest,* a monthly periodical; (3) *Members' News Bulletin,* published occasionally.

the member boards for discussion and recommendations. In December, the general Committee on Legislation and Taxation meets at the headquarters in Albany and prepares a suggested program for the Board of Directors, which acts upon it before the legislative session opens in January. The execution of this legislative program is left to the executive vice-president of the Association, who is, in effect, the legislative agent of the Association. From Albany he issues weekly bulletins to the members and recommends specific pressure techniques. The Committee on Legislation of the Real Estate Board of New York meets weekly during legislative sessions to examine all legislation which bears directly or indirectly on real estate. On every bill is registered the action of the Board in writing, the introducer of the bill, the committee to which it has been referred, and the leader of the particular branch of the legislature in which the bill has been introduced. The committee also supervises the activities of the legislative agent of the Board, who attends the committee meetings.[7]

One of the principal aims of these real estate organizations is to relieve the real estate interests of their "disproportionate" burden of taxation by broadening the tax base to provide a more "equitable" distribution of the load.[8] To achieve this end they are never at a loss to suggest fresh sources of revenue. In 1934, for example, the Association launched an organized campaign for the adoption of its "comprehensive 10-Point Tax Program on behalf of homes, farms and other real estate," the chief point in which was a two per cent sales tax levy.[9] The Association was also responsible for the establishment, in 1935, of the State Committee for Real Estate Tax Limitation, whose purpose was to obtain an amendment to the state constitution

---

[7] The legislative agent of the Board is Edward P. Doyle, a well known figure in Albany official circles for 50 years, first as a member of the legislature and since then as a lobbyist. He moves familiarly in Albany officialdom, using cigars as calling cards, and calling legislators by their first names. Interviews, Edward P. Doyle, Mar. 4, 1933, and Ray Hofford, Executive Vice-President of the Real Estate Association of the State of New York, Jan. 27, 1933, Sept. 5, 1935.

[8] See *Second Report of the N. Y. State Commission for the Revision of the Tax Laws,* 1932, Legislative Document No. 77, p. 60.

[9] See *Report of the Legislative Activities of the Real Estate Association of the State of New York on Behalf of the Owners of Homes, Farms and Other Real Estate,* 1934. Real estate interests have also advocated increased taxes on gasoline and liquor and lowering of the income tax brackets.

limiting taxes on real property to two per cent of its assessed valuation.[10]

The legislative influence of the real estate interests may best be observed, however, in the multiple dwelling law campaign in 1928 and 1929. A Temporary Commission,[11] created for the purpose of revising the tenement house law in the cities of New York and Buffalo, had sponsored a bill which the realty interests of the state did not approve. The New York Allied Property Owners' Committee was, therefore, organized in 1928 to defeat this legislation. In the face of ardent support of the bill by newspapers, civic groups, and welfare organizations, the realtors, 500 strong, stormed the legislature for the public hearing, and succeeded in delaying the consummation of the commission's work.[12] Thereupon three new members, representing the realty interests, were added to the commission, and a new bill was introduced into the legislature in 1929.[13] This time the tables were turned. Although the realtors now actively supported the revised tenement house bill, vigorous opposition came from New York City's Democratic administration, which attacked the bill as a violation of the home rule amendment and the city's zoning regulations.[14] Hearst newspapers throughout the state decried the legislation as "un-American." Such diverse groups as the New York State Federation of Labor and the New York Academy of Medicine denounced the inadequacy of the provisions. Yet, in spite of this opposition, the real estate lobby was able to obtain the

---

[10] Other organizations concerned in the establishment of this committee included chambers of commerce, banks, taxpayers' associations, Empire State Gas and Electric Association, Citizens' Budget Commission, and the New York Central Railroad. A complete list of these appears in the *New York Teacher,* published by the Teachers' Union of the City of New York, Feb., 1936, p. 65. The directors of this committee are official representatives of cooperating groups, but membership is open to any property owner. See *New York Times,* Oct. 27, 1935, and Sept. 22, 1935; *Real Property,* official quarterly of the Real Estate Association of the State of New York, Aug., 1935, and issues since then.

[11] This commission was composed of eight legislators and three additional members appointed by the Governor to represent the public.

[12] The 1928 bill was introduced after the Temporary Commission had toiled for eight months, during which time many public hearings were held and hundreds of witnesses were heard.

[13] The realty interests insisted that without their direct representation on the commission, no "intelligent, practical" report or bill could be drawn.

[14] This new bill applied only to New York City.

enactment of the bill, to prove its validity in the courts, and to win for it annual amendments. This success was due in part to the unusual political situation in which most of the Democratic legislators from New York City voted against the bill, the Republican-controlled legislature passed it, and the Democratic Governor, F. D. Roosevelt, signed it. For the most part, however, it was the pressure backed by the support, money, and talent of the real estate interests which was responsible for passage of the act.[15]

Banking

The bankers, another basic economic group, have always been active in legislative matters in New York State. However, with public opinion holding them most accountable for the economic crisis, banking legislation has inevitably increased in recent years. To protect their interests, bankers have cooperated, therefore, with such active organizations as the New York State Bankers Association. Organized in Buffalo in 1894, this body is today representative of some 800 national banks, state banks, trust companies, investment banking houses, and savings banks incorporated under the laws of New York.[16]

Specialized groups in the Association are the savings banks and the trust companies, which have state associations of their own.[17] All 135 savings banks in the state are members of the Savings Bank Association of the State of New York, estab-

[15] In the New York City office of Harold Riegelman, counsel to the Temporary Dwelling House Commission and the Multiple Dwelling Law Committee, created in 1929, are some 18 volumes which tell the whole story of this campaign. These volumes contain the personnel and reports of the commissions, the text of bills prepared and passed by the legislature, amendments to the law since 1929, minutes of the hearings held by the commissions and the legislature, the record of the court proceedings testing the constitutionality of the laws, and extensive press and magazine comments. See *Real Estate Magazine,* published by the Real Estate Board of New York, Apr., 1928.

[16] Eighty-two per cent of the eligible banking institutions in New York State were members of this Association in Sept., 1935. It is supported largely by dues computed upon a graduated scale of the capital, surplus and undivided profits of the commercial members and the surplus fund of the savings banks. In 1933–1934 it operated within an annual budget of approximately $35,000.

[17] Fifty-four of the 135 savings banks and 124 of the 135 trust companies in the state were members of the New York State Bankers Association in Sept., 1935.

lished in 1894.   This organization, although usually cooperating with the State Bankers Association, often acts alone in cases affecting savings institutions particularly.[18] The Trust Companies Association of the State of New York, organized in 1904, exists almost wholly for the purpose of watching legislation affecting the interests of its members. Eighty-four trust companies in the state were members of this group in 1935. National and state banks that act in a fiduciary capacity are now also eligible for membership.   Meetings of the executive and legislative committees of the Trust Companies Association are held frequently, but for the members there is only an annual meeting, held in February.[19]

The structure of the New York State Bankers Association parallels that of the various other bankers' associations in the state.   A Council of Administration of 20 members is composed of the officers of the Association, the two most recent past presidents, and, also, the chairmen of the eight groups into which the Association is divided on a geographical county basis.[20]   In addition, there are two representatives for each of the five classes from which the Association draws its membership: national banks, state banks, trust companies, savings banks, and investment banking houses.   One of the most important and active committees of the Association is the State Legislative Committee, composed of five members, for whose work $1,000 was allowed in the Association's annual budget for 1933–1934.   This committee submits a detailed report of its activities to the members assembled at the midwinter and summer annual meetings.

Prior to the depression, many banking bills had been suggested and even drafted by bankers' associations.   With constantly increasing supervision by the State Department of Banking during the economic depression, however, much of the banking legislation originates with the State Superintendent of Banks and the Department of Taxation and Finance,

---

[18] See Frederic B. Stevens, *History of the Savings Bank Association of the State of New York,* Garden City, N. Y., Doubleday, Page, 1915.

[19] Interview, Henry L. Servoss, Secretary, Dec. 13, 1935.

[20] Each of these groups selects its own officers, holds meetings, and reports back its activities to the Association at its annual convention.   Over 100 county and committee meetings have been held in the course of one year. *Proceedings of the New York State Bankers Association,* 1932.

or grows out of recommendations from specially-created legislative investigatory committees. For this reason the Association, through its State Legislative Committee, encourages wholehearted cooperation with these departments and keeps close watch on the sessions of the special investigatory committees and the legislative standing committees to which bills have been referred. The results of this scrutiny and study are transmitted to the Association's members through frequent letters, bulletins, and circulars from the State Legislative Committee, the executive manager, or the secretary of the Association.[21] The influence of the individual banks in their home towns and cities, however, is the chief weapon of bankers' associations. Members are urged to exert pressure on their local legislators and other persons "in authority or influential at Albany," by seeing, by writing, or by wiring them.[22] Party leaders inside and outside of the legislature, in the local community and at Albany, are contacted in this very personal way.[23] With the local bank necessary to the very existence of the local community, and frequently to the dominant political party organization, the bankers' groups do not hesitate to communicate with political leaders responsible, perhaps, for some recalcitrant legislator who is "not cooperating." This is apparent in the following excerpt from a letter of the secretary of one of the bankers' associations to the chairman of the Republican State Committee:

> In our efforts to further the passage of the Fearon-Wallace bill equalizing the state franchise tax on savings

[21] Representatives of the savings banks and the trust companies associations are more in evidence at Albany. The members of the Council of Administration or of the State Legislative Committee of the New York State Bankers Association are usually present in Albany only when their attendance is necessary at public hearings before investigatory or legislative standing committees. Interviews, W. G. Brown, Executive Manager, Apr. 4, 1933, and Clifford F. Post, Secretary, Sept. 26, 1935.

[22] *Bulletin,* Mar. 9, 1933.

[23] Emphasis upon this particular method saves the Association from attacks by individual members on controversial banking legislation on which there is no general agreement among members of the Association. For example, the chairman of the State Legislative Committee of the New York State Bankers Association appeared in 1933 before the public hearing at Albany on the subject of branch banking and expressed only the views of the members of the Legislative Committee, which is usually the official stand of the Association. The individual members of the Association and of the legislature were asked to inform themselves mutually about local banking sentiment.

banks, we find as our chief opponent the Chairman of the Senate Finance Committee (a Republican) who recently in a letter to a friend expressed the following thoughts on the question . . . [24]

The associations are equally generous, through resolutions at conventions or in bulletins to members, in singling out legislators who have done "fine work." [25]   The influence of the individual member banks is such that they are sometimes called upon to name representatives to advisory or investigatory commissions or to the Banking Board.[26]

Favorable newspaper publicity is also an element in these pressure techniques.   The New York State Bankers Association maintains a list of some 150 upstate newspapers to which it dispatches news releases from time to time, and at frequent intervals representatives of New York City newspapers visit the city offices of the Association for news.   But for such publicity, too, the banking associations depend, in general, chiefly upon the local banks.

Very occasionally the banking associations suggest to their members that they communicate with individual depositors and stockholders to urge pressure on the legislature.   Such a procedure, however, is in general believed to be ineffective, especially when they desire to reach large numbers.[27]

Insurance

In the third basic field of economic endeavor, insurance, cooperative action has been achieved largely through national,

---

[24] Letter from the general secretary of the Savings Bank Association of the State of New York to W. Kingsland Macy, Mar. 31, 1931.

[25] In recent years, there has not been much naming of names, realizing that the public temper may be such as to interpret every boost as a knock.

[26] Both the New York State Bankers Association and the Savings Bank Association were represented on the important State Budget Advisory Commission.   In 1932, the New York State Bankers Association participated in the nomination of candidates to the newly created Banking Board in New York. When Joseph A. Broderick resigned as State Superintendent of Banks, the Governor sought the advice of the individual banks rather than that of the Association in naming a successor.   Interview, C. F. Post, Secretary, Sept. 26, 1935.

[27] The Savings Bank Association reported, for example, that there were 6,400,000 accounts in the savings banks of the state on Jan. 1, 1935.   The bankers realize, however, that in legislative matters the interests of the bankers and the depositors are not identical.

rather than state, organizations. The most influential of these has been the Association of Life Insurance Presidents, organized in 1906, with headquarters in New York City, for the purpose of "dispelling the mystery from life insurance in state legislative bodies."[28] The origin of this Association is bound up with an investigation authorized by the New York State Legislature in 1905, which disclosed that insurance interests with a less formal and more secret organization had employed unethical methods in promoting or opposing legislation.[29]

The Association of Life Insurance Presidents, having assumed the task of purging these methods, had grown by 1934 to a membership of 68 life insurance companies representing total assets of more than $20,000,000,000 and insurance in force of more than $91,000,000,000.[30] In a period of 17 years the Association examined 22,000 legislative measures, including, during this same period, the 1,700 statutes or amendments which were passed by state legislative bodies in the United States.[31] For these achievements the Association has relied, for the most part, upon the member companies resident in the particular states. At Albany, where insurance legislation is unusually voluminous, the attorney of the Association is regularly registered and appears as its representative in company with the counsel of several of its large New York member companies.[32]

Manufacturing

In the large and influential economic field of manufacturing, the chief pressure group is Associated Industries, Inc., an asso-

---

[28] George T. Wight, Secretary and Manager of the Association, "Removing Mystery from Life Insurance," *Spectator,* July 17, 1924, reprinted in pamphlet form by the Association.

[29] *Hearings before the Joint Committee of the Senate and Assembly of the State of New York, Appointed to Investigate the Affairs of Life Insurance Companies,* 10 vols., Albany, 1906.

[30] Originally the Association had 13 members with total assets of about $2,000,000,000 and insurance in force of some $9,000,000,000. Seven of the 68 members are Canadian companies. *Proceedings of the 29th Annual Convention of the Association of Life Insurance Presidents,* Dec., 1935.

[31] George T. Wight, *op. cit.*

[32] The American Life Convention, established in 1905, with headquarters in Chicago, is composed largely of some 130 small legal reserve life insurance companies (1935). This Association cooperates with the Association of Life Insurance Presidents, 35 members of the Association of Life Insurance Presidents being associated with the American Life Convention as well. See *Proceedings, op. cit.,* 1935, p. 91.

ciation of manufacturers, merchants, and industrial and mercantile property owners. Organized in May, 1914, with permanent headquarters at Buffalo, it is composed of some 1,500 firms, corporations, and individuals "who give employment to about two-thirds of the total number of wage earners engaged in manufactures in the State of New York" and is, therefore, "one of the largest associations of its kind in the United States." [33]

Although the organization comprises officers and a Board of Directors of 38 members, the policies of Associated Industries are directed by the general secretary, assisted by an Executive Committee of nine persons.[34]

In addition to protecting its members from "unreasonable and unnecessary legislation," the Association maintains a Legal Bureau and a Tax Bureau headed by experts who answer questions and often publish their answers in the Association's official monthly publication, the *Monitor*. There is also a Technical Advisory Bureau of 25 engineers and practical factory managers, whose services are offered free of cost by their employers. The work of this bureau is divided into two divisions: Inspections and Variations, and Industrial Codes. The Division of Inspections and Variations investigates orders of the State Department of Labor referred to it by members

---

[33] *Monitor,* monthly publication of Associated Industries, Inc., May, 1934, p. 232. Dues are based on payrolls of members, computed on the basis of 30¢ for each $1,000 of total payroll for the preceding year. The minimum for members is $10 annually, and for members owning industrial or mercantile properties, $25 annually, regardless of payroll. Subsidiary companies are eligible to remain as members without payment of separate dues. During the depression years a large number of the subsidiary companies took advantage of this privilege. The organization grew from a membership of 39 in 1914 to 1,859 in 1930, when its income was about $100,000. Though there was a steady decline in membership and income from 1930 to 1933, the fiscal year ending Feb. 28, 1935, showed an improvement. Its income during the depression years has been about $60,000. See annual reports in *Monitor*, May, 1934, and May, 1935. For the recruitment of members a field service is maintained. In 1930 a professional agency was employed to plan and execute a special campaign for new members. See *Monitor,* May, 1931, p. 271.

[34] The Board of Directors, elected by the members at the annual meeting, selects the officers, all of whom except the general secretary and the district vice-presidents must be members of the Board of Directors. The president appoints the Executive Committee from among the members of the Board of Directors. Mark A. Daly has been secretary of Associated Industries since its inception in 1914. During this period the organization has had five presidents. *Monitor,* June, 1934, p. 17.

of the Association. If the division deems it advisable, appeals are taken to the State Industrial Board. This division also makes applications for variations from provisions of the labor law affecting construction and maintenance of buildings.[35] The Industrial Codes Division is represented on all advisory committees of the State Department of Labor which draft the rules and regulations interpreting the labor law in the State of New York. This agency, it has been said, has saved members of the Association more than $1,000,000, and is the only one of its kind in existence.[36]

The Association also maintains a Traffic Managers' Council, composed of the traffic managers of member firms. The council advises members on traffic problems in their respective territorial districts, and undertakes special assignments for various groups concerning rates and classifications.[37]

The Educational Bureau of the Association, in addition to publishing the *Monitor,* has sponsored, since 1925, annual statewide safety campaigns in which a wide variety of industries cooperate to reduce accidents.[38]

Associated Industries maintains intimate contacts with the New York State Society of Industrial Medicine, a society which keeps industry informed of the latest methods and practices in industrial medicine and surgery. For many years, *The Industrial Doctor,* the monthly publication of this Society, was distributed by Associated Industries through its Educational Bureau to industrial practitioners, whose activities are of vital importance to members of Associated Industries because of their connection with Workmen's Compensation provisions.[39] So, although Associated Industries came into existence largely as a defensive organization against the "riot of social legislation" enacted by the New York Legislature in 1913 and 1914, it has evolved into an organization which instructs its members in how "to live with these laws whether

[35] The Technical Bureau handled 2,769 appeals in 14 years. *Monitor,* June, 1932, p. 10.
[36] *Monitor,* June, 1932, p. 10, and May, 1934, p. 232.
[37] *Monitor,* May, 1934, p. 233. *Cf. A Broadcast of Services to New York Industry,* published by Associated Industries, 1930, p. 6.
[38] *Monitor,* May, 1934, pp. 222, 233.
[39] *The Industrial Doctor* was recently combined with the national journal, *Industrial Medicine,* published in Chicago.

they like them or not." [40]   Its chief function, however, remains
legislative.

For a score of years the legislative activities of Associated
Industries have been conducted by Mark A. Daly, its general
secretary.   This rotund, jovial figure is among the best known
of "lobbyists" on Capitol Hill, his name having become syn-
onymous with that of the Association he represents.   His
methods in influencing legislation are known as the "Daly
Lobby." [41]   During the legislative session, Mark Daly and
his assistant are installed at the Associated Industries' Albany
headquarters in the Ten Eyck Hotel, where Daly prepares
bulletins of information about various bills for distribution
among the Association's membership.[42]

The secrecy which has always surrounded the Daly lobby
has been dispelled in recent years by the chief adversaries of
Associated Industries, such as organized labor and certain welfare organizations, particularly women's groups.[43]   During the
campaign for a 48-hour law for women, in 1920, for example,
the New York State League of Women Voters published a
*Report and Protest to the Governor, the Legislature and the
People of the State of New York: The Daly Lobby and Propaganda as a Danger Confronting Popular Government.*   In this
leaflet Associated Industries was shown to be "the dominant
obstructionist influence."   The League had been "reliably
informed" that this Association had raised a fund of between
$100,000 and $200,000 for propaganda purposes to support the
"so-called" New York League for Americanism, and that this
propaganda, "conducted under the pretense of patriotism, has
been calculated to arouse, by unscrupulously false and mis-

---

[40] Mark Daly, *Monitor*, May, 1935, p. 228.
[41] Daly was honored at the twentieth anniversary meeting of Associated
Industries in 1934.   For 17 years prior to his association with this organization,
Daly was a newspaper man.   See *Monitor,* June, 1934, p. 16 and June, 1936,
p. 6.
[42] *Monitor,* May, 1935, p. 227.
[43] Recently, however, Associated Industries and the New York State Federation of Labor joined forces in opposition to the competition of prison-made
goods.   Both cooperated, as do other organizations and individuals, with the
Campaign Committee Against Unfair Competition of Prison-Made Products,
the National Committee on Prisons and Prison Labor, serving as a national
clearing house.   Furthermore, *Monitor* devotes much space to the annual
legislative program of the New York State Federation of Labor.

leading statements, popular prejudice against and misunderstanding of such a measure as that providing for workmen's
cooperative illness insurance as well as other measures of
human welfare." The secretary and active director of the New
York League for Americanism was said to be "a man who has
long been employed by certain insurance interests to wage
propagandist warfare" against such legislation, and his task
of "accelerating" public opinion was performed by "tricky
methods." A list of these methods followed.

Mark A. Daly was depicted as a lobbyist who employed the
funds at his disposal and his intimacy with certain influential
members of the legislature [44] "to prevent the impartial consideration of such legislative measures as he sees fit to condemn. His methods are intended to defeat such measures
before they even reach the floor of the Assembly." These
methods were illustrated by showing how an amendment to
the Workmen's Compensation Law was defeated in 1919.
Though agreed upon at a conference with Daly, the bill failed
to come out of committee because Daly said the bill was "not
to be moved." Thereupon, the individuals concerned informed Speaker Sweet that the bill had been agreed upon by
all. The Speaker had replied that since this was so, the bill
would go through at once. After all had withdrawn, Daly
immediately returned to the Speaker's office. And so, although the bill finally passed the Assembly, two days before
the close of the session it was tabled in the Senate. The
influence of Daly with the Speaker was further illustrated by
the selection of Assemblyman Bewley, Daly's roommate, to
introduce the minimum wage law for women in 1919. The
assemblymen of the majority party who bolted the party
caucus, moreover, were punished by "demotion," i.e., by their
assignment to unimportant committees or by the withholding
of committee chairmanships in spite of the fact that length
of service in the legislature would normally have entitled them
to such superior assignments.

At the instigation of the Daly lobby, it was said, petitions
had been obtained through "subtle methods of coercion," with

---

[44] John Sullivan, former President of the New York State Federation of
Labor, stated in interview that he saw Daly order legislators around as though
they were errand boys.

the knowledge of members of the Assembly, in order to lend support to the arbitrary position of the Speaker against certain welfare laws, as in the case of the measure for workmen's cooperative illness insurance. These petitions had come from the officers of insurance companies, closely associated with the Daly lobby, and did not originate with the employees. They had been circulated by individuals who were blindly prejudiced against the proposed legislation. It was further stated that often false information had been given as an inducement to secure signatures.[45]

One evidence of the great influence of Associated Industries in the New York State Legislature had been the sympathetic reception given to its program by the Republican party. An analysis of the votes cast in the legislature on measures in which Associated Industries has been interested since its organization shows that, with few exceptions, successful enactment was due to Republican support. With the Democratic party Associated Industries identifies organized labor, its chief adversary at Albany. The members of the Association have been warned that "if the minority (Dem.) ever should become the majority in the legislature it will be flatly committed to the passage of the bills [of organized labor] despite the fact that the leaders of the minority are too intelligent not to know that the measures are unfair and uneconomic." [46] In 1935 the Democrats controlled both houses of the Legislature and the Governorship. Mark Daly said at that time: "No legislature since 1913 did as much damage to business as did the 1935 session. There was a very remote, outside hope that Governor Lehman might mitigate the blow a little by vetoes during the thirty-day-bill period, but . . . the hope was unrealized

---

[45] Associated Industries again brought unfavorable publicity upon itself when its Board of Directors, on Jan. 10, 1924, called upon Governor Alfred E. Smith to appoint a Moreland Act Commissioner to investigate the charge made by Associated Industries that the state insurance fund in the Department of Labor was inefficiently administered. Governor Smith, announcing that he, as his own commissioner, would undertake the inquiry, subpoenaed several officers of Associated Industries, Mark Daly among them. The inquiry, ostensibly directed at the administration of the Workmen's Compensation Law, was actually focussed upon the activities of the accusers. When the inquiry began, the officers of the Association admitted that they could prove none of their contentions, and the matter was dropped. Cf. New York World, Jan. 24, 1924, and Mar. 14, 1924.

[46] Monitor, June, 1932, pp. 5, 6 and June, 1936, p. 6.

except in a few relatively minor instances. The 'big stuff' all became law." [47]

Daly employed the effective technique of concentrating on the committee holding a particularly obnoxious bill, so that the bill would not reach the floor for debate or vote. For this reason Associated Industries frowned on the practice of discharging committees from further consideration of a bill, especially when the Republicans had made it a caucus issue and had pledged sufficient votes to prevent the Democrats from overriding the action of the committee. Daly, citing a particular instance where the Democrats had made motions to discharge committees from further consideration of bills, praised the Republican senators, all of whom "stood by their guns and refused to be stampeded or intimidated; and that the same thing was true of all the Republican members of the Assembly except . . ."—then appeared in Daly's report the full name, address, district, and county of the four Republican assemblymen who joined with the Democrats in voting for the discharge.[48]

Thus Associated Industries has wielded great influence in Albany when the legislature has been controlled by Republicans. Even when only one house has been so controlled, its pressure has been a redoubtable force, for its chief interest lies in blocking rather than promoting legislation, in postponing or emasculating social legislation as long as possible to thus "save as much money for industry as possible, even if it cannot be done indefinitely." [49] In this connection, Associated Industries is always prepared with a compromise measure as an alternative or as a basis upon which to trade.[50]

With the traditional Republican allies of Associated Industries no longer in control at Albany, Mark Daly now speaks frankly of "employers getting into politics with no reservations" by putting into the legislature men who understand the

---

[47] *Monitor,* May, 1935, p. 227. The "big stuff" was chiefly such progressive social legislation as unemployment insurance and liberal reforms in the Workmen's Compensation Law and the Public Health Law.

[48] *Monitor,* June, 1932, p. 5. See also *Monitor,* May, 1934, p. 206.

[49] Interview, Mark Daly, Feb. 1, 1933.

[50] In 1934, for example, when the passage of the labor-sponsored Unemployment Insurance bill was imminent, Associated Industries prepared a compromise measure to be passed in its stead. *Monitor,* May, 1934, p. 205.

problems and responsibilities of business and thus "raise the standards of legislative brains." [51]

The influence of Associated Industries does not depend entirely, however, on the vicissitudes of the Republican party or on the efficiency of *sub rosa* pressure methods. The Association represents a substantial number of influential manufacturers in New York and is the largest organization of its kind in the state. Even if for no other reason, its officers have been called upon to serve on important advisory governmental commissions. For example, Mark Daly has been a member of the New York State Budget Advisory Commission. In 1933, moreover, he was appointed by the Governor to the important Minimum Wage Advisory Committee, and in 1935 to the equally important State Advisory Council on Unemployment Insurance and the Commission on Interstate Compacts.

Associated Industries is not, of course, the only vigorous pressure body representing organized business men.[52] Another such group that deserves notice is the New York State Economic Council, Inc., an organization which grew out of the failure of the legislature to reappoint the joint legislative Industrial Survey Commission in 1929. Beginning in 1926, this commission had studied economic and industrial condi-

---

[51] *Monitor,* June, 1935, p. 24.

[52] Unlike most other states, no state chamber of commerce exists in New York. The Chamber of Commerce of the State of New York, founded in 1768, is local in character and unique in organization. This group functions on the town meeting, rather than the more common corporation plan. Each member is entitled to attend the monthly meetings of the chamber, to voice his opinion, and to vote. Officers and committees report directly to the chamber. Reports in full to be discussed at the meeting are sent to each member a few days in advance. Action on proposals is, therefore, slower, for fewer subjects are considered at one time. Such an organization has made necessary a membership limited to 2,000 resident and 250 non-resident members. These are individual business men, not corporations. Lawyers are excluded. Dues are $100 a year. Although the membership quota is usually filled and a waiting list maintained, this was not the case during the economic depression. The number of members as of Oct. 1, 1935, was 1,150. The chamber presents opinions on legislative matters through resolutions and reports, accepted by its members at their monthly meetings. When these deal with legislation pending at Albany, copies are submitted to the Legislature and the Governor. The chamber believes that these reports "are regarded as being expressive of the careful and studied opinion of a group of New York's most important business men." See pamphlet, *Chamber of Commerce of the State of New York: Its Organization and Activities,* undated.

tions in New York State for the guidance of business men in making industrial progress. Two of the public members of the commission, Messrs. James W. Gerald and Merwin K. Hart, in order to continue this work, planned a statewide congress to be held in New York City in the spring of 1929. From this congress a Committee of Twenty-five, composed mostly of business men, was appointed to place before the people of the state a program aimed at maintaining the economic supremacy of the state, in which the advice and leadership of business men would be the directing forces.[53] To execute the "long range" program formulated by this committee, there was incorporated in November, 1930, the New York State Economic Council, with the members of the Committee of Twenty-five as its directors.[54]

The legislative influence of the Council has deepened with the depression. It has clamored for the curtailment of public expenditures so as to make possible the drastic reduction in taxes which it considers "an absolute prerequisite to the return of any kind of prosperity." [55] Advocating a pay-as-you-go policy in balancing the budget rather than increased indebtedness, it has become the open enemy of such social legislation as compulsory unemployment insurance and workmen's compensation.[56] It has opposed mandatory expenditures upon local governments, has strongly advocated the reduction of the salaries of public employees, and has opposed the general or sympathetic strike. It has even advocated the disenfranchisement of all persons on public relief rolls.[57] Consequently, like

---

[53] See pamphlet, *Statement of the Committee of Twenty-five of the New York State-Wide Economic Congress,* Oct. 22, 1929.

[54] The Council, supported by voluntary contributions, has an annual budget of approximately $60,000, and maintains offices in New York City and Utica and during the legislative session, at Albany.

[55] *Economic Council Bulletin,* Jan. 16, 1933.

[56] At the public hearing on the pending unemployment insurance bills at Albany in 1934, the president of the Economic Council was the only one present who was opposed to any form of unemployment insurance. *Bulletin of the New York State Federation of Labor,* Apr. 3, 1934.

[57] Other significant recommendations in the Economic Council's program are county reorganization, general revision of the pension laws, coordination of taxes to avoid duplication, a uniform budget system, opposition to any form of compulsory health or sickness insurance or to any extension of New York's old age security, limitation of real estate taxes to 2 per cent of the true values, and repeal of the veterans' preference clause in the state constitution. *New York Times,* Aug. 6, 1934.

Associated Industries, the Economic Council supports a program that redounds materially to the interests of private business. In this program the business man occupies an unshackled position of leadership for the maintenance of high economic standards in the state.

To this end the Economic Council has built up an organization of 50,000 "taxpaying members," [58] organized in local county councils. These county councils are independent units which deal with problems in their own locality, under the direction of their own leaders. In legislative matters, however, they cooperate with the State Council. Although this support is voluntary, the state organization considers it the function of each county council:

> 1. To furnish the State Council with important or unusual facts or incidents as to Federal or State expenditures within the county, and with information as to public opinion within each county on problems of State and Federal public expenditures;
>
> 2. To consider, and in its discretion to act upon, any State or Federal problem put up to it by the State Council;
>
> 3. To use the full influence of its leaders and its membership with the legislators of the County on behalf of any Federal or State proposition upon which the County Council has acted, thus pooling its strength with that of the other County Councils;
>
> 4. Where requested by the State Council to undertake to furnish data on any subject of general interest which the State Council is studying;
>
> 5. To report immediately any economy or other substantial result obtained by the County Council, or by any other agency within the County; and
>
> 6. To cooperate generally with the State Council.[59]

---

[58] The Economic Council has realized that to function effectively it must have as wide a base of membership as possible. To confine its membership to merchants chiefly would make the organization too vulnerable for attack because the boycott can be used so effectively against merchants. Interview, Merwin K. Hart, Apr. 18, 1933. Cf. *New York Times*, Aug. 6, 1934. In addition to merchants and manufacturers there are also farmers and professional men in the membership.

[59] *Economic Council Bulletin*, Jan. 16, 1933, p. 2.

The State Council, in turn, assists the county councils in their local activities, particularly with information and suggestions for public economies.   In this way the state and the county councils cooperate to draft, introduce, and press the enactment of bills in the legislature.

To reach the voter directly, the Economic Council has compiled a mailing list of the names of representative business men, farmers, and professional men.   A quota is assigned to each county for individual communication with the most influential voters.   On the basis of this list some 16,000 letters have been dispatched twice a month, sometimes more frequently during legislative sessions.[60]   In these letters economic conditions in the state and nation are reviewed and interpreted, their readers being urged to express their opposition to or approval of pending legislation directly to the members of the legislature.   In a recent campaign, during which this "representative" mailing list was compiled, citizens were asked to sign cards, agreeing to write to their legislators five times during the year when requested by the Council, provided they approved the Council's recommendations.

In addition, the Economic Council has also been able to secure the cooperation of other organizations, because many of its influential members are also affiliated with other groups.[61]   In the City of New York several of the Council's members are also members of the Citizens' Budget Commission.   Many of its members, appointed to such important administrative and advisory commissions as the Governor's Budget Advisory Commission, have in this way been able to exert influence upon the legislature through the executive branch of the government.[62]   To supplement this force, the Council utilizes such common pressure techniques as the prepa-

---

[60] Interview, Col. Arthur F. Cosby, Secretary of the New York State Economic Council, Oct. 8, 1935.

[61] The Council has a large Board of Directors recruited from many counties in the state.   About 30 of its 74 members, however, are from New York City.

[62] In Mar., 1935, the New York State Economic Council sponsored and assisted in forming the New York State Committee for the Revival of Private Enterprise.   This committee "independent of party or politics" is composed of about 100 men and women representing 50 of the 62 counties of the state. The program of the committee is very similar to that of the Council itself. See pamphlet published by this committee, *Revive Private Enterprise*, a radio address by Merwin K. Hart, Mar. 15, 1935.

ration of special letters for newspapers and the procural of
advance statements from legislators on its program. This
"questionnaire method" has not been very effective and is not
utilized frequently.

Thus the Economic Council, much like Associated Industries, is considered by many labor, welfare, and governmental
employee organizations, a reactionary body and an enemy of
social progress.

There are two other organizations which are somewhat similar in aim to the Economic Council in that they represent
strong pressure directed by a number of big business interests at New York State's legislators for the purpose of preventing an increase in specific taxes. These are the New York
State Automobile Association and the New York State Motor
Truck Association,[63] both of them offering similar services to
their members. Of these services, which are rendered by
numerous specialized committees with a secretary and a paid
staff, there are two classes. In the first class are benefits which
do not require special legislation, such as emergency road
service, travel information, or the elimination of speed traps
for the benefit of the car owner generally. The services in the
second class consist of legislative proposals which favor the
automobile owner. In recent years these services have consisted chiefly of pressure for appropriations to develop and
improve roads and against any increase in taxes on motor
fuel. Results of such legislative activity are announced to
the members of the Associations through legislative bulletins,
publications, specially prepared brochures,[64] and long distance
telephone calls.

---

[63] The New York State Automobile Association was organized in 1903, the
Motor Truck Association in 1910. In 1933 the Empire State Motor Truck
Owners Association, Inc., organized in 1931, with headquarters in Albany, and
serving chiefly upstate commercial vehicular operators, was amalgamated with
the Motor Truck Association of America, with headquarters in New York
City. There are in the New York State Automobile Association 50 local
automobile clubs and their branches, representing 100,000 individual passenger
car owners. Membership in the Motor Truck Association numbers more than
2,200 "leading" individual and industrial firms operating commercial vehicles.
The annual budget of the Motor Truck Association is about $46,000 (1934).

[64] In Dec., 1932, for example, a large brochure of statistics was prepared and
widely distributed by the New York State Automobile Association, containing current facts regarding taxation of the motorist in New York State and
the nation as a basis for publicity and as a defense weapon if the Governor
suggested another increase in gasoline taxes to meet the 1933 deficit.

Although unsuccessful in blocking increases in automotive taxes during the depression years, the Associations waged energetic campaigns against them, often winning a compromise measure. Such was the campaign waged against Governor Roosevelt's attempt to increase the gasoline tax from two to four cents in 1932. The two cent increase was defeated in that year by a mass movement, encouraged and directed by the automobile associations, in which hundreds of thousands of signatures, letters, and telegrams deluged the members of the legislature. This technique, wide and convincing in its appeal, is illustrated by the following excerpts from a bulletin dated February 2, 1932, sent by the secretary of the New York State Automobile Association to the local automobile club members:

GAS TAX INCREASE BATTLE HALF WON

For the past three weeks, two million motorists of New York State as represented by 52 automobile clubs have been pounding away at the legislature, with the result that to-day the Republican majority issued a statement that they would not grant the Governor's request (Governor Roosevelt, a Democrat) for a two cent gas tax and would limit the increase to one cent.

The battle is half won; at the present moment, we have 61,730 signatures on file in this office (petitions placed on display in garages and gas stations through the suggestion chiefly of local automobile clubs). Scores of clubs are working on this proposition as never before, redouble your efforts now for a few more days and we have hopes of preventing any increase in the gas tax whatsoever.

Signatures, by the tens of thousands must come into this office immediately. You must get many, many motorists of your vicinity to write and telegraph your representatives in the legislature vigorously opposing any increase whatsoever.

Last night (here the names of ten officers of the state and local clubs are given) called on a large number of senators and assemblymen at the Capitol. The demonstration was very effective.

Next Monday, we will need the help of many more representatives of local clubs. If you possibly can, please plan to visit Albany on that date.

As soon as this bulletin is finished, I leave for New York
City where I address sixty-five salesmen of the New York
Automobile Club to-night on the subject "Beat that Three
Cent Gas Tax"—that will be our slogan from now on.

To-day's receipts total 6,808 (signatures), including
.... from Albany; .... from Adirondack,
etc. . . .

To support this essentially negative program, the Associations had to suggest other taxable sources which they, by extensive statistical reports, sought to show to be better able to
bear taxation.   In 1933, for example, they favored a general
sales tax as a more fitting substitute for increased gasoline
taxes.   At times, however, pressure for new legislation has
been found undesirable by the automobile associations for
fear that concessions more harmful to their interests would be
wrung from them.[65]   Furthermore, the Associations have suggested recommendations for the reduction of highway costs in
order to discourage increased taxes that would fall directly on
automobile owners.[66]

In the execution of this legislative program, the two automobile associations generally work together,[67] employing highly

---

[65] In 1933, for example, the New York State Automobile Association did
not press a quarterly registration fee of automobiles instead of the usual
annual fee for fear of raising the gasoline tax issue again.   Interview, Warner
Bates, Secretary of the New York State Automobile Association, Sept. 4, 1935.

[66] Thus, in 1932, the Legislative Committee of the New York State Automobile Association submitted to the legislature a plan in which "no increased
tax will be necessary on motor vehicles with the great reduction in highway
costs if the state will recognize the Highway Classification Plan which follows." See other reports of the Highway Committee of the New York State
Automobile Association.

[67] The New York State Automobile Association, however, has suggested that
the motor truck owner bear a larger share of the tax burden since the
latter derives greater benefits and profits therefrom.   The railroads too,
feeling the keen competition of motor vehicles, particularly the passenger
traffic of buses, have exerted great pressure at Albany for greater governmental regulation and increased governmental revenue from buses as one
means of checking their competitive character with railroads.   The New York
Motor Truck Association, in cooperation with other associations, such as the
New York State Farm Bureau Federation, was instrumental in preventing
the original and more exacting motor truck tax bill from passing in 1932 and
in repealing the compromise measure before it took effect in 1933.   The support of such outstanding personages as Alfred E. Smith and hundreds of motor
truck owners who were urged to bring direct pressure upon the legislature
proved effective.   Interviews, L. G. Stapley, Manager, New York State Motor
Truck Association, Feb. 3, 1932, and Jan. 28, 1933, and with T. D. Pratt,
Secretary of the New York State Motor Truck Association, Oct. 9, 1935.

experienced legislative agents to superintend the pressure at Albany.[68] In their attempts to block legislation for the increase of gasoline and motor vehicle taxes they have frequently received the assistance of numerous individual petroleum companies and organizations, such as the American Petroleum Institute [69] and the Petroleum Industries Committee of New York.[70]

And so it is seen that, both in aim and in achievement, the automobile associations' pressure at Albany supplements that of its kindred organizations, Associated Industries and the Economic Council.[71]

Public Utilities

By far the most influential of the moneyed lobby groups are those representing the fifth basic economic field in New York: the public utilities. Of the three most active constituents of this field—the gas and electric companies, the telephone company,[72] and the railroads [73]—the lobbying tech-

---

[68] Among these are Lewis G. Stapley, a former member of the State Legislature and of legislative committees that formulated much of the New York State motor vehicle legislation and T. D. Pratt, who has been engaged in "legislative work" for 21 years. Interview, T. D. Pratt, Oct. 9, 1935.

[69] Under the auspices of this institute a pamphlet was published, reprinted from *Collier's Weekly*, by John T. Flynn, entitled *Bootleg Gasoline.*

[70] See the pamphlet published by this committee, *Dangers in Doubling New York Gasoline Tax,* Jan., 1932. It should be noted that the diversion of gasoline and motor vehicle taxes to the general fund from use "for the construction, maintenance and repair of highways and bridges," as provided for in the Tax and Motor Vehicle Laws of 1929, was also opposed by the New York State Highway Chapter of the General Contractors of America, organized in 1926 with headquarters at Albany and primarily interested in construction problems on the New York State highways. The director of this chapter examined some 600 bills introduced into the regular session of the legislature in 1932 for their possible effect on highway construction. Similar opposition came from the New York State Construction Council, organized in 1932 as an emergency agency by the New York State Highway Chapter for the sole purpose of answering attacks on highway appropriations. The economic emergency and the state budget deficit, however, proved too much for the highway contractors. Interview, Harry R. Hayes, Managing Director of the New York State Highway Chapter, Jan. 30, 1933.

[71] Although the Economic Council, the Automobile Association, and the Motor Truck Association are not strictly speaking "manufacturing" associations, it seemed convenient and not illogical to consider them along with Associated Industries in this section.

[72] The New York Telephone Company, which possesses a monopoly of the telephone service in the state, is regularly represented at legislative sessions by counsel, usually three in number (J. H. Griswold, F. H. Ferris, and H.

niques of the first may be studied to best advantage. In recent years these techniques have been publicly exposed in a series of investigations conducted by the Federal Trade Commission [74] and a special committee appointed for the purpose by the New York State Legislature.[75] An analysis of the utilities' lobby has been facilitated by the facts revealed in these investigations, and by the activities of the gas and electric companies after Mayor La Guardia announced that he would seek legislative approval of the establishment of a municipally-owned electricity plant for New York City.

The operation of this lobby is centralized in the Empire State Gas and Electric Association, a statewide organization with which are affiliated about a third of all the privately-owned gas and electric companies in the state,[76] but who sell

Hendrickson). As members of the legal department of the company, these attorneys concern themselves with legislation which affects also the parent organization, the American Telephone and Telegraph Company. These registered counsel of the New York Telephone Company are thus regarded in official and unofficial circles as the spokesmen of the gigantic Bell System. An investigation of the American Telephone and Telegraph Company was undertaken by the Federal Communications Commission in 1936.

[73] The Associated Railroads of New York represents the railroad interests in New York State. This Association, organized informally, is composed of railway companies whose annual gross revenues exceed a million dollars. It has no officers, counsel, or by-laws, but is managed by two committees, the Operating Committee and the Law Committee, the latter concerned chiefly with legislative matters. Its frequent meetings, held 10 or 15 times each year, chiefly during the legislative session, are under the chairmanship of Frank A. McNamee, Jr., popularly known at Albany as "the railroad lobbyist." Mr. McNamee also represents the New York Central Railroad. It should be noted that railroads are, in addition, regularly represented at Albany by members of the legal profession. Until his death in 1935, for example, Ross M. Lovell represented half a dozen railroads as counsel. See legislative appearance statements in files of the Secretary of State.

[74] These were begun in 1928 and were authorized by the U. S. Senate in Resolution No. 83, 70th Congress, 1st session. Reference to the testimony and exhibits of this investigation on utility corporations are hereinafter referred to as *F.T.C. Hearings*, 1928, and *Exhibits*, 1929.

[75] The Joint Legislative Committee to Investigate Public Utilities, appointed in 1934.

[76] Mention should also be made of the New York State Association of Municipal Electrical Utilities, whose membership is composed of representatives of 35 of the 53 municipally-owned electrical plants in New York State, all but one of these being in communities with a population less than 25,000. Approximately one-tenth of the communities of 1,000 or more inhabitants supply their own light and power under municipal ownership. Some

more than 90 per cent of the current generated in the state.[77] This Association, however, is really the agency through which is often administered the pressure dictated by the three largest gas and electric utility systems in the state, the Consolidated Edison Company of New York, the Niagara Hudson Power Corporation, and the Associated Gas and Electric Company.[78] Each of these three systems is itself a powerful pressure group. When all three unite to promote or oppose a bill, therefore, their influence is manifestly far-reaching. However, the influence of the gas and electric lobby may be exerted through an individual operating company, through the intermediary or

---

three-fourths of the municipal systems in the state purchase all or most of the current that they sell, instead of generating it themselves. See *N.Y. S. Commission for the Revision of the Tax Laws, Fourth Report,* 1934, p. 81; *State of New York, Final Report of the Joint Legislative Committee to Investigate Public Utilities.* Legislative Document, 1936, No. 78, p. 54 (hereinafter referred to as *Final Report*).

[77] There are some 160 such companies in the state. Fifty-two of the largest of these are members of the Association. Federal Trade Commission, Hearings on Utility Corporations, (Senate Resolution, No. 83, 70th Congress, 1st session), Washington, Government Printing Office, 1928, part 4, p. 234 and interview with George H. Smith, Engineer of Empire State Gas and Electric Association, Dec. 12, 1935. There are three classes of members in the Association: operating companies, individuals, and associate members. Of these, only the operating companies may vote at meetings. Holding companies are not eligible for membership. Dues paid by the members defray the Association's annual budget of approximately $30,000. *F.T.C. Hearings,* 1928, part 4, p. 232. A managing committee of five members, including a representative from each of the three large gas and electric systems of the state, is appointed by the Executive Committee to direct the activities of the Association. In addition, there are seven technical committees, or sections of the Association, as well as a women's section. A monthly bulletin, in which there generally appear discussions of a technical nature, also informs members of important legislation at the state Capitol. The Association does not maintain a representative at Albany, since counsel of the individual companies make this unnecessary. At times, however, the Association may call together a group of utility executives in order to formulate a unified plan of legislative pressure.

[78] With the Consolidated Edison Company were affiliated, in 1934, 21 New York companies, with total assets of $1,363,241,977. In the Niagara Hudson Power Corporation there were 42 such companies, with total assets of $652,-403,966. The Associated Gas and Electric Company represented 164 companies in many states, with total assets of $901,105,493. The corporate structure of these systems, with the interlocking corporate relationships, is highly complex, the Associated Gas and Electric Company having been called the most complicated holding company system in the U. S. The need for the simplification of this corporate structure, to which public attention has been called in recent years, has resulted in many changes of late. See *Final Report, op. cit.,* p. 74.

"top" company of one of the systems, or through the Empire State Gas and Electric Association.[79]

By the very nature of the private control of public utilities, successful lobbying in its interest has necessitated a great deal of publicity work, directed chiefly at conciliating and persuading public opinion to support or oppose utilities' legislation at Albany.   In 1919, with the close of the World War, the national utility associations launched "probably the greatest peacetime propaganda campaign ever conducted by private interests in this country," [80] under the leadership of the National Electric Light Association, "the largest, most important, and most active of the utility associations engaged in publicity activities." [81]   In the course of this campaign, special publicity bureaus were organized to spread both national and state utility propaganda.[82]   In New York such an agency, known as the New York State Public Utilities Information Bureau, an "offspring of the Empire State Gas and Electric Association," [83] was established in 1922, its membership being

---

[79] When the state legislation concerned has national importance, cooperation may also be extended by national groups of privately-owned companies, such as the Edison Electric Institute and the American Gas Association.

[80] *Summary Report of the Federal Trade Commission to the Senate of the United States, Pursuant to Senate Resolution No. 83, 70th Congress, 1st session, on Efforts by Associations and Agencies of Electric and Gas Utilities to Influence Public Opinion,* Washington, Government Printing Office, 1934, p. 391 (hereinafter referred to as *Summary Report*). See Robert Bruce Raup, *Education and Organized Interests in America,* New York, Putnam, 1936, ch. 2.

[81] *Summary Report,* p. 23.   The National Electric Light Association was dissolved soon after the investigation by the Federal Trade Commission opened in 1928 and was superseded by the Edison Electric Institute, organized in 1933. See *Edison Electric Institute Bulletin,* Apr., 1933.

[82] Before the Federal Trade Commission investigation opened, there were 28 such state publicity bureaus or committees in 38 states, all modeled more or less upon the original bureau which had been established in Illinois.   These committees had served as publicity conduits for such national utility groups as the National Electric Light Association, the American Gas Association, the Joint Committee of National Utility Associations, and the American Electric Railway Association. See *Summary Report,* pp. 21, 43, and *F.T.C. Hearings,* 1928, part 4, p. 252.

[83] *F.T.C. Hearings,* 1928, part 4, pp. 189, 184. See also *F.T.C. Exhibits,* 1929, part 4, pp. 200, 201. Because of the unfavorable publicity given to these information bureaus by the Federal Trade Commission investigation, they too were dissolved with the National Electric Light Association. The annual budget of the New York State Bureau for 1926–1927 was approximately $40,000. *F.T.C. Exhibits,* 1929, part 4, p. 184. (Exhibit No. 1672A.)

much the same as that of its parent organization. The publicity campaigns launched by the Bureau were intended to reach not only the millions of stockholders and employees interested in dividends and salaries paid by the utilities, but the general masses as well. For this reason the publicity media employed by the Bureau were chiefly the press, the schools, and the radio.

Frederick W. Crone, the Director of the Bureau, a man of wide journalistic experience,[84] supervised the preparation of weekly bulletins and their distribution to about a thousand newspapers throughout the state. As a result, an unusually large amount of favorable editorial comment and prominent news items was published,[85] often reproduced word for word from the bulletins, without disclosing the source of the information.[86] Such favorable editorial expression was often encouraged by reciprocation in the form of goodwill advertising, upon the reasoning that "it is extremely difficult to interest the newspapers in your welfare unless you are interested in the welfare of the newspapers."[87] "Advertising to be effective should be regular and continuous, not spasmodic. Occasional advertising arouses suspicion"—this was the advice given by New York utility men.[88] Thus the New York State Public

---

[84] Mr. Crone had had 15 years of experience as reporter and editorial writer for the *New York Tribune* when he became the Bureau's director on May 1, 1922. For five of these years he had also been a legislative correspondent at Albany, and during his directorship he retained his membership in the Newspaper Club of New York. Before the establishment of the Bureau, luncheons to which local newspaper men were invited had been held by public utility officials in seven cities of the state. At these meetings the plans for the Bureau had been outlined to the newspaper men and their advice sought. *F.T.C. Hearings,* 1928, part 4, p. 228; *F.T.C. Exhibits,* 1929, part 4, p. 202.

[85] See Exhibit No. 1670, *F.T.C. Exhibits,* 1929, part 4, p. 183, for articles in these bulletins. In 1922 the newspaper space acquired as a result of these bulletins was five columns a week. By 1924 this had grown to 372 solid columns. This amount of reprint, the Bureau boasted, "would make a copy of the New York Times forty-six pages thick devoted every line to items about gas and electric industry." *Cf. F.T.C. Exhibits,* 1929, part 4, p. 196, *F.T.C. Hearings,* 1928, part 4, p. 227. For a five-month period in 1927 the Bureau reported 460 solid columns of reprint. The actual amount of newspaper reprint was more than this, for the Bureau did not clip reprinted material from all the newspapers to which the committee's news bulletins had been sent. See *Summary Report,* pp. 64, 406.

[86] *F.T.C. Hearings,* 1928, part 4, p. 185; *F.T.C. Exhibits,* 1929, part 4, p. 196.

[87] *Summary Report,* p. 74.

[88] *F.T.C. Exhibits,* 1929, part 4, p. 198.

Utilities Information Bureau established an industry advertising service "to help swing the pendulum of public opinion in the direction of the privately-controlled utilities." [89]   In the first year of its existence, a copy of goodwill advertising which it furnished to the utility companies appeared in 55 newspapers and reached over a million people.[90]   Newspaper advertising by the utilities, confined chiefly to local papers throughout the country, cost approximately $30,000,000 in 1927.   One-third of this amount constituted the newspaper advertising expenditures of the individual electric and power companies in the country.[91]   In explaining how the advertising appropriation of a public utility is determined, F. L. Blanchard, director of advertising of H. L. Doherty & Company stated: "It may be that a renewal of the company's franchise will come up before the city council, or bills that would injure its business are up for passage in the State Legislature, in which case it will be necessary to spend a larger amount of money in advertising than ordinarily . . ." [92]   The policy followed in placing these advertisements is illustrated by a telegram of H. C. Hopson, of the Associated Gas and Electric Company, introduced into evidence before the United States Senate committee investigating the activities of the utilities in their campaign to defeat the Federal Wheeler-Rayburn bill in 1935:

> *Times*, of course, is under strong influence from Morgan and Carlisle sources. We must therefore expect that we will be in receipt of very unpleasant attacks from that quarter at more or less frequent intervals. Am inclined to think that we ought to withhold patronage of this paper

---

[89] *F.T.C. Exhibits,* 1929, part 4, p. 196.

[90] *F.T.C. Hearings,* 1928, part 4, p. 228. The forms of these advertisements are listed in Exhibit No. 1672B, *F.T.C. Exhibits,* 1929, part 4, p. 184. Director Crone testified that he advocated large advertising accounts with newspapers merely for the value there was in advertising. Crone further stated that it made him "mad" when he heard utility men at the national conventions of the National Electric Light Association urge advertising in order to open the columns of the newspapers to the power companies. *F.T.C. Hearings,* 1928, part 4, p. 190.

[91] *Summary Report,* p. 76. *Cf.* Ernest Greenwood, *You, Utilities and the Government,* New York, D. Appleton-Century, 1935, p. 199; H. S. Raushenbush, and H. W. Laidler, *Power Control,* New York, New Republic, 1928, p. 25.

[92] *Summary Report,* p. 77.

in line with our former practice, in view of their settled habit of taking all biased, lying, distorted statements which they can get hold of and shooting an editorial first and leaving us later to protest against it. Their influence as an advertiser is not great; practically all their readers are already being slurred up by the articles of other enterprises. If we can get other papers like Hearst and Gannett people to switch over, also Scripps Howard, it would do more good than twenty *New York Times*.[93]

Sometimes the utilities secured more direct control of newspapers through financial investments. The International Paper Company, for example, a subsidiary of the International Paper and Power Company, invested heavily in the *Brooklyn Daily Eagle,* the *Knickerbocker Press and Evening News* of Albany, and the *Ithaca News-Journal,* among others.[94] Archibald R. Graustein, President of the International Paper Company, indicated that the policy of financing newspapers grew out of the need for additional markets for paper. His company, he said, had gone "into the red" in 1928 because of the loss of a large account to a competitor who had given financial assistance to newspapers.[95]

To extend the range of publicity so secured, the New York State Information Bureau established a Speakers' Bureau, the secretary of which, Frank Regan, was a former newspaper man.[96] Through subcommittees in 10 districts throughout the state, each in the charge of a district chairman, this bureau supplied speakers for any occasion. In the course of its work it also published a specially prepared *Speakers' Handbook,* which was distributed to utility company employees in an attempt to train them for public speaking.[97] The women em-

---

[93] *New York Times,* Aug. 17, 1935, p. 26.

[94] These were part of the chain of publications owned by Frank C. Gannett. In May, 1929, after the Federal Trade Commission investigation, Mr. Gannett reassumed their ownership. See H. S. Raushenbush, *The Power Fight,* New York, New Republic, 1932, p. 21.

[95] See *Summary Report,* pp. 85–88; *F.T.C. Hearings,* 1928, part 14, pp. 62, 79–82.

[96] *F.T.C. Hearings,* 1928, part 4, p. 192.

[97] The original plan of distributing 3,500 copies of this handbook was interrupted by the Federal Trade Commission's investigation, and only 900 copies were disposed of. The handbook discussed such subjects as customer ownership, holding companies, and government ownership. *F.T.C. Hearings,* 1928, part 4, p. 194; *F.T.C. Exhibits,* 1929, part 4, p. 167.

ployees were expected to maintain close contact with women's clubs. The district chairwomen of the Women's Section of the Empire State Gas and Electric Association, for example, were urged to become members of the League of Women Voters, an organization which favored "public ownership," so that they, as members, could influence meetings and suggest speakers from the Information Bureau.[98] Addresses were also delivered to chambers of commerce, boards of trade, church clubs, Rotary Clubs, Kiwanis Clubs, elementary and high schools, and colleges, a monthly report being made to the Bureau of the number of addresses, the size of the audiences, and the column inches obtained in newspapers as a result of these speeches.[99] A bulletin of the Empire State Gas and Electric Association commented thus upon the success of the New York State Information Bureau: "It is, perhaps, the committee's most valuable accomplishment that its material is accepted as facts put forth by the utilities in good faith and used by newspapers, speakers, and commercial organizations as authentic." [100]

The propaganda activities of the utilities were systematically extended into the schools.[101] "If a fair presentation of the economics of utility management and operation could be gotten before the students of our schools, we would find a different impression held by the general public within a few years regarding the utilities," wrote the secretary of the southeastern division of the National Electric Light Association.[102]

Besides utility speakers,[103] thousands of copies of pamphlets

---

[98] *F.T.C. Hearings*, 1928, part 4, p. 243. During the five-month period from Nov. 1, 1927, to Mar. 31, 1928, 2,840 addresses were made under the auspices of the Speakers' Bureau, to audiences aggregating 281,578 people. Of this number 1,250 addresses were made by the women to audiences totalling 135,158 persons. See Exhibit No. 1648, *F.T.C. Exhibits*, 1929, part 4, p. 167. As a result of these addresses 359.5 columns of newspaper publicity were obtained in addition to the reproduction of bulletin material. *F.T.C. Hearings*, 1928, part 4, p. 196.

[99] *F.T.C. Hearings*, 1928, part 4, pp. 192–198. One of these monthly reports under the heading "Materials for Speakers" included a model speech by Mr. Paul Clapp, Managing Director of the National Electric Light Corporation.

[100] *F.T.C. Hearings*, 1928, part 4, p. 213.

[101] See *Summary Report*, pp. 139–221.

[102] E. T. O'Connell to J. F. Gilchrist, chairman of the Illinois Committee on Public Utility Information, Jan. 29, 1925. *Cf. Summary Report*, p. 141.

[103] The Public Utilities Information Bureau maintained a Committee on School Activities which was merged with the Speakers' Bureau in 1928. All

found their way into the schools. Two pamphlets prepared chiefly for the schools were distributed by the New York State Information Bureau in 1927. Thirty thousand copies of the pamphlet *Servants of Progress* went into 490 schools, while 10,000 copies were given to two utility companies for use in school campaigns. Seventy-four thousand copies of *Know New York State* were distributed in the same way. This pamphlet was so arranged that on each page a favorable reference was made to electric and gas companies. In some of the schools these pamphlets were used as textbooks or as supplementary references.[104] Sometimes the utilities distributed cinema films which were shown in schools, and they sponsored talks illustrated by slides.[105] Courses in public utilities were introduced into many colleges throughout the country, and attempts were made to make such instruction a part of the curriculum in lower schools. William A. Prendergast, chairman of the New York Public Service Commission, was approached by members of the New York Information Bureau in the matter of public utility instruction in the New York schools and colleges, in the hope that the Commissioner might use his influence with the State Board of Education in this direction.[106] "How in heaven's name," asked M. H. Aylesworth, at that time Managing Director of the National Electric Light Association, "can we do anything in the schools of this country with the young people growing up, if we have not first sold the idea of education to the college professor?" A definite plan was thus inaugurated to lend financial assistance to college professors directly or indirectly.[107] For exam-

the members of this committee were officers of the utility corporations. Director Crone testified that this committee was not active and was in existence only "a year or two." *F.T.C. Hearings*, 1928, part 4, p. 193.

[104] *F.T.C. Hearings*, 1928, part 4, pp. 199–204, 216. Additional pamphlets were also prepared by the bureau and distributed in large numbers outside the schools. *F.T.C. Hearings*, 1928, part 4, pp. 208–212.

[105] *F.T.C. Hearings*, 1928, part 4, pp. 199, 200, and *F.T.C. Exhibits*, 1929, part 4, p. 189.

[106] *F.T.C. Hearings*, 1928, part 4, p. 223. Director Crone could throw no light on the establishment of such courses in the colleges in New York State. *F.T.C. Hearings*, 1928, part 4, p. 218.

[107] The testimony before the Federal Trade Commission does not list colleges or universities in New York or their professors among the recipients of generous utility favors. *Cf.* Ernest H. Gruening, *The Public Pays*, New York, Vanguard Press, 1931, p. 66, and *Summary Report*, p. 154.

ple, Professor Richard T. Ely, Director of the Institute for Research in Land Economics and Public Utilities at Northwestern University, requested and was granted financial aid from the National Electric Light Association and from several of the state committees including the New York Bureau.[108] Dr. H. M. Diamond, while head of the Economics Department at Lehigh University, was employed by the National Electric Light Association. His article, "Whole Fabric of United States Built in Opposition to Government Ownership," appeared in the *Bulletin* of the New York State Information Bureau, was transmitted to newspapers throughout the state, and was printed in bulletins of other utility associations.[109]

The New York Bureau also participated in the nation-wide campaign inspired by J. B. Sheridan, Director of the Missouri Committee to rewrite textbooks used in the schools of each state which were "deficient" in their treatment of public utilities, so that the "obsolete and public ownership trend noticeable in many of the textbooks then in use (1924) would be greatly modified, if not entirely eliminated." [110]   In his report to Mr. Sheridan, the director of the New York Bureau indicated that not all the textbooks used in the schools of the state had been examined, because books used in New York City were sufficiently varied to be considered representative of all in use in the state.   The director, moreover, stated:

> In any general consideration of this matter it may not be inappropriate to note that while the textbook is the basis of instruction, the teacher under present day methods has wide latitude in the presentation of the subject. Among school teachers in the large cities, and notably in New York City, there is a considerable proportion of the so-called liberals or radicals. In New York City this is so much the case that during the war it was found neces-

---

[108] This Institute "volunteered to undertake studies of economic questions in New York State if desired." *Minutes of New York State Committee,* Jan. 15, 1926, *F.T.C. Exhibits,* 1929, part 4, p. 193. Many public utility officials showed "great interest" in the work of the Institute and contributed to its financial support. *Summary Report,* p. 162.

[109] *Summary Report,* p. 157.

[110] *Summary Report,* p. 187. See Exhibit 1668A, *F.T.C. Exhibits,* 1929, part 4, p. 180.

sary to apply a sort of patriotism test and varieties of repression. . . .[111]

It should also be noted that when 7,000 copies of Edward Hungerford's *Story of Public Utilities* were prepared by the utilities, the first edition of 3,000 copies, distributed in Rochester schools, bore a foreword written and signed by the president of the Rochester Board of Education. Although this volume had not been prepared directly by the New York Information Bureau, a committee including utility companies, representatives of Rochester city departments, and a member of the Rochester Board of Education prepared and financed it, through the agency of F. W. Fisher, of the Rochester Gas and Electric Corporation, chairman of the New York Committee on School Activities. Local utility companies were also asked to use their influence in introducing the book in schools of other cities.[112]

In addition to the newspapers and the schools, the radio was utilized by the public utilities to reach even greater numbers of people. When M. H. Aylesworth, for example, was promoted from the managing directorship of the National Electric Light Association to the presidency of the National Broadcasting Company,[113] "he took occasion to tell the public policy committee, National Electric Light Association, of the value and possibilities of radio in the promotion of their public relations work."[114] When Mr. J. B. Sheridan called Mr. Aylesworth's attention to the fact that a J. B. Rutherford of Toronto, Canada, had been permitted to make "an address in which he commented in very unfavorable terms upon the operation of public utilities," Mr. Aylesworth replied that the

---

[111] Dated Dec. 22, 1924. Exhibit No. 1668B, *F.T.C. Exhibits*, 1929, part 4, p. 181. *F.T.C. Hearings*, 1928, part 4, p. 253.

[112] *F.T.C. Hearings*, 1928, part 4, p. 206, *Summary Report*, p. 196. The utility interests were also anxious to see James N. Mavor's *Niagara in Politics* placed in schools and libraries in the state. *F.T.C. Hearings*, 1928, part 4, p. 248, *Summary Report*, p. 114.

[113] The National Broadcasting Company was controlled by General Electric Company, the Westinghouse Electric & Manufacturing Co., and the Radio Corporation of America (Raushenbush and Laidler, *Power Control*, p. 27), but is now owned entirely by Radio Corporation of America (Moody's Manual of Investments, 1935). M. H. Aylesworth resigned as president of the National Broadcasting Company, Dec. 27, 1935.

[114] *Summary Report*, p. 299.

speaker had been permitted to do so in order to avoid the accusation that the National Broadcasting Company was a monopoly. This was, he added, "just one of those things which is not apt to occur again in the very near future." [115]

Where companies do not actually own broadcasting stations, time has been bought from broadcasting companies throughout the country for the transmission of public utility programs. Recently, for example, the Consolidated Edison Company of New York instituted a series of Sunday night programs to counteract the announcement of Mayor La Guardia that he would seek legislation in 1936 to legalize the establishment of a municipal plant in New York City. The New York Information Bureau was responsible for a series of ten talks on home economics and gas use, delivered by members of the women's section of the committee in 1925, as well as six broadcasts by public utility men over the broadcasting station of the Rensselaer Polytechnic Institute at Troy.[116] The director of the New York Bureau reported that in addition to the public speaking that had been done in New York, there had been "98 radio talks on general utility matters, reaching during the year (1926) an aggregate audience of more than 10,000,000."[117]

This well-organized publicity campaign, by its very nature, elicited hearty cooperation from numerous business men's organizations and clubs which had been addressed by the utilities' speakers, particularly bankers, insurance companies, chambers of commerce, and boards of trade. George F. Oxley, for example, Director of Publicity of the National Electric Light Association, sent to all State Public Utilities Information Bureau directors telegrams stating that "quick action was needed" against the Congressional Boulder Dam Bill. When this telegram was received by the New York director, the matter was referred by him to the Chamber of Commerce of the State of New York, which later submitted a report expressing

---

[115] *Summary Report*, p. 301.

[116] *F.T.C. Hearings*, 1928, part 4, p. 198.

[117] In 1929 the secretary of the Federal Radio Commission estimated the total radio audience as 38,000,000 people. *Summary Report*, pp. 300, 301.

opposition to the Boulder Dam legislation.[118] A folder, *Your Rights as a Capitalist,* prepared from material submitted by Mr. Oxley, was circulated by Haley Fiske, President of the Metropolitan Life Insurance Company, to millions of policy-holders, state utility commissioners, public utility information bureaus, and public libraries. This folder pointed out that since the insurance companies had invested heavily in public utility securities, any unfair treatment of the utilities in the form of an extension of the government ownership principle would constitute unfair treatment of the mass of the people through their insurance:

> Plans for municipal, state or federal ownership of public utilities often sound well as presented by their advocates. But before assenting to them every policyholder should examine them carefully, asking himself how political ownership can possibly give him results to compare with those attained through private ownership. . . . The ownership of the light and power companies is now in the hands of more than 2,500,000 direct investors in the public utility stocks, and indirectly in the hands of millions more of bank depositors and holders of life insurance policies through their ownership of public-utility bonds. This is people's ownership under public regulation, and as such should be defended against assault from those who would wantonly destroy public utility investment values.[119]

Such warm cooperation is perhaps not surprising when it is realized that during the years 1929–1934 the Consolidated Edison Company of New York spent $2,505,185.23 in dona-tions, contributions, dues, and other charges to clubs, associa-tions, and scientific and social organizations, an average of over $417,000 per year. This money, most of which was charged to operating expenses for fourteen companies of the Consolidated Edison Company of New York, was distributed in large part as follows:

---

[118] *F.T.C. Hearings,* 1928, part 4, p. 245. The presidents of the Chamber of Commerce of the State of New York, the Merchants Association of New York, and the New York Board of Trade were among the active sponsors in organ-izing a "Citizens Committee of 500" to oppose Mayor La Guardia's municipal power plan. *New York Times,* Nov. 28, 1935, Mar. 25, 1936.

[119] *Summary Report,* p. 119. See also Ernest H. Gruening, *op. cit.,* p. 213.

Total 6 Years

American Gas Association.. $435,038.19
Chambers of Commerce:
   United States.. 56,716.99
   Other Chambers of Commerce (31)......................... 57,952.71
Edison Electric Institute and/or National Electric Light Association.. 686,015.91
Empire State Gas and Electric Association...................... 123,800.06
Kiwanis Clubs (7)... 841.37
Lions Clubs (14).. 1,349.75
Public Policy Fund.. 13,373.14
New York State Committee on Public Utility Information...... 23,672.87
Regional Plan Association..................................... 32,952.40
Rotary Clubs (9).. 1,224.56

The Westchester Lighting Company alone also made payments to approximately 150 organizations. The New York State Joint Legislative Committee to Investigate Public Utilities, in commenting upon these expenditures by the Consolidated Edison Company of New York, stated: "The function of some of these organizations is undoubtedly to disseminate propaganda for the utility companies while operating in the guise of independent organizations under names which make them appear to be independent in the eyes of the general public. Many of them, we believe are supported through the large support afforded by the utility interests . . . Many of these contributions are probably commendable from a stockholder's standpoint but certainly should not be paid by consumers who have no say in selecting the organizations which in many instances probably work directly against their interests." [120]

Another source of cooperation has been the large army of small utility stockholders, "the widows and orphans," and the employees of utility companies, who have a material interest in private ownership of utilities. In the campaign conducted by the Consolidated Edison Company against a municipally-owned plant in New York, the stockholders—even those who

---

[120] *Final Report, pp.* 47, 48. *Cf. New York Times,* Nov. 1, 1935. The Public Service Commission announced that public utilities supplying gas, electricity, water, and telephone service in New York State made similar payments totalling $744,000 in 1934 and $670,000 in 1935 of which 86 per cent for each year was charged to operating expenses. The 1934 figures were based on reports from 552 companies, for 1935 on 411 companies. *Cf. New York Times,* July 27, 1936.

owned only one share—were the targets of the company's constant propaganda, while the support of employees of the utility companies in New York City was won by picturing the threats to their jobs implied in a program of public ownership. More than 6,000 employees held an overflow meeting in New York City to protest against Mayor La Guardia's utilities' program. Announcement was made that public utilities employees' headquarters would be opened in all boroughs of the city, and pledges were circulated, in which the employees agreed to enlist the support of their friends in the fight against the Mayor's power program. "We are organized and will stay organized," said the leader of this group, "until politicians in New York City realize that the municipal power plant question in New York City is loaded with enough voltage to jolt them right out of office." [121] Thus, at opportune times, letters and telegrams from thousands of stockholders and employees have poured into the offices of legislators in Albany.

Attempting to conciliate the mass of the people by organized publicity and by eliciting the cooperation of other groups, however, did not constitute the entire campaign "to disparage all forms of public ownership and operation of utilities and preach the economy, sufficiency, and general excellence of the privately-owned utilities." [122] A great deal of direct pressure was also exerted on the individual legislators. Advocates of public ownership of utilities were dubbed "enemies of society." "My idea would be not to try logic, or reason, but to try to pin the Bolshevik idea on my opponent," was the advice given by a public utility official.[123] Special pamphlets were prepared and distributed to members of the legislature when the Governor launched a power program inimical to private utility interests. Of such pamphlets as *Water Power in New York State —What Its Development Will Mean for the Public,* 1926, and *River Regulation in New York State,* 1927, a total of 250,000 copies were distributed as propaganda against Governor Alfred E. Smith's water power program.[124] The New York State Public Utilities Information Bureau, moreover, subscribed to

---

[121] *New York Times,* Oct. 30, 1935.
[122] *Summary Report,* p. 391.
[123] *F.T.C. Hearings,* 1928, part 2, p. 7, and part 4, pp. 214, 219.
[124] *F.T.C. Hearings,* 1928, part 4, pp. 208–212.

200 copies of the *Public Service Magazine,* which were sent to members of the New York State Legislature.[125]

More important than these, however, was the influential position of utilities' representatives at Albany. For example, Senator Warren T. Thayer, chairman of the New York Senate Committee on Public Service for many years, was at the same time a paid lobbyist of the Associated Gas and Electric Company, as was disclosed in the investigation of Senator Thayer's conduct by the Judiciary Committee of the New York Senate. This investigation was requested by the senator himself after certain letters from him to officials of the Associated Gas and Electric Company and the J. G. White Management Corporation had been introduced into evidence before the Federal Trade Commission and published in the press. The evidence showed that the senator, who owned a majority of the corporate stock of the Chasm Power Company, had agreed to sell his interest to Wallace E. Pierce, a representative of the Associated Gas and Electric Company, in an option in September, 1924. Although this option, which was originally to extend until November 1, 1924, was not exercised, it was twice renewed after the elections in November, 1924, when the Republicans regained control of the Senate. The contract was finally closed on January 17, 1925, five days after Senator Thayer had become chairman of the Committee on Public Service. Between 1926 and 1932, furthermore, Senator Thayer received a stipend of $3,600 annually from the Associated Gas and Electric Company.[126] An excerpt from the letter written by the senator to S. J. Magee, Vice-President of the Associated Gas and Electric Company, on March 15, 1927, indicated why these payments were made: "The Legislature adjourned last Friday . . . I hope my work during the past session was satisfactory to your company, not so much for the new legislation enacted, but from the fact that many detrimental bills which were introduced we were able to kill in my committee." [127] In

---

[125] The stock of the Chicago company which published this magazine was owned by public utility companies. *F.T.C. Hearings,* 1928, part 4, pp. 191, 227.

[126] Significantly, the last semi-annual payment was made to Senator Thayer in May, 1932. Thereafter payments stopped, when it was obvious that Thayer could not remain as chairman of the Committee on Public Service when control of the Senate returned to the Democrats in Nov., 1932.

[127] *State of New York, Proceedings of the Judiciary Committee of the Senate*

another letter Thayer stated that he had taken up the matter of amending a bill with Senator W. W. Westall, of Westchester county, who had "prepared an amendment to the bill which will make it satisfactory to your people. When this bill is reprinted I will send you a copy of it for your consideration and to see if the objectionable features have been eliminated." [128] Thus, as Paul J. McCauley, counsel for the New York Senate Investigating Committee, stated, "It is clear, he (Thayer) was reporting to his employer." [129]

That Senator Thayer was not the only representative of the utilities in official Albany was indicated by Governor Lehman in his campaign for reelection in 1934: "Ex-Senator Thayer may have been less prudent than his colleagues but no one believes that Thayer alone bore the whole brunt of battle for the utilities. It took more than one man to protect their interests as well as they have been protected by the 'Old Guard'." [130] Some four months before the Thayer letters were made public, moreover, W. Kingsland Macy, chairman of the New York Republican State Committee, said publicly that the Republican leaders of the Assembly were tools of the corrupt

---

in the Matter of Investigation Requested by Senator Thayer, Legislative Document, 1934, No. 102, p. 464. *Cf. New York Times,* Mar. 30, 1934. Thayer stated he was anxious to do satisfactory work for the utility company because a large number of their employees and stockholders lived in his district. *Proceedings,* p. 216, and *New York Times,* May 11, 1934.

[128] *Proceedings,* p. 466, and *New York Times,* Mar. 30, 1934.

[129] Obviously Senator Thayer was at this time voting against bills which the power companies did not want. The record of the Senate for 1923 and 1924, before Thayer's money negotiations with the utility company, however, disclosed that the senator was voting in favor of identical bills. To explain this, the senator said: "The record, the journal of the Senate is wrong. There was a short roll call and they shouldn't have so recorded me, because I didn't vote for such bills." *Proceedings,* p. 454. In 1927 Thayer, it was charged, had also committed a misdemeanor in violation of section 44 of the General Corporation Law (now section 671 of the Penal Law), when he submitted a bill of $400 to the Chasm Power Company for expenses incurred by him in a village election of trustees who favored the granting of a charter to the Chasm Power Company. *Proceedings,* pp. 239, 453, 454. Senator Thayer resigned a few days before the Senate found him guilty of "official misconduct." *Proceedings,* pp. 443, 444, 457. For full details in the Thayer case see Legislative Document, 1934, No. 102, and *New York Times,* Mar. 30 through June 20, 1934.

[130] *New York Times,* Oct. 24, 1934. It should be noted, however, that the Joint Legislative Committee to Investigate Public Utilities found no further evidence of improper relationships between state officers and the public utilities. *Joint Report,* 1936, p. 33. See *infra,* p. 82.

and reactionary forces of the power interests through H.
Edmund Machold, former Republican Speaker of the Assembly and Mr. Macy's predecessor as state chairman.[131] He
accused Machold of aligning the Republican party with the
"corrupt" Tammany organization so that Democratic votes
would

> protect the power interests if in return the power interests
> would swing their influence to protect Tammany from
> investigation . . . The trouble is not that Mr. Machold
> believes in the private ownership of public utilities, but
> that he apparently believes in the private ownership of the
> State Government . . . The representative of the power
> interests (Machold) sits in his office in 15 Broad Street,
> and through the clerk of the Assembly, issues orders, pro-
> motes this bill or that, directs who shall be put at the head
> of committees, and in seeing that the interests of his cor-
> poration (Niagara Hudson Power Corporation) are always
> protected, as against the interests of the people of the State
> of New York, nullifies the laws of the State and the Con-
> stitution itself . . . The issue is honest government vs.
> invisible government.[132]

The pressure of the utilities within the legislature is thus
unusually effective because many of the legislators themselves
are counsel, officers, directors, or stockholders of utility companies.[133] The application of this pressure may be vividly

---

[131] It should be noted that the Senate was controlled at this time by
Democrats.

[132] *New York Times,* Dec. 9, 1933. The *Final Report of the Joint Legislative Committee to Investigate Public Utilities,* Legislative Document, 1936,
no. 78, p. 32, contains this comment on Macy's charge against Machold:
"From the letters which have been offered in evidence it did appear that an
officer of public utilities who had previously been very active in state affairs
had been consulted on political matters but not on matters relating to utilities." *Cf. New York Times,* Dec. 19, 1934. To gain the support of legislators, the officers of the utilities have contributed to party campaign funds
as private citizens. Even Chairman Macy solicited campaign funds from a
utility official shortly after he had made the charge against Machold. Letter
to G. D. Cortelyou, President of Consolidated Edison Co. of N. Y., Aug. 13,
1934, in *New York Times,* Dec. 20, 1934. (Exhibit 36 of *Final Report,* 1936.)
Letters concerning a contribution by an officer of a public utility to a local
campaign were offered in evidence before the Joint Committee, though the
officer denied that the contribution had actually been made. *Final Report,*
p. 32.

[133] During roll calls on utility bills in 1934 several legislators asked to be
excused from voting for this reason. *New York Times,* Apr. 6, 1934. *Final*

seen in the events growing out of the public utility program of Governor Lehman, which had been defeated even in the Democrat-controlled Senate in 1933. When Governor Lehman resubmitted his twelve-point program early in the legislative session of 1934, both the opponents and the proponents of the program were well prepared for the fight. At an unprecedented legislative hearing occupying three weeks, large numbers of utility officials and representatives of banking and business organizations recited the stock arguments. An important public utility official [134] charged even that the Governor violated President Roosevelt's recovery program, since the essence of that program was "fair competition." [135] When by March 26 the legislature had not acted on his program, the Governor explained it directly to the people over a statewide radio hook-up:

> In fact, I believe the officers of the large utility companies know that the consumers of this state will demand the enactment of this legislation. Their realization has prompted them to adopt extraordinary methods. From the opening day of the Legislature the lobbyists of the public utility companies have been on guard. Gradually their number has increased. They are always busy. But apparently this year the officials of these large companies have felt that this usual method of killing legislation looking toward more efficient and expeditious protection of the interests of the consumer will not be enough. New and additional means of destruction must be called into operation, they believe. And so they are carrying on a concerted effort to frighten the small and frequently uninformed investor. The statements made are absolutely unjustified by the facts of the case . . . As a matter of simple fact, I have no hesitation in saying that in the six years that I have been in Albany . . . I do not recall a

---

Report, p. 33, and exhibit no. 63. Dr. William L. Love, while a member of the legislature, was retained by the Consolidated Edison Co. as a consulting specialist on compensation cases. *New York Times,* Mar. 8, 1935.

[134] Floyd L. Carlisle, chairman of the Board of Directors of Niagara Hudson Power Corporation.

[135] This statement was made on Feb. 20, 1934, before the NRA was declared unconstitutional and before "big business" opened its organized attacks on President Roosevelt preparatory to the national election campaign of 1936. See *New York Times,* Feb. 21, 1934.

single instance where a public utility corporation either
made constructive suggestions with regard to control or
voluntarily cooperated in the efforts of the State to bring
about sound measures of control and supervision. Their
attitude has continuously been one of opposition and
obstruction.[136]

Four days after this address the newspapers published the
startling Thayer letters which the Federal Trade Commission
had had in its possession since 1929,[137] and Governor Lehman
and Chairman Macy called promptly for an investigation of
the power lobby in the state. A resolution authorizing the
Judiciary Committee of the Senate to investigate Senator
Thayer's alleged official misconduct was introduced at the
senator's request and passed by the Senate on April 3, 1934.
But this was not enough. A broader inquiry into the "wicked"
power utilities in New York State was demanded, and on
April 20, 1934, the legislature authorized by joint resolution
the creation of a Joint Legislative Committee to Investigate
Public Utilities. An initial appropriation of $250,000 was
made and John E. Mack was named counsel. Although its
primary purpose was to ascertain if improper relationship
existed between members of the legislature and the public
utilities, the committee, after having spent $577,000, found
no further evidence of this kind.[138] When, however, Governor
Lehman's utility program was finally passed, a number of
legislators complained that they had voted "under stress" because there was so much "hysteria in the air." [139]

---

[136] *New York Times,* Mar. 27, 1934. This address was characterized by the
Times as the most aggressive verbal onslaught on the "interests" by a governor
in many years. Yet there was a note of conservatism, designed to carry
reassurance to the holders of public utility securities, who for the first time
had been summoned to fight the Lehman measures.

[137] *New York Times,* Mar. 30 and Apr. 12, 1934.

[138] The counsel of the committee justified this large expenditure of public
funds on an investigation which did not achieve its avowed purpose by showing that the work of the committee, by disclosing pernicious utility practices
in improperly inflating the rate base and in excessive payments to so-called
affiliated service corporations, or to their affiliated companies, helped to bring
about reductions in gas and electric rates, in 1935, aggregating $15,000,000.
Final Report, 1936, pp. 10, 78. *New York Times,* Feb. 9, 1936.

[139] *New York Times,* Apr. 6, 1934. The circuitous methods sometimes
adopted by the utilities to achieve their ends is shown in the incidents attending the referendum on a municipal plant for the City of Auburn in Apr., 1935.
In Jan., 1935, the City of Auburn passed the resolution calling for the referen-

In this way the public utilities have resorted to almost all forms of large scale pressure techniques to exert some control over state legislation. In cooperation with banks, insurance companies, and other business groups, they have attempted, first, to build up favorable public opinion through the press, the school, the radio, and their own employees and stockholders. Upon this foundation of favorable public opinion they have proceeded to build a cooperating element within the legislature. To this end, legislators are carefully circularized with utility literature. Furthermore, they count on a friendly outlook from some legislators who, with their families, are undoubtedly found among the large number of utility stockholders. In addition, it is to be noted that some legislators are retained as counsel or hold executive positions in utility companies, not to speak of the "Senator Thayers" who are illegally in the pay of the utilities.

Summary

Because the utilities have been able to pass their lobbying expenses on to the consumer in good times as well as in bad, they have developed publicity projects on a much wider scale than the other economic pressure groups of the state. With the Republican party in New York (closely identified with the industrial groups) no longer in control at Albany, the industrial groups cannot confine their pressure techniques to contributions to party funds, to employment of lawyer-legislators, and to the deep respect and attention which they believe should be theirs because they represent powerful property interests. They have, therefore, found it necessary to emulate

---

dum because of dissatisfaction with the privately-owned Empire Gas and Electric Company. Before the referendum took place, reduced rates went into effect and a still lower schedule was announced prior to the election to take effect on Jan. 1, 1936. As a result of this strategy, the voters rejected the municipal plant. An investigation by the Joint Legislative Committee disclosed that the Empire Gas and Electric Company had engaged a citizen prominent in local politics to conduct a campaign against the referendum, through a "Citizens Committee" which was the unwitting tool of the operating company and its paid agent. An examination of the books of the Empire Gas and Electric Company indicated that the company spent more than $43,000 in the municipal election. Engineers were employed and engaged by the utility company to bolster up material which was passed on to the unwitting Citizens Committee, which did not see the literature issued in its name. *Final Report*, 1936, p. 84.

some of the mass techniques best developed by their opponents.   They have stressed, for instance, the education and
activity of their employees [140] and have grown more attentive
to the power of the ballot box.[141]   In addition, they have
pointed out that business men are not sufficiently represented
in our lawmaking bodies,[142] and have urged that they take a
more active interest in proposed legislation.[143]

[140] For example, Thomas I. Parkinson, President of the Chamber of Commerce of the State of New York and of the Equitable Life Assurance Society,
has urged business men to use their influence with their employees to counteract the "demagogic and foolish doctrines" of the Roosevelt administration
by explaining to them how such doctrines affect the businesses from which
they derive a livelihood. *New York Times,* Jan. 28, 1936.   When a lawyer
claiming to represent 19,000 employees of the Endicott Johnson Corporation
opposed the unemployment insurance bill at a public hearing, his motives were
openly attacked by the legislators.   *Cf. Monitor,* June, 1935, p. 25.

[141] *Monitor,* June, 1935, p. 24 and June, 1936, p. 7.   Annual meeting of the
National Association of Manufacturers, 1935, *New York Times,* Dec. 5, 1935.

[142] There are, however, comparatively more members engaged in commercial enterprises in the New York State Legislature than in Congress. See
Appendix A.

[143] Thomas I. Parkinson, in *New York Times,* Feb. 28, 1936.

CHAPTER IV

The Phalanx of Farmers

THOUGH the Empire State is ordinarily thought of as the dominant industrial center of the Union, it is also the home of a significant body of agriculture. It is, therefore, not surprising that New York farmers present diverse and complex problems to their lawmakers. In the solution of these problems the private agricultural pressure groups play a leading part. Two conditions, however, must be clearly realized before the activities of these groups can be adequately understood. First, there is the unusual relationship that exists between the history, organization, and functions of all the unofficial agricultural organizations and those of the official agencies, institutions, and movements through which agricultural education has developed in New York State. Second, the date is comparatively recent when the farmers of New York realized that organized and united effort among themselves was necessary if agriculture was to achieve an economic equality with industry.

The Agricultural Setup in New York State

The close interdependence of official and unofficial agricultural agencies began after the passage of the Morrill Act in 1862. Under this act, a gift of public land was made to the State of New York for the establishment of a college of agriculture and the mechanic arts. The grant in New York was made to what was at that time a new university, Cornell. Subsequently, in 1893, 1904, and 1906, the state provided funds for the support of a State Veterinary College and a State College of Agriculture.[1] Thus, a unique situation has developed, in that an institution supported in large measure by private endowments receives support from the state for

---

[1] From the College of Agriculture, in 1925, the Department of Home Economics developed as a separate college.

three of its constituent colleges.   Moreover, although state aid is given to other, less important farm-educational institutions,[2] Cornell University has been allotted successive grants from the federal government for specific agricultural purposes.[3] Consequently, three divisions of the Cornell Colleges of Agriculture and Home Economics (research, resident teaching, and extension) have exerted a very powerful influence on agriculture throughout the state.   Something of the relationship of the College of Agriculture to the agricultural community is portrayed in the words of Dean Ladd:

> Nearly all of our research work is undertaken because of troubles that occur on farms somewhere in the state. Some farmer has a trouble that he cannot solve.   He reports it to the college.   Perhaps his local Grange or his Farm Bureau passes a resolution concerning it and asks that some work be undertaken to prevent this difficulty. Oftentimes a group of people go to the legislature and ask for an appropriation to make a study of some particular problem.   As a result the college or experiment station starts experimental workers on the problem.[4]

It is the extension departments of the colleges, however, that reach the largest number, through the services of the Farm Bureau, the Home Bureau, and the junior extension units known as the 4H clubs.   The Farm Bureau "was not created to meet a special emergency or to correct any injustice, but as a deliberate constructive movement . . . to make farming an efficient and profitable business, rural home life

[2] At Syracuse University the state supports the College of Forestry without the assistance of federal funds. Six agricultural secondary schools at St. Lawrence University and at Alfred University, and at Morrisville, Cobleskill, Farmingdale, and Delhi, almost wholly state-supported, are supervised by the State Department of Education. In addition, about 125 high schools give instruction in agriculture and home economics with the aid of federal funds and under the supervision of state and federal vocational-educational boards.

[3] In 1879, an Agricultural Experiment Station was set up at Cornell University, supported by both federal and state funds. In 1923 the State Agricultural Experiment Station, founded in 1882 as a separate state-supported station at Geneva, was also placed under the administration of the university. *Cf.* Dr. Cornelius Betten, "A Century's Progress in Agricultural Education," address at the 100th Anniversary of New York State Agricultural Society, Albany, Jan. 20, 1932 in *Bulletin* prepared by the New York State Agricultural Society.

[4] Dean C. E. Ladd, *Journal of Proceedings, N. Y. State Grange—Patrons of Husbandry, 60th Annual Session*, Geneva, 1933, p. 62.

fuller and richer, and to improve the community life of the country as a whole." [5] The prototype of the Farm Bureau was established as a department of the Binghamton Chamber of Commerce in Broome county in 1909. John H. Barron was appointed the first county agent in 1911. Financed jointly by the Binghamton Chamber of Commerce, the D. L. & W. Railroad, and the United States Department of Agriculture, he studied farmers' problems and aided in their solution. The work received "advice and encouragement" from the New York State College of Agriculture, and thus incorporated the first principle of successful county agent activity "service through education." [6] Perhaps it was because of the fact that the county agent movement received its stimulus from an urban source that it was at first difficult to secure the cooperation of the farmers in this work. [7] Nevertheless, the county farm and home bureau association movement likewise originated in Broome county in 1914.

As county agents were appointed in the several counties, equipped both with practical experience and technical education, they organized county farm bureaus as agencies through which they might familiarize themselves with local problems, and thus perform their work more effectively, while at the same time developing in the farmers themselves the essential concept of self-help and self-responsibility.

Just as the Farm Bureau developed around the county agent, the Home Bureau grew up around the home demonstration agent, and attempted to accomplish for the rural home and rural community what the Farm Bureau was doing for agriculture as a business. Established first in August, 1914, in Erie county as a subordinate branch of the Farm Bureau, under Miss Katherine Mills, first home bureau agent in the state, it was, two years later, made coordinate with the Farm Bureau, and has remained so ever since.

---

[5] C. B. Smith, of the States Relations Service, U. S. Department of Agriculture, quoted in A. C. True, *A History of Agricultural Extension Work in the United States, 1785–1923,* Washington, U. S. Government Printing Office, 1928, p. 167.

[6] *Cf.* M. C. Burritt, *The County Agent and the Farm Bureau,* New York, Harcourt, Brace, 1922.

[7] *Cf.* M. C. Burritt, "The Rise and Significance of Agricultural Extension," in *Annual Report of the Dean and Director of N. Y. State College of Agriculture at Cornell University,* Ithaca, 1922, p. 107.

These two phases of county extension work, as well as the third and later development—the 4H clubs, conducted in the interests of boys and girls between the ages of ten and twenty years, under the direction of county club agents—are centralized in the Director of Extension of the Colleges of Agriculture and Home Economics. He is assisted by a state leader for each of the three departments, with headquarters at the colleges in Ithaca. These various state leaders not only supervise the work of their respective county agents [8] but direct the activities of thousands of volunteer assistants who carry out the state programs through the local farm and home bureaus and the 4H clubs. These county agents and club leaders are selected by the County Farm and Home Bureau Associations upon the recommendation of the Director of Extension through his three state leaders.[9]

In order more effectively to meet the terms and conditions for rural extension work stipulated in the federal Smith-Lever Act of 1914, the Capper-Ketcham Act of 1928, and the State Farm Bureau Law of 1930,[10] the newly revised constitution

[8] The county agents in these three fields are public officers, part of whose salaries is paid from public funds authorized by federal and state law, $900 from federal sources and $900 from state funds being set aside for such payment in each department, provided the conditions stipulated by statute have been met by the county.

[9] L. R. Simons is Director of Extension of the Colleges of Agriculture and Home Economics. E. A. Flansburgh, state agricultural county agent leader, supervised in 1934 the work of 51 county agents, 27 assistants, and a large number of workers among farm bureaus totalling 25,891 members (1933). The seriousness of the economic depression is reflected in the fact that four counties temporarily abandoned their county farm agents, and that the total farm bureau membership for 1933 showed a decrease of almost 15,000 since 1931. See infra, p. 100. Mrs. R. G. Smith, state home demonstration leader, supervised in 1934 the activities of 34 county and 3 city home demonstration agents, 7 paid assistants, and a large number of other paid and volunteer workers. In 1930, 43 counties and 3 cities maintained demonstration agents. The total home bureau membership in 1933 was 22,013, representing a decline of over 5,000 since 1931. See infra, p. 108. W. J. Wright, state club leader, supervised in 1934 the work of 32 county club agents assisted by 8 associates and many volunteer workers. 4H club membership was at its peak in 1933, with 26,861 boys and girls enrolled. In those counties where there is no county club agent, club work is in charge of the home demonstration agents and others. In the agricultural counties of New York, 18,047 persons volunteer their time and services to help carry forward the extension work in these three fields. Interviews with Dean Ladd, Director Simons, E. A. Flansburgh, and assistants to Mrs. Smith and W. J. Wright, in Ithaca, June 25 to July 14, 1934.

[10] As amended, ch. 769 of laws of 1930. See an unpublished and undated outline of these by Director Simons, "Basic Legislation for Extension Work,"

provides for a County Farm and Home Bureau Association, one in each county, composed of three departments: (1) a Farm Department, known as the Farm Bureau; (2) a Home Department, known as the Home Bureau; and (3) a Junior Department, known as the 4H Clubs. Such at least has been the organization since 1931.

At the annual meeting of the Association, the enrolled members of the Farm Bureau and the Home Bureau each elect their respective executive committees of seven members. In joint session they elect the seven members of the junior executive committee and the president of the Farm and Home Bureau Association. Each executive committee of seven elects its own officers, and both together elect from their own number the vice-president and the secretary of the Association and appoint at the same time an Association treasurer, who may or may not be a member of one of the executive committees.

The Board of Directors of the County Farm and Home Bureau Association in each county is composed of the president of the Association, the 21 members on the executive committees of the three departments, and a representative nominated by the county Board of Supervisors and elected in joint session by the executive committees. The president of the Association and the chairmen of the three departments constitute a central committee to which the Board of Directors may delegate certain duties and responsibilities.

The extension services of the three departments of the County Farm and Home Bureau Association, including the salaries of the state and county agents and their paid assistants, rest largely upon two main sources of income: (1) public moneys derived from county, state, and federal sources, and (2) moneys received from the payment of membership dues.

---

revised in 1936 after the passage of the Bankhead-Jones Act of 1935. The Smith-Lever Act provides for the allotment of federal funds to the state's College of Agriculture for annual specific projects in cooperation with the U. S. Department of Agriculture. The Capper-Ketcham Act provides for further federal funds, 80 per cent of these to be used for the salaries of county agents. The Farm Bureau Law provides for the allotment of state funds, administered by Cornell University, for projects and salaries. To secure these state funds, each county must first raise $2,500 within the county for each line of work.

A meager income is also obtained from a miscellany of private sources.

The accompanying chart indicates how large a proportion of these funds comes from public sources: [11]

EXPENDITURES IN RURAL EXTENSION WORK IN NEW YORK STATE

1931[a]	From All Sources	From Public Sources		From Dues and Other Miscellaneous Sources
Farm Bureaus (55 counties)..	$641,255.16	county— state[b]— federal[c]—	58.3%—$374,252.78 41.7%—$267,239.88 7.7%— 49,675.00 8.9%— 57,337.90	41.7%— $267,002.38
Home Bureaus (41 counties)..	275,732.85	county— state[b] } federal[c] }	84.5%—$232,927.24 58.5%—$161,374.43 26.0%— 71,552.81	15.5%— $42,805.61
Junior Extension (33 counties)..	240,938.59	county— state[b]— federal[c]—	88.4%—$213,037.29 53.39%—$128,646.47 23.05%— 55,530.89 11.98%— 28,859.93	11.6%— $27,901.30 (No dues paid)
Total..........	$1,157,926.60		70.8%—$820,217.31	29.2%—$337,709.29

[a] 1931 represents the peak year prior to the passage of the Bankhead-Jones Act by Congress in 1935.   In the following years of the depression the decrease in the sum from all sources was due largely to the failure of the county to vote its $2,500 annually for each of the three departments of the County Farm and Home Bureau Association in accordance with the state law, and a falling off in membership dues in the farm and home bureaus.   Following the passage of the Bankhead-Jones Act, extension funds for 1935-1936 from federal, state, and county sources reached a new high of $1,540,250.08.

[b] New York State Farm Bureau Law operating under amended form of Chapter 769 of laws of 1930.

[c] Authorized by Federal Smith-Lever Acts of 1914, Supplementary Lever Appropriation, and the Capper-Ketcham Act of 1928.

Thus, although not all of its funds are derived from public sources, the County Farm and Home Bureau Association is primarily a public organization.[12]   In consequence, it is necessary for the Association to meet the requirements laid down

[11] Based on summary of Financial Reports submitted to Director of Extension by County Farm and Home Bureau Associations.   See also, in Library of College of Agriculture, Cornell University: *Ten Year Financial Summary for Farm Bureaus, 1917–1926* and *Seven Year Financial Summary for Home Bureaus, 1920–1926.*

[12] Decision in *State Bank of Commerce of Brockport, N. Y.* versus *Howard G. Stone, as Treasurer of the Farm Department of the Monroe County Farm and Home Bureau Association,* July 22, 1932: "The defendant (the County Farm Bureau Association) is a public county association . . . authorized and directed to perform governmental functions; the moneys held by it for such purposes must be considered to be public funds." (144 N. Y. Miscellaneous 393.)

in the laws.[13] To this end annual agreements are formally drawn and entered into between:

1. The United States Department of Agriculture and the New York State College of Agriculture;

2. The County Farm and Home Bureau Association and the New York State College of Agriculture; and

3. The County Board of Supervisors and the County Farm and Home Bureau Association. These latter must be approved by the New York State College of Agriculture.

In dealing with private agricultural groups in New York State, consequently, one must always keep in mind their dependence upon official agencies.

Moreover, the unification of private farmers' organizations, it should be remembered, is a very recent occurrence. The two agencies chiefly responsible for such unification as has taken place are the New York State Conference Board of Farm Organizations and the Governor's Agricultural Advisory Commission.[14] Both of them came into existence after the World War. Prior to the federation of the various agricultural organizations, pressure at Albany in the interests of agricultural legislation emanated from the seven private organizations which today wield their influence largely through the New York State Conference Board of Farm Organizations.[15]

New York State Grange

The first and oldest of these is the New York State Grange, which grew out of an organization founded on April 16, 1868, in Chautauqua county, by Oliver Hudson Kelley. Fredonia Grange No. 1, as it was called, was the first New York member of the national fraternity of farmers established in the previous year by Kelley [16] as the National Grange—Patrons of

---

[13] *Cf. supra*, pp. 88, 89, and note 10.

[14] See *infra*, pp. 123, 129.

[15] See *infra*, p. 130, note 133 on the historic New York State Agricultural Society.

[16] With Kelley had been associated six others. See Kenyon L. Butterfield, in *Cyclopedia of American Agriculture*, edited by L. H. Bailey, New York, Macmillan, 4th edition, 1912, Vol. IV, pp. 294–297; L. L. Allen, *A History of the New York State Grange from 1873 to 1933*, Watertown, N. Y., Hungerford,

Husbandry. One purpose of the National Grange was to soothe the feeling of hostility which existed between the farmers of the North and the South as a result of the Civil War.

On November 6, 1873, representatives of 21 newly formed New York granges met in Syracuse and organized a State Grange. The State Grange grew so rapidly that by March 18, 1874, when its first annual meeting was held in Albany, the number of granges in the state had increased to 164. To-day, the New York State Grange records a membership of 133,008 men and women over the age of fourteen. It is organized in 877 subordinate and 52 Pomona (county) Granges, and holds about 22,000 meetings throughout the state annually. If we include the 7,644 children organized in 256 juvenile granges throughout the state, meeting twice a month, a total of approximately 30,000 grange meetings are held in the state annually, and New York may be said to have the largest grange membership of any state in the Union, greater than the combined grange membership of the states west of the Mississippi.[17]

Local units are permitted to draft their own constitutions and regulations, subject to certain stipulations set forth in the constitution of the National Grange. These units are known as subordinate granges,[18] and may be formed by 13 persons more than 14 years of age, of whom four must be members of the sex opposite to that of the majority of the members. When there are three or more such subordinate granges in a county, permission may be secured from the State Grange for the organization of a Pomona, the county unit of the Grange.

Holbrook, 1934, and E. P. Herring, *Group Representation before Congress,* Baltimore, Johns Hopkins Press, 1929, pp. 114–117.

[17] The N. Y. State Grange has recorded a steady increase in the number of dues-paying members within recent years, when other agricultural organizations in the state were losing members because of the economic crisis. *Cf. Journal of Proceedings,* 1934, pp. 49–52. Up to 1933, 10,018 Silver Star Certificates and 204 Golden Sheaf Certificates were awarded to members of the New York Grange. *Cf.* Allen, *op. cit.,* p. 107. The membership of the National Grange is approximately 800,000.

[18] Of the 877 subordinate granges in 55 counties of the state, Steuben county holds the record for the state with 44 subordinates. *Cf. Journal of Proceedings,* 1934, p. 50.

There may be but one Pomona in a county.[19]   Membership in
the Pomona is open to all fourth degree members [20] of the
subordinates who are in good standing.   The Pomona confers
the fifth degree.[21]

The sixth degree is conferred by the New York State Grange
at its annual session.   At this session an accounting of the
year's activities is rendered both by the officers and the committees and plans for the following year are made.   Such an
annual session is attended by some 400 voting delegates, one
for each 400 Pomona members or major fraction thereof, and
one delegate at large for each Pomona.[22]   It is they who elect
both the officers [23] of the Grange for the coming biennium, and
the Executive Committee.   The latter, composed of the Master and the secretary, ex officio, and three additional members,
one of whom is elected every year for a three-year term, acts
for the order when the State Grange is not in session.[24]   The
detailed administrative work is delegated to standing committees appointed by the Master.   The most important of these
are the Committees on Legislation, Service and Hospitality,
and the Revolving Scholarship Fund.

In each county a Deputy Master is appointed by and repre-

---

[19] Form of *Constitution and By-Laws* for subordinate and Pomona in pamphlet issued in 1932 by New York State Grange, pp. 51–80.

[20] The ritual of the Grange is somewhat similar to that of the Masonic
Order, though changed and much extended.

[21] There are 52 Pomona Granges in the 55 agricultural counties of the state.
Two Pomona Granges have been organized in five smaller counties: Putnam,
Westchester, and Rockland counties form one; Suffolk and Nassau the other.
In the remaining fifty counties there is a Pomona for each county.

[22] Special meetings of the Grange may be called by the Executive Committee.   This is not customary, although, in 1930, 30 special State Grange
meetings were called for the purpose of conferring the sixth degree upon an
extraordinarily large number of candidates (nearly 13,000) in preparation for
the installation of seventh degree members at the National Grange annual
meeting in Rochester, N. Y., that year.   The seventh degree was given to
11,125, Governor F. D. Roosevelt among them.   This was the largest class
received into the National Grange in one session.   In 1930, $44,000 was turned
over to the National Grange from New York.   Each state has two voting
delegates at the National Grange, regardless of size of membership.   Interview, Master F. J. Freestone, at Interlaken, N. Y., July 11, 1934.   *Cf.* Allen,
op. cit., p. 104.

[23] The officers, elected biennially, are: Master, Overseer, Lecturer, Steward,
Assistant Steward, Treasurer, Secretary, and Gate Keeper (Ceres, Pomona,
Flora).

[24] *By-Laws of the N. Y. State Grange,* Art. VII.

sents the State Master in his activities among the branches of the Grange in the county.[25]   In addition, there is now a Juvenile Deputy Master, usually the wife of the Deputy Master, who supervises the administration of juvenile granges within the county, a division of the Grange's activity which has, since 1929, assumed greater importance.   The membership of the juvenile granges is composed of boys and girls between the ages of 5 and 14 years.   From these children, the future leaders of the Grange are developed.[26]   The children's meetings, held twice a month, usually at the same time the meetings of the subordinates are held, are marked by educational and recreational programs prepared by the subordinate lecturer under the supervision of a matron.   In connection with these programs, prizes are often awarded as a technique of stimulating activity.   Such has been the progress of the movement that New York ranks first in the United States in juvenile grange membership.[27]   The importance of the junior grange movement can perhaps be better understood if it is remembered that about half of the members of these junior granges graduate sooner or later into the subordinates.

The budget of the State Grange is usually in excess of $50,000 per annum.   Its income is chiefly derived from the 28¢ membership dues levied upon the subordinate and juvenile granges, and from initiation fees paid by subordinate and sixth degree members.[28]   The chief items of expense are the salaries

---

[25] These 52 county deputies have organized the N. Y. Association of County Masters for the better coordination and discussion of county problems, but without official standing in the State Grange.   The juvenile county deputies have followed suit.

[26] The first juvenile grange was established in Wayne county in 1904. Although in 1907 a resolution authorized the Grange Master to appoint a state deputy for the superintendence of juvenile grange work, a plan for such organized activity was not formulated until 1922.   The present system was adopted in 1929.   See Allen, op. cit., pp. 70, 80, 103.

[27] As of Sept. 30, 1933, there were 900 juvenile granges in the United States with an approximate membership of 24,000; as of Dec. 1, 1933 there were 237 juvenile granges with 7,050 members in New York State.   Allen, op. cit., pp. 143–146.

[28] Interview with State Master at Interlaken, N. Y., July 11, 1934:

(a) The *Juvenile Grange* turns over to the State Grange treasury 1¢ per member per quarter.   The Juvenile Grange fee is 15¢ for new members and 5¢ quarterly dues per person.

(b) The *Subordinate Grange* pays to the State Grange treasury 9¢ per member per quarter, of which 6¢ per member quarterly is retained by the State

and disbursements of officers and committee members, and the cost of the annual session, which frequently runs as high as $15,000.[29]

Since the dissemination of information is one of the chief purposes of the State Grange, great importance is attached to publicity. Thus, both a State Grange correspondent and a Grange historian are maintained.[30] They cooperate with members, officers, and lecturers in the preparation of pamphlets, articles on agriculture, and the issuance of a quarterly bulletin by the Pomona Lecturers' Association. In addition, the State Grange pays for three pages devoted to State Grange news in the *National Grange Monthly,* the official organ of the National Grange and the most systematic medium for the distribution of grange information in the United States. Additional publicity is also secured at the well-attended annual state fair, where grange projects are displayed in a building on the fair grounds.

Probably the chief reason for the wide influence which the State Grange exerts is to be found in its social and moral character, for, by virtue of the 30,000 annual meetings held in 600 grange halls throughout the state, the Grange stands next to the church and the school as the most important spiritual force in the rural community.[31] Under the guidance of official grange chaplains, meetings are opened and closed with prayer. Special Sundays are set aside annually as "Go-to-Church" days. And strong opposition is aroused against "the sale of

---

Grange and 3¢ quarterly given to the National Grange. The State Grange receives also $1 of the fee paid by men and 50¢ of the fee paid by women joining the subordinate grange.

(c) The State Grange derives no income from the *Pomona Grange.* Pomona fees and dues are very low and the Pomonas retain it all.

(d) *Sixth degree members* pay a $2 fee but no dues, upon joining the State Grange, of which $1 is retained by the State Grange and the other half turned over to the National Grange.

[29] Four dollars per day is paid to Deputy Masters and committee members, $2.50 per day to delegates to the annual session and an additional $2.50 per day if accompanied by their wives. Delegates, officers, and deputies also receive 5¢ for each mile of travel to the annual session, though this does not cover their full expenses. See *Journal of Proceedings,* 1934, pp. 38–45, 157.

[30] The office of correspondent was created in 1902; that of the historian, in 1923. The latter recently prepared a published history of the State Grange, in celebration of its 60th anniversary.

[31] About 300 Protestant pastors are Grange members.

intoxicants, . . . a foe as deadly in its influence as a crafty enemy within the household . . ." [32]

Moreover, the Grange conducts an educational program among its adult and juvenile members. Under the supervision of a partially salaried state lecturer who is assisted by the voluntary services of a lecturer for each subordinate and Pomona in the state, programs are marked out and discussion stimulated. And in an effort to improve the quality of such educational work, annual regional conferences of lecturers are held. At these conferences the state lecturer meets with and advises his subordinates, distributing and discussing the material in the lecturers' handbook, which is prepared annually. Since the formation of the Pomona Lecturers' Association in 1930, a still further effort has been made to increase the quality of service through the issuance of a professional bulletin and the development of a closer relationship among the lecturers. In addition, a Mid-Atlantic Lecturers' Conference brings together the lecturers of all the middle Atlantic States annually. No less important is a short course of lectures on contemporary problems offered by Cornell University. [33]

Though the Grange is not so well equipped with trained teachers as it might well be, and is consequently unable to conduct an extensive educational program, it does stress the practical experience of its teachers and strives within the limits of its resources to accomplish what it can. It gives both financial and moral support to any program of an educational character launched by other bodies. Thus, the program of the Geneva Experiment Station [34] and the teaching of agriculture

---

[32] Fred J. Freestone, at annual session, Lake Placid, N. Y., Feb. 6, 1934. Cf. Journal of Proceedings of New York State Grange, pp. 11, 12. Mr. Freestone, in an interview, stated that hotels and restaurants in Lake Placid were keenly disappointed when the 1934 session of the Grange, which attracted about 1,500 people, consumed practically no intoxicating liquors of any sort.

[33] Allen, op. cit., pp. 138–142.

[34] In recognition of this support, a member of the Grange served on its Board of Directors until the Experiment Station was merged with Cornell University in 1923, and since then the director of the Station reports annually to the Grange. Since 1909, a Grange representative has also served on the Board of Trustees of Cornell University, W. F. Pratt from 1909 to 1930, and H. E. Babcock since then. See Allen, op. cit., p. 104. Cf. Report of Trustees in Journal of Proceedings, 1934, p. 108. It should be noted that the N. Y. S. Grange and the N. Y. S. Agricultural Society are the only two organizations

in high schools have the full support of the Grange. Moreover, since 1923 a revolving scholarship fund, built up by contributions from subordinates, Pomonas, and the State Grange, as well as from individuals, is maintained for the purpose of building character and loyalty among grange members by helping young boys and girls in the Grange to obtain a better education. In 1934 the fund amounted to more than $45,000. From this some 438 loans had been made, averaging $200 each, giving assistance to students in 24 different professions, in more than 40 different schools, and located in 13 different states.[35]

Among the services rendered by the Grange is that of life, fire, and automobile liability insurance, at allegedly great savings to its members. Such insurance is issued by the Farmers and Traders Life Insurance Company and the National Grange Mutual Liability Insurance Company,[36] both sponsored and largely officered by the State Grange. In addition, 28 mutual fire insurance associations require membership in the Grange for eligibility to be insured. From these associations the State Grange receives considerable revenue.

Another service rendered by the Grange is the elimination of the profits of the middleman through sponsorship of an agency of cooperative trading.[37] Organized in June, 1920— sponsored by the Grange, the Dairymen's League,[38] and the State Farm Bureau Federation [39]—the Grange League Federation acts as a cooperative buying and selling agency for grange members who care to make use of its services.[40]

---

in the state thus represented on the Board of Trustees of the land-grant institution of New York.

[35] *Journal of Proceedings,* 1933, p. 113; 1934, pp. 55, 117. This plan was the successor to the four $50 scholarships at Cornell University, given by the Grange for almost 20 years, but abandoned in 1923 in favor of the revolving fund.

[36] The business of this company is confined to grange members. Formal campaigns are conducted and prizes issued to secure members for these grange insurance companies. See Allen, *op. cit.,* pp. 132–137.

[37] See *infra,* pp. 117–119.

[38] See *infra,* pp. 110–117.

[39] See *infra,* pp. 100–107.

[40] The Grange made its first organized attempt at cooperative trading in Monroe county in 1878, with arrangements for reduced prices on purchases by grange members. In 1883 the Grange secured control of the Union Trade Association, a pioneer cooperative, founded unofficially in 1874, and for 20 years this was managed by Henry H. Goff, Secretary of the State Grange.

More important from the point of view of this study, the State Grange has, from its very inception in 1873, attempted to influence the course of legislation in Albany and in Washington. Much of its legislative activity since 1918, however, has been carried on through the New York State Conference Board of Farm Organizations,[41] over which the Grange Masters have often presided, and through representation on the Governor's Agricultural Advisory Commission,[42] as well as on other advisory and administrative boards.[43] In the course of years, moreover, the procedure by which the Grange formulated its legislative program has been radically modified. In the first annual session of the State Grange, the draft of a proposed bill to be introduced into the State Legislature was first presented and discussed by the grange members. Then a committee was appointed by the State Master to arrange for the bill's introduction at Albany and to lay before the legislators and the Governor the wishes of the Grange with reference to it.[44]

The newer procedure of the Grange in formulating its legislative policy is much more representative in character. The Pomona and subordinate granges have been encouraged to appoint standing committees on legislative matters. These legislative committees, or individual members of the Pomona and subordinate granges, raise a great many problems, quasi-legislative in character, for discussion at the annual meetings. In consequence of these discussions, resolutions calling for specific legislative action are frequently passed. These are then submitted to the State Grange at its annual session for approval.

The State Grange, in recognition of the importance of an intelligent legislative policy, and of the physical impossibility of group examination of hundreds of resolutions, appoints ses-

---

In 1918 the Union Trade Association was supplanted by the Grange Exchange, Inc., plans for which had been prepared by a committee headed by Prof. H. H. Wing, of Cornell University. The fact that this undertaking almost ruined the Grange itself led, in 1920, to the organization of the G.L.F., from whose transactions the Grange does not derive any financial benefits today.

[41] See *infra*, pp. 124, 132.
[42] See *infra*, p. 129.
[43] The Master of the New York State Grange, Fred J. Freestone, was in 1934 a member of the Governor's Agricultural Advisory Commission, New York State Planning Board, and the St. Lawrence Power Commission.
[44] Allen, *op. cit.*, p. 47.

sional committees to examine the resolutions and report their recommendations to the assembled delegates of the State Grange. About ten such sessional committees topically examine these resolutions, reporting favorably or unfavorably to the assembled delegates, who, in turn, generally adopt the reports of these committees.[45] In addition, the State Grange maintains a standing committee on legislation, composed of three important officers of the Grange: the state master, the secretary, and the chairman of the Executive Committee. This committee, immediately after the close of the annual session of the State Grange, prepares its annual legislative program, copies of which are placed on the desks of the legislators at Albany. It has happened on several occasions, however, that Pomona and subordinate granges, in ignorance of the position taken by the State Grange, have passed resolutions differing from those agreed upon by the State Grange, have forwarded them to their representatives at Albany, and have thus diminished the influence of the order.[46] To check such contrary action by the granges, and to provide a more opportune annual meeting date, it was ordered at the sixty-first annual session of the State Grange in February, 1934, that future annual sessions be held in December, a month before the New York Legislature meets, rather than in February, as previously.

Thus, as a non-partisan, non-political organization, the State Grange, though it does not formally endorse individual candidates for office, attempts to influence the course of agricultural policy in New York by the formulation of a legislative program and by participation in the activities of various governmental commissions. It is a fraternity enabling thousands of farmers to assemble in their numerous grange halls to attempt to work out a solution of their problems. It is more than that; it is a cross-section of rural New York, and as such is politically significant—the more so because the overwhelming majority of its constituents are over twenty-one years of age and can, if they so desire, wield great influence at the ballot box.

---

[45] See *Journal of Proceedings* of any recent year.
[46] Allen, *op. cit.,* p. 86. *Cf. Journal of Proceedings,* 1933, p. 19.

New York State Farm Bureau Federation

The second statewide agricultural organization to which it is appropriate to direct attention is the New York State Farm Bureau Federation, which was organized in February, 1917. In that year, M. C. Burritt, then the state leader of county agents, called a meeting of representatives of the 34 county farm bureaus at the State College of Agriculture. The New York State Farm Bureau Federation was formed. Shortly thereafter, similar federations were formed in other states, and in 1919 the National Federation was organized. The chief purpose of the Federation, according to Mr. Burritt, was the "strengthening of the farm bureau organization . . . for the primary purpose of carrying out a constructive educational program for the improvement of agriculture, in which there will be utilized every facility of science and practice, including a partnership with the public agricultural institutions . . ." [47]

The unit of membership in the New York State Farm Bureau Federation is the county farm bureau, whose members decide whether or not their county farm bureau shall join the State Federation. In 1933, of the 51 active farm bureaus in New York State, 50 were members of the New York State Farm Bureau Federation. Membership figures for the ten-year period preceding indicate that 92 per cent of the county farm bureau members had been members of the State Federation.

Year	County Farm Bureau Membership	Members in N.Y.S. Farm Bureau Federation
1924	28,398	25,559
1925	29,388	24,704
1926	28,476	24,660
1927	29,213	26,781
1928	30,431	28,644
1929	34,931	32,969
1930	39,056	37,939
1931	40,111	39,035
1932	36,087	34,162
1933	25,891	24,045

[47] Quoted in A. C. True, *A History of Agricultural Extension Work in the United States*, 1928, p. 164.

Every county farm bureau in good standing and holding a membership in the State Federation is represented in the Federation by one voting delegate, and by one additional voting delegate if the membership of the county farm bureau is 900 or over. Each delegate is selected by the executive committee of the farm bureau of the County Farm and Home Bureau Association in his county, and although the delegate must not be the county agent or manager, he is practically always a member of the executive committee of the county farm bureau.[48] At their annual meeting, these county delegates elect the Board of Directors of the Federation. The directorate is made up of the president, first and second vice-presidents, and treasurer, all elected annually, together with four directors who are elected for four-year terms, spaced in such a fashion that the term of one of these directors expires annually. In addition, the Director of Extension of the College of Agriculture is an ex officio member of the board.[49] Although the Board of Directors selects the general secretary of the Federation, it is the delegates assembled at their annual meeting who elect the delegates to the national association, the American Farm Bureau Federation. These state delegates, in turn, choose the Board of Directors of the national association. Thus, every farmer who joins a county farm bureau becomes a member of the State Federation, if his county bureau joins the state organization; and he becomes also a member of the American Federation if the state organization joins the national group.

Although legally the county farm bureau is a "public association," the State Federation is not, for the income of the State Farm Bureau Federation is derived almost wholly from dues paid into the county farm bureau by the farmer members, and not from public sources.[50] The dues paid by farmers

---

[48] Art. III, Sec. 1 and 2, *Constitution and By-Laws of the N. Y. S. Farm Bureau Federation*. In 1933, only two counties were represented by more than one voting delegate: Albany and Dutchess counties were each represented by two delegates in the annual and special meetings of the State Federation. When membership of the State Federation was at its peak, there were 17 counties with two voting delegates each. Thus, this group of voting delegates in the State Federation ranges in size from about 50 to 70.

[49] In 1933, an honorary life member was elected to the Board of Directors.

[50] *Cf. supra*, p. 90, and *infra*, note 52.

desiring to join a county farm bureau vary in the different counties of the state from $2 to $5 annually. Of this, $1 is forwarded to the State Federation by the county member bureau, one half of this dollar is retained by the State Federation, and the other half goes to sustain the work of the American Farm Bureau Federation.[51]

Thus, although the county farm bureau and the State Federation are separate organizations, it can readily be seen that the county bureaus control the policies of the State Federation by reason of the fact that the selection of the officers and other members of the Board of Directors is made by voting delegates chosen by the county bureaus.[52]

To conduct the varied activities of the State Federation, an annual budget of between $20,000 and $25,000 [53] is required.

---

[51] E. P. Herring, *Group Representation Before Congress*, 1929, pp. 117–124; *Constitution and By-Laws of N. Y. S. Federation of Farm Bureaus*, Art. IV.

[52] See *supra*, p. 101, and note 12. Because of the close, interlocking connections among the publicly supported county agent, the semi-official county farm bureau, and the non-public, unofficial State Federation, it was found necessary for the American Farm Bureau Federation and the United States Department of Agriculture to enter into a memorandum of agreement, in 1921, outlining the policy governing the relations between the farm bureau and the extension service, in order to quiet the complaints of other farm organizations in the United States that the American Farm Bureau Federation was the recipient of material advantages because of close contacts with county farm bureaus and county agents. See A. C. True, *A History of Agricultural Extension Work in the United States*, 1928, pp. 168–170. *Cf.* C. B. Smith, and M. C. Wilson, *The Agricultural Extension System of the United States*, New York, J. Wiley, 1930, pp. 152, 378. This memorandum is not applicable to New York State where the rural extension work is carried on through agencies and under conditions quite different from those in most other states. Interview, July 14, 1934 and letter, Sept. 21, 1936, L. R. Simons, Director of Extension at Cornell.

[53] Expenditures for the fiscal year, Nov. 1, 1932 to Nov. 1, 1933, were $19,431.39. Of this amount, exclusive of dues to the American Farm Bureau Federation, which totalled $14,277, "officers' salaries and travel, including president, secretary, and treasurer represented 22%. Cost of operating the office (office space placed at disposal of State Federation by College of Agriculture in Ithaca, rent free), including stenographer, telephone and telegraph, postage, equipment, supplies and printing, represented 8%. Cost of preparing press releases, extra mimeographing and work on *Bureau Farmer*, (the organ of the national organization) amounted to 2%. Cost of the annual meeting, 3½%. Directors *per diem* and expenses, plus a small budget for speakers, 2%. Expenses of committees, including legislation, marketing, transportation, tuberculosis eradication, vigilance, 13%. Cost of *Bureau Farmer* represented 10%."
In 1933 and 1934, the State Federation tried to recover a small portion of its decreased income, resulting from a serious decline in membership, by charging a small registration fee for tours conducted by the State Federation.

These activities are for the most part conducted under the auspices of various standing and special committees appointed by the president. Indeed, the policies of the Federation itself are frequently the result of studies and recommendations made by these committees. There are always, of course, the standing committees on Dairy, Marketing, Poultry, Transportation, Organization, TB Eradication, Fruit, Vigilance, and Legislation.[54] In addition, the Federation from time to time appoints special committees to study particular problems. For example, in 1933, a special committee of 20 member farmers was appointed to study the problem of the prevention and control of mastitis. With the aid of some 32 experts which it called to its assistance, this committee made an exceedingly interesting and valuable report.[55]

Although the State Federation interests itself at times in federal legislation affecting farmers,[56] it is to the State Legislature at Albany that it most often addresses itself. A formal legislative program is drafted and presented to the Governor

---

Other minor sources of income for the State Federation come from advertisements sold for the state section of the *Farm Bureau* magazine and from the operation of a rural information service. See report of treasurer in general secretary's summary of the minutes of annual convention, Nov., 1933.

[54] The scope of all these committees is reflected in their titles, except the Vigilance service of the Federation. This service makes available to members reward signs for posting farm property. Many rewards have been paid to individuals giving evidence leading to arrest and conviction of persons guilty of stealing from posted farms. The service has helped to prevent and discourage thefts.

[55] This committee reported May 25, 1934. Copy of report in *American Agriculturist*, June 9, 1934, pp. 12–13.

[56] With the expansion of federal powers during the economic emergency, the State Federation sought for the farmers of New York a just share of federal rural relief. The State Federation claimed some credit for the "changed" monetary policy of the Roosevelt administration. "The position taken by the New York State Farm Bureau Federation and the American Farm Bureau Federation on the monetary question is outstanding. Dr. Warren put it to us point blank that his job was to find the facts; it was ours to get these facts to the people. For two years our representatives carried on educational work with the directors and delegates of the American Farm Bureau Federation, none of whom understood the monetary problem. We were entirely successful. As a result, the American Farm Bureau Federation in the annual meeting last December (the first representative body in the United States to do so), made detailed recommendations as to a monetary policy to be pursued. We were able to convince Franklin D. Roosevelt even before he entered the White House that the policy was sound, and it is being carried out at the present time." From address of President C. R. White, at annual meeting of State Federation, Syracuse, Nov. 9, 1933.

and the legislative leaders before the legislature convenes, in the hope that it may serve as a guide to the further development of the state's agricultural policies. In the transmission of the legislative program, the Governor and legislative leaders are frequently told that the "program expresses the thoughts of 24,000 individual farmers in 48 agricultural counties," who "represent approximately 90,000 persons or 70,000 adults." In this fashion the Federation attempts to indicate, to the political leaders addressed, something of the voting strength of the Farm Bureau Federation. Most of the provisions in this legislative program are drawn from resolutions passed at the annual meeting of the State Federation in November. The resolutions are submitted at the annual meeting by the various county delegates attending the convention, by the officers and directors of the State Federation, and by the individual farmer members.[57] The execution of the legislative program then devolves upon a legislative committee of three, composed of the president and secretary and one other member, assisted by a paid legislative representative of the Federation at Albany. It may mean either planning and carrying through extensive surveys in anticipation of the enactment of legislation, or the accumulation of additional data to influence legislation already enacted into law, which is either supported or opposed by the Federation.

A survey made by the Federation after the legislature authorized a 65 per cent surtax upon motor truck registration illustrates the method frequently pursued by the State Federation. During the summer of 1932, after this legislation was enacted to take effect in March, 1933, the Federation made plans at once to collect information showing the influence of this surtax upon the operation of farm trucks. With the assistance of the Department of Agricultural Economics and Farm Management of the New York State College of Agriculture, facts derived from 9,000 questionnaires distributed to farm motor truck owners were tabulated to show that the new

[57] Of the 24 resolutions passed at the convention in November, 1933, 14 required state legislative action for execution. At times the resolutions committee of the convention recommends that no action be taken on some resolutions submitted, suggesting to the convention that these be referred to the Board of Directors for further consideration and action. *Annual Meeting,* Nov. 11, 1932.

taxes, because of the high rate, would be prohibitive, so that the state in 1933, under the increased rates, would receive less than one half the revenue derived from farm trucks under the 1932 rates.

After a summary of the questionnaire had been looked over by the county boards of supervisors, county farm bureaus, many legislators, and the Governor, it was officially presented to the legislature at a committee hearing on February 8, 1933. Copies of the summary were sent to the editors of some 175 daily and 575 weekly newspapers as well as to many radio stations throughout the state. In addition, *Farm Economics,* the publication of the Department of Agricultural Economics and Farm Management of the New York State College of Agriculture, the County Farm Bureau monthly newspapers, and the *Bureau Farmer,* the official monthly publication of the American Farm Bureau Association,[58] all published the report. Moreover, the National Highways Users' Conference in Washington sent briefs of the report to all daily newspapers in the United States. To exert still further pressure, the Board of Directors of the Federation issued to the Associated Press a statement advising farmers not to license their trucks until the legislature had modified the law. Although many other organizations engaged in a campaign against the surtax,[59] the Federation's survey was undoubtedly an important factor in stirring up public opinion against the new rate, and perhaps contributed as much as anything else to its final repeal.

Through a series of bulletins prepared by its Legislative Committee, members of the Federation are kept informed as to the progress of their program. At the close of the legislative session these reports of progress are published in summary form and a detailed analysis is made of the Federation's legislative achievements. An analysis of the summary of these legislative reports sent to members of the Federation in 1934 may, perhaps, reveal to some extent the significance of the Federation's work. At the close of the legislative session of 1934, the Federation listed 62 bills and budgetary items

[58] The New York State Farm Bureau Federation contributes an 8 page insert in the *Bureau Farmer.*

[59] Motor truck associations, automobile associations, oil companies, automobile manufacturers, and the N. Y. S. Conference Board of Farm Organizations.

of interest to agriculturists which it had either supported or opposed upon introduction into the legislature. Of these, the summary shows that:

> 27 were supported by the Federation and passed by the legislature; and of this number 4 were vetoed by the Governor.
>
> 11 were not supported by the Federation and not passed by the legislature.
>
> 17 were supported by the Federation but were not passed by the legislature.
>
> 2 were not supported by the Federation, were passed by the legislature, but were vetoed by the Governor.
>
> 5 were not supported by the Federation, were passed by the legislature, and were signed by the Governor.

On 38 of the 62 bills, the action taken by the legislature was in accord with the position taken by the Federation. If one could assume that the legislature followed the bidding of the Federation alone the statistical measure of the Federation's influence on the legislature during the regular session of 1934 would be 61 per cent. Such an assumption, however, is in no way warranted, for undoubtedly a number of other organizations contributed to the passage and defeat of the various measures.

Nevertheless, the fact that the New York Farm Bureau Federation is the only individual farm organization maintaining a paid representative in the state Capitol for the purpose of presenting its views to the legislators undoubtedly makes it one of the most effective of the farm organizations.[60] On occasion, however, the Federation prefers even more personal and direct contact with the legislature. This is revealed in the fact that it is the president of the Federation and not its legislative agent who appears before the various committees during public hearings. In this fashion it hopes to drive home

---

[60] Bert W. Miller represented the New York State Farm Bureau Federation at Albany from the organization of the Federation in 1917, until his appointment as assistant director of the Milk Control Board in 1933. His tasks have been assumed by the secretary of the Federation. The New York State Conference Board of Farm Organizations had also used the services of Mr. Miller. See *infra,* pp. 127, 132.

the fact that the program of the Farm Bureau Federation is in reality the program of a large section of authentic farmers rather than the idiosyncrasies of a paid lobbyist.[61] Needless to say, the fact that at least 20 of the members of the New York Legislature are or have been members of the Farm Bureau Federation does not in any way diminish the Federation's influence.[62]

New York State Federation of Home Bureaus

The third organization to which we turn our attention is the New York State Federation of Home Bureaus. It was organized in October, 1919, at the close of the World War, the first in the United States. This new organization was brought into existence by virtue of the rapid development of the extension work at the College of Home Economics [63] which made necessary a statewide organization for the county home bureaus [64] similar to that which had been launched by the farm bureaus years before. Thus, the Federation was organized. Its purpose was the "strengthening and improving the existing institutions of rural community life, namely the rural school, the country store, the country weekly, the rural church, and recreation for farm people." In an effort to achieve its objective, "it endeavors to cooperate with other existing agencies for the betterment of home and community life, and to furnish the organized homemakers of the state an opportunity to express themselves on problems concerning civic and social welfare and on matters affecting the home." [65]

[61] Interviews with C. R. White, President of the New York State Farm Bureau Federation, and Bert W. Miller, in Albany, Feb. 1, 1933.

[62] Interview with E. S. Foster, Secretary, Aug. 10, 1933. For example, Fred Porter, formerly chairman of the Ways and Means Committee, was a first and second vice-president of the Federation, and Frank Smith, formerly chairman of the Assembly Committee on Agriculture, was a director of the Federation from 1919–1924.

[63] This was due particularly to the generous provision by both the federal and state governments, during the World War, for conservation agents in the counties to assist homemakers in the war conservation program.

[64] Cf. supra, p. 87. The movement has now spread to a sufficient number of states to warrant the opinion that the time is now ripe for the organization of an American Home Bureau Federation to replace the Home Department of the American Farm Bureau Federation. Interview with Miss C. Morton, of the College of Home Economics, in Ithaca, July 2, 1934.

[65] Mrs. A. E. Brigden, first president of the Federation, quoted in an unpublished paper, *A History of Extension Service to Women in New York State,*

The unit of organization in the State Federation of Home Bureaus is the county and city home bureau, and, as in the case of the county farm bureaus, each local home bureau decides for itself whether or not it wishes to join the State Home Bureau Federation. Each member bureau in good standing is represented by one voting delegate and two alternate delegates, selected by the Executive Committee of the member organization. The individual membership in the county home bureaus of the state has varied from 11,089, organized in 25 county and two city home bureaus in 1919, to 27,675, organized in 41 county and three city home bureaus in 1931.[66] Although, as in the case of the farm bureaus, most county home bureaus are members of the New York State Federation of Home Bureaus, the organization operates with a modest annual budget, since its chief source of income is an assessment of 20 cents per member levied by the State Federation on the various county and city home bureaus.[67]

In order to assure more adequate representation from all parts of the state in the work of the Federation, and more effectively to execute its program, the state is divided into four districts: Northern, Southeastern, Western, and Central. Each district has its own chairman and other officers and operates under its own individual by-laws. Moreover, each district holds one to four meetings a year, in which problems are considered and recommendations are made to the Board of Directors of the State Federation. Each of the four districts is represented on the Board of Directors by one member, elected by the State Federation at its annual meeting, for a four-year term, one elected annually. In addition to these four members, the Board of Directors is composed of the annually elected officers of the Federation, the Counselor to the Federation and the Director of the College of Home Economics.

---

by Franc Hall Morse, Secretary of Literature, New York State Federation of Home Bureaus. See also planks in the ten-year *Program,* adopted by the Federation at its first annual meeting, Oct. 26, 1920. *Cf.* Art. I, Sec. 2, *Constitution and By-Laws of the New York State Federation of Home Bureaus.*
　[66] *Cf.* records in files of College of Home Economics in Ithaca.
　[67] *Constitution and By-Laws of New York State Federation of Home Bureaus,* Art. IV. *Cf.* letter of Mrs. George M. Tyler, President of State Federation, Aug. 3, 1934.

The activities of the Federation are conducted through some ten state committees that work with similar committees in district, county, and local units. The more important of these committees are those on Legislation, Marketing, Rural School, Libraries, and Publicity. Since the Federation is aware of the value of publicity, it capitalizes thoroughly any opportunity afforded it. In the *Bureau Farmer,* the official publication of the American Farm Bureau Federation, for example, one page is devoted to news of the New York State Federation of Home Bureaus.

Through its Legislative Committee, the Federation prepares a program for submission to the legislative leaders of the state. Only rarely does it attempt to present its case to the legislature directly, but relies, rather, upon the support of the Conference Board [68] for the prosecution of its legislative program. Nevertheless, through its representation on the Governor's Agricultural Advisory Commission [69] and other administrative and advisory boards to which its representatives are appointed, the Federation does attempt to influence the agricultural policy of the state, particularly as it relates to the welfare of women in rural communities. To this end, the Legislative Committee of the State Federation studies such legislation as may be introduced into the State Legislature, making extensive use of the bulletins of information prepared by the Women's Joint Legislative Forum which are mailed weekly to the legislative chairmen.[70]

And so it is correct to conclude that the influence of the Federation of Home Bureaus in the field of legislation in New York is secondary only to that of the Grange or the Farm Bureau Federation. For its importance must be judged as that of the representative of women in the rural communities of the state on the Conference Board of Farm Organizations and the Governor's Agricultural Advisory Commission. Furthermore, as an organized group of women, it assists the State Colleges of Agriculture and Home Economics in their tasks of improving the conditions of agriculture in the state

---

[68] See *infra,* p. 124.
[69] See *infra,* p. 129.
[70] See *infra,* p. 216, for this Forum. *Cf.* letter of Mrs. Eliza K. Young, chairman of the Legislative Committee of the New York State Federation of Home Bureaus, Aug. 13, 1934.

generally, and the welfare of women in the rural parts of the state in particular.

Dairymen's League Cooperative Association

The fourth organization to which our attention must be given is the Dairymen's League Cooperative Association, Inc., which grew out of the old Dairymen's League. The latter organization traces its rise in 1906 to the Orange County Pomona Grange.[71] The League, however, did not begin to function until 1910, after it had secured members who owned a total of 50,000 cows.[72] It immediately began a concerted drive to raise the price of its members' products. About half its members, organized in local associations in various sections of the six states which today constitute the New York Milk Shed,[73] customarily sent their milk to New York City. The prices paid to the dairymen for these shipments were practically controlled by three large distributors: The Milk Exchange, Borden's Condensed Milk Company, and the Sheffield Farms-Slawson Decker Company. So tight was this control that a farmer had merely the alternative of selling to one of these distributors or turning his milk into butter and cheese.[74] When, in the fall of 1916, however, the Dairymen's League ordered its members to withhold their milk until the dealers agreed to a price set by the League for a period of six months, about 40,000 nonmember dairymen [75] cooperated with the League members in an 11-day strike which brought the surprised distributors to terms.[76]

This and other similar achievements together with the great strike of January, 1919, when the farmers withheld their milk from the market for 19 days, made the League a very powerful instrument in obtaining for the farmers of the New York Milk Shed—almost all of whom were members of the League

---

[71] See *supra,* p. 92.

[72] Required under the Act of Incorporation in the State of New Jersey, 1907.

[73] New York, New Jersey, Pennsylvania, Vermont, Connecticut, and Massachusetts.

[74] *Report of the Joint Legislative Committee to Investigate the Milk Industry,* Legislative Document 114, Apr. 10, 1933, p. 101.

[75] The League had, at this time, only 15,000 members, and $5,000 in its treasury.

[76] Herman Steen, *Cooperative Marketing: The Golden Rule in Agriculture,* Garden City, N. Y., Doubleday, Page, 1923, p. 177.

by this time—what they deemed an equitable price. The close of the World War, however, created problems in the milk industry [77] which could not be solved by a mere bargaining agency. In 1920, consequently, there was incorporated under the laws of New York, the Dairymen's League Cooperative Association, a non-stock, non-profit organization. Beginning May 1, 1921,[78] the Association secured some 50,000 contracts from milk producers in the area of the New York Milk Shed. The Association, like the League, acts as a bargaining agency in connection with the sale of milk produced by its members. Since the surplus milk problem was one with which the Association was particularly designed to deal, it early purchased sundry wholesale and retail establishments in various cities throughout the state. The Association has, therefore, developed outlets for its produce, and ranks today third among the milk distributing organizations in the metropolitan area.[79]

A bona fide producer of milk or dairy products, or the owner of a dairy farm, upon becoming a member of the League, signs a formal pooling contract, in which he agrees to deliver to the Association all the milk produced by him during the period of the contract, usually one year. The pooling plan recognizes the right of each member to receive the same basic price for his milk as is paid to each other member, regardless of whether it is sold as fluid milk or manufactured into butter, cheese, condensed milk, ice cream, or other products. Under the classified price plan of the Association, a feature much discussed and criticized, the price received by a member bears little relation to the price for which his milk is sold, although freight rates, butterfat content, and other differentials are taken into

---

[77] Chief of these problems was that of the difficulty of marketing large quantities of surplus milk at suitable prices. Such a problem had not, of course, existed during the war, for such milk was purchased by condensaries to meet foreign orders. Condensed milk, indeed, sold at the same price as fluid milk in New York City. See *Milk Report, op. cit.,* pp. 100–106, and Albert Manning, "A Complete History of the Dairymen's League," *Bulletin 121,* Department of Farms and Markets of State of New York, July, 1919, pp. 406–411.

[78] The old Dairymen's League ceased its operations in 1922.

[79] *Milk Report, op. cit.,* pp. 108, 123.

consideration in computing the price. This explains the variation in the prices actually paid the producers.[80]

The services offered by the League to its members include,
in addition to its guarantee of a market for their milk and
milk products, the protection of the farmers from the dis-
honesty on the part of distributors. To this end, the Association insists on the right to audit the books of such dealers as
buy the produce of its members, both to verify the various
classifications of the milk purchased and to forestall such losses
as would arise from unanticipated bankruptcies.[81] Moreover,
the League maintains a highly organized Home and Health
Educational Department to deal with problems which fall into
this category. In addition, it represents the farmers' point of
view at hearings before local boards of health when rules and
regulations relative to dairy farms are contemplated. No less
important is the League's constant service to both the farmer
and the consumer in stimulating the production of a higher
quality of milk, by supervising the accuracy of weights and the
effectiveness of tests, and by maintaining strategically located
plants in various cities, where milk supplies are constantly
watched to assure the consumer of an adequate supply of high
quality milk in the event of an interruption of any kind from
other sources or an unusual increase in consumption.[82]

Approximately 76 per cent of the members of the League [83]
are milk producers in New York State who produce 38 per cent
of the milk delivered to plants in the state. The membership
on May 1, 1921, when the pooling plan was adopted, was
50,843, and has varied since then from 74,887, in 1922–1923, to

---

[80] *Ibid.*, pp. 109–118.

[81] This is the common reply made by officials of the League to the criticism
that the classified price plan gives the dealers an opportunity to obtain milk
at a low price by making false reports of their use of it. *Milk Report, op. cit.*,
pp. 111, 124. Officials of the League are frank to admit that the League's
auditors have found some dealers dishonest in this respect, and that dealers
have been forced to turn back money to the League to cover these irregulari-
ties. Interview, D. J. Carter, Editor of the *Dairymen's League News*, July
20, 1934. A bill providing compulsory audit of dealers' books was defeated
in 1936. *Cf. New York Times*, Aug. 23, 1936.

[82] Testimony of F. H. Sexauer, President of the League, in *Milk Report,
op. cit.*, pp. 123–125.

[83] A member is a producer who has signed the marketing agreement.

43,504 at the close of the abnormal fiscal year, 1934.[84] In 1932, moreover, the League inaugurated a selective membership policy in order that, with the volume of milk production deflated by a decreased membership, there might be less difficulty in marketing the League's surplus supplies.

The members of the League are grouped into local units. There are 825 of these units, regularly incorporated under the laws of the six states in the Milk Shed, and each unit is a separate and distinct corporation, with its own annually elected officers and directors. Since a member of the local association may or may not be a member of the League, the latter is a distinct and separate organization, often referred to as the "parent association." [85] To provide for adequate territorial representation of the large number of producers who are scattered over the wide New York Milk Shed, and to overcome the physical difficulties attendant upon gathering together 50,000 members, the territory served by the Association is divided into 24 sections, called directors' districts. Each district elects one member to the League's Board of Directors. The local association serves as the nominating unit for the directors, eight of whom are elected annually for a three-year term. A meeting of each local association is called, on the first Saturday in May, in those districts where a director is to be selected. At this meeting a delegate is chosen to attend the district meeting. The delegate, who is generally under instructions from the local unit, casts at the district meeting a vote equal to the number of members present at the local meeting in which the delegate was selected. The secretaries of the several district meetings then notify the secretary of the parent association of the nominations made. The latter then prepares for distribution to the local associations, ballots carrying the name of each nominee for director. On the fourth Saturday of May of each year, a meeting of all the local associations is called. At these meetings each member casts one vote for each of the directors to be chosen, whether his name appears

---

[84] Since there were in 1934 approximately 84,000 producers in the New York Milk Shed, more than half of these were members of the League. *Cf.* letter of W. M. Requa of the statistical department of the Dairymen's League, Jan. 31, 1936 to the writer.

[85] *Cf. Pocket Manual of Dairymen's League Cooperative Association,* 1928, p. 28.

on the ballot or not. A director is thus nominated by the membership within his district, and elected by all the members in all the districts. The ballots are then sealed, transmitted to the secretary of the Association, and canvassed by a specially constituted committee. The candidate who receives a plurality of the votes cast is elected as director.[86]

The results of these elections are reported to the annual meeting held in June, made up of delegates representing the local associations, and immediately afterward the Board of Directors selects the officers of the League: president, first vice-president, second vice-president, secretary, and treasurer. The Board of Directors selects, in addition, four from its own number who, with the president of the League, act as an Executive Committee and give their full time to the conduct of the Association's business. From the organization of the League in 1921 until March 31, 1934, 36 individuals have served on the League's Board of Directors of 24 members.[87] The League explains this limited variation in its directing personnel [88] by pointing out that experienced men are wanted and valued by the rank and file of its membership, that the League has been exceptionally fortunate in securing such men, and that the repeated reelection of these directors attests to the confidence which they inspire in the membership.[89] The detailed execution of the League's business, however, is delegated to special committees,[90] on which local associations are represented by the presence of a voting delegate.

---

[86] *By-Laws of Dairymen's League Cooperative Association,* Art. IV, Sec. 5.

[87] During this same period, ten persons served on the Executive Committee of five members. Officers of the League (with the exception of the treasurer and the secretary) and members of the Executive Committee must be chosen from the Board of Directors.

[88] It is perhaps pertinent to bear in mind here, that several members of the board were removed through death and not through failure of reelection.

[89] Interview with D. J. Carter, Oct. 18, 1934.

[90] These committees are: Membership, Production, Sales, Legal, Accounting, Financing, Engineering, Purchasing, Home Department, Health Education, Costs and Statistics, Traffic, Office Manager, and *Dairymen's League News* (official weekly publication of the League). See *Milk Report, op. cit.,* p. 126, and *By-Laws,* Feb., 1932. The Home and Health Departments were recently combined. A rather unique department in a cooperative association, it was organized for the purpose of enlisting rural women in a movement to spread the idea of the League's cooperative marketing and the value of dairy products to one's health, to thus increase the consumption and sales of dairy products. The women are kept informed of the League's business by the

Since it is a non-stock, non-profit cooperative organization, conducted for the mutual help of its members and nonmembers,[91] the League is financed largely through the issue of certificates of indebtedness to members, in return for loans made to the organization by means of monthly deductions from milk checks. Although the maturity of these certificates of indebtedness was originally set for five years, it has gradually been extended to ten. The certificates carry an interest rate of 6 per cent. The financial strength of the League is indicated by the fact that these certificates of indebtedness can be sold readily at par almost any time. The League values its assets, moreover, at approximately 23 million dollars, its liabilities at 18 million, and about two-thirds of the latter is represented by the certificates of indebtedness referred to above.[92]

The peak year in the gross sales of the League was that ending March 31, 1929. In that year the League's business grossed well over 85 million dollars. Since then, although the volume of business has not fallen radically, the gross receipts from sales has diminished steadily. In consequence, the gross receipts for both 1933 and 1934 totalled only 55 million annually.

As might be expected of an organization which represents "the most important branch of agriculture in New York State, yielding fully one-half the total income from all farm products" [93] in the state, the Dairymen's League has, again and again since its organization, acted as the spokesman of the dairy industry in matters of legislation. In spite of its vigorous opposition, the milk control law of 1933 was passed by the Legislature and signed by the Governor, but not until a num-

---

director of the district at the district meetings, attended by an associate delegate, a woman representative of each local association. Interview with Laura Ellenwood, of Home Department of D.L.C.A., July 20, 1934. Accounts of activities in annual reports of D.L.C.A.

[91] For limitations placed upon services to nonmembers, see Art. I, Sec. II of By-Laws as amended Apr. 20, 1932.

[92] From condensed balance sheet, Jan. 31, 1933, in Milk Report, op. cit., p. 130. On Mar. 31, 1934, there had been issued certificates of indebtedness amounting to approximately $35,867,000. Of these, approximately $10,598,000 are outstanding, the remainder, including $15,748,000 before maturity, having been retired. From Annual Report, 1933–1934, p. 52.

[93] State of New York, Legislative Document No. 59, 1933, p. 9.

ber of amendments suggested by the League had been incorporated in its text.[94]

The League, a member of the Conference Board, finds it can best further the interests of its clientele by an active interest in and cooperation with the legislative program of the Board,[95] designed as it is to benefit agriculture in general, rather than the dairy farms in particular. Frequently, therefore, the Dairymen's League Cooperative Association, representing half of all the milk producers in the Milk Shed, has attempted, without the assistance of the Conference Board, to fight for particular projects in a very complicated industry. Such was its position in the case of the milk control bill, already referred to, and in the case of its campaign to reduce railroad rates in 1932 and 1933.[96] In attempting to find solutions for the problems of its industry, the League has materially benefited those who have not been associated with it. What these latter producers do, of course, vitally affects the entire milk industry, and the difficulty of dealing with them is increased by the fact that, not being organized,[97] they may at times receive higher prices for their milk, particularly in the fluid form, than members of the League. At such times, naturally, League members become disgruntled[98] and forget the many other advantages offered by membership in the League.

---

[94] The League realized that this important legislation could not be discussed on its merits. At the time disgruntled farmers were striking, dumping milk, and threatening even greater violence. Furthermore, it was understood that the immediate effect of the law would result in an increase in prices to the farmers. It had been maintained by the League that the law, providing for governmental control of the milk industry, would create new and complex problems in a milk shed that extended over more than one state, the interstate aspects of which could not be covered by the New York State law. That the League was justified may be seen in the decision of the Supreme Court, in the Seelig Case (294 U.S. 511) in 1935, declaring that New York State could not provide for a minimum price to be paid producers for milk originating outside of the state. Although the law, of course, despite the cooperation of the League, was difficult to enforce, the League derived some satisfaction from the adoption by the Milk Control Board, created under the act, of the classified price plan of the League. Interview with D. J. Carter, Oct. 18, 1934. Cf. Dairymen's League News, Oct. 16, 1934.

[95] See infra, pp. 124, 132.

[96] Annual Report, 1932–1933, pp. 18–19.

[97] Unsuccessful attempts to organize these producers are discussed in Milk Report, op. cit., pp. 132–134.

[98] Legislation to permit the examination of the books of the League has been introduced almost yearly since 1927, but has always failed of passage.

The only other important producers' organization in the New York Milk Shed is the Sheffield Producers' Cooperative Association, Inc. This organization was formed in 1922, and numbered, in 1934, a membership of 16,000. It deals, however, solely with the Sheffield Farms Company. Its producers are not compelled to sign a contract and are free to withdraw from the Association at any time. Moreover, though the Association has been able to pay the producer a higher average composite price for the milk it has taken than has the League, it has accepted little or no responsibility either for surplus milk or for the farmer's marketing problems.[99] It is not, needless to say, a member of the Conference Board.

The Dairymen's League Cooperative Association is, therefore, preeminently the representative of organized dairy farmers of New York State, especially in the field of dairy legislation. Thoroughly experienced, it has "gone over the road of about all the problems and possibilities a farmers' organization can face," [100] and is "the best example of regional planning in the whole United States." [101]   As such, it is one of the chief members of the Conference Board of Farm Organizations.

Cooperative Grange League Federation Exchange

The fifth private, statewide agricultural group, entirely different in organization and purpose from those already discussed, is the Cooperative Grange League Federation Exchange, Inc., known as the G.L.F. It was organized in 1920, as the successor to the New York State Grange Exchange, Inc., under the sponsorship of the New York State Grange, the Dairymen's League Cooperative Association, Inc., and the New York State Farm Bureau Federation.

The original purpose of the organization was to supply the

See *Annual Report,* 1933–1934, pp. 9–42, where the League's president, in his annual address, discusses such trying problems.

[99] E. O. Fippin, *First Principles of Cooperation in Buying and Selling in Agriculture,* Richmond, Garrett and Massie, 1934, p. 229.

[100] *Ibid.,* p. 230.

[101] *Cf.* pamphlet, *Opinions of State and Federal Spokesmen on Agricultural Cooperation in the New York Milk Shed,* issued by Dairymen's League Cooperative Association, Inc., July, 1930. See the report of the Federal Trade Commission made pursuant to House Concurrent Resolution 32, 73rd Congress, 2nd Session on conditions in the New York Milk Shed filed with Congress on Oct. 1, 1936.

farmers of New York, New Jersey, and northern Pennsylvania with farm supplies of better quality than those which they had secured before, at the lowest possible cost. In order to make the purchasing and distributing services of this organization effective, farm service agencies were established in the various communities. These service agencies were local cooperative corporations organized by the farmers in their respective neighborhoods. The individual farmers subscribed for preferred capital stock in the corporation, and the G.L.F. subscribed to the common stock. Additional working capital is loaned to the individual corporations by the G.L.F. Each local agency cooperates with representatives of the G.L.F. through an elected advisory committee. All the local agencies, of which there were approximately 130 in 1934, are united under the managerial, financial, and accounting control of the G.L.F.

The G.L.F. is, consequently, a single organization which handles the financing for all the individual corporations. It lends adequate funds to individual farm service agencies, until their fixed assets and warehouse equipment have depreciated to one dollar. Furthermore, they are not financially independent of the G.L.F. until a reserve equal to the preferred stock which the farmers have purchased, and a working capital reserve equal to the average amount of money which the farm service agency uses throughout the year, have been set up. After this solvent position has been reached, earnings are returned to the patrons (the farmers) in the form of a patronage dividend, computed on the basis of the individual patron's business to the total volume of business in the farm service agencies.[102]

The farmers have recently requested additional services from their local agencies, with the result that subsidiary corporations have been organized to aid in the marketing of farmers' produce, to help provide working capital credit, and

---

[102] As of June 30, 1934, 20 agencies had already paid patrons' dividends. "The benefits of using the farm service agency by farmers will always accrue to them, as the parent corporation (the G.L.F.) is limited by law to a dividend return of 6% on its one class of (common) stock. The average investment in common stock for each agency is $75." Interview with E. V. Underwood, Secretary-Treasurer of G.L.F. in Ithaca, June 29, 1934.

to market beans and eggs. These subsidiary corporations promise to become important factors in future farm operations.

Thus, the G.L.F. is a cooperative stock corporation, owned by 35,000 farmers and controlled by 13 directors, rendering service to some 110,000 farmers in New York, New Jersey, and northern Pennsylvania. The directors are elected by the individual stockholders of the G.L.F. Three directors are nominated by each of the three sponsoring organizations, the New York State Grange, the Dairymen's League, and the New York State Federation of Farm Bureaus. The patrons of the G.L.F. in Pennsylvania and New Jersey by caucus nominate the remaining four directors.

In addition to the 130 farm service agencies, 40 independent cooperatives and 500 dealers handle G.L.F. supplies,[103] so that the G.L.F. is believed to be one of the largest cooperative purchasing organizations in the world, doing approximately 23 million dollars in wholesale, and 12 million dollars in retail, business annually.

In so far as the G.L.F. exerts an influence upon the course of public policy in the agricultural field, it does so as a member of the Conference Board.

New York State Vegetable Growers' Association

The sixth organization to which attention should likewise be directed is the New York State Vegetable Growers' Association, established at Ithaca, on February 22, 1911, at the instigation of a few vegetable growers seeking the benefits of organization and unification in a state that probably ranks second in vegetable production of the United States. Adhering as closely as possible to its avowed object "to organize and federate the interests of those engaged in vegetable growing to the end that larger crops of constantly improving quality may be grown and marketed with increased profit," the organ-

---

[103] "In the G.L.F. the farmers possess a most powerful and effective means for coping with the problem of the purchasing of farm supplies and the marketing of all farm products except milk possessed by farmers anywhere in the world . . . all in all, both the financial fitness and the ability to give service demonstrated by this Cooperative, which had its origin in the Grange in 1874, justifies our faith in it, and is one of the bright spots in an otherwise discouraging economic situation." From Master's address at annual session of the New York State Grange, Feb., 1933. See E. O. Fippin, *op. cit.*, pp. 91, 234.

ization is the strongest of all the state organizations of vegetable producers, both in number and activity.

To the 27 interested vegetable growers with which the organization began operation under the presidency of C. R. White,[104] many more were soon added until, with a membership of 3,300, the Association today represents practically all sections of the state in which vegetables are grown for the market. The World War somewhat interrupted the activities of the Association. Since then the unit of membership has been changed from an individual to affiliation membership of local vegetable growers' associations—so that today, although individual membership is still permissible, 17 affiliated associations constitute a vital part of its membership.

The income of the Association is derived from dues paid both by the affiliated groups and by individual members, from the sale of space for exhibits at the annual meetings, and from advertisements in the Association's *Bulletin*. The Association's average income during the five years, 1929–1934, was about a thousand dollars annually.[105]

Since the Association has always been chiefly educational and representative rather than commercial in character, it has exerted a powerful influence in stimulating the undertaking by the State College of Agriculture of research upon projects connected with the growing of vegetables. This alone has necessitated the addition of new workers to the state research extension offices. The utilization of the results of these research studies has been highly beneficial to the vegetable growers and their industry. Moreover, the Association's well-planned and well-attended annual meetings have developed into real educational forces and have, in the opinion of Professor Paul Work, been its greatest contribution.[106] The programs of these meetings permit an exchange of ideas among

[104] Late president of the New York State Farm Bureau Federation.
[105] Letter of Lewis H. Gasper, Secretary-Treasurer, Jan. 15, 1935.
[106] Interview with Prof. Paul Work at Ithaca, July 12, 1934. *Cf. Agricultural Bulletin 240* of Department of Agriculture and Markets, July, 1930, pp. 163–165. Three hundred attended the meeting in Buffalo, Jan., 1934. About 1,500 attended the joint meetings of the Vegetable Growers' Association and the Empire State Potato Club in Jan., 1932. This represented an attendance two or three times that of previous meetings. See *Market Growers' Journal,* Feb. 1, 1932.

the farmers, the state specialists, and experts brought in from other states. Section meetings concentrating upon the distinctive interests of particular groups—upland, muckland, and potato areas—still further vitalize the discussion. Moreover, the annual [107] and summer meetings make possible the use of interesting and instructive exhibits. In addition to holding its own meetings, be it said, the Association cooperates with and supports the work of the Junior 4H clubs, arranging for exhibitions and judging contests among the "young farmers" of the state.

The Board of Directors of the Association is composed of one accredited representative from each of the affiliated local associations, all of whom meet the night before the annual meeting to formulate a list of problems facing the respective locals for discussion and action at the annual meeting. An executive committee of five members conducts the activities of the Association between meetings. In addition, there are a number of standing committees concerned with the solution of specialized problems of the vegetable growing industry. One of these is a legislative committee, whose members go to Albany if the occasion arises. At the annual meetings, the Association by resolution expresses its position on specific bills, urging cooperation with other groups interested in the same legislation. It usually seeks the support of the Conference Board, of which it has been a member since 1928, for any measure in which it is particularly interested, since the Vegetable Growers' Association alone can wield little legislative influence beyond the recording of numerous resolutions passed at its annual meetings.

The Association issues a quarterly *Bulletin,* of from 8 to 16 pages, in which the activities of the local associations are discussed and news of interest to vegetable growers is presented.

In affiliation with the New York State Vegetable Growers' Association, the potato growers of the state have developed a statewide body under the name of the Empire State Potato Club. This Club has at times worked with the Vegetable Growers' Association in planning joint annual meetings and exhibits. The Empire State Potato Club has applied for rep-

---

[107] Annual meetings are held in January in different cities. Syracuse and Buffalo are the most favored.

resentation in the Conference Board, but has not yet been admitted.

In consequence, although the New York State Vegetable Growers' Association has maintained close connections with the Vegetable Growers of America, and has urged even closer relations,[108] the State Association is, nevertheless, primarily devoted to serving the interests, both legislative and educational, of the vegetable growers of New York State.

New York State Horticultural Society

Among the agricultural organizations in New York State existing for the purpose of advancing the common interests of agriculture is the New York State Horticultural Society, the seventh and last of the statewide organizations we will discuss.   Organized in 1855 for the purpose of promoting horticulture in New York, it is among the oldest active societies in the state.   Its membership of less than 1,000 comprises the most progressive horticulturists in the state.[109]

It is at the annual meeting of the Horticultural Society, held in January in the City of Rochester, that the officers of the Society and the personnel of the executive committee and other committees are selected.   The Society operates on an annual budget of less than $10,000, received largely from membership dues and the renting of space at its exhibition grounds. Since the secretary is its only salaried officer, a considerable portion of the income of the Society is expended on prizes to exhibitors at the meetings of the Society.[110]

The Society is primarily interested in securing and disseminating scientific and practical information on fruit growing. For this purpose, it holds winter and summer meetings at which the fruit growers of the state listen to a series of papers

---

[108] See *Market Growers' Journal*, Sept. 15, and Nov. 11, 1933 for functions and membership plan of the V.G.A. of A.   The national association's membership in Jan., 1934, was 25,000.   *Cf. Bulletin* of N.Y.S.V.G.A., June, 1934, and *Market Growers' Journal*, Feb. 1, 1934.

[109] The increased services placed free of charge at the disposal of the fruit growers of the state by extension service agents is undoubtedly the most important factor in explaining that only 10 per cent of the fruit growers of the state are members of the Society.   The Society's services to its members are, therefore, seriously restricted because of this gratuitous policy.

[110] Report of the secretary-treasurer, in *Proceedings of the Annual Meeting*, 1932, p. 84.

delivered both by research students from the College of Agriculture and Experiment Stations and by practical fruit growers. In addition, their programs may present such subjects as the necessity of improved transportation facilities, a better and more uniform system of packing and packaging, the possibility of developing better marketing systems for their products by improved systems of crop reporting, and the cooperative purchase of supplies.[111]

The Society, of course, is interested in securing such legislation as may be advantageous and in preventing such as may be detrimental to its industry. To this end the Society maintains a legislative committee of three, who attend public hearings at Albany when occasions arise. At the annual meeting of the Society, moreover, resolutions are passed, a number of which call for legislative action, though the truly effective agency for legislative action for this organization has been the Conference Board, on which the Horticultural Society is represented by three members. It is because the Society has thus cooperated through the Conference Board in presenting a united front for agriculture that its legislative influence as a single organization has become unimportant.[112]

New York State Conference Board of Farm Organizations

Thus, in the period prior to 1916, the only truly statewide organization in New York, with a widespread membership which probably included the best elements of the state's agricultural population, was the Grange. A successful milk strike in 1916 brought recognition to the Dairymen's League, Inc. Between 1910 and 1917, the farm bureau movement grew steadily in numbers and influence, with a somewhat corresponding, though slower-moving, home bureau movement. Long before 1917, however, a number of progressive agricultural leaders had recognized the absolute necessity of unifying these farm organizations of the state into a single unit. They realized, however, that any such attempt would probably prove abortive unless the Grange gave the movement its sympathetic support. But the Grange leaders were reluctant, for,

---

[111] See Preamble of the *Constitution* of the Society.
[112] Interview with E. A. Flansburgh, State Farm Bureau agent, in Ithaca, June 29, 1934.

as they saw it, theirs was the outstanding agricultural organization in the state at the time, and had everything to lose and nothing to gain by the recognition of other agricultural organizations in the state.

However, by 1918, the unsettled conditions growing out of the war, particularly in the dairy industry, made the time ripe for a united front among the agricultural organizations of the state. A meeting was called of the representative farm organizations in the state at the Murray Hill Hotel in New York City on May 25, 1918, for the purpose of discussing plans for the establishment of a centralized agricultural agency. At this meeting, a temporary organization was established under the chairmanship of R. D. Cooper, of the Dairymen's League, Inc., and was called the New York State Conference Board of Farm Organizations. This organization was made permanent at a meeting called a month later. Since that time, the chairmanship of the Conference Board has been held by the ranking officers of the New York State Farm Bureau Federation, the New York State Horticultural Society, the New York State Vegetable Growers' Association, and, most frequently, however, the New York State Grange.

The original member organizations of the Conference Board were the New York State Grange, the Dairymen's League, Inc., the New York State Farm Bureau Federation, and the New York State Horticultural Society, though representatives of other agricultural groups attended by invitation from time to time. The Dairymen's League, Inc. gave way to the reorganized Dairymen's League Cooperative Association, Inc.[113] which retained its membership on the Conference Board. On February 15, 1923, the motion prevailed to include in the Board's membership the New York State Federation of Home Bureaus. In 1928 the Grange League Federation [114] and the

---

[113] *Cf. supra,* pp. 110, 111.

[114] The G.L.F. took the place on the Conference Board of the Cooperative Council, organized in 1922 by H. E. Babcock for the purpose of discussing trade problems. The council included in its membership the Dairymen's League and some ten other business organizations selling such agricultural products as potatoes, maple products, fruits, vegetables, wool, livestock, and milk. In 1923, the Cooperative Council was invited to attend all meetings of the Conference Board with full voting power. With representation on the Conference Board, the legislative program of the Cooperative Council was soon enacted into law and its influence as a separate and distinct organization

New York State Vegetable Growers' Association were given representation on the Conference Board, thus completing the representation of these seven organizations on the Conference Board as it exists today.

In 1924 the Conference Board appointed a committee to study its program and methods and to define the qualifications for membership on the Board. The recommendations of this committee may be summarized as follows:

> 1. That associations statewide in membership and educational in character be eligible for membership.[115]
>
> 2. That the accredited representatives of the constituent members of the Conference Board shall be the president, the secretary, and three others duly selected by the member associations.[116]
>
> 3. That upon unanimous agreement in the Board, each member organization, through publicity and other ways, shall strive to carry out the recommendations of the Conference Board.
>
> 4. That the scope of the Conference Board's activities shall include:
>
> > (a) matters of legislation;
> > (b) state appointments of specific interest to agriculture;
> > (c) matters of public policy affecting the farmer;
> > (d) educational programs affecting rural communities; and
> > (e) the transmission of information to the general farmer on matters vitally concerning him.
>
> 5. That meetings of the Board shall be called at the discretion of the president of the Conference Board or upon the request of member associations.
>
> 6. That the officers of the Conference Board shall consist of a president, a vice-president, and a secretary-treas-

---

declined, so that when a number of its members failed, the council as such went out of existence in 1928. *Cf. Minutes of Conference Board,* Feb. 15, 1923, and interview with H. E. Babcock in Ithaca, July 3, 1934.

[115] The Dairymen's League and G.L.F. differ radically from the other five organizations on the Conference Board in that they are essentially *commercial,* although they are statewide in character and although certain phases of their activities are educational in character.

[116] This total of five was later decreased to three.

urer, elected annually, and that the Executive Committee
of the Conference Board shall be composed of the presidents of the member organizations or alternates designated
by such presidents.[117]

With a few changes, the recommendations were accepted.
The Board meets informally every three months or so and
operates under no set rules. Indeed, it has not even been
considered necessary or advisable to draw up a constitution.[118]
The officers of the Conference Board receive no salary for
their services on the Board; the nominal expenses of the Board
are defrayed from a fund built up by a ten-dollar assessment
upon each member organization.[119]

In about fifty recorded meetings [120] held between 1918 and
1933, the Conference Board has discussed and tried to reach
a unanimous agreement on the broad questions of agricultural
policy affecting New York State arising in federal, state, or
county spheres. Thus it has attempted and for the most part
has succeeded in acting as a clearing house for the major agricultural organizations in the state, and as the spokesman of
organized agriculture.[121] Although not concerned solely with
legislation, the Conference Board prepares a formal legislative
program each winter and presents it to the legislature and to
the Governor. This legislative program usually incorporates
the position which the Conference Board has unanimously
adopted on such broad agricultural questions as taxation, highway construction, cooperative development, bovine tuberculosis eradication, agricultural research and education, and
government economy. Each member organization is bound
to support this program, by following the instructions prepared for its consummation. Each individual organization
is left free to deal with additional, perhaps less important,

---

[117] *Minutes of the Conference Board*, Dec. 17, 1924.

[118] This matter was, however, considered at the meeting of Feb. 2, 1922.

[119] Its annual disbursements, covering printing, telephone, telegraph, and
postage, are under $100.

[120] Many informal meetings, of course, were held without being officially
recorded, for between 1920 and 1925, with the whole cooperative movement
under attack, it was considered best to commit as few matters as possible to
writing. Interview with Mr. Babcock, July 9, 1934.

[121] It was claimed that the aggregate membership represented by the Conference Board's members in 1927 reached 225,000. *Cf. Minutes of the Conference Board*, Jan. 19, 1927.

problems affecting its own membership. The individual organization is permitted, furthermore, to assume in its own name whatever position it wishes on matters upon which the Conference Board cannot unanimously agree.[122] Quite frequently, the New York State Farm Bureau Federation presents its own legislative program to the Conference Board and attempts to persuade the Board to support it *in toto*—adding to it such proposals as may be suggested by other organization members, provided there is unanimous agreement.

Because of the fact that the New York State Farm Bureau Federation maintains a paid legislative agent at Albany during the entire session, it has been found expedient and economical for the Conference Board to use him as its own legislative agent.[123] In addition, the Board has attempted to maintain friendly relations with all governmental officials in administrative and legislative positions which affect agriculture. Frequently, the Board has made recommendations relative to choice of personnel for these positions by formal resolutions. At other times, less formal but more effective ways of exerting influence have been found. When vacancies occur in the Council of Agriculture and Markets [124] or the Board of Regents, for example, it is not unusual for the Conference Board to suggest to the legislature the names of those who might well fill them.[125]

The membership and the chairmanships of certain commit-

[122] For example, in the meeting of the Conference Board on Feb. 16, 1933, only one organization, the New York State Vegetable Growers' Association refused to concur in a resolution endorsing the principles of changing the monetary system so that the purchasing power of the dollar might be measured or governed by the commodity price, and for the appointment of a committee by the Conference Board to create among other groups a public opinion favorable to the commodity dollar. Individual organizations, however, particularly the New York State Farm Bureau Federation, working with Professor Warren of Cornell, strongly advocated the commodity dollar. *Cf. supra,* p. 103, note 56.

[123] Such an assignment was given by the Conference Board to Bert W. Miller, Jan. 1, 1924. E. S. Foster, who is secretary of the Federation and secretary-treasurer of the Conference Board now represents both organizations at Albany. See *supra,* p. 103 and note 60.

[124] Abolished in 1935.

[125] See *Minutes of Conference Board:* Jan. 8, 1924: Board of Regents; Dec. 17, 1924: Board of Regents; Jan. 18, 1924: Council of Agriculture and Markets; Feb. 13, 1929: Trustee of Cornell; Feb. 2, 1922: Conservation Commissioner.

tees in the Senate and Assembly itself, however, are of even greater concern to the agricultural organizations. It is in connection with such appointments that the Conference Board's influence is most noticeable.[126] The Conference Board and its individual member organizations, however, unlike the American Farm Bureau Association, do not compile formal records of legislative members to help elect the friends of organized agriculture and to defeat its foes. Instead, it places before both nominating conventions and candidates a program of agricultural needs in New York State, the program being considered of paramount importance. Thus, in July, 1920, for example, the Board drafted the full text of an agricultural plank which it submitted with a letter to the chairman of the Republican Platform Committee and requested that it be incorporated in the Republican state platform for that year.[127]

Thus, the agricultural Conference Board serves as the unifying agent of the farm organizations of New York State in coordinating and thereby strengthening the legislative power of the farmer.[128]

---

[126] Frank M. Smith, chairman of the Assembly Committee on Agriculture from 1925 to 1934, is a member of the Board of Directors of the G.L.F., and was a director of the Farm Bureau Federation from 1919–1924. Before the Democratic control of the Senate in 1933, Senator L. C. Kirkland was chairman of the Senate Agriculture Committee, as well as a director of the G.L.F., which he has represented at meetings of the Conference Board. Since it was a matter of some concern to the agricultural organizations that the ranking Democrat on the Senate Agriculture Committee, Senator S. J. Wojtkowiak of Buffalo (nicknamed by farmers Senator "Watch your coat and hat" because they did not trust him) should not succeed Senator Kirkland as chairman because of his unsympathetic attitude toward organized agriculture, the members of the Conference Board used their influence in securing the appointment of the Democratic Senator Byrne of Albany and in urging him to return to this post in 1934, at some sacrifice to himself.

[127] *Minutes of Conference Board,* July 23, 1920. Since this time, it has been customary for a representative of the Conference Board to draft agricultural planks for both the Democratic and Republican state platforms in New York, which the political parties are usually anxious to secure. (Interview with Mr. Babcock, July 3, 1934.) On Sept. 6, 1932, the Conference Board appointed a Program Committee to draw up for the Board an agricultural program which was placed before the gubernatorial candidates in that year. For a statement of the Conference Board's views to political parties in 1936, see *American Agriculturist,* Sept. 26, 1936.

[128] Occasionally jealousy arises among its members as intimated in the statement of Fred J. Freestone, Master of the New York State Grange: "This agricultural united front should continue and will do so, provided no individual organization on the Conference Board claims credit for helpful

Governor's Agricultural Advisory Commission

Ten years after the creation of the successful Conference Board, rural New York was once more the recipient of sympathetic attention when, in November, 1928, Franklin D. Roosevelt, as Governor-elect, organized the Governor's Agricultural Advisory Commission "for the specific purpose of a cooperative study of the outstanding needs of the rural population of New York State." [129]   Though there may have been political motives for the establishment of this Commission,[130] an examination of its personnel will disclose that no attempt was made by either Governor Roosevelt or Governor Lehman to appoint a majority of Democrats, and that the Commission is completely non-partisan.   In addition to the presidents of the seven agricultural groups that constitute the Conference Board, who represent their organizations on the Governor's Advisory Commission, the membership includes four master farmers, agricultural specialists, the Director of Extension of the New York State Colleges of Agriculture and Home Economics of Cornell University, and Dr. G. F. Warren, of the Department of Agricultural Economics.[131]   Moreover, though, the official agencies of the government are represented by the Commissioner of the Department of Agriculture and Markets, the Commissioner of the Public Service Commission, and the

---

legislation that was secured through united effort." *Cf. Journal of Proceedings of New York State Grange,* Feb. 6, 1934, p. 9.

[129] State of New York, *Public Papers of Franklin D. Roosevelt,* Albany, 1930, pp. 414–417.

[130] In addition, of course, to its value as a rural vote-getter, the Commission could make the Democratic Governors who sponsored it less dependent upon the advice and suggestions of the State Department of Agriculture and Markets, the 11 members in the governing council of which, representing the 9 judicial districts of the state, were selected by a traditionally Republican State Legislature. It should be noted that an act of the legislature, on Feb. 4, 1935, dissolved this council and substituted a single commissioner, appointed by the Governor. It may be significant to note that since this change in the organization of the state department, the Commission has met infrequently.

[131] During Governor Roosevelt's administration, when Henry Morgenthau, Jr., was chairman of the Commission, the secretaryship was held by C. E. Ladd, then Director of Extension, and since made Dean of the College of Agriculture. When Mr. Morgenthau was called by President Roosevelt to Washington, Dr. Ladd was appointed in his place as chairman of the Commission by Governor Lehman. It is chiefly because of the efforts of both these chairmen that the Commission became an important advisory body, rather than a mere rubber stamp of the Governor.

chairmen of the Senate and Assembly Committees on Agriculture, Taxation and Retrenchment,[132] unofficial agencies are likewise represented by the editor of the *American Agriculturist* and the president of the historic New York State Agricultural Society.[133] Thus, at least 15 of the 53 persons who have been members of the Commission [134] are, or have at one time been, closely identified with organized agriculture in the state, and these have been the most dynamic and influential personalities in the group.

In defining the scope of its work, at its first meeting held on January 15, 1929, the Commission accepted a broad view of its duties, looking not merely to the examination of subjects that would benefit directly the agricultural industry in the state but also to such social problems as agricultural education and research, health, and other related subjects that would "make the home life of our agricultural population more attractive." [135] Any early ambition which the Commission may have entertained to *represent* agriculture was soon dele-

---

[132] When, under Governor Lehman, the Senate came into Democratic control and these formerly Republican committee chairmen were supplanted by Democrats, the Governor reappointed the former Republican senators as additional members of the Commission, and B. A. Pyrke, former Commissioner of Agriculture and Markets.

[133] The New York State Agricultural Society, which celebrated its centenary in 1932, was for many decades a constructive force in the agricultural life of the state, early sponsoring the establishment of an agricultural college and other farm organizations, and, in general, encouraging progressive agricultural movements. In time, all its functions were absorbed by other groups, so that its chief distinction today is that the president of the Society is an ex officio member of the Board of Trustees of Cornell University. See George E. Peabody, *History of the New York State Agricultural Society,* unpublished Master's essay (no date), on file in library of College of Agriculture at Ithaca, New York; "New York State Agricultural Society—Its History and Its Objects," Agricultural Bulletin of the Department of Agriculture and Markets of State of New York, *Bulletin 161,* Jan., 1924, which contains a copy of the constitution of the Society; Bulletin prepared by the New York State Agricultural Society in celebration of its 100th Anniversary held at Albany, N. Y., Jan. 20, 1932; L. H. Bailey, editor, *Cyclopedia of American Agriculture,* 4th edition, 1912, Vol. IV, ch. VIII, p. 387; and U. P. Hedrick, *A History of Agriculture in the State of New York,* Albany, published by the state for the New York State Agricultural Society, 1933, pp. 120–122.

[134] On Governor Roosevelt's Commission there were 26 members, three of whom were women; on Governor Lehman's Commission there have been 27 members, two of whom are women.

[135] Report of the Commission, Jan. 16, 1929, in State of New York, *Public Papers of Governor Franklin D. Roosevelt,* Albany, 1929, pp. 477–478.

gated entirely to the Conference Board, the Commission itself becoming purely an *advisory* body to the Governor. Under this happy arrangement, legislative proposals originate in the Conference Board, which is influential in the legislature, and these proposals are then recommended to the Governor by his Advisory Commission for enactment into progressive agricultural legislation.[136]

The Commission has, in the past, met four or five times a year, though it may often be called together hurriedly to prepare a report for the Governor on some special agricultural emergency which may have arisen. On many occasions the Commission has found it a desirable procedure for the chairman to appoint subcommittees to study and report on specific problems before actual discussion and recommendation by the full Board. Very often, too, the Commission has submitted to the Governor a detailed report of the reasons for its conclusions on particular problems, together with its recommendations. It has been customary, moreover, for either the subcommittees of the Commission or the full Commission to call upon persons not affiliated with it to appear and present their opinions on the problems which it is considering.[137]

Summary

And so the farmers of New York State have learned the value of cooperative action in legislative matters, first, through the establishment of a large number of organizations covering all phases of agricultural life,[138] and, later, through the creation

---

[136] Comparison of the minutes of the Conference Board with the reports of the Advisory Commission will disclose marked similarity in both discussions and recommendations. Minutes of the Board are in the files of the New York State Farm Bureau Federation, Roberts Hall, College of Agriculture, Ithaca, N. Y. Reports of the Commission may be found in the *Public Papers of the Governors,* compiled annually.

[137] The Governor himself has attended meetings of the Commission. Since the enactment of the law in 1935 which gave the Governor the power to select the head of the Department of Agriculture and Markets, the Commission has met infrequently.

[138] U. P. Hedrick, Director of the New York Experimental Station, in *A History of Agriculture in the State of New York,* 1933, p. 133: "There are more than 4,000 organized agricultural bodies in New York, covering every conceivable phase of plant and animal industries." These, however, probably include many bodies that are organizations merely in name, and others that have a very small membership or are local units of larger organizations.

of the highly effective New York Conference Board of Farm Organizations. That the latter organization, moreover, is so influential in the legislature is due to the interrelation, in both personnel and organization, of the governmental and unofficial agricultural groups in the state.

The most influential members of the Conference Board are the Grange, the Farm Bureau Federation, the Dairymen's League Cooperative Association, and the Grange League Federation. All of these groups have active educational functions, but two of them, the Dairymen's League and the G.L.F., engage, in addition, in commercial activities.

Probably the most vigorous and progressive of the groups represented in the Board is, however, the New York State Farm Bureau Federation, which has never permitted extraneous considerations, such as that of temperance, to divert its attention from its chief object, the improvement of the farmers' economic position. In this connection, it has always stressed the importance of agricultural research. The New York State Grange, on the other hand, although better established and more truly representative of rural New York because of its very large membership, lacks what the Federation possesses: an organization geared to act with speed, composed of a small membership with a larger proportion of younger men, guided by experienced and progressive leaders. To keep the more conservative Grange working in cooperation with the more progressive Farm Bureau Federation has been the secret of the success of the Conference Board.

CHAPTER V

Welfare Dynamics

PROBABLY no private welfare organization in the State of New York has engaged in so many diversified legislative activities as the State Charities Aid Association. In addition to being the oldest of the statewide, non-sectarian welfare agencies thus concerned with the enactment of social welfare legislation,[1] this Association is unique among voluntary charitable organizations in the United States because of its concern with many different phases of welfare work.[2] In other states the various activities are handled by many separate organizations.

The State Charities Aid Association was organized on May 11, 1872, at 19 West 31st Street, New York City, under the leadership of Louisa Lee Schuyler, granddaughter of Alexander Hamilton. Its avowed purpose was the alleviation of the deplorable conditions in the poorhouses and almshouses of the state, "where the young and old, men, women and children, the sick, the insane and decrepit, the virtuous and the vicious, [were] mingled together without proper care, without classification."[3] Volunteer committees of taxpayers and citizens in each county of the state were to visit the poorhouses and almshouses in their respective counties. A central association, with headquarters in New York City and a membership similar to those of the visiting committees of the counties, was to have attached to it a professional personnel whose services were to be available to the members of local committees in connection

---

[1] See *Directory of Social Agencies of the City of New York,* published for the Welfare Council of New York City, Columbia University Press, 1935. Particular mention should be made of the New York Child Labor Committee, organized in 1902, which has long played a leading role in child labor reform in New York State.

[2] A possible exception is the Pennsylvania Public Charities Association.

[3] Address by Louisa Lee Schuyler, Feb. 25, 1915, published by the SCAA in the pamphlet, *Forty-Three Years Ago, or the Early Days of the State Charities Aid Association, 1872–1915.*

with any problems relative to tax supported or public elee-
mosynary institutions on which they were competent to advise.
This, in broad outline, was the original structure of the State
Charities Aid Association.

Early in its career the Association was granted, by state
law, the privilege of obtaining from any Supreme Court Justice
an order which would enable it to visit, inspect, and examine
any county, town, or city almshouse in the state. In 1893,
the scope of the law was extended to include all state institutions of a similar character. In the same legislative enactment, provision was made for the submission of an annual
report by the State Charities Aid Association to the State
Board of Charities and to the State Commission in Lunacy
"upon matters relating to the institutions subject to the visita-
tion of [the] board." [4] Armed with this authority, unique in
that it had been granted to a private organization, the State
Charities Aid Association has established visiting committees
for practically every county in the state. The counties comprising New York City are served by the very active New
York City Visiting Committee.[5]

It is largely because of the basic work performed by these
visiting committees that the activities of the State Charities
Aid Association have so frequently resulted in legislative enactments that in and of themselves constitute milestones in the
development of the public health and charity work of the
state.[6]

Some 170 committees,[7] each concerned with a particular
phase of social work, carry on the activities of the Association.
Thirty-six of these are working for better care of needy chil-

---

[4] *Right of Entrance Law.* New York Consolidated Laws, ch. 55, *State
Charities Law,* Art. 3, Sec. 30, 31, 32. The functions of the State Commission
in Lunacy have been taken over by the New York State Department of
Mental Hygiene.

[5] This committee evolved from the Visiting Committee for Bellevue and
other hospitals, founded Jan. 26, 1872, before the organization of the SCAA
itself.

[6] For a brief summary of the achievements between 1872 and 1929, see the
pamphlet published by the SCAA, entitled, *Milestones in Health and Welfare,*
and the *Annual Reports* since then, especially for 1932. See also *SCAA News,*
Mar., 1922.

[7] The number of committees varies from year to year. See the SCAA
pamphlet, *They Approve,* May, 1930, p. 13, and *Annual Reports.*

dren; 63 are engaged in efforts to promote public health generally; 14 are popularizing the principles of mental hygiene; and 58 are carrying on the work for which the Association was organized—namely, visiting public charitable institutions.

Each phase of the work is supervised by a special section of the trained staff at the central headquarters in New York City, while the work as a whole is coordinated under a central directing Board of Managers, 11 of whose 33 members are elected annually by the members of the Association for a three-year term.[8]

The membership of the Association falls into three classes. The first class consists of regular members, or the members of the Central Committee[9] and those of the county and city visiting committees. The second class is composed of corresponding members, who are not residents of the State of New York. The third class is made up of contributing members, who donate money to, but do not actually participate in, the work of the Association.[10]

The Association maintains a Department of Information and Membership, which has the twofold function of handling all matters pertaining to membership, and, in addition, securing such publicity as is deemed advisable. The *SCAA News,* a monthly periodical which enjoys a circulation of 25,000 is, consequently, under its direction.

The officers of the Association consist of a president, three vice-presidents, a treasurer, and a librarian, all elected annually

---

[8] The constitution also provides for honorary members of the Board of Managers who "shall be persons of long experience and distinguished service in the Association, or of notable interest in its purpose." These honorary members exercise the same powers as other members of the Board, except that of voting. The Association notes with interest that many men of public affairs, such as Elihu Root, Charles E. Hughes, Henry Morgenthau, Henry L. Stimson, John W. Davis, Owen D. Young, Carl Schurz, Joseph H. Choate, and the Theodore Roosevelts, were attracted to the Board of Managers or resumed active participation in the work of the Association "after they had had experience in public affairs from the official side and had won their honors in the field of public service, which is impressive evidence of their opinion as to the value and usefulness of our Association in the field of preventative philanthropy and social welfare." (From the *SCAA News,* Feb., 1930, pp. 2, 3.)

[9] These must be residents of New York City or its vicinity.

[10] Members of the Association who accept official positions in any institution subject to the inspection of the various visiting committees must sever their connections with the Association.

from the incoming Board of Managers, and a secretary. The latter is, in effect, the chief executive officer of the Association. His duties include not only the organization of visiting committees and the initial selection [11] of their members, but also the study of welfare legislation and the formulation of plans for the extension and improvement of the work of the Association.[12] Aided by members of the Association's trained staff, the officers frequently lend assistance to other welfare organizations, by delivering public addresses and contributing articles to a variety of publications for the purpose of stimulating an interest in social problems in different fields.

To superintend effectively the three additional phases of welfare work which have grown out of the Association's original program—Child Welfare, Public Health, and Mental Hygiene—specialized departments are maintained. Work in the field of child welfare is divided among the Department of County Children's Agencies, the Department of Child Placing and Adoption, and the Mothers and Babies Department.[13]

---

[11] The formal appointment of such committees and visitors is made by the Board of Managers. The committees thereafter add to their own membership.

[12] Thus, the expansion of the SCAA in both actual influence and public esteem is due largely to the enlightened and vigorous activity of Mr. Homer Folks, Secretary of the Association since 1893. See the *New York Times*, July 10, 1936, for a review of the career of Homer Folks on the occasion of the dedication of the Homer Folks Tuberculosis Hospital at Oneonta, N. Y. when Governor Lehman hailed the secretary of the SCAA "as an eminent humanitarian, social engineer extraordinary, and statesman in public health and welfare."

[13] For record of SCAA accomplishments in the interest of child welfare in New York State see:

1. Pamphlet, *County Organization for Child Care and Protection*, Children's Bureau Publication, No. 107 of the U. S. Department of Labor, Washington, 1922, section by H. Ida Curry on "County Organization for Child Welfare in New York State by the New York State Charities Aid Association."

2. White House Conference on Child Health and Protection, called by President Hoover in 1930, *Organization for the Care of Handicapped Children*, Vol. IVA, New York, Century, 1932, pp. 119–121.

3. In 1922, Miss Emelyn Peck, of the SCAA staff, made a complete compilation of New York laws referring to children and placed it at the disposal of the Children's Code Commission recently appointed. (See *SCAA Annual Report*, 1922, p. 16.)

4. Pamphlet, *For Each Child—The Care He Needs*, published by the SCAA, 1936.

The Department of County Children's Agencies [14] has been instrumental in securing the appropriation of public funds, in nearly all counties outside of New York City, for the creation of county children's agencies which assist public welfare officers and judges of Children's Courts in supervising the welfare of the thousands of children who are each year maintained in boarding or private homes and public institutions. Frequently this department makes specific recommendations for appointment of these agents from a specially trained personnel. In this fashion it has assisted in maintaining a high degree of competence among the welfare workers so employed. In addition, the Department of County Children's Agencies endeavors to assist the local authorities by:

1. Advising public officials concerning the administration of various welfare activities (such advice frequently relates to the administration of relief to families and adults, as well as children);

2. Helping local children's agents and local county committees to create a body of public opinion that will insure the maintenance of sound principles and high standards for child care in the different localities; and

3. Advising local agents in their multitudinous case work problems.[15]

The Department of Child Placing and Adoption finds homes and foster parents for homeless and neglected children, provides temporary board for them before, and supervises their care after, their placement. Organized in 1898, this department placed its 5,000th child in January, 1934.[16] Its staff of trained workers frequently makes as many as 15,000 visits, chiefly to potential foster parents, in the course of a year.[17] The efforts of this staff have been directed particularly to the

[14] This department has been under the superintendency of Miss H. Ida Curry since its organization in 1907.

[15] From the *SCAA Annual Report,* 1933, pp. 31, 32, and interviews with Miss H. Ida Curry, Dec. 13, 1932 and Aug. 14, 1935.

[16] For early reports of child placing by a Joint Committee of the SCAA and the Association for Improving the Condition of the Poor, see *Modern Methods of Saving Motherless Babies,* which consists of annual reports of these two Associations to their Board of Managers from 1898 to 1904. See also *Annual Report,* 1934, p. 29.

[17] *Annual Report,* 1934, p. 29.

extension of the range of homes in which children can be placed, so that they may be removed from neighborhoods in which their circumstances are known. A special effort is made to place children outside of New York City.[18] The efficiency of this department is strikingly revealed in a stock-taking study of some 910 children who had been so placed. The study showed that 615 of these children, or 77 per cent of them, grew up to be decent, law-abiding citizens, respected in their communities.[19]

The Mothers and Babies Department seeks proper employment for widowed, deserted, unmarried, or otherwise distressed mothers, attempting, wherever possible, to avoid separating the mother from her child. Thus, though it has often been necessary to provide a boarding home for the child while the mother has been given employment, in many cases both mother and child have been placed in a suburban home, where both have been maintained in return for the mother's services. Frequently, in addition to medical attention, legal assistance is provided for mothers in efforts to secure financial aid from fathers who have deserted. Organized in 1893, the Mothers and Babies Department, with Miss Mary R. Mason as its superintendent, has helped over 40,000 mothers to support their children.[20]

---

[18] Interview with Miss Sophie Van S. Theis, superintendent of this department, Dec. 8, 1932. Of the 123 children placed with families in 1931, 87 came from county agencies for dependent children and only 36 from New York City societies and institutions. *Annual Report,* 1931, p. 38.

[19] All 910 children had become 18 years of age or over. The study also showed a marked difference between children who, when placed, had been under 5 years of age and those who had been 5 years old or more. Eighty-six per cent of the former grew up to be desirable citizens, but of the latter only 72 per cent developed favorably. Similarly, 7.6 per cent of those over 5 grew up to be anti-social, but only 2.6 per cent of those under 5 developed so unfavorably. It should be noted that approximately 80 per cent of the 910 children studied had had a predominantly "bad" background. Nearly half of the 910 children, moreover, had remained with their own families for 5 years or more. A summary of this study, *How Foster Children Turn Out,* appears in *SCAA News,* July, 1924. See also the tribute paid to the department by Miss Grace Abbott, former chief of the Children's Bureau, U. S. Department of Labor, in *SCAA News,* Feb., 1930, p. 5.

[20] *Annual Report,* 1931, pp. 46, 47. A total of 1,013 employment opportunities were filled in this one year by distressed mothers, many of them under 20 years of age. The department has suffered a setback because of the depression, showing a decided decline in the number of positions found and filled. *Cf. Annual Report,* 1934, p. 36.

The work of the SCAA in the field of Public Health is conducted by the Committee on Tuberculosis and Public Health. Organized in 1907, it is known as the State Committee and represents the National Tuberculosis Association in the State of New York. Financed largely by the annual sale of Christmas seals,[21] it is affiliated with 63 county and city organizations in an effort to fight tuberculosis and promote public health in three ways:

1. By developing and fostering in the general public a growing concern and sense of responsibility for the problems of tuberculosis and associated public health problems;

2. By promoting the enactment of needed health legislation; and

3. By undertaking new activities and demonstrating their effectiveness by actual use.[22]

Thus, in addition to its function as a supervising and controlling body for affiliated local health associations, the State Committee conducts vigorous educational campaigns, by means of the press, radio, and speaker's platform, sometimes for the purpose of disseminating information relative to the public health,[23] often for the purpose of obtaining the enactment of health laws.

A concrete illustration of such work may be seen in the reports of a Special Health Commission appointed by Governor Franklin D. Roosevelt, May 1, 1930. This commission recommended, among other things, the enactment of several pieces of remedial legislation. Immediately thereafter, the Committee on Tuberculosis and Health launched a vigorous campaign for the purpose of rallying public opinion to the support of the commission's proposals. In this connection it:

1. Secured the endorsement of the bills by approximately 100 health, welfare, and civic organizations;

2. Distributed leaflets and bulletins, totalling 100,000, which supported the proposals;

---

[21] It is not unusual, when special health projects have been undertaken, for such organizations as the Milbank Memorial Fund and the Metropolitan Life Insurance Company to lend financial assistance. See *Annual Report,* 1931, pp. 19, 84, 85.

[22] *Annual Report,* 1931, p. 19.

[23] *Ibid.,* p. 27.

3. Provided a press bulletin service, which stimulated favorable editorial comment, in hundreds of newspapers throughout the state;

4. Sent letters to thousands of prominent citizens;

5. Organized special meetings in support of the measures under various auspices; and

6. Dedicated two sessions of the annual conference of the State Committee and its local committees on Tuberculosis and Public Health to a discussion of the new State Health Program.[24]

But the work of the State Committee did not stop there. In conjunction with the Committee on Publication of the Special Health Commission, it conducted an elaborate campaign for the purpose of stimulating public understanding and support of the "New State Health Program" recommended by the commission in its final report to the Governor on December 31, 1931. In the course of this campaign, a luncheon meeting was held at the Executive Mansion in Albany, attended by the Governor and the members of the Health Commission, at which addresses made by Mr. Henry Morgenthau, Dr. Simon Flexner, and Dr. Livingston Farrand were broadcast via the radio. In each case a suggested draft of these addresses was prepared by the SCAA and submitted to the speakers. Both the meeting and its purpose were widely publicized in the daily and weekly newspapers of the state. The issue of the *SCAA News* for April, 1932, was entirely devoted to the new health program. Through the efforts of the Association a series of Sunday feature articles on four phases of the program was placed in seven newspapers in the state. Moreover, letters were sent to a number of public health experts in the United States and Europe, and the replies were utilized to evoke editorial comment in at least 100 newspapers throughout the state. With the assistance of the Academy of Medicine and the New York Tuberculosis and Health Association, two radio broadcasts were arranged over a nation-wide hookup of 70 stations. An upstate newspaper [25] was persuaded to devote a full page of its Sunday rotogravure section to pictures relative

---

[24] *Ibid.*, p. 21.
[25] *Buffalo Courier-Express*, Aug. 14, 1932.

to the new health program. Forum meetings were organized everywhere, at which speakers from the Health Commission, Health Department, and the State Committee of the SCAA presented material in support of the proposals of the Health Commission. Though it was originally estimated that the expense of this publicity campaign would be $2,300, it actually cost $157.33, because so many of its features were donated to the cause.[26]

The work in the field of mental hygiene is concentrated in a New York State Committee on Mental Hygiene, which cooperates with the National Committee for Mental Hygiene as well as with various local organizations, in an effort to promote mental health (a) by developing and improving mental hygiene resources throughout the state, and (b) by encouraging preventive mental hygiene education among professional groups and the general public.[27] Composed of 72 men and women, most of whom are members of the medical profession,[28] the State Committee works primarily through the agency of thirteen county committees and the New York City Committee on Mental Hygiene, the chairmen of these bodies being members of the State Committee. On the basis of information supplied by the county visiting committees, some 10,000 pamphlets on mental hygiene have been distributed annually to parents, teachers, nurses, social workers, and public officials. A Speakers' Bureau and an Information Service supply speakers to clubs [29] and give such advice relative to the perplexing problems of mental health as it can.

This State Committee also prepares an annual report for the State Commission in Lunacy,[30] on much of the material on which the various campaigns for the improvement of conditions in state institutions for the insane have been based. In

---

[26] These facts are from the files of the SCAA State Committee. For further progress in the campaign, see *Annual Reports* since 1931.

[27] The depression has compelled the department in recent years to emphasize its educational program almost exclusively.

[28] Other members are psychologists, psychiatrists, and sociologists, as well as non-professional men and women who contribute time and money.

[29] Especially the parent-teacher groups and the New York State Federation of Women's Clubs. Interview with Miss Katherine C. Ecob, Executive Secretary, Dec. 5, 1932.

[30] See *supra*, p. 134, and *First Annual Report of the SCAA to the State Commission in Lunacy,* Dec. 1, 1893, p. 23.

1930, for example, the State Committee on Mental Hygiene played a leading part in the promotion of a $50,000,000 bond issue for state institutions. It organized a special subcommittee, with headquarters in the offices of the Association, for campaign purposes. Through the activities of this subcommittee, endorsements of the bond issue were secured from leading welfare organizations throughout the state and from officials of state and county political committees. It is estimated that a specially prepared handbook, several popular leaflets of information, and two special issues of the *SCAA News* reached half a million persons. In addition, some 300 public addresses and 25 radio broadcasts were arranged. Motion pictures of state hospitals and prisons were shown in theaters throughout the state; posters were displayed in public places, railroads, and subways; and the envelopes containing official mail of all state departments, as well as that of the SCAA, state institutions, and the New York Prison Association, bore the stamp: "Vote YES on the Bond Issue for State Institutions." [31]

The expenditures of the SCAA for its work as a whole, at one time in excess of half a million dollars,[32] are financed primarily by voluntary contributions from interested individuals; a small fraction comes from endowments, never from government subsidy. Not infrequently special grants for short-term projects within the scope of individual departments are secured from the Milbank Memorial Fund, the Russell Sage Foundation, the Rockefeller Foundation, or the Metropolitan Life Insurance Company. When expenditures exceed receipts, the deficit is met by the general fund of the SCAA, which finances the expenditures of most of the departments of the Association. The Department of Tuberculosis and Public Health, however, is financed chiefly through the sale of Christmas seals, although special grants are frequently made for particular health campaigns. The County Children's Agencies are financed largely by grants from the Russell Sage and Rockefeller Foundations; the boarding-out work of the

---

[31] *Annual Report,* 1931, pp. 28–37. See also loose-leaf notebook in the office of the SCAA Mental Hygiene Department, containing newspaper clippings.

[32] Expenditures for 1930–1931: $713,420.16; for 1933–1934: $365,130.60. See *Annual Reports.*

Child Placing and Mothers and Babies Departments is aided annually by the *New York Times'* well-advertised Christmas campaign for the "One Hundred Neediest Cases."

Following the practice of other eleemosynary organizations, the SCAA conducts, from time to time, campaigns for contributions, in the course of which attractive brochures, explaining the need for funds and the necessary amounts, are widely circulated. Bequests entitled *When You Make Your Will* are solicited, and the proper legal form is supplied.

As has already been indicated in our sketch account of the activities of the SCAA, one of the basic functions of the organization is its official supervision of an ever increasing number of welfare and health bills introduced into the State Legislature annually.[33] For this purpose the Association established, in 1927, a Welfare Legislative Information Bureau. This bureau, under the direction of Miss Elsie M. Bond, devotes more time to the intensive study of state social welfare legislation than any other organization in the state, distributing the results of its research to subscribing social agencies.[34]

The bills studied fall into six categories: Child Welfare, Health, Mental Hygiene, Public Relief, Unemployment, and Miscellaneous. On the basis of an intensive study of these bills, two types of reporting service are offered by the bureau. One, known as the final report, takes the form of a series of informational bulletins [35] on bills of interest to the subscriber, including, on request, copies of particular bills. The second, known as the current report, is more detailed, and includes, in addition to bulletins and copies of bills, such specialized service as frequent reports on the progress of certain bills and

---

[33] In 1929, for example, the SCAA considered it necessary to follow 300 bills, at that time before the legislature. In 1934, the Association followed 698 bills involving 467 legislative proposals.

[34] In 1927 there were only 19 subscribing agencies. The service is not yet self-supporting, though the agencies contribute toward the expenses incurred. The data gathered by the bureau is, of course, also utilized by the various departments of the SCAA.

[35] During the regular and extraordinary sessions of the legislature of 1934, the bureau issued 191 bulletins. The first, or introductory, bulletin usually contains the names, addresses, and districts of all legislators, legislative leaders, and members of such committees as interest the subscribing agency, and a summary of the Governor's annual message.

a discussion of their merits and of the legislature's reaction to them.[36]

It should be observed that the purpose of this bureau is chiefly that of supplying factual information on bills and not of supporting or opposing them, though, of course, such information is the first step in a campaign to defeat or promote legislation. Information on bills which might interest specific departments in the SCAA is transmitted by the bureau to the heads of such departments, who, in turn, ultimately determine, with the approval of the Board of Managers, the policy of the Association with reference to such bills. In 1935, six bills were in this way supported and 20 were opposed. Of the six, all were passed by the Legislature, and all but one were signed by the Governor; of the 20, all but three were passed by the Legislature, but 15 of these were vetoed by the Governor.[37] Thus, the Welfare Legislative Information Bureau is concerned only with the first step in systematic lobbying in the interest of social welfare legislation.

One can, perhaps, obtain a clearer picture of the lobbying techniques of the SCAA through an analysis of a specific piece of legislation than in any other way. The activities of the SCAA in its long campaign to substitute a unified public welfare law for the 148 laws relating to the public welfare functions of the state,[38] may, consequently, serve as an example.

The effort to revise the welfare laws of the state began in 1925 with the creation by the SCAA of a special committee on the Revision of the Poor Law.[39] This committee consisted of eight interested citizens. The chairman was Judge Peter Cantline, of Newburgh, who had had extensive experience in

[36] *Annual Report,* 1934, p. 40. Interviews with Miss Elsie M. Bond, Oct. 18, Nov. 20 and 21, 1932.

[37] One was signed by the Governor after it had been so amended as to remove the Association's objection to it. From *minutes* of the Board of Managers, May 16, 1935. The Board of Managers, at this meeting, followed the unusual procedure of passing a resolution expressing the Association's admiration of Governor Lehman for the skill and courage he displayed in dealing with the unusually large number of welfare bills that year.

[38] This law which was drafted chiefly by Miss Elsie M. Bond of the SCAA was characterized as "one of the finest pieces of draftsmanship that ever came into the state from an outside source" by State Senator George R. Fearon in an address on Oct. 9, 1929.

[39] This was the orginal title of the law now known as the Public Welfare Law.

the interpretation and administration of the old poor laws. Its executive secretary was Miss Elsie M. Bond, at that time an assistant secretary of the association, and a widely experienced social worker.[40]

The special committee formulated as its objectives:

1. The repeal of the obsolete poor law and a large number of special statutes, and substituting therefor one coherent general statute dealing with the subject of public relief;

2. The centralization, as far as possible, of the administration of poor relief in the county; and

3. A delineation of the powers and duties of the various public welfare officials, together with some indication of the methods by which these duties were to be carried out.[41]

A preliminary survey was made by the committee to ascertain what changes, or suggestions for changes, in the poor laws and their administration had recently been made by the State Legislature, the State Conference of Superintendents of the Poor, the Conference of Mayors, and similar groups. It was learned from this survey: that the State Legislature had, in 1924, appropriated $5,000 for the codification of the poor laws by a specially appointed commission;[42] that the State Conference of the Superintendents of the Poor had passed resolutions approving the discontinuance of the obsolete Town Overseers of the Poor and the creation in their place of Deputy Superintendents; and that the Conference of Mayors had appointed a committee to draft a report on the poor law for submission to the 1926 meeting of the conference.

All data relevant to the revision of the poor law was then compiled. This compilation included the results of a comprehensive study of poor law administration in Dutchess county, made in 1914, recent drafts of model poor laws and incidental material gathered both by the SCAA and the State Board of

---

[40] The Russell Sage Foundation contributed a substantial sum of money to help defray the expenses incurred in this undertaking.

[41] Letter from Miss E. M. Bond to Edith Foster, of the Wisconsin Conference of Social Work, Oct. 9, 1930.

[42] In 1925 and 1926 additional sums were appropriated for this purpose by the legislature.

Charities, and various data concerning the laws and practices of other states.

On the basis of this survey, on December 9, 1925, Miss Elsie Bond presented to the Board of Managers a plan of procedure. Briefly summarized, her proposal was:

1. To familiarize herself with the existing poor law, section by section, making particular note of conflicts, where such existed, and of criticisms which had already been expressed;

2. To call together a group of persons, including representatives of the State Board of Charities, the State Commission for Mental Defectives, the State Conference of Poor Law Officials, the New York Department of Public Welfare, the poor law officials from nearby counties, and others interested in the administration of the poor law, including representatives of the larger private charities, such as the Charity Organization Society (C.O.S.), the Association for Improving the Condition of the Poor (A.I.C.P.), Catholic Charities of the Archdiocese of New York, the United Hebrew Charities, and the Federation of Institutions for Protestant Children; and to arrange for the organization of similar groups in Buffalo, Rochester, and Albany, and, possibly, other cities;

3. To solicit from these groups suggestions as to the difficulties in the present law and its administration;

4. To assemble such data as might be necessary to present a picture of the operation of the present system and its costs;

5. To formulate, in consultation with the groups, various suggestions for changes;

6. To present the proposed changes to the legislative leaders, for the purpose of gauging the legislative reaction;

7. To draft a bill for introduction into the legislature;

8. To select strategic legislators to introduce the bill in the Senate and Assembly, and to interest members of each house in the bill, so that they would be willing and able to defend it later in the session;

9. To distribute copies of the bill, with suitable explanatory material, to organizations and individuals throughout the state who might be persuaded to sponsor it;

10. To prepare suitable newspaper publicity material for the purpose of building up popular support; and, finally,

11. To explain the bill to members of the legislature, to answer questions concerning it, to see that the bill was effectively presented at public hearings, and to stand by the bill until its passage.[43]

Needless to say, it was not possible to follow these steps in the order indicated, for conflicts that would necessitate changes of plan were bound to arise. The first of these conflicts arose when the State Association of County Superintendents of the Poor introduced the so-called Clark bill, which did little more than codify the existing laws, retaining many of their most complicated features.

The realization that passage of this bill would delay a real revision of the poor law for many years prompted the SCAA to draft a bill of its own and cause its introduction into the legislature. This bill set up the county as the unit of administration, and provided for an *appointed,* rather than an elected, county commissioner. The opposition to the SCAA bill was immediate. One member of the State Association of County Superintendents of the Poor proclaimed that his chief purpose in Albany was "to defeat Homer Folks' bill and press the Clark bill, which the Superintendents wanted"; and stated that "Folks was trying to give the Superintendents what he (Folks) thought was good for them, not what they wanted." [44]

Neither of these bills passed. This, in and of itself, was effective strategy on the part of the SCAA, for the political situation in New York was such that almost anything might have happened. The legislature was controlled by the Republicans, who under no condition would allow Governor Alfred E. Smith to further his presidential aspirations by claiming credit for the passage of so important an item of welfare legislation as the Homer Folks bill, no matter what they thought of the bill itself.[45] On the other hand, these same Republicans felt that it would be undesirable to make any changes "back home"

---

[43] Taken from the files of the SCAA on Revision of the Poor Law.
[44] Letter of Miss Bond, from Albany, to Miss Curry, Mar. 8, 1927.
[45] Letter from Miss Bond to R. C. Atkinson, of the Ohio Institute, June 1, 1928.

which might in any way upset the local political situation. Thus the stage was set for the passage of the Clark bill, which undoubtedly would have been enacted into law had not the SCAA been able to draft, even on very short notice, a much superior measure and to secure its introduction by an influential legislator (Senator George R. Fearon), gathering support for it through extensive publicity.

It was clear to the leaders of the SCAA that the removal of opposition *outside* of the legislature was necessary before any real progress could be made within that body. Long experience had taught them that, regardless of the merits of a bill, individual legislators would vote against a bill if they were subjected to powerful local pressure. After the adjournment of the legislature in 1927, the SCAA began its attempt to reconcile the poor law superintendents [46] by organizing a Joint Committee composed of representatives of the State Department of Social Welfare, the Legislative Committee of the State Association of County Superintendents of the Poor, and the SCAA. Although the Joint Committee agreed to leave much of the drafting of the bill, its publicity, and its management in the legislature to the SCAA, the poor law officials—who, after defeating the bill twice in the legislature, almost wrecked the Joint Committee itself in 1928—were not reconciled until a third draft of the bill, providing for a permissive, rather than a mandatory, establishment of the county as a unit, was accepted in 1929.[47]

The next step in the campaign was pressure and publicity. Representatives of the SCAA went from county to county lining up support and unearthing opposition. In this county field work the different departments of the SCAA cooperated, but the children's county and the local tuberculosis agents, assisted by specially assigned field workers bore the brunt of the battle. In approaching local political leaders, careful preliminary arrangements were made, in order that the "right" persons might be reached. To this end information was gath-

---

[46] It was realized that even if a progressive poor law were enacted by the legislature in 1928, without the support of these officials, the administration of the law would be seriously impaired by recalcitrant poor law officials.

[47] Miss Elsie M. Bond, in *Social Service Review*, Sept., 1929, p. 420, published quarterly by the University of Chicago Press, Chicago.

ered by SCAA representatives throughout the state. For example, a list of officers of the *Republican* county committees in upstate New York, in the files of the SCAA, bears after each name a notation. Some of these notations are very brief— "OK," "helpful," "best," "key person"; others are somewhat more lengthy, as the following comments on one of the county committees indicate:

> X County: L——, Chairman, Republican Committee, is considered a "figure-head." County Judge T—— is real leader. Mrs. J——, Vice-Chairman, is ineffective. R——, Secretary, friend of M——, Superintendent Poor. M—— is a friend of H—— and H—— will speak to M—— concerning the bill.[48]

Persons of local political importance were approached either by representatives of the SCAA or through persons of influence in the county who were willing to give active support to the bill. That indirect, rather than direct, pressure was sometimes the more effective is illustrated in the report of a field worker from Saratoga:

> At first he (C——, ex-supervisor of the Town of Saratoga) thought it (the bill) wouldn't do, but after I convinced B——, of the City of Saratoga Springs, then C—— decided it might be O.K. He told me confidentially that it would do away with graft, and because of that it might hit Saratoga too hard. He said he would be for it though, for he knew it was a good thing.[49]

In addition, an attempt was made to minimize opposition from private groups adversely affected by the provisions of the law. "If you hear of any criticism or misunderstanding of the bill," wrote Miss Bond to the secretary of the New York State Conference of Mayors, "I should be very grateful if you would let me know. We are always glad to talk these matters over with people who are interested in the bill and correct any ambiguities in it." [50] Amendments of minor importance were included in the bill to satisfy the State Council of Catholic Charities. When the Christian Scientists appeared before

---

[48] From the files of SCAA under date of Feb. 3, 1928 and Feb. 10, 1928.
[49] Letter from Miss Helen Locke to Miss Curry, of the SCAA, Mar. 13, 1927.
[50] Letter to William P. Capes dated Feb. 15, 1929.

Senator Fearon in February, 1929, with some sixteen amendments to the bill which might in effect have changed the Medical Practice Act of the state, however, the SCAA first sought the opinion of the State Departments of Education, Health, and Public Welfare, as well as that of the various medical associations, and then fought the amendments tooth and nail.

In addition to dealing with professional politicians and organized pressure groups, an attempt was made to build up public support generally. To this end a special educational campaign was inaugurated in 1927. The campaign was not confined to the periods of legislative sessions, but, on the contrary, was renewed with even more vigor after the adjournment of a legislature in which the bill had been defeated. Thus, on April 13, 1927, after the first defeat of the bill, Miss Bond, writing to Mr. John M. Glenn, of the Russell Sage Foundation, said: "We are planning to have the revision of the poor law widely discussed throughout the state during the coming year. I have several engagements to speak in several cities."

In addition to such speaking tours, made by several representatives of the SCAA, study groups were organized by the Association's county committees. In counties where the Association was not represented, the Superintendent of the Poor was urged to encourage the formation of such groups, in order that the problem might be thoroughly studied before the next legislature met.

It was necessary, moreover, to supply these groups with literature relating to the proposed poor law as a basis for discussion. Hence, several pamphlets and leaflets were prepared and distributed in large numbers, not only to the study groups, but also to such individuals and groups as might in any way help the cause of poor law revision. Particular attention was paid to county officials, members of the State Legislature, and newspapers.[51] Some of these leaflets were expository in character, analyzing certain technical aspects of the bill, whereas others were essentially briefs for the law. One leaflet showed, in parallel columns, the provisions of the old poor law and the

---

[51] It should also be noted that the monthly issues of the *SCAA News* were an important element in the educational program.

changes proposed in the Clark bill and the SCAA bill, respectively, so that the reader might see at a glance the salient points in and the differences between the two bills. Another contained a chart showing a "Comparison of Administrative and Financial Systems in Cities under the Poor Law and the Proposed Public Welfare Law." But whatever the content, the primary purpose of the pamphlets was to build up public opinion in support of the SCAA's proposed law.

At frequent intervals special news releases were prepared for the press, and not infrequently the Association stimulated favorable editorial comment. Reprints of such comment were distributed by the SCAA. That newspaper publicity was considered of the utmost desirability may be seen in a letter of instruction from Mr. Folks to the county agents,[52] requesting them to secure the consent of prominent persons in each county to the publication of interviews. The material for these interviews was often prepared in the office of the SCAA and forwarded to prominent persons for their approval. Very often the SCAA actually handled the news releases of these interviews.

The organization exerted the utmost care in preparing a list of important persons in each county who were to be asked to support the proposed bill. The importance of these persons was determined either by their individual prominence or by their connection with a legislator or political leader. Care was taken, however, to rally support for the bill from as many different walks of life as possible.

In addition, favorable endorsements were sought, received, and transmitted to Albany from many varied and representative professional, civic, and religious organizations.[53] The New York State League of Women Voters was asked to make the revision of the poor law part of the League's legislative program for 1929,[54] and overtures were made to secure the

---

[52] Dated Feb. 19, 1929.

[53] Especially from the Greater New York Federation of Churches, the New York State Council of Churches, the City Club, the Women's City Club, the Jewish Federation, the Charity Organization Society, the Association for Improving the Condition of the Poor, and the Brooklyn Bureau of Charities.

[54] Letter from Miss Bond to Miss Dorothy Kenyon, Feb. 11, 1928.

support of the American Legion for the sections in the poor
law dealing with veteran relief.[55]

Frequently copies of the proposed bill accompanied literature distributed by the SCAA, with the request that the
recipient address a letter to the proper legislators if he considered the bill worthy of support.[56] The files of the SCAA
are thus replete with letters from prominent persons throughout the state, stating that they favor the legislation and will
communicate, by letter or telegram, with the legislators suggested. Moreover, although the support of Governor Roosevelt had been assured in advance, the Association, nevertheless, after the bill had been passed by both houses, requested
all organizations that endorsed the bill to write to the Governor, asking his approval.[57]

Such painstaking care in removing sources of opposition and
in cementing friendly goodwill "back home" lightened the
difficulty of working with the legislators themselves, so that
the Association could concentrate its pressure on the leaders.[58]
"If we can secure Mr. McGinnies' (the Speaker) approval of
a draft of the bill before it is introduced, we ought to have
much less trouble in the legislature," wrote Miss Bond to
Commissioner C. H. Johnson on January 4, 1929. Accordingly, before the introduction of the bill into the legislature
the Joint Committee discussed it in detail with the Speaker.
Such discussions with friendly leaders were particularly helpful in disclosing the exact sources of opposition, so that the
Association could either strike back or effect some compromise.[59]

---

[55] Here, too, characteristically, the SCAA attempted to ascertain in advance
as much as it could about the chairman of the Legislative Committee of the
New York Department of the American Legion, in order to secure the best
results from such a conference. Bond-Prevost correspondence, Nov., 1928.

[56] For example, a letter distributed Feb. 20, 1929, making this request, contained a summary of the provisions of the bill, a pamphlet prepared for general distribution, and reprints of editorial comment from two of the New York
City daily newspapers, together with a copy of the resolutions, approving the
law, adopted by the Board of Managers of the SCAA.

[57] Letter from Elsie Bond to Leo M. Doody, President of the State Association of County Superintendents of the Poor, Mar. 20, 1929.

[58] It should be noted, however, that representatives of the SCAA, particularly Miss Bond, talked at great length about the bill with a number of
legislators.

[59] For example, the Speaker called the attention of the SCAA to the fact
that the State Commissioner of Public Welfare had filed a list of eighteen

To introduce the bill into the legislature, the Association selected Senator George R. Fearon and Assemblyman Herbert B. Shonk, men who carried weight in their party councils, who were sincerely interested in the enactment of the law, and who had unswerving confidence in the Association. Neither of these men would give amendments to the bill any consideration unless they bore the approval of the SCAA.[60]

At the public hearings on the proposed poor laws, the SCAA arranged for the presence of advocates from as many different fields as possible, although those who had direct contact with poor law administration in the counties and the cities were given the greatest prominence.

Thus, during the campaign to secure the passage of a modernized public welfare law, the SCAA made use of pressure techniques in two directions; one in the direction of building up popular support, the other in the direction of breaking down specific sources of opposition. Under trained leadership, through the establishment of study groups, through the dissemination of specially prepared factual material, and with the cooperation of sympathetic organizations, prominent and influential persons, and newspapers, it succeeded in creating a favorable and enlightened public opinion. Step by step it removed sources of opposition, either through compromise or through persuasion. Finally, in 1929, after four years of diligent prodding, the new public welfare law was passed unanimously by both houses of the legislature.

As one might expect, the SCAA commands the respect and admiration of the legislators at Albany, not only for its achievements, but also because of the integrity of its aims and honesty of its methods.

---

amendments to the bill in 1928, of which the Association had no advance notice, despite the fact that the Department of Public Welfare was represented on the Joint Committee.

[60] Excerpt of a letter from Senator Fearon to Miss Elsie Bond of the SCAA:

"Enclosed find letter from Corporation Counsel of New York . . . together with copy of letter from ——— (Commissioner of Charities in New York City), proposing amendments to the Public Welfare Law. If any of the amendments suggested are constructive suggestions, I assume, of course, that you will adopt them, otherwise not."

Dated Feb. 27, 1928. Senator Fearon's reply to the Commissioner of Charities in New York City was drafted by the SCAA, Mar. 2, 1928.

In the first place, it is generally recognized that the legislation sought by the Association is for the amelioration of the plight of the poorest, weakest, and most downtrodden people in the community.[61]

In the second place, it is realized at Albany that the SCAA supports or opposes legislation only after careful study by trained welfare workers,[62] and that its campaigns for this item of legislation or that are characterized by restraint and patience. The conservative attitude that the SCAA maintains toward the legislative process is interestingly revealed in a sentence of its secretary, Homer Folks: "If legislation came more easily, it would not stick; you would get more laws than you could digest."[63]

In the third place, because of the educational campaigns conducted by the Association, bills sponsored by the SCAA practically always have the support of many other social organizations, as well as of thousands of citizens scattered throughout the state.

Finally, the fact that the SCAA shuns the idea of "disciplining" legislators when a bill bearing its support has been defeated, as not within the scope of the Association's objectives, likewise contributes to the favorable attitude in Albany. On the other hand, the Association does seek to reward the honest assistance given it by legislators, by giving their names publicity in the *Annual Reports* and in the titles of the bills, and occasionally by recommending and endorsing them for reelection.[64]

---

[61] Funds for the improvement of state institutions come out of general taxes or from bond issues. The SCAA did not, like many other groups, oppose the appropriation of funds for projects sponsored by others, in order that its own welfare legislation might command greater sums. On the contrary, the Association willingly agreed to conduct campaigns for bond issues of interest to other organizations, as it did on many occasions beginning with 1923. See *SCAA News.*

[62] *Cf.* the remarks of Speaker McGinnies and Senator Knight (majority leader) to this effect in *SCAA News,* Sept., 1930, p. 3.

[63] Interview, Jan. 11, 1933.

[64] In Nov., 1932, for example, when the strong opposition of the teachers' groups was threatening the reelection of Senator Fearon, the secretary of the SCAA sent letters to the Association's local committees, praising the senator's work in public welfare. These letters were made public throughout the state. Copy, dated Nov. 1, 1932, is in the Association's files.

Thus, while there are many pressure groups which are, perhaps, more influential than the SCAA, few are so highly esteemed at Albany. Others ask for and secure much more legislation from the State Legislature; the SCAA, however, receives much more respect and, in proportion to its activities, can show impressive results.

CHAPTER VI

The Professions

GROUP pressure directed at the legislators of New York
State proceeds chiefly from three major sources: labor,
business, and agriculture. No study of pressure techniques
can be complete, however, without some consideration of the
minor, though equally pertinacious, groups that exert a noticeable influence on the State Legislature—if for no other reason
than that they are so numerous and variegated. The multiplicity of these bodies, indeed, makes it almost impossible to
treat all of them adequately. Since many of them, however,
are similar in aim and organization, it is possible to group
the most important ones under seven divisions and thus to
consider their general character. These organizations are discussed in this chapter and the one following. To an analysis
of the recognized professions of education, medicine, and law,
always alert at Albany to protect their interests, the present
chapter is devoted.

Education

The first division is that of education, involving the largest
item in the budget of New York State, and, consequently, the
most important of the minor streams of pressure. Educational
groups in the state, composed chiefly of teachers, differ from
the other groups that we have considered in that they are, for
the most part, local and territorial in organization but statewide in influence. This paradox grows out of the fact that, on
the one hand, the salaries, pensions, and tenure of the New
York State teachers are protected by state legislation, but, on
the other, they are confronted with a diversity of peculiarly
local problems. Many special educational statutes, for example, apply solely to New York City and not to cities in other
parts of the state, because New York City, with its unusually
large school system, faces unique problems requiring unique
solutions. In New York City alone, therefore, there are more

than eighty local organizations[1] that deal with educational matters of greater or less importance to them. On the other hand, there are perhaps a score of additional educational groups that draw their membership from areas outside of the metropolis and whose main interest is the solution of problems affecting only their respective memberships. These "upstate" groups are for the most part federated in the New York State Teachers' Association.

Although the pressure techniques employed by "upstate" groups differ from those used by New York City organizations, the state's educational organizations have been drawn together by important statewide problems. Their hardest campaigns have been fought over the maintenance of existing salary laws, pension systems, and state control of education against the onslaughts of a large and powerful array of business organizations.[2] Since unified and cooperative effort has been necessary for success in such campaigns, several centralized statewide organizations have been developed, composed of the various local groups in the state.

Upstate New York. Prior to 1929 the unifying agency for upstate educational groups in matters of legislation was the New York State Department of Education, headed by the Board of Regents.[3] In December, 1929, the Department of Education attempted to concentrate and centralize under its guidance most of the powerful upstate organizations through the creation of a Regents Joint Legislative Committee,[4] made up of the Regents Committee on Legislation of the Department of Education, the State Commissioner of Education and

[1] Many of these are, of course, organizations in name only, their influence being insignificant. Others are very active and persistent.

[2] *Cf.* Address of Prof. J. K. Norton of Teachers College, Columbia University, before the annual convention of the National Education Association, *New York Times,* July 4, 1935. It should be noted that exceptionally vigorous campaigns have been waged by teachers during the depression against salary cuts and other forms of educational retrenchment.

[3] The Board of Regents is composed of 12 members, one elected each year by the legislature in joint session. The chief executive officer of both this board and of the state's educational system is the Commissioner of Education, elected by the Board of Regents for an indefinite term. *New York Legislative Manual,* 1935, p. 435.

[4] Interview with Ernest E. Cole, Deputy Commissioner of Education, Sept. 5, 1935.

his assistants, and representatives of eight major educational groups: (1) the New York State Teachers' Association, (2) the New York State School Boards Association, (3) the Council of City and Village Superintendents, (4) the State Association of District Superintendents, (5) the New York City Board of Education, (6) the Associated Academic Principals, (7) the New York State Congress of Parents and Teachers, and (8) the Parochial Schools.[5]

The Regents Joint Legislative Committee attempted from the first to avoid controversial questions that would divide the members and to devote its attention solely to the support or defeat of educational legislation desired by all. During a legislative session the Joint Committee met several times, considered pending bills, and dispatched memoranda to the Legislature and the Governor, indicating the position taken by the committee on the various bills. On several occasions since the establishment of the Joint Committee, however, the teachers' groups have accused the State Department of Education of a breach of trust.[6] Thus, while the relations between the Department and the teachers' groups have, in general, been cordial, a somewhat strained feeling has developed in recent years, reflected in the infrequent meetings of the Joint Committee currently, in contrast to former years.

The most important of the upstate organizations is the New York State Teachers' Association, organized at a "state convention of teachers" in Syracuse, on July 30, 1845, to promote the interests, standards, and conditions of teachers and schools in the state.[7] Since that time the Association has grown to 46,000 members "actively engaged in any branch of educational work or . . . regularly retired under the New York State Retirement System."[8] All but 400 are teachers in edu-

---

[5] The Conference of Faculties of Teachers' Colleges and Normal Schools, though represented in the early meetings of the Joint Committee, later dropped out. The first meeting of the Joint Committee was held Dec. 14, 1929.

[6] In 1933, for example, the State Department of Education supported the "destructive" Pratt bill and agreed to a decrease in state aid to local education, to the deep chagrin of the educational groups.

[7] *New York State Education,* the monthly publication of the Association, Dec., 1930, p. 359. *Cf. Constitution of the New York State Teachers' Association,* Art. II.

[8] *Constitution,* Art. III. Associate members, with restricted privileges, are

cational institutions of upstate New York. The number of New York City teachers in the Association is negligible. A great deal of influence is exerted in the Association, however, by the district superintendents and school principals, who constitute a very powerful bloc among the non-teacher members. Since about 60 per cent of the Association's members work in "non-tenure" areas, where a superintendent's recommendation to the local school board may cost a teacher his position, the district superintendents are able, in large part, to control the Association. Consequently, the officers of the Association, the leading members in the standing and special committees, and a large proportion of the members of the House of Delegates are superintendents or principals, rather than classroom teachers.[9]

The officers of the Association and the Executive Committee constitute the executive and administrative agencies of the New York State Teachers' Association. The Executive Committee is composed of the president, vice-president, and retiring president of the Association, together with one member from each of the zones into which the state is divided. An executive secretary devotes his full time to the work of the Association under the direction of this committee. The legislative agency of the Association is the House of Delegates, which elects the president and vice-president, annually, and the other members of the Executive Committee.[10] The representatives of the House of Delegates are selected from specially constituted territorial units of the state. The number of delegates from each unit depends upon the number of members in the Association who reside in that unit.[11] Some 600 delegates

---

also provided for. These number about 125. Of those eligible for regular membership in upstate New York, 97 per cent are members of the Association.

[9] It should be noted, however, that classroom teachers constitute about 50 per cent of the membership of the House of Delegates, the standing and special committees. Interview, Dr. Arvie Eldred, Sept. 4, 1935. Recently, also, the Classroom Teachers' Committee was made a standing committee of the Association. *New York State Education*, Jan., 1935.

[10] The zone representatives on the Executive Committee serve for three years, of whom one-third is elected annually. The Executive Committee selects the executive secretary and treasurer, who serve at the pleasure of and sit with the Executive Committee without the power to vote. Art. IV of the *Constitution*.

[11] Members of the Association belonging to institutions of higher learning,

usually attend the annual meetings of the House of Delegates, which are held in November. Although this representative governing body was established because of the difficulty of convoking the full membership of the Association in any one city, an attempt is made, nevertheless, to stimulate member participation in the activities of the Association through sectional meetings. For this purpose the state is divided into nine zones, in each of which annual meetings, open to Association members living in the area, are held in October. At these meetings professional problems are discussed, delegates are elected, and standing committes are organized.[12]

The Association maintains committees, appointed by the president, on Legislation, Finance, Resolutions, Welfare, NEA Relationship, Elementary Teacher Training, Classroom Teachers, and Study of Tenure in Non-Tenure Areas.[13] In addition, there is an Advisory Committee of past presidents of the Association, and an Editorial Advisory Committee under the chairmanship of the president.

The New York State Teachers' Association spends approximately $100,000 annually. Its expenditures include the salary, traveling expenses, and clerical assistance of the general secretary; the cost of its building in Albany; the expenses incurred by the zones; and the deficit in the operation of the Association's monthly publication, *New York State Education*.[14] A good deal of money is also expended on publicity and legislative campaigns.[15] The income of the Association comes chiefly from the annual membership dues of from one to three dollars,

---

such as universities, colleges, and state normal schools, are entitled to representation in the House of Delegates. All elective officers of the Association and members of the duly appointed standing and special committees and the presidents of the various zones into which the Association is divided are ex officio members of the House of Delegates. Art. VII of the *Constitution*.

[12] Annual reports of these zone meetings have been published by the Association.

[13] Four of these committees are standing committees of the Association: Finance, Resolutions, Welfare, and Classroom Teachers. See Art. VI as amended. For recent reports of the activities of these committees see *New York State Education*, Nov., 1934.

[14] The Association, in addition, publishes two educational monographs a year on professional subjects of interest to its members, under the direction of the educational research division.

[15] For details of the Association's budget, see *New York State Education*, Nov., 1933, and Nov., 1934. *Cf.* Art. IX of the *Constitution*.

depending upon the salary or annuity of the member, and advertisements in the monthly magazine.[16]

Since the enactment of educational legislation has slowly evolved as the major activity of the Association,[17] its Legislative Committee has assumed great importance.[18] As its chief weapon in its legislative campaigns, the committee employs publicity of various kinds. During legislative sessions, for example, two series of bulletins are issued each week, sometimes even more frequently. The first of these series contains descriptions of educational bills introduced into the Senate and Assembly, their numbers, introducers, and committees to which they have been referred. The second series contains a concise but frank exposition of the forces aiding or hindering educational legislation, together with factual answers to the arguments of opposition groups. These bulletins, sent chiefly to superintendents and principals, urge their readers to: "Read, use, file (or post) this bulletin; pass the information along; keep local groups informed; and keep headquarters informed."

During the years of the retrenchment drive, the publicity agencies were more varied. Under the supervision of a professional publicity agent, facilities for gathering and distributing facts were extended, and the assistance of the State Education Department in this direction was invoked. Some 3,000 letters left the Association's headquarters during each week of a legislative session, and a regular weekly radio broadcast was initiated.[19] In addition, attempts were made through the Classroom Teachers' Committee to organize local groups of teachers as media for passing on information.[20] Cooperation

---

[16] The income from dues yields about five times the income from advertisements in the monthly magazine.

[17] See "These Eighty-Five Years," *New York State Education*, Dec., 1930; C. Kirk Hyland, *A History of the New York State Teachers' Association*, New York, E. L. Kellogg, 1883.

[18] This importance is reflected in the fact that the Legislative Committee is composed of the members of the Executive Committee, and is allowed complete freedom in solving legislative problems. See *New York State Education*, Jan., 1934, p. 275.

[19] Interview, Dr. Arvie Eldred, Feb. 8, 1933.

[20] Prominent members of the Association even composed a song which was publicized, "Stand by the Schools." *New York State Education*, Nov., 1933, p. 172.

was secured from other organizations interested in teacher legislation.

Thus, the New York State Teachers' Association lays claim to credit for making the teachers' lobby one of the most formidable in the state. This it has achieved, in the words of its president, not by "buttonholing" legislators nor by "finding jobs for their sons. We have only had one type of ammunition, one type of weapon, and that is gathering and using of facts. It has been a process of education all the way through, and we are gradually coming to realize that education is not merely the process of informing children, but also a process of informing parents as well; and our job doesn't stop with the classroom, it goes far beyond that." [21]

Closely associated with the New York State Teachers' Association is the New York State School Boards Association, a statewide organization of some 500 local school board members which, in 1932, was greatly strengthened by the amalgamation of the two strongest upstate school boards.[22] Since members of school boards are, for the most part, average citizens rather than trained educators, they generally look to their superintendents of schools and other educational groups to take the lead in protecting educational interests. The purpose in merging the school boards into an association, therefore, has been to stimulate a "more positive and aggressive attitude" among their members.[23] As the Association considers itself "a buffer between the taxpayer and the teacher," [24] however, its concessions to the taxpayer when it has taken a "more positive and aggressive attitude" have brought it in conflict with larger, more influential teachers' organizations.[25] The most effective

---

[21] *New York State Education*, Jan., 1934, p. 275; E. H. Staffelbach, "Policy-Making by Teachers' Organizations—State Association Standpoint," in *The Annals of the American Academy of Political and Social Science*, Nov., 1935.

[22] These two organizations were the New York State Association of Central Rural School District Boards and the larger Associated School Boards and Trustees of the State of New York. A total of 519 member boards were recorded in Nov., 1934—among these are central (120), city (43), village (57), and rural school boards (299). Among the recent members is the Board of Education of the City of New York.

[23] *New York State School Boards Association Bulletin*, Nov., 1933, p. 22.

[24] Letter of W. A. Clifford, Executive Secretary, Aug. 14, 1935.

[25] The School Boards Association, for example, sponsored a bill in 1933 providing that when a teacher reaches the age of 60 and is eligible for retirement, further service should be at the discretion of the school board. The

work of the reorganized and strengthened School Boards Association, therefore, has been done in cooperation with other educational groups in the state, particularly the New York State Teachers' Association.

The School Boards Association conducts its affairs through its officers and a Board of Directors, composed of the officers and the chairmen of the districts into which the state is divided. There are also a number of committees, of which the important ones are the Executive Committee, the Editorial Advisory Committee, and the Legislative Committee. Meetings of county and district groups are held in addition to a regular annual meeting. These local meetings are addressed by leading educators of the state, group discussions being invited, while at the annual meeting it is customary to exhibit school building and equipment materials. Information is disseminated through the Association's *Bulletin,* issued five times a year, supplemented by a special bulletin which is distributed to members during legislative sessions, giving a complete record of the status of pending educational bills.

The remaining upstate groups represented on the Regents Joint Legislative Committee are organized largely on the model of the New York State Teachers' Association, with which they are all, for the most part, closely allied. These organizations represent specialized groups of the more comprehensive Teachers' Association, to which they look for leadership in the solution of two types of problems, professional and legislative.[26]

The Council of City and Village Superintendents, composed of some 180 superintendents of schools [27] in the cities and villages of the state, and the New York Association of District Superintendents, made up of over 200 superintendents in rural communities,[28] are particularly influential locally because they

New York State Teachers' Association strenuously fought this bill and succeeded in defeating it. *New York State School Boards Association Bulletin,* Nov., 1933, p. 23.

[26] These groups are, of course, fully organized, with officers and standing committees, the most important being the Legislative Committees. Annual conventions are held for both business and social purposes. As would be expected, the memberships of the various groups overlap.

[27] In addition, there are about an equal number of associate members, not superintendents of schools. Letter of James B. Welles, Superintendent of Schools, Roslyn Heights, N. Y., Mar. 13, 1933.

[28] In the rural sections the superintendents are selected for a five-year term

have personal contacts with legislative members and leaders of farm, parents', and other organizations in their communities.

More professional in its interests is the Associated Academic Principals of the State of New York,[29] founded in 1885 "for the promotion of the interests of secondary education and a closer acquaintance among the principals." In 1934 the membership consisted of 634 principals and assistant principals of secondary schools. Its constitution provides for a council, serving in an advisory capacity, composed of one member from each senatorial district in the county. This member is also the chairman of the Associated Academic Principals of his district.[30]

Of much greater influence is the New York State Congress of Parents and Teachers, organized in 1897, twice incorporated in New York State under different names. It is affiliated with the National Congress of Parents and Teachers. Its objects are: (1) to develop trained parenthood; (2) to raise the standard of child life; and (3) to encourage closer relations between home, school, church, and state.[31] Its membership of 85,000, composed, for the most part, of the parents of school children in upstate New York, is organized in 1,100 congress units [32] for

---

by specially selected school directors. There are two such directors in each town, whose only duty is to select the rural superintendent, for there are no school boards in these districts. All of the rural superintendents' terms expired in 1936.

[29] See *New York State Education,* Mar., 1935, p. 473. *Cf. Constitution of Associated Academic Principals of the State of New York* and letter of its president, R. L. Butterfield, Mar. 7, 1933.

[30] There is also a New York State Association of Elementary Principals, which is not, however, represented on the Regents Joint Legislative Committee. Organized in 1929, it consists of more than 400 supervisors, teachers, and assistant principals of elementary schools who are members of the New York State Teachers' Association or the New York City Principals' Association. This represents about 40 per cent of those eligible to membership from upstate. *New York State Education,* Mar., 1935, p. 472.

[31] Address of President Frances H. Blake at the annual convention of the State Congress in Syracuse, Oct., 1933. *Journal of Proceedings,* p. 16. *Cf.* Mrs. Blake's discussion of the "Aims of Parent and Teacher Activity" in *New York State Education,* Feb., 1935, p. 373.

[32] About half of the 22,000 local units of the National Congress are thus located in New York State, but the total national membership is more than a million and three-quarters. New York State is the fifth ranking state in the National Congress of Parents and Teachers. See *New York Parent-Teacher,* bulletin of the New York State Congress of Parents and Teachers, Sept., 1935.

the more effective execution of the educational work of the State Congress. To the annual convention of the Congress each unit sends its president and one delegate for every 25 of its members, and these, together with the members of the Board of Managers of the State Congress and the county chairmen, determine the policies of the Congress. Between annual conventions, the Board of Managers and the Executive Committee transact the organization's business. To promote the plans of the Congress, the state is divided into 15 districts, each with a district director appointed by the Executive Committee. The district directors are assisted by the county chairmen within their respective districts.[33]

To meet its annual expenditures of some $15,000, the State Congress relies chiefly on Founder's Day gifts and dues.[34] By this means it is able to publish its 12- to 16-page bulletin, *New York Parent-Teacher,* and to contribute monthly articles to *New York State Education* and the national organ, *National Parent-Teacher Magazine.*

Since the chief interest of the State Congress is child welfare, it has been most active in supporting bills which affect the welfare of the child by maintaining the educational standards of the state and improving general social welfare.[35]

In matters of legislation the National Congress has advised state branches and their local units to:

---

[33] See *By-Laws of the New York State Congress of Parents and Teachers.* The district directors are members of the Board of Managers.

[34] Upon payment of dues, members become affiliated with the local, state, and national branches of the Congress. The dues are 15¢ per capita for all members of each local congress unit, 10¢ of which is retained by the State Congress, the remaining 5¢ being turned over to the National Congress. There are no salaried officers. The State Congress also maintains a student loan fund of about $2,700, supported by life membership dues and other gifts, through which students are aided by loans averaging $100, at 2 per cent interest. See *New York State Congress of Parents and Teachers Directory and Guide,* 1933–1934, p. 13.

[35] *Journal of Proceedings,* Oct., 1933, p. 23. In 1933, for example, the State Congress sponsored a bill to retain the Division of Child Development and Parent Education in the State Education Department, and secured an appropriation of $16,000 to make this possible. In the same year it vigorously opposed the destructive Pratt bill, as well as bills that would undermine centralized school district laws and abolish motion picture censorship in the state. *Cf.* letter of President Frances H. Blake, Jan. 3, 1934. In July, 1933, Governor Lehman appointed the president of the State Congress to the Committee of Public Education in New York State and in July, 1935, to the Advisory Committee to wipe out crime.

1. **Find out** community needs which require legislative action. Secure support of public opinion through resolutions, publicity, etc., to aid in securing enactment of legislative provisions to meet needs. Attend hearings before proper legislative body—city or county—and follow through to final enactment. This effort will reveal state needs to meet which, cooperation with state chairman is essential.

2. **Cooperate** with state committee in study of education and child welfare laws. Compare with laws of other states on similar subjects and ascertain which are producing best results. Ask for class or conference at your convention and follow with local study group on legislation.

3. **Study** legislative program of National Congress as set forth in Plan of Work and Annual Legislative Program. When projects are endorsed, mail copies of endorsements or resolutions to your Senators and Representatives in Congress and to your state and national chairmen. Stand ready to send personal letters or telegrams in large numbers to Senators and Representatives.

4. **Compare** state and national laws with State and National Congress resolutions to determine whether local needs can best be met through enactment of new law.

5. **Teach** organization the necessity of all chairmen desiring legislation conferring with and working through the legislative chairman.

6. **Oppose** objectionable legislation concerning child welfare.

7. **Urge** intelligent voting basing conclusions on scientific research not on snap judgment or someone's personal opinion.[36]

The chairman of the Legislative Committee of the State Congress, accordingly, is present in Albany once a week during legislative sessions. During recent years, moreover, the radio has been resorted to more and more in order to carry the message of the Congress into thousands of homes.[37] By these means the Congress has developed pressure techniques that

---

[36] National Congress leaflet, undated, entitled *Legislation-Committee Activities and Projects.*

[37] *New York Parent-Teacher,* Sept., 1935.

render its cooperation invaluable to other women's, civic, and welfare organizations in the state. Since the Congress also possesses direct contact with the home and the school, educational groups, especially the New York State Teachers' Association, have not been reluctant to enlist its support in their campaigns for legislation.[38]

City of New York. The many educational associations that exist in New York City have, since 1924, worked together for legislation through the centralizing agency of the Joint Committee of Teachers' Organizations.[39] Operating informally, without a constitution or by-laws, this Joint Committee is supported by the voluntary contributions of New York City teachers. Originally the Joint Committee was established for the purpose of centralizing teachers' activities in the campaign for increased salaries. Since 1933, however, the Joint Committee has extended the scope of its interests to include such matters as tenure, pensions, and state aid for education.

The Joint Committee constitutes the most representative group ever organized among separate local teacher organizations, for with it are affiliated 80 local organizations with individual memberships ranging from three members, in the Association of Physicians to Examine Candidates for Licenses, to over 8,000 in the Kindergarten–6B Teachers' Association. Until September, 1936, each affiliated organization regardless of its numerical size was represented on the Joint Committee by one delegate with a voting power of one unit. Under the new plan, from one to five delegates, depending on the size of

---

[38] The State Congress of Parents and Teachers is primarily an upstate organization. Its counterpart in New York City is the United Parents Association of the City of New York, whose membership is restricted to inhabitants of the metropolis. Unlike the State Congress, the United Parents Association discourages teacher membership, preferring to represent only the mothers and fathers of school children and to cooperate with the separately organized teachers. Affiliated with the Association are some 207 public and private school associations, including 27 high school groups, 94 parents' associations, 61 parent-teacher organizations, and 25 mothers' clubs. In addition, there are some 500 individuals. The Association is thus representative of some 70,000 families. Its business is conducted by a Delegate Assembly of about 300 members, which meets once a month, and a paid executive director (LeRoy E. Bowman). It also publishes a monthly magazine, *School Parent*. Its annual budget is in excess of $20,000.

[39] See W. W. Wattenberg, *On the Educational Front*, New York, Columbia University Press, 1936.

the organization, are elected to the committee, each with one vote. In this way, the number of delegates of the Joint Committee has been increased from 80 to 147. The aggregate membership in the 80 organizations represented on the Joint Committee is 60,000.[40] Practically every member in the City of New York public school system is affiliated with at least one of these local organizations.[41]

Most of these associations have a complete organization of officers and committees. They hold several meetings of the full membership annually and attempt to solve their own group problems. Membership in the Joint Committee has not deprived them of their individual identity, for the larger organizations have active legislative committees, and all reserve the right to oppose bills endorsed by the Joint Committee, although such action is rarely taken.

Despite the fact that four meetings, attended by delegates of the member organizations, are held annually, the policies of the Joint Committee are determined by an Executive Committee of 21 members, one-third of whom are elected annually for a three-year term.[42] This committee, working largely through subcommittees, is concerned with the reconciliation of factions within the Joint Committee in order that united action may facilitate the enactment of legislation.[43] Seven of its members constitute the Legislative Subcommittee of the Joint Committee, which drafts bills and maintains intimate personal contact with legislators during legislative ses-

[40] The basis of representation on the Joint Committee is as follows: organizations with a membership of 100 or less, one delegate; a membership of 101 to 1,000, two; membership of 1,001 to 2,000, three; 2,001 to 5,000, four; and more than 5,000, five. *New York Times,* May 29, 1936.

[41] There are 37,000 members of the teaching, administrative, and supervising staffs of elementary and secondary schools in the City of New York. Many teachers join several organizations, so that there is overlapping membership in a number of instances.

[42] Most of the members of the Executive Commiteee are also members of several of the local organizations. In this way practically all of the 80 local groups have some voice in the deliberations of the Executive Committee. It should be noted that the Teachers' Union, after its reorganization in Oct., 1935, lost its place in the Executive Committee. See "What's Wrong with the Joint Committee?" in *The New York Teacher,* Nov., 1936.

[43] In the campaign for salary increases in 1927, for example, the Executive Committee prepared some 100 salary schedules in an attempt to secure unanimity among the different groups. Interview, Mrs. Anna R. Pettebone, Secretary, June, 1933.

sions.[44] Moreover, bulletins, issued bi-monthly, are posted in every school in the city and are distributed directly to the teachers through the affiliated member organizations. These bulletins keep the teachers informed of the activities of the Joint Committee and contain specific suggestions for assistance. One such suggestion,[45] for example, reads:

How every teacher can help—

The district in which you RESIDE is represented in the State Legislature by a Senator and an Assemblyman. If unknown to you, learn their names.

Write to them. In your own language urge the enactment of the measures we sponsor.

Do not use a "form" letter. Do not telegraph, but appeal individually by letter.

Start writing these letters at once. Mail them, if possible, this week. Make it an intensive letter-writing campaign concentrated within a few days and not spread thinly over several weeks.

Do not stop there. Seek the active cooperation of Parents' Associations and Civic Organizations in your school district. They can help effectively by individual letters to the legislative representatives of their district, and, if time permits, by formal action in support of our bills.

If you wish to study these bills, write to the Joint Committee for copies. They will be forwarded IMMEDIATELY.

United action will win for us, and nothing else can.

During the legislative session of 1935, the Joint Committee, through its Legislative Subcommittee, issued from Albany a daily news release to various newspapers in New York City, explaining specifications of proposed legislation affecting the teachers and the schools.

In addition to these activities, the Joint Committee submits a list of questions to local and state candidates for public office of the Democratic, Republican, and Socialist parties each year.

---

[44] In recent years the Joint Committee has utilized the services of a full-time, salaried Public Relations Secretary.

[45] *Bulletin of the Joint Committee of Teachers' Organizations,* Jan. 28, 1935.

The replies from each candidate are published in full in a *Bulletin,* which is sent to every teacher in the City of New York about a week before election. The teachers are urged carefully

> to consider these Candidate Pledges, and *vote on November 6th* as will best serve to uphold Uncurtailed Public Education in this City and State, and to safeguard Your Own Rights as Teachers devoting their lives to this vital service for the public good.
>
> Here are their Definite Pledges—not voiced in campaign speeches or in press interviews—but Deliberately Made in Writing by the Candidates over Their Own Signatures and filed with the Joint Committee.
>
> These are Pre-election Promises in the most binding sense, for which the Candidate *this time* will be held rigidly accountable.
>
> Aroused Public Sentiment—and the party leaders know it—will never again condone or tolerate the violation of major campaign pledges publicly made and officially attested for vote-getting purposes.[46]

Vividly colored placards, urging teachers to "REGISTER, ENROLL in a political party, and VOTE," are sent by the Joint Committee to every school in New York for posting. A systematic campaign is thus waged to utilize the teachers' ballots in the election of friendly members to the State Legislature.[47]

Of the member organizations in the Joint Committee of Teachers' Organizations, four deserve special notice.[48] The first of these is the Brooklyn Teachers' Association, which was, until 1935, the largest local teachers' association in the United States.[49] Its membership, composed of primary and secondary

---

[46] *Bulletin of the Joint Committee of Teachers' Organizations,* Oct. 30, 1934.

[47] The records of legislators from New York City in the session of 1935 disclose that they adhered strictly to the pre-election pledges made in their replies to the Joint Committee's questionnaire of 1934.

[48] These four associations are represented on the reorganized Joint Committee by the maximum number of five delegates. The important Kindergarten–6B Teachers' Association elects five delegates, too. See *infra,* note 49.

[49] From a membership of 329 in 1874, when the Association was founded, it grew to 9,000 members in 1933. With the decrease in this number to 7,500, in 1935, however, the Kindergarten–6B Teachers' Association succeeded to the position held by the Brooklyn Teachers' Association, with a membership of

school teachers, principals, and superintendents in the Borough of Brooklyn, was said to have represented 95 per cent of the teachers of Brooklyn.[50]

The chief directive agencies of the Association, in addition to its officers, are the Board of Trustees, the Executive Committee, the chairmen of the committees, and the Board of Representatives. The Board of Trustees is composed of forty members, elected in each school under the supervision of a director-representative for each school, named by the president. This director-representative is the liaison agent between the members in the individual school and the officers of the Association.[51] The Board of Trustees with the president of the Association constitutes the nominating committee that annually names all the officers of the Association, designates the banks in which the funds of the Association are deposited, and administers the special funds of the Association.

The Executive Committee, which meets monthly from September to June, inclusive, is composed of the officers, the trustees, the chairmen of the 15 standing committees, and the former active presidents of the Association. The members of all these committees are appointed by the president of the Association.

The Board of Representatives consists of the members of the Executive Committee and the representatives elected in the respective schools, the number of such representatives being proportionate to the number of active members of the Association in the school. At its regular annual meeting, the

---

8,400. The Kindergarten–6B Teachers' Association is particularly active in promoting salary legislation, utilizing, for this purpose, its efficient Legislative Committee and its monthly bulletin. *Cf.* Interview with President Johanna M. Lindhof, June 23, 1933. Mayor La Guardia appointed Mrs. Lindhof to the Board of Education of the City of New York in May, 1936. The deep significance of this appointment can be understood when it is realized that, for the first time, a teacher participates in formulating the educational policy of the New York City school system.

[50] Letter of Augustus Ludwig, President, dated Nov. 13, 1933. As in the case of the New York State Teachers' Association, the presence in the Association of principals and superintendents accounts partially for the large teacher membership.

[51] Each school district in the Borough of Brooklyn is represented on the board by two trustees elected for a four-year term. Each school in the district is permitted to submit the name of one nominee. A preferential voting ballot is used for the election.

Board of Representatives considers the budget prepared by the Executive Committee of the Association, which it may reduce but not increase. If no independent nominations have been made, the Board of Representatives at this regular meeting also ratifies the slate of officers submitted to it by the Nominating Committee. Thus, the Board of Representatives is not so powerful as the Board of Trustees, but is, in fact, little more than a ratifying body.[52]

The Brooklyn Teachers' Association is unique among local educational organizations in having preserved a record of its activities over a period of some 60 years in the minutes of its meetings. A study of this record reveals that the Association has taken part in almost every important change in the schools of Brooklyn since 1874. Among other things, it:

1. Sponsored activities looking to the establishment and extension of facilities for higher education;[53]

2. Sponsored the establishment of parent-teacher associations to bring the home and school closer together; and

3. Has offered, through a network of standing and special committees, valuable services to teachers, such as a program of courses,[54] legal advice, salary, pension and tenure protection, benefits of trade, and commercial discounts.

In addition to these activities, all legislation at Albany affecting teachers is carefully watched and studied by the Committee on Legislation,[55] through which the Association

---

[52] The Association is supported largely through the annual dues of one dollar paid by each member. Although the annual report of the treasurer indicates annual receipts and expenditures in excess of $30,000, approximately two-thirds represents income and disbursements of the Lectures and Studies Committee. This service of the Association is self-supporting. See report of treasurer in *Annual Report of the Treasurer.* The Association also publishes a magazine, *The Brooklyn Teacher,* which has a circulation of 1,300 monthly, and an *Annual Report.*

[53] In Sept., 1874, the Brooklyn Teachers' Association formally debated "Resolved, that the educational facilities of Brooklyn demand the establishment of a high or normal school." *The Brooklyn Teacher,* Sept., 1933, p. 6.

[54] The Association was, for this purpose, chartered by the Regents of the University of the State of New York in 1898. For a summary of the Association's activities, see *Annual Reports.*

[55] Since 1920, Miss Isabel A. Ennis has been chairman of the Committee on Legislation, bringing to this post the advantages of long experience in teacher legislation. She was one of the leading figures in the vigorous campaign for

supported favorable legislation for years prior to the establishment of the Joint Committee of Teachers' Organizations. Because of the advantages accruing from united action, however, the Brooklyn Teachers' Association, through its representation on the Joint Committee, brings the influence and support of the Association to the coordinating agency.

A second member organization of the Joint Committee that deserves notice is the militant and progressive Teachers' Union of the City of New York, organized in 1916—constituting Local No. 5 of the American Federation of Teachers, affiliated with the American Federation of Labor.[55a]

The objects of the Union, as stated in its constitution, are:

1. To increase the efficiency of the schools in democratic education
   (a) By promoting good teaching.
   (b) By improving conditions of work.
   (c) By providing systematic study of school problems by teachers.
   (d) By promoting the participation of teachers in school administration.
   (e) By cooperating with associations and other educational forces.

2. To protect teachers against oppressive supervision.

3. To provide for the protection of teachers' interests by legal and other means.

4. To prevent discrimination in education on account of sex, color, religion, or political beliefs.

5. To prevent political, religious, or economic domination of the schools.

These objects have brought the Teachers' Union into the vanguard of almost every campaign to maintain or improve the educational standards of the state. The Union has fought to protect the teacher from laws curtailing his liberties, such as the Lusk laws of 1921, the restrictive residence laws, oaths of allegiance especially designed for teachers, unfair appoint-

---

equal pay for teachers from 1905 to 1912. Interview with Miss Ennis at Albany, May 5, 1936.

[55a] A State Federation of Teachers was launched late in 1936. See *The New York Teacher*, Jan., 1937; and the Feb., 1937 issue for "The Teachers' Union 1917–1937."

ments, unwarranted delays in promotions and other restrictions on academic freedom.

The 5,000 members of the Teachers' Union are chiefly classroom teachers in the public elementary and secondary schools of New York City. Although principals, teachers in private schools, and professors in colleges and universities [56] are also represented, superintendents of schools are not eligible for membership. The officers of the Union are elected annually and are subject to recall. In addition to the president, there are four vice-presidents, one representing the elementary schools, one the high schools, one the private schools, and one the colleges; a secretary-treasurer; a recording secretary; and a legislative representative. These officers are nominated by a committee on nominations and elections, whose report is approved or amended by the Executive Board and by the Assembly of Delegates. The latter Assembly was created because of the difficulty of transacting detailed business at large membership meetings.[57] The Assembly of Delegates is elected by the Union members in each school where there are at least seven such members in the school, or on a borough basis for schools with fewer than seven Union members. It holds meetings monthly.

The Executive Board of the Union is composed of 26 members, elected annually, by means of proportional representation, on a secret ballot.[58] The Executive Board administers the affairs of the Union, subject to the review of the Assembly of Delegates. Its meetings, except when in executive session, are open to all members of the Union.

As a closer bond between the Executive Board and the membership of the Union, a school in which there are Union members elects a school representative, subject to recall, who, in addition to collecting dues, soliciting memberships, and distributing literature, submits grievances or recommendations to the Executive Board.

The important standing and special committees of the

---

[56] The Teachers' Union established a college section in 1935 and a private school section in 1936. The status of these sections is somewhat autonomous.

[57] The constitution provides that at least four membership meetings shall be held annually, at which questions of policy are decided.

[58] The candidates are nominated in the same way as the officers of the Union.

Union, appointed by the president, are: Membership, Legislative, Teachers' Interests, Academic Freedom, Legal Aid and Grievance, Trade School, Elementary School, Anti-War and Anti-Fascist, and Research. All of these committees must submit reports to the Executive Board, and no committee can take final action without the consent of the Executive Board or the Assembly of Delegates. An amendment to the constitution, moreover, must be endorsed by at least five members of the Union and submitted to the Executive Board for revision and approval before submission at the next meeting of the Assembly of Delegates and the membership meeting.

The highest dues of any teachers' organization in New York, are paid by members of the Teachers' Union because of its contributions to the American Federation of Teachers and the New York State Federation of Labor. The schedule, being graded, is based on the earning capacity of the members.[59] The Union's budget in 1936 was approximately $30,000.

In cooperation with other teachers' organizations, such as the Joint Committee, the Retirement Board, and the upstate New York State Teachers' Association, the Teachers' Union frequently plays the directive role in campaigns for legislation. One reason for its power in this direction is the fact that it selects legislative representatives who are well trained.[60]

During legislative sessions, the Teachers' Union publishes weekly bulletins which, like those of other organizations, explain succinctly both the situation at Albany and the action expected from its members. In addition, the Union issues a monthly publication [61] and special pamphlets.[62]

---

[59] The schedule is:

Salary Range	Yearly Dues	Initiation
Less than $1,500	$ 3.00	$ .50
$1,500–$3,168	6.00	
$3,169–$3,573	9.00	
$3,574–$4,185	12.00	.... 1.00
More than $4,185	15.00	
Retired or on leave	3.00	

[60] Dr. Abraham Lefkowitz, chairman of the History Department at Commerce High School, New York City served from 1916 to 1935, when he was succeeded by Dr. Bella V. Dodd, of Hunter College. Interviews, Dr. Lefkowitz, June 20 and Aug. 9, 1933 and Dr. Dodd, Dec. 20, 1935 and July 23, 1936.

[61] This was called *The Union Teacher* until 1935, when, with the reorganization of the Union, it was enlarged and named *The New York Teacher*. This reorganization was the result of factional dissensions which had grown in the

The position of the Teachers' Union at Albany is unique among teachers' organizations because of its affiliation with the powerful State Federation of Labor.

The third organization represented in the Joint Committee of Teachers' Organizations that merits special notice is the High School Teachers' Association, membership in which is open to any person employed under a regular license in any senior public high school in New York City. Consequently, its 6,000 members, consisting of teachers, principals, assistant principals, librarians, teachers-in-training, substitute teachers, and teacher-clerks, represent about two-thirds of the regular-licensed employees of New York City's high schools. The membership is represented on the Association's Board of Representatives, which is composed of the officers of the Association, the Executive Committee, and one representative for each 10 members in each school.

The conduct of the Association's business is delegated to some 15 standing committees, whose recommendations are acted upon by the Executive Committee and the Board of Representatives. Though there is a Legislative Committee, whose duty is to keep an eye on state legislation affecting the Association's members, legislative pressure is largely left to the Joint Committee. The Association devotes much of its attention, however, to studies of such problems as arise in the high schools. In 1936, for example, the annual luncheon of the Association was held jointly with that of the High School

---

Union for many years. In Oct., 1935, all the officers, including the legislative representative, a majority of the members of the Executive Board, and some 500 others, having failed to convince the American Federation of Teachers to revoke the charter of the Teachers' Union, withdrew from the Union and formed a new group, The New York Teachers Guild. Although not affiliated with organized labor, this group promised that it "will cooperate to the fullest extent with the labor movement and will . . . endeavor to awaken in all teachers a labor-consciousness and a feeling of solidarity." (*New York Times,* Oct. 2, 1935.) On Jan. 1, 1936, however, when The Teachers Guild comprised 700 members, the Teachers' Union increased the number of its members to more than 3,000.

[62] For example, the former legislative representative of the Teachers' Union, Dr. Abraham Lefkowitz, prepared a number of valuable pamphlets during the recent educational crisis in New York State. Prominent among these are: *The Cry of the Children or the Demands of the Profiteer, The Educational Budget and the Financial Crisis,* and *Teachers and the Economic Situation.* In 1936, the Union published *The College Teacher and the Trade Union.*

Principals' Association of New York City, the highlight of this event being a round table discussion of youth's problems.

A fourth member of the Joint Committee, the Teachers Welfare League, draws its 5,200 members from the public elementary and secondary schools of the City of New York. In legislative matters, its particular attention is devoted to the pension system, since the president of the Welfare League is also secretary of the Teachers' Retirement Board and one of its three teacher members.[63]

Summary. The teachers' lobby has become one of the most militant and effective in the state chiefly because the multitude of educational organizations of which it is composed has learned to suppress its jealousies and petty differences and to act in unison—the upstate groups through the New York State Teachers' Association, the New York City groups through the Joint Committee of Teachers' Organizations. Because of the differences in educational needs between these two divisions of the state, the New York City groups have developed more militant pressure techniques than the comparatively placid upstate associations. These techniques include feminine "lobbyists," who, by training and personal force, are able to exert direct influence on legislators,[64] and contact with local political leaders to whom legislators owe their nomination. In general, therefore, the aggressive leadership comes from the more progressive New York City organizations, the upstate groups cooperating.

There are other reasons, too, for the efficiency of the teachers' lobby. The extensive activities undertaken during legislative sessions, for instance, are made possible, despite legal

---

[63] The Teachers' Retirement Board is composed, in addition to three teacher members, of the president of the Board of Education, the comptroller of the City of New York, and two additional members appointed by the Mayor, one of whom must be a member of the Board of Education. The relationship between the Welfare League and the Retirement Board consists of cooperation between the two bodies in drafting, endorsing, and pressing pension legislation. Pressure is, for the most part, personal in nature, contacts being maintained with legislators and the Governor. Interview, F. Z. Lewis, June 27, 1933.

[64] Interview, William R. Lasher, President of the Joint Committee of Teachers' Organizations, June 23, 1933.

prohibitions,[65] by the comparative ease with which funds can be raised among the teachers. With these funds that are made available so promptly, techniques both new and old are employed. During the defensive campaign waged against the repeal of mandatory legislation and further salary cuts in 1933, certain influential newspapers in New York City devoted much space to the reports of the Citizens' Budget Commission, to the detriment of the teachers' arguments. The Joint Committee of Teachers' Organizations promptly utilized the columns of an old magazine, *School,* for the twelve-week period during the legislative session, to answer the attacks of the Citizens' Budget Commission and other groups unfriendly to the teachers. Furthermore, in recent years, greater use has been made of the radio in reaching the public. When an educational bill is pending, representatives of the teachers' organizations, especially from New York City, are so much in evidence in the corridors, galleries, and on the floor of the legislative chambers, that such uncomplimentary epithets as "racketeers" and "nuisances" have been hurled at teachers' representatives. At public hearings representatives from all over the state appear in tremendous delegations. From those who remain in their classrooms, floods of telegrams, letters, and petitions,[66] pour into the legislators' offices within two hours after the request is made by the teachers' legislative agents stationed at Albany. The legislative agent of the Joint Committee of Teachers' Organizations, in such a case, communicates with the president of the New York Principals' Association. The latter soon reaches the principals of more than 300 schools in New York City, each of whom calls his teachers together and issues to them the "instructions" that have come from Albany.

Upstate, where teachers are more scattered, the New York State Teachers' Association finds it more effective for letters and telegrams to come from prominent citizens, rather than from the teachers themselves. For this purpose, therefore, the Association seeks cooperation from labor, civic, parents',

---

[65] Section 525 of the Charter of the City of New York provides that moneys may not be contributed by teachers or educational administrators "to any fund intended to affect legislation increasing their emoluments."

[66] Letters are preferred to telegrams, except where time is an important element.

and women's groups. The secretary of the New York State Teachers' Association travels about 50,000 miles a year, discussing educational problems at the meetings of a wide variety of organizations, to which local legislators are invited and asked to participate in the discussions.[67] At the suggestion of the New York State Teachers' Association, a Plan and Scope Committee, composed of representatives of labor, parents', and civic organizations, was established during the summer of 1935 to assure the cooperation and support of these groups for the educational program of the Association before the opening of the legislative session.

One weapon used by the teachers is innate in the dignified position which education holds in the state. No legislator wishes to be branded an enemy of education. When salary cuts are imminent, therefore, the cry of "Economy at the Expense of our Children" is raised and much of the battle is already won. Agencies with prestige, such as the Citizens' Budget Commission in New York City, with a membership drawn from bankers', merchants', and civic organizations, often serve as a refuge for opposition legislators.

The chief weapon of the teachers, however, is the ballot box. Many of the associations have followed the practice of asking candidates for the Governorship and the Legislature for their views on educational problems. Contacts of this sort are encouraged by local teacher associations, so that the legislator is aware of the pressure in his own district. Both individual teachers and organizations usually receive prompt, favorable, and cordial replies.[68]

The possibilities of a pressure group of 85,000 "educators" acting in concert, aided by parents', labor, welfare, and civic

---

[67] Interview, Dr. Arvie Eldred, Sept. 4, 1935.

[68] Eighty-three per cent of the Democratic, Republican, and Socialist candidates for the State Legislature from New York City replied to the questionnaire submitted to them by the Joint Committee of Teachers' Organizations during the political campaign of 1934. Most of the candidates' answers to the eight questions listed in the questionnaire disclosed a most favorable attitude to the teachers' programs. See *Bulletin of the Joint Committee of Teachers' Organizations*, Oct. 30, 1934. *Cf.* John K. Norton, "Preparing for the Next Legislature," *New York State Education,* Oct., 1934, p. 43. Not infrequently, voluntary groups of teachers band together for the purpose of conducting non-partisan campaigns in the interests of specific candidates, such as the Non-Partisan Teachers' Committee to elect Frank J. Prial for comptroller in Oct., 1933.

associations, challenge one's imagination. The teachers' lobby
in the State of New York has made a good start toward
this goal.

Medicine

Of the organized professions, aside from the teachers, who
constitute additional streams of legislative pressure in New
York State, the most influential are those of medicine and
law. Medical practitioners are more numerous than lawyers,
and the number of organizations constituting the medical
lobby is, in consequence, distinctly larger.

Most important of the medical organizations is the Medical
Society of the State of New York, whose origin dates back
to a state law enacted on April 4, 1806, which authorized
qualified physicians of each county to organize themselves
into a county medical society for the purpose of examining
and licensing candidates for the practice of medicine, and
to organize a state medical society under the control of these
county societies. The state Society, founded February 2,
1807, had the same powers as its component county societies
and, in addition, could act as a Board of Appeal if candidates
were rejected by a county society.[69] The avowed purpose
of the Society, however, was chiefly the improvement of the
medical profession by federating into one compact organization the medical practitioners of the state and by securing
the enactment and enforcement of just medical laws.[70]

The membership of the state Society, consisting of all active
members in good standing of the component county medical
societies,[71] is divided into eight district branches. Each district branch governs itself under a constitution and by-laws
not inconsistent with those of the state Society.[72]

---

[69] *New York State Journal of Medicine*, 1931, p. 97.

[70] *Constitution of the Medical Society of the State of New York*, Art. I.

[71] Only one society in each county may be affiliated with the state Society.

[72] For reports of the activities of the district branches, see the convention
number of the *New York State Journal of Medicine*, Apr. 15, 1935. *The
Medical Directory of New York, New Jersey and Connecticut*, 1934, recorded
21,278 physicians in New York State, while the secretary of the New York
State Medical Society reported 13,172 dues-paying members, or 62 per cent
of these physicians. The Society is supported largely by the $10 dues paid
by the members. For details in the Medical Society budget, see annual
report of the treasurer in the *New York State Journal of Medicine*, Apr. 15,
1935, p. 368.

The chief governing agencies of the State Medical Society are the officers, a House of Delegates, a Council, an Executive Committee, a Board of Trustees, and a Board of Censors. The House of Delegates, the legislative body, is composed of delegates elected by the component county medical societies [73] and of the officers of the Society, the chairmen of standing committees, the trustees, and the past presidents and secretaries of the Society. The officers, trustees, and chairmen of the standing committees of the Society are elected by the House of Delegates.

The Council, composed of the officers of the Society, the chairmen of the standing committees, the editor-in-chief of the Society's official organ, the *New York State Journal of Medicine,* and the retiring president of the Society, constitutes the administrative body of the Society. It acts for the House of Delegates when the latter is not in session. The Council's most important duty is to select the Executive Committee of five members, three of whom must be councilors. These, together with the president, the secretary, the treasurer, and the immediate past president, conduct and supervise the daily work of the Society.

The five members of the Board of Trustees, one elected each year for a five-year term, manage the financial affairs of the Society and approve the budget of the Society, which is initiated by the Executive Committee.

The Board of Censors is composed of the president, the secretary, and the eight district councilors, who are the presidents of their respective districts. This board reviews appeals from decisions on discipline, privileges, rights, or standing of members of the component county medical societies.[74]

In addition to these agencies, there are a number of regular and special committees, such as those on Public Health, Economics, Public Relations, Insurance, Medical Research, and

---

[73] There is one delegate for each state assembly district in the county.

[74] A further appeal from the Board of Censors to the House of Delegates of the Society is possible. See pamphlet on *Principles of Professional Conduct of the Medical Society of the State of New York,* adopted June 1, 1931, and the *Constitution and By-Laws of the Medical Society of the State of New York.*

Legislation,[75] as well as a Legal Department, which assists members who are sued for malpractice.

At Albany, the Society is permanently represented by a legislative agent, a member of the medical profession, whose function it is to study and report on medical bills introduced into the legislature. In a recent session the legislative committee of the Society was thus furnished with information about 200 bills affecting the medical profession. At times, the legislative committee and the Albany representative invite the opinions of the county society legislative chairmen before deciding on a definite position, in order that the Society may, as far as possible, represent the views of the medical profession of the entire state. Despite this precaution, however, local medical societies, both member and nonmember groups of the state Medical Society, have at times opposed the position assumed by the legislative committee.[76] As a further assurance of united action, therefore, a conference is held in Albany early in the legislative session, attended by the county legislative chairmen, the legislative representative, and the legislative committee of the state Society. Bills affecting the medical profession, introduced or about to be introduced, are discussed at this conference in an attempt to effect unanimous agreement.[77]

While the legislative chairmen of the county societies inform local legislators of the position thus assumed, the state Society prepares a statement for each bill. One of these statements reads as follows:

Re:

The Medical Society of the State of New York is

IN FAVOR (*or* IN OPPOSITION)

of the above bill and asks your support of it for the following reasons:

This statement, submitted to the introducers of the bill, the chairmen of the legislative committees to which the bill has

---

[75] See annual reports for detailed accounts of the activities of these committees in the convention issue of the *New York State Journal of Medicine*.

[76] Interview, Dr. Harry Aranow, chairman of the Committee on Legislation of the Medical Society of the State of New York, Aug. 3, 1932.

[77] *Legislative Bulletin,* Feb. 4, 1935.

been referred, and the majority and minority leaders of the legislature, is also sent to the Governor if the bill is passed.

The progress of legislative bills of interest to the Society is recorded in bulletins [78] issued by the legislative committee of the Society, and in the descriptive letters accompanying copies of the bills that are sent to the legislative chairmen of the county societies, the Council of the state Society, and the editors of the county medical journals. The following excerpt from a legislative bulletin issued during the closing days of a session sheds some light on the legislative procedure, in which bills lying dormant for weeks come to life suddenly through the pressure of the Society:

> You have not had a bulletin in several days owing to the fact that adjournment of the Legislature seemed to be a daily possibility, but at this hour the end is not yet in sight. Several very important bills remain to be acted upon and an agreement upon them seems impossible to be reached.
>
> During this hectic time our troubles have been multiplying. On Wednesday the O'Brien osteopathy bill passed the Senate and was referred to the Committee on Rules in the Assembly, where it is still resting and we hope we can keep it there. On Wednesday, also Senator Feld reported out his chiropractic bill. On Thursday it came up for final reading in the Senate, was debated and referred to the Committee on Finance because it bears a clause that will require the expenditure of money. Later in the day the Finance Committee reported it back and it is now on the third reading calendar. Yesterday it was reached, but laid aside temporarily. It may be reached again today.
>
> On Thursday Senator Feld reported out the Berg Physiotherapy bill and it is now on the Senate third reading calendar and may be reached this morning.
>
> A podiatry bill appeared in the Assembly the other day and was promptly passed. On careful reading it is doubtful whether it is a good bill. We are holding it up temporarily in the Senate while we continue a study of it.

---

[78] Wide publicity is given to these bulletins. They are published in the *Journal of Medicine*, which is issued twice a month and is forwarded to each member of the Society.

Last night Senator McCall introduced in the Senate the Bernhardt antivivisection bill. The Bernhardt bill, of course, was an Assembly bill and has been definitely killed in committee, but Senator McCall's introduction of it in the Senate makes it necessary for us to kill it there. We hope to keep it in the Senate Codes Committee.[79]

Personal contacts with legislators are also an important element in the maneuvering of medical legislation. The legislative committee of the Society, for example, suggests to its county legislative chairmen that they call meetings of the members of their legislative committees to ascertain the names of the family physicians to the legislators. These physicians are then carefully informed of the legislative proceedings as they are reported in the bulletins, so that the legislators may be suitably advised.[80] In addition, letters are sent by prominent local physicians to such legislators as are suggested by the Society's legislative representative at Albany, who keeps a watchful eye on the results of the pressure applied in a particular locality. A great effort is also made to secure lay support for the passage or defeat of legislation. The county legislative chairmen are urged to inform their patients of this need.[81] And at public hearings on bills in which the Society is interested, the legislative representative of the Society is always accompanied by a number of prominent physicians and laymen.[82]

The Medical Society has been very emphatic in making known to the legislature and the general public that its interest in legislation is not based solely upon its desire to guard the material interests of its members, but to protect the interests of the general public. It opposes the influential lobby of osteopaths and chiropractors on these grounds, and attacks the "deadly serious" annual attempt of the endowed antivivisection society to secure the passage of its "dog bill" as a barrier to the development of scientific knowledge.[83]

---

[79] *Legislative Bulletin,* Apr. 8, 1933.
[80] *New York State Journal of Medicine,* 1931, p. 109.
[81] *Legislative Bulletin,* Mar. 3, 1933.
[82] Lay support carries potential weight at the ballot box. The Bronx Medical Society, in 1934, used its influence in an unsuccessful campaign to defeat for reelection Senator Berg of the Bronx.
[83] Interviews with Dr. Joseph S. Lawrence, legislative agent, Jan. 27, 1933,

Legislative activities of the Society thus bring it in contact with other organized groups in the state, chiefly health and welfare organizations whose positions on specific bills the Society either supports or opposes. Some of these are:

The New York State Osteopathic Society.
The New York State Chiropractic Society.
The Christian Scientists.[84]
New York Antivivisection Society.
New York State Nurses' Association.
American Association of School Physicians.
Sanitary Officers Association.
New York State Association of Public Health Laboratories.
New York State Pharmaceutical Association.

Furthermore, the Society's interest in the workmen's compensation law has often brought it into close contact with organized labor, the manufacturers, and the insurance companies. For example, until a satisfactory compromise was reached on the workmen's compensation law passed in 1935, the Medical Society supported Associated Industries and the insurance companies against organized labor. Similarly, the Society's support of a hospital and physicians' lien bill have brought the physicians, the bar associations, and the insurance groups together. In this case the Society offered to compromise by trading support for bills:

> We are informed that insurance companies and agents are soliciting the interest of physicians in opposing . . . bills for the creation of an exclusive State Insurance Fund. As you are aware, it is our intention to oppose the advancement of these bills. We are pleased to have this opportunity of cooperating in opposing the bills, but it is

Sept. 3, 1935, and Dr. Harry Aranow, chairman of the Committee on Legislation, Aug. 3, 1932.

[84] The Christian Science Committee on Publications for the State of New York presses the interests of the Christian Scientists at Albany. This committee, composed of just one person, is practically a general public relations committee, is appointed alternately each year by the readers of the three largest churches of Christ Scientist in the state and represents all the churches of the state. William W. Porter is the present Christian Science Committee on Publications for the State of New York. The personnel of this committee does not change at frequent intervals. In 1935 Mr. Porter went to Albany to seek an amendment to the jury duty bill, providing for the exemption of Christian Science practitioners. Both the bill and amendment failed to pass in the 1935 session of the legislature.

well to remember that our friends, the insurance companies and agents, are the principal ones opposing the advancement of our hospital and physicians' lien bill. We recommend, therefore, that before pledging your (county medical societies, chiefly) cooperation, you ask them in return, to withdraw their opposition to the lien bill.[85]

One of the most vigorously opposed organizations is the New York State Chiropractic Society, chartered in 1912 as a membership corporation, and representative of several hundred of the state's 1,500 practicing chiropractors.[86] This Society functions through a Board of Directors, an Executive Committee, several standing committees, and the 13 separate district societies affiliated with it. Its annual expenditures of $18,000 are defrayed by membership dues and assessments. Almost every year since its organization the Society has had a bill introduced into the legislature, providing for the licensing of chiropractors, and even though such a bill passed in the 1920 session, it was vetoed by the Governor.[87]

Despite the powerful opposition that comes chiefly from the Medical Society of the State of New York, however, the influence of the chiropractors has grown steadily at Albany. Its legislative activities are in charge of a legislative committee headed by the president of the Society, and of a legislative agent at Albany. A monthly *Bulletin,* with a circulation of about 100,000, carries the message of the chiropractors to laymen and members of the profession. An even wider public is reached through at least six public meetings held in strategic centers of the state, frequently with radio hook-ups. Lectures, demonstrations, and exhibits are the features of these public meetings, which are attended by legislators, public officials, and press representatives. Openly stressing among their members the importance of electing friendly legislators, the legislative committee of each district society contacts the legislative candidates to determine their attitude on chiro-

---

[85] *Legislative Bulletin,* Jan. 15, 1935.

[86] Dr. Sol Goldschmidt, former President of the Society, in interview, Sept. 24, 1935, was not willing to disclose the exact membership of the Society.

[87] In the sessions of 1934 and 1935 the chiropractors did not introduce their customary bills. The Society hoped in vain to enlist the support of the Board of Regents in the State Department of Education.

practic regulation. On the basis of such interviews, members are informed who such friendly candidates are.[88]

Another group whose legislative activities the Medical Society of the State of New York usually opposes is the New York State Osteopathic Society, composed of some 450 practicing osteopaths. In 1907, when a law was passed granting the license to practice osteopathy to those who had met the preliminary and professional educational requirements and passed a licensing examination,[89] this organization won a significant victory early in its history. Further concessions to permit osteopaths to use drugs and perform minor surgical operations have been the source of recent friction between the medical and osteopathic societies at Albany. In 1934 a bill providing for such privileges was passed by both the Senate and the Assembly, but vetoed by the Governor. A public hearing, however, preceded the veto—an indication of the effectiveness of the pressure exerted by the osteopaths.

In this connection, like the medical men and chiropractors, the osteopaths have made valuable contacts with state legislators through their patients, but unlike these groups they have made no open or systematic attempts to elect or defeat legislative candidates. They have at times secured promises from political leaders, however, that legislators would be left free to vote as they saw fit on osteopathic legislation.[90]

There are other organizations, however, which cooperate with the Medical Society of the State of New York in its legislative campaigns at Albany. One of these, the New York Academy of Medicine, is composed of some 2,000 Fellows who are, for the most part, physicians in metropolitan New York. Although the Academy and the Medical Society are separate and independent organizations, most of the Academy Fellows are members of the county medical societies affiliated with the Medical Society of the State of New York. The Academy is primarily interested in research aimed at the advancement of

---

[88] It should be noted that the New York State Chiropractic Society was not called upon to defend the charge of corruption brought by the medical men in 1932, although for a while it appeared that this charge would be subject to an investigation by Judge Samuel Seabury.

[89] An osteopath is a member of the State Board of Medical Examiners.

[90] Interview, Dr. Alexander Levitt, former President of the New York State Osteopathic Society, Oct. 30, 1935.

the science, rather than the economics, of medicine. Through
its Committee on Public Health Relations, however, the Academy keeps an eye on legislation affecting public health and
the practice of medicine. Recommendations to the legislature frequently result from its extensive investigations in these
fields. As a result, the Academy has built up a splendid record
of public service, chiefly in the administrative departments of
New York City.[91]

"Although we do not maintain a lobby at Albany," reads
one of the Academy's bulletins, "we pester the legislators at
each session with many missives sent by wire or by post." [92]
This pressure, though occasionally exerted by the Academy
on its own initiative,[93] is most frequently an adjunct to the
more vigorous legislative activities of the state Medical Society, and is of an educational nature.

Another organization that often cooperates with the Medical Society of the State of New York is the New York State
Nurses' Association, founded in 1901, chiefly for the advancement of the educational and professional standards of nursing.[94] The membership of this Association consists of 15,387

[91] See the annual reports of the Committee on Public Health Relations and
the *Bulletin* of the Academy, published monthly, for a record of such achievements. The Academy was instrumental in securing the transfer of the mari-
time quarantine at the Port of New York from state to national control.
Bulletin, Mar., 1926. See also pamphlet published by the Academy, *Veteran
Legislation and Its Relation to Health.*

[92] *Bulletin,* July, 1931, p. 258, and interview, Dr. E. H. L. Corwin, executive
secretary of the Committee on Public Relations, Apr. 29, 1932. Interview,
Dr. F. P. Reynolds, secretary of Committee on Medical Education, Mar. 16,
1933, and Dr. Iago Galdston, chairman of Press Relations Committee, Apr.
29, 1932.

[93] The law passed by the New York Legislature to develop spa treatment in
therapeutics at Saratoga Springs was sponsored by the Academy. See *Bulletin,* July, 1931, p. 528.

[94] This Association also cooperates with the American Nurses' Association,
with which it is affiliated; the New York League of Nursing Education, which
is primarily interested in nursing education and service; and the New York
State Organization for Public Health Nursing, which strives to effect a better
understanding and appreciation of nursing services on the part of the general
public. The latter organization possesses both lay and professional members.
Representatives of the New York League of Nursing Education and the New
York State Organization for Public Health Nursing are members of the Advisory Council of the New York State Nurses' Association, and may participate in the Board of Directors meetings without vote. These same privileges
are accorded the State Board of Nurse Examiners. *By-Laws of the New York*

registered nurses, representing 47 per cent of the registered nurses in the state, most of whom are found in the 14 district associations affiliated with the Association. Each of these district associations is made up of the alumnae associations within that area, which, in turn, are composed of graduate nurses of the local schools.[95] With the dues paid by the district associations, on a per capita basis of $2 annually, the Association expends about $30,000 annually for its administrative and legislative expenses, for benefits paid to needy nurses, and for its allotment of dues paid to the American Nurses' Association.[96] Since 1902, the Association has utilized the *American Journal of Nursing* as its official organ. In addition, in 1929, it began the publication of its own *Quarterly News.*

Like the state Association, with its six officers, its Board of Directors of eleven, its Executive Advisory Council, and its standing and special committees,[97] each district association and each alumnae group has its own constitution, officers, Board of Directors, and committees paralleling for the most part those established for the state Association.[98]

In cooperation with the New York League of Nursing Education, the New York State Organization for Public Health Nursing, and the State Board of Nurse Examiners, the New York State Nurses' Association seeks favorable state legislation. Its chief interest has long centered in the Nurse Prac-

---

State Nurses' Association, Art. 4, 8. Of these organizations, the New York State Nurses' Association is most active in pressure for legislation.

[95] In 1935 there were 152 alumnae associations. Graduate nurses who have had their training in schools outside of the district in which they reside join the district association as individual members. Letter of Emily J. Hicks, R.N., Executive Secretary, Jan. 3, 1936. Individual members in the district association are urged to retain contact with their alumnae association as non-resident members, paying non-resident dues. Honorary membership is also conferred, upon the unanimous recommendation of the Board of Directors at the annual meeting, on persons who have rendered distinguished service or valuable assistance to the nursing profession. *By-Laws,* Art. II, Sec. 2.

[96] Bulletin advertising, convention registration fees, and contributions are additional minor sources of revenue. *Annual Reports of Officers and Committees,* 1934, p. 6.

[97] Among the important standing committees are the Nurses Service Committee, the Public Information Committee, and the Legislative Committee. An important special committee was appointed recently to study the Nurse Practice Act. For accounts of the activities of these committees see *Annual Reports of Officers and Committees* for any recent year.

[98] Three of the 14 districts maintain offices. *Annual Reports of Officers and Committees,* 1935, p. 5.

tice bill, which became law in 1903 and was amended in 1920. In recent years the Association has made extensive studies in an effort to find what additional changes are needed and what steps may be taken to secure them.   In addition, the Association is also interested in general public health measures and joins with organizations which sponsor such bills.[99]   The executive secretary and the legislative committee of the Association utilize, for this purpose, the cooperation of the district legislative committees, which usually include in their membership, among others, the legislative chairmen of the alumnae associations.   A weekly bulletin is sent from Albany by the executive secretary to the chairman of each district legislative committee, and through her to the chairmen of alumnae associations' legislative committees.   These bulletins list and summarize bills of interest to nurses and report their progress.[100]

The chief pressure technique employed by the Association, however, is that of personal calls on legislators.   To this end, shortly after January 1st, there are dispatched to each district legislative chairman forms partially filled out in duplicate, one copy to be returned to state headquarters and the other to be retained by the district legislative chairman.   In addition to such routine information concerning each legislator in a particular district as his name, address, district, party, and business, this form also indicates the legislator's religious faith, his club membership, and his influential friends.   Blank spaces are included for "Representative who interviewed him" and "Report of interview."   When she receives the list of senators and assemblymen residing in her district, each district legislative chairman is instructed to indicate which legislative chairmen of the alumnae associations reside near legislators.   The instructions state: "These are key persons to interview, wire or write to legislators, in emergency.   As soon as you receive these forms, begin to study them immediately, in order to determine how best and through what channels you can reach each legislator if the emergency call comes from the state chairman."   Thus the state Association learns at first hand the

---

[99] See report of the Legislative Committee in *Annual Report of Officers and Committees*, 1935, p. 21.

[100] On occasion, the clipsheets of the Women's Joint Legislative Forum are attached and forwarded with these legislative bulletins. See *infra*, p. 217.

attitude of individual legislators toward nurses' bills pending before the legislature, and is able, by distributing detailed instructions to district chairmen, to see that wires, telephone calls, and letters reach legislators promptly when the necessity for such communication arises. With so well-ordered a system of legislative pressure, therefore, the cooperation of the New York State Nurses' Association is of much value to other groups.

Law

Just as the organized physicians of New York State exert legislative pressure chiefly through the Medical Society of the State of New York, so the lawyers act through the New York State Bar Association. Organized in 1876 for the purpose of promoting the scientific and professional standards of jurisprudence, the Association possesses about 5,000 members, most of whom are active practitioners of the legal profession in New York State.[101] The Association operates within an annual budget of approximately $45,000, derived almost entirely from the $10 annual dues paid by its members.

The directive agencies of the Association are the officers and the Executive Committee. Each of the nine judicial districts in the state is represented in the Association by a vice-president and by three members on the Executive Committee of 27. These three members also compose the district executive committee. The judicial district is likewise the basis of representation for many of the Association's standing and special committees.[102] A new slate of officers of the Association and of the members of its committees is elected at the annual meeting of the Association, after presentation by a committee on nominations.

The headquarters of the Association, supervised by the secretary,[103] is located in Albany, within reach of the Capitol.

---

[101] There are three classes of membership in the Association: active, associate, and honorary. Associate membership is open to members of the legal profession in good standing outside of New York. Among the honorary members are judges in the federal and higher state courts and numerous governmental officials who are resident members of the bar of the State of New York.

[102] See *Constitution and By-Laws* of the Association and the reports of these committees in the annual reports of the Association.

[103] Charles W. Walton, Secretary of the Association, served in the New York State Senate from 1915 to 1923.

From these headquarters is issued the monthly *Bulletin* of the
Association, containing scholarly discussions of legal matters
and reports of the legislature's business.[104]

   The state Association maintains close relations with the
county and local bar associations, as well as with regional federations of associations, in an effort to promote among them
cooperation and unified action.[105]   One reason for this is the
comparatively small membership of the New York State Bar
Association as the representative of the state bar.[106]   In this
respect it is sometimes outshone by a local group, such as the
Association of the Bar of the City of New York.[107]   To maintain leadership in legislative pressure activities, the cooperation of these local associations is consequently indispensable
to the state organization.[108]

   The legislative activities of the Association are in the charge
of a Legislative Committee of nine members, appointed by the
president.   After carefully studying bills introduced into the
legislature, this committee presents its attitude to the chair-

---

[104] It should be noted that there are important sections in the Association:
the Judicial Section made up of federal, state, and local judges residing in
New York State; and the District Attorneys' Section, until recently the District Attorneys' Association of the State of New York.   Each elects its own
officers and has its own constitution and by-laws.   These sections meet separately each year for conference, discussion, and interchange of ideas on the
duties, responsibilities, and welfare of their respective groups.   These discussions are followed by reports of activities and recommendations to the state
Bar Association.   See reports of the officers and the meetings of the Judicial
Section and the District Attorneys' Section in recent annual reports of the
New York State Bar Association.

[105] Integration of these local units has been achieved through the establishment of the group called the Presidents of the Federated and Local Bar Associations and the Committees on Character and Fitness of the State of New
York, which recently became a permanent section of the state Bar Association.
There are in New York State 57 county bar associations, 18 local bar associations, and 7 federations of bar associations with representation in this group.
See *Annual Report of the New York State Bar Association,* 1934, pp. 53, 870.

[106] There are about 30,000 persons who have been admitted to the bar in
New York.   The number actually in practice is not known.   Probably not
more than one out of every five practicing attorneys is a member of the state
Association.

[107] The Association of the Bar of the City of New York, through its Committee on State Legislation, also carefully examines and reports on bills pending in the State Legislature.   About 22,000 of the state's 30,000 practicing
lawyers, it should be noted, are to be found in the City of New York.

[108] There have been joint meetings of the presidents of the local bar associations and members on similar committees of these associations.   See *Annual
Report of the New York State Bar Association,* 1932, p. 43.

men of those committees in the legislature that may be considering the bills. In addition, such measures as are recommended by the numerous other committees of the Association are likewise under the Legislative Committee's control.

In order that the views of the legal profession may be brought before the legislators more frequently and directly, the state Bar Association, early in 1936, authorized the employment of a legislative reporter to be stationed at Albany for the purpose of keeping all local bar associations in the state informed on proposed or pending legislation of interest to the profession. The reporter does not have the authority to speak for any bar association or to transmit its views unless specifically authorized to do so by its president.[109]

That the New York State Bar Association has become a leader among the bar associations of the state is shown in the direct representation of the state Bar Association in the Commission on the Administration of Justice.[110] The state Association was largely responsible for the creation of this commission, in 1930, for the purpose of investigating thoroughly the judicial system of the state and to submit reports and recommendations to the legislature.[111] On this commission of sixteen are four members of the New York State Bar Association, appointed by the Governor and the legislative leaders, on the nomination of the president of the Bar Association, and six additional appointees of the Governor and six members of the legislature itself.[112] The commission has been continued since 1931 by annual authorization of the legislature, and as a result of its studies and recommendations the legislature has enacted much constructive judicial legislation.

Still wider opportunities for service have been given the state Bar Association with the recent establishment in New York State of a Judicial Council, a Law Revision Commission, and the Crime Conference called by Governor Lehman. Such has been the recognition of the Association's influence that

---

[109] New York Times, Jan. 6, 1936.
[110] Annual Report, 1932, p. 337.
[111] The necessity for such a survey was suggested by President William C. Breed in 1929.
[112] New York Legislative Manual, 1935, p. 504.

special committees of the state Bar Association have been established to aid these judicial agencies in carrying out their recommendations.[113]   Since these bodies are called upon to make recommendations to the legislature, greater legislative activity is required of the state Bar Association.   This activity takes the form, first, of study and, second, of pressure in promoting or defeating bills of a juridical nature.[114]

---

[113] *New York Times,* Oct. 20, 1935.   See *Annual Reports,* particularly in recent years.

[114] Isidor Lazarus, chairman of the Committee on Professional Economics of the state Bar Association, deploring the small membership in the Association, suggested that it could enroll a preponderance of the lawyers of the state if it embarked on a program of action, notably for the economic betterment of the legal profession. *Cf. New York Times,* Jan. 31, 1937.   For the objectives of the recently formed "progressive" National Lawyers Guild, which established a New York chapter, see *New York Times,* Dec. 16, 1936. The president of the Guild is Frank P. Walsh, chairman of the Power Authority of the State of New York.

CHAPTER VII

Other Groups

Public Service

A FOURTH[1] stream of minor pressure on the New York State Legislature proceeds from a host of organizations of public officials and employees[2] who are primarily interested in legislation affecting the administration of their particular offices. More effectively to achieve favorable legislation of this kind, these organizations, like the teachers' groups, have banded together in statewide associations, of which many are very active at Albany. Since most of these groups are strikingly similar in structure, it will suffice to examine six of the most active and influential ones to see the general pattern.

The Association of State Civil Service Employees of the State of New York, with headquarters in the state Capitol building at Albany, aims to extend the principle of merit in public employment and to advance the interests of civil service employees in general.[3] From 1910, when it was founded, to 1928, the activities of the Association were almost entirely social and its membership was limited to state employees in the classified civil service who were stationed at Albany. When, in 1928, membership was extended to all state employees[4] the number of members in the Association grew from 800 in 1928, to 12,200 in 1935.[5] With the annual dues of one

---

[1] See *supra*, ch. VI.

[2] See *A Directory of Organizations in the Field of Public Administration,* published by the Public Administration Clearing House, Chicago, 1936, p. 161. For the discussion of teachers, see *supra*, ch. VI.

[3] *New York Legislative Manual,* 1935, p. 494.

[4] Municipal, county, and other local civil service employees are not eligible for membership because the Association feels that such exclusion makes for a more compact organization, freer from internal dissension. The interests of state employees are held to be identical, whereas the interests of all civil service employees are not. Interview, William J. Pierce, Financial Secretary, Aug. 9, 1933. *Cf. The State Employee,* May, 1935, p. 9.

[5] There are approximately 30,000 state employees in New York. Of this number, 22,500 in the competitive and non-competitive services are eligible

dollar paid by each of these members, the Association is able to carry on its activities and show a favorable financial balance.[6]

The activities of the Association are directed by its officers, an Executive Committee, a General Committee, and a Special Advisory Committee. The officers constitute the executive division of the Association and receive no compensation for their services. The Executive Committee consists of the officers and one representative elected by each of the 18 administrative departments in the state. The General Committee, composed of representatives of such organizations as the State Hospital and the Highway Engineers' Association, as well as of the five administrative districts of New York, works with the Executive Committee in determining the Association's policies. Special committees are maintained on Retirement Fund, Budget and Salary, Educational and Recreational Activities, Program and Work, and Legislation. Annually a Special Advisory Committee of about 100 persons, representative of every office, institution, and bureau, wherever located in the state, is appointed.[7] By this means the state employees benefit from the advice and guidance of over 150 of their fellow workers who serve on the committees of the Association.

Among the outstanding accomplishments of the Association are the establishment of the retirement fund, the reclassification of state employees, the development of sound civil service practices, and favorable salary adjustments. In 1929, particularly, the Association played a part in securing the partial salary adjustment, and since then has fought vigorously against salary decreases.[8]

---

for membership in the Association. The remaining 7,500 constitute labor, exempt, and unclassified groups. The formation of local chapters of state employees was recently begun with the establishment of chapters in New York City and Buffalo.

[6] In 1934, the treasury balance was about $7,000. See *The State Employee,* Nov., 1934, p. 11.

[7] The State Hospital Association is represented by a special committee of five persons who meet with the other committees on all important matters.

[8] *New York Times,* Jan. 3, 1934. A well illustrated booklet on *Facts About Salaries Paid State Employees in New York State,* was prepared by the salary committee of the Association and placed before the Governor's Citizens Advisory Committee on Budget Economies in Nov., 1932. This, however, did not prevent reductions in the salaries of employees receiving more than $2,000 when the Governor and Legislature attempted to balance the budget in 1933. These reductions were restored in 1935. See summary of activities of the

Opposition to the Association's demands has come from industrial groups, particularly in the matter of salary adjustments. Moreover, the New York City civil service employees, under the leadership of Frank J. Prial, and the large and influential group of state employees who are in the exempt and unclassified groups and not eligible for membership in the Association, have often opposed the Association's recommendations.

In addition to its primary concern with civil service matters, the Association maintains some social activities. In 1931 a summer vacation camp was established in the Adirondack Mountains, which has afforded state employees the advantages of a vacation at low cost. Similarly, a number of courses in cultural and technical subjects are offered state employees through the medium of the Association.[9]

The Association's Committee on Legislation, consisting of three members under the leadership of the president of the Association, is assisted by the counsel to the Association in handling legislative problems. Hundreds of special statements explaining the Association's attitude toward legislation appear in the weekly bulletins that are distributed during legislative sessions, and in the official monthly periodical, *The State Employee*. The endorsement of bills favorable to the welfare of state employees is vigorously sought in the state platforms of both major parties. In addition, the Association seeks to discover the position of the candidates for the Governorship on matters of interest to state employees, and during the course of political campaigns it publishes such data.[10] Beyond this, however, the Association plays no further part

---

Association from 1929 to 1934 in report of retiring president, *The State Employee*, Nov., and Dec., 1934.

[9] During 1932–1933 these courses were taken by 265 state employees stationed in Albany. The following year a broader program was offered with arrangements to accommodate state employees throughout the state. *Program of the Institute of the New York State Civil Service Employees*, 1933–1934. In 1934 the Albany center of New York University, sponsored by the Civil Service Employees Association in cooperation with New York University, was established for the benefit of state employees. Three hundred and sixty-five state employees were registered during the first semester. *The State Employee*, Nov., 1934, p. 12; Jan., 1935, p. 5.

[10] See *The State Employee*, Oct.-Nov., and Dec., 1932.

in campaigns, for as an Association it does not endorse candidates for office.[11]

A second influential organization of public officials is the New York State Conference of Mayors, which represents at Albany such cities and villages in the state as have a population of at least 3,000.[12] Since the Conference is concerned exclusively with problems of efficient municipal administration, the basis of membership is the municipality. At an annual meeting the mayors elect the officers of the Conference, with the exception of the executive secretary, who is selected by the Advisory Committee, an executive body acting for the Conference between meetings.

The work of the Conference, financed chiefly, as it is, from the public funds of the member municipalities, under the authorization of state law, is largely educational. A Bureau of Municipal Information, supplying valuable facts to officials of cities and villages, is one of its most active agencies.[13] In addition, a Bureau of Training and Research operates training schools and institutes for municipal officials, alone or in cooperation with other agencies,[14] and conducts studies of municipal administration in conjunction with Syracuse University and other institutions.

An important part of the Conference's work is concerned with legislation. Although the Conference often offers assistance to the legislature in the preparation of bills, it does not

---

[11] Interview, Miss Beulah Bailey, President of the Association, Sept. 4, 1935. The Association looks to the Governor to veto legislation granting special privileges to individuals in the civil service, when such bills cannot be blocked in the legislature. All but two of such bills, for example, were vetoed by Governor Lehman in 1933. *The State Employee*, May-June, 1933, p. 6. For a recent program laid before Governor Lehman by the Association, see *The State Employee*, Jan., 1935, p. 3.

[12] The membership of the Conference represents the 60 cities, 54 first class villages, and 62 second class villages in New York State.

[13] In one year a total of 2,244 requests from officials was received and studied by the bureau, and more than 30,000 reports were distributed. See *Annual Report*, 1935, p. 100.

[14] During one year this bureau operated 39 training schools for 10 groups of municipal officials, with a total attendance of 7,652 officials. The Municipal Training Institute of New York State, chartered on Jan. 1, 1935, has since operated the Conference's training schools, in cooperation with the Conference and other agencies. *Annual Report*, 1935, pp. 23, 101.

actually draft bills or request their introduction.[15] Nevertheless, a legislative program adapted to municipal needs is prepared by the Advisory Committee, in consultation with the municipalities, and presented to the Governor and the State Legislature at the beginning of each regular session.[16] Moreover, a Legislative Committee of seven members meets every week during the legislative session and studies all bills introduced that affect municipal administration. Summaries of the Conference's action on these bills are then sent to the member municipalities and villages.

In 1935 the Conference studied 322 bills introduced into the legislature. The Conference approved 54 and disapproved 100. Of the approved bills, 27 passed the legislature, and four were vetoed by the Governor. Of the 100 bills disapproved, 25 passed the legislature, but of these all but nine were vetoed by the Governor. In other words, 74 per cent of the Conference's recommendations were effective. It is by virtue of such accomplishments that the New York State Conference of Mayors occupies an important place among the governmental pressure groups at Albany.[17]

Legislation specifically relating to any one of the larger cities is the concern of a special representative sent from the city affected. This may be the Mayor or some other high official. More often, however, it is a specially-designated person known to the legislature as the representative of the city administration.[18]

Somewhat similar to the State Conference of Mayors is the Association of Towns of the State of New York, founded in February, 1933, as a centralized agency for united opposition to a growing movement for the abolition of town government

---

[15] See Art. IX, Sec. 4 of the *Constitution of the New York State Conference of Mayors*.

[16] In 1935 this program contained 33 recommendations, of which the Governor and Legislature approved 12. *Annual Report, 1935,* p. 101.

[17] Interview with William P. Capes, Executive Secretary of the Conference at Albany, Feb. 1, 1933 and Sept. 6, 1935. See also pamphlet published by the Conference, *Municipal Cooperation and Its Results.*

[18] The City of New York is represented by a well known figure in official circles, Reuben A. Lazarus, Assistant Corporation Counsel, whose activity for the city at the state Capitol covers a continuous period of more than twenty years. Interview, Mar. 12, 1936. Buffalo, too, has been represented for more than twenty-five years by Andrew Ronan, Assistant Corporation Counsel.

in New York State.　For this purpose the Association of Towns maintains an office in Albany during legislative sessions, from which pressure is directed for and against bills relating to town government.　In addition, its Committee on Laws and Legislation works with its executive officers to prepare a constructive legislative program, while every township bill introduced into the legislature is studied and watched. Periodically the Association reports to its members on the reception and progress of such bills.　Thus, despite its recent inception, the Association of Towns has become a clearing house of ideas and a distributor of valuable information on town government as well as a pressure group worthy of attention.[19]

More influential and much older than the Association of Towns is another public service organization, the Firemen's Association of the State of New York.　Established in 1872, this Association has grown in number and strength until its membership today represents more than 150,000 volunteer firemen in the state.[20]　By state law two per cent of the public tax revenues derived from foreign stock fire insurance premiums is set aside for the support of volunteer fire organizations in return for the gratuitous services rendered by their members to the state.　This fund constitutes the income of the Association.[21]

Of the two chief services rendered by the Association to its members, the first is the maintenance of a home for incapaci-

---

[19] Two years after its establishment, 251 towns representing 52 counties in the State of New York were members of the Association.　(July, 1935.)　A town becomes a member of the Association by the adoption of a resolution and the payment of annual dues.　Dues are computed upon the assessed valuation of the towns.　By state law the towns are permitted to contribute to the support and maintenance of the Association (chapter 412 of the laws of 1933).　Individual membership in the Association is open to present or former town officers upon the payment of $2.00 dues per year.　See *The Town Crier, the Official Year Book of the Association of Towns of the State of New York,* 1935.

[20] See W. H. Swartwout, "New York State Firemen's Association: An Historical Sketch," *Firemen's Journal,* Aug., 1933.　The membership is composed of volunteer firemen, volunteer fire departments, fire districts, firemen's benevolent associations, exempt or veteran firemen's associations, and county and regional associations of local volunteer firemen's groups.

[21] For the fiscal year ending June 30, 1935, this amounted to approximately $80,000.　It should be noted that in New York City and Buffalo, provision for volunteer firemen's organizations is also made in the city charters.

tated ex-volunteer firemen at Hudson, N. Y. Founded in 1895, this home, under the supervision of a special Board of Trustees, has cost the Association more than $100,000 annually.[22] The second service is concerned with the protection of firemen's interests in the State Legislature from the hostile pressure exerted by such groups as the New York State Conference of Mayors and the Citizens' Budget Commission of New York. For this purpose the Association has sought to affiliate with it all volunteer firemen's organizations in the state, so that a unified legislative program might be formulated and a definite plan of action adopted. Thus, the annual conventions and the legislative committee of the Association are widely representative of local firemen's groups.[23]

The chief agency of the Association is its Law Committee, which maintains permanent offices in Albany, under the chairmanship of the Association's attorney. In October of each year, the Law Committee, at a meeting of the executive officers of the Association and representatives of the various regional and county organizations, tentatively formulates a legislative program. Such a program may include proposals for the advancement in prestige and power of volunteer firemen in general, but for many years its chief objective has been to prevent any change in the two per cent tax law referred to above.

When this program has been formulated, copies are distributed to the law committees of all the local associations for criticism or approval. On the basis of the reaction of these local committees, the Association's Law Committee determines its final program. The introduction of the bills, arranged by the chairman of the Law Committee, is accompanied by interviews with the Governor and other influential officials.

With such a centralized plan of action, the Association's recommendations have commanded serious attention at Albany, and more than 80 per cent of them have been enacted into law.[24] An important reason for this is the voting strength

---

[22] *Proceedings of the Firemen's Association of the State of New York,* 1935, pp. 93, 190.

[23] The four-day annual convention is attended by some 800 delegates. See *Proceedings.*

[24] Significantly, Seth T. Cole, the salaried chairman of the Association's Law Committee and, therefore, its legislative agent at Albany since 1934, has been

of the 150,000 volunteer firemen who, with their families, command respect in the smaller communities, and who can often dictate the political future of certain members of the legislature. Friendly legislators are generously praised by the Law Committee in its reports to the local groups, and even greater publicity is given them at annual conventions. Caustic comment is often made on their opponents.[25]

What the Firemen's Association of the State of New York does for volunteer firemen, the New York State Firemen's Legislative Committee does for approximately 20,000 paid firemen in the state. Organized in February, 1932, the committee is affiliated with the International Association of Fire Fighters and the American Federation of Labor. The committee, composed of six representatives of local paid firemen's associations in the state, operates informally, without a constitution or by-laws. At a meeting held at least once a year, usually in December, the committee receives representatives from different parts of the state, who bring with them legislative proposals. On the basis of these proposals, a legislative program for the paid firemen is prepared and submitted to the legislature and the Governor. It is the committee's task to translate this program into law and to protect the paid firemen from inimical legislation. The local firemen's associations are kept informed of the progress of the bills and the pressure that is required from them. Like similar organizations, the committee also urges local groups to cooperate in supporting candidates for the legislature who are friendly to firemen's interests. Although it frequently distributes questionnaires to ascertain candidates' views, the committee

---

at the same time head of the Law Bureau of the State Department of Taxation and Finance. See detailed report of the Law Committee of the Firemen's Association of the State of New York for 1935 in *Officers Report,* p. 141, and in *Proceedings,* p. 238. See also the *Annual Report of the New York State Conference of Mayors,* 1935, p. 18.

[25] Among others, Governor Lehman addressed the convention of August, 1934, during his campaign for reelection. In his address he reviewed his approval of many bills to "increase the protection and benefits accorded to the volunteer firemen," and said that he would not look with favor upon attempts to deprive them of the two per cent tax revenue. *Proceedings,* 1934, pp. 222, 416.

looks to the larger national organizations with which it is affiliated for additional support in its legislative endeavors.[26]

The final pressure group of public employees deserving notice is the State Police Conference, composed of police organizations in the cities, counties, towns, and villages of the State of New York. Founded in 1924, this organization represents approximately 38,000, or 98 per cent, of the policemen of all ranks in the state.[27]

The organization of the Conference is very simple. Delegates of the local police organizations meet in convention annually. The president of the Patrolmen's Benevolent Association of the city in which the convention is held automatically becomes president of the State Police Conference for that year. There is only one additional officer, a secretary, who holds this position for an indefinite period. The Conference has no constitution, no by-laws, and no budget. Such expenses as are incurred at the annual convention are defrayed by the local member organizations and from the proceeds of a social function held at the time of the convention.

The Conference's committees function, for the most part, only at the time of the convention, except for the Legislative Committee. Since the latter is the most important agency of the Conference, it is assisted by special committees appointed from time to time to conduct particular studies. Usually the legislative work of the Conference begins in the annual convention, at which the Resolutions Committee receives such suggestions as the delegates may wish to submit. On the basis of these suggestions, a program is prepared and submitted to the delegates for their approval before the convention adjourns. The Legislative Committee of four members is then elected. Two of these four members belong to the Patrolmen's Benevolent Association of New York City, which has 18,000 police members.[28] This Legislative Committee prepares the bills and forwards them to the local member organ-

---

26 Interview, Vincent K. Kane, President of the Uniformed Firemen's Association of Greater New York and a member of the New York State Firemen's Legislative Committee, Nov. 6, 1935.

27 The City of Endicott, built up around a single industry, is not represented in the State Police Conference.

28 It has been the practice of the convention to reelect the same men for many years.

izations of the State Conference for approval. Unlike the procedure in most organizations, the legislative program of the Conference is prosecuted in Albany by the Legislative Committee rather than by a specially assigned legislative agent.

In its annual legislative program, the State Police Conference has found it advisable to concentrate on one or two major planks. In addition, in recent years its chief aim has been to block legislation inimical to the interests of the police. The Conference relies upon local organizations to exert the pressure necessary to win over individual legislators. In addition, resolutions by civic organizations endorsing police legislation are invited. Because of their unique relation with the general public, however, the police do not seek pre-election pledges from legislative candidates to guide them in voting.[29]

Veterans

The legislative activities of organized war veterans, although conducted chiefly in Washington, constitute also one of the more powerful of the minor pressures directed at the New York State Legislature. This fact becomes apparent when one realizes that there are more veterans' laws in New York than in any other state in the Union.[30] Such pressure comes, for the most part, from the New York departments maintained by seven organizations of veterans, listed below in the order of origin:

1. The Grand Army of the Republic.
2. The United Spanish War Veterans.
3. The American Legion.
4. The Disabled American Veterans of the World War.
5. Veterans of Foreign Wars of the United States.
6. The Army and Navy Union of the United States.
7. The Jewish Veterans of the Wars of the Republic, Inc.

---

[29] Interview, Thomas P. Cummings, Secretary of the Patrolmen's Benevolent Association of New York City, Nov. 6, 1935. *Cf.* letter of Peter Keresman, Secretary of the State Police Conference, Oct. 31, 1935.

[30] It has been so admitted by officials of veterans' organizations. Interview, J. J. Fitzpatrick and Joseph Fitzgerald, legislative representatives at Albany of the United Spanish War Veterans and the Veterans of Foreign Wars of the United States, Feb. 8, 1933. *Cf. New York State Veterans Laws,* 1932, 1935.

Chief among these, in number of members and extent of influence, is the New York State Department of the American Legion, whose membership, consisting of 75,000 honorably discharged World War veterans, is equivalent to three times the combined membership of all other veterans' organizations in the state. Composed of younger, more energetic men, the American Legion has thus been able to assume leadership among veterans' groups [31] and to build more extensively on the foundation laid before the World War by the Grand Army of the Republic and the United Spanish War Veterans. The veterans' lobby in New York may, therefore, be adequately understood by an examination of the New York Department of the American Legion.

historical

This department, founded in Rochester in the fall of 1919, within a few months after the birth of the national body, is organized on a pyramidic territorial arrangement. The smallest unit is the Post. Above it are the county, district, and state divisions. The annual department convention, the legislative body, is composed of county delegates and alternates,[32] whose deliberations, like those of other veterans' organizations, are published at the expense of the state.[33] The executive

---

[31] It should be noted, however, that the Legion is sometimes opposed by other veterans' organizations and occasionally by some of its own Posts, though cooperation is more frequent. This opposition was combined with the hostility of such groups as the State Charities Aid Association and the New York State Association of Public Welfare Officials, for example, when the Legion sought in 1935 to amend the Public Welfare law so that veteran relief might be administered by joint veteran welfare committees selected on a proportional basis. The bill passed the legislature in 1935, but was vetoed by the Governor. *Proceedings of the American Legion, Department of New York,* 1935, p. 135.

[32] Each county is entitled to four delegates, four alternates, and one additional delegate and alternate for every 250 members. At recent conventions there have been some 600 such delegates and 600 alternates. The latter have the same privileges as the delegates, including service on committees, but vote on the floor of the convention only in the absence of delegates. Representation from 32 counties constitutes a quorum. *By-Laws,* Art. IV.

[33] Fifteen hundred dollars is appropriated annually for the publication of 5,000 copies of the *Proceedings of the American Legion, Department of New York. Cf. New York State Veterans Laws,* 1932, p. 51, and *Proceedings,* 1935, p. 116. The department is represented on the National Executive Committee of the American Legion by one member and one alternate elected for two years by the department convention. It is also represented at the national convention by five delegates-at-large, five alternates-at-large, and one additional delegate and alternate for each 1,000 members. These are also elected at the department convention.

officers are the department commander,[34] three vice-commanders, a treasurer, a department chaplain, and a department historian. There is also a department adjutant, who has secretarial functions, and a department judge advocate, the legal adviser of the organization.[35] Both of these are appointed [36] by the department Executive Committee, the administrative agency between conventions, which is composed of the commander, vice-commanders, and treasurer, as well as the national executive committeemen and the district commander of each of the nine judicial districts in the state. The nine district commanders, as the chief executives of their respective district units,[37] are also the links between the department, the county units, and the Posts, within their districts.

The Post, the local unit of the Legion, may be organized by 15 members under a charter issued by the national commander with the approval of the county committee and the department Executive Committee. The dues paid by the members of the 840 Posts constitute the chief source of income of the larger units, including the state department and the national organization.[38] The department's budget, totalling some $40,000 annually, defrays expenses incurred for its admin-

---

[34] The commander is the executive head of the department, and, though not eligible for reelection, he is a life delegate to all department conventions.

[35] Departmental activities are conducted also through various standing committees. For a list of such committees, see *By-Laws*, Art. III.

[36] The adjutant serves indefinitely, the judge advocate for one year.

[37] District units have their own by-laws, committees, and officers, the latter being elected annually by the district delegates to the department convention. County units, similarly organized under the supervision of the department Executive Committee, exist in 61 counties, the legislative body being the county committee. There is no such unit in Hamilton, since this county is largely forest land, with a population of some 4,000. County officers are elected by the county committee, composed of one representative from each Post in the county, with one additional representative for each additional 100 members or major fraction thereof.

[38] Although the constitution of the department sets a minimum of $2 a year for dues, they vary among the Posts from $3 to $10. The average dues are $5 or $6, higher where a club-house is maintained by the Post. The Post turns over to the county an amount determined by a regularly convened county convention, usually 25¢ or 50¢; $1.50 per member is paid to the department. Of this amount, 50¢ per member is retained by the department, the balance of $1 per member being forwarded to the national organization. For the fiscal year ending Sept. 30, 1935, the New York Department turned over to the national organization $73,625. *Proceedings*, 1935, p. 43. *Cf. Constitution and By-Laws of the American Legion, Department of New York.*

istrative work, field work, welfare work,[39] conventions, and the
publication of the *New York State Legionnaire,* a bulletin
distributed from time to time to the executive officers of the
various units in the state.[40]

To assist the Legion in its activities, there is an American
Legion Auxiliary, composed of mothers, wives, daughters, and
sisters of honorably discharged veterans, which is concerned
particularly with educational and welfare work, such as the
rehabilitation of disabled veterans and the maintenance of
health camps for children.[41] Organized in much the same way
as the Legion itself, the Auxiliary has 24,640 members, holds
its own conventions, and spends about $23,000 annually.[42]
Legislative activities undertaken by the Auxiliary are dependent upon the endorsement of the Legion itself; the Auxiliary
never follows a policy which does not coincide exactly with
the Legion's stand. The women are expected to win support
for the Legion's program by letters and telegrams to legisla-

---

[39] Funds are raised from special sources to send home at Christmas time
veterans without means domiciled in hospitals in the state. The American
Legion Mountain Camp on Big Tupper Lake, owned and operated by the
New York Department of the American Legion, offers two services. One is a
convalescent area for the care of sick World War veterans, supported from the
proceeds of poppy sales and donations, which is open five months of the year.
The second is a recreational area, with accommodations for 675 guests, open
to members of the American Legion and their families for vacations at
nominal cost. The recreational and convalescent areas are one mile apart.
Proceedings, 1935, pp. 61, 199.

[40] *Proceedings,* 1935, p. 62. The national organization publishes *The American Legion,* a monthly that is forwarded to each member of the American
Legion. It should be noted that Legion headquarters at different points
throughout the state require no expenditure for rent. Other veteran organizations in New York State receive similar advantages, including the use of
public buildings in localities without expense or at nominal rent. See *New
York State Veterans Laws,* 1932, pp. 106–111.

[41] *Proceedings of the American Legion Auxiliary, Department of New York,*
1935. The Auxiliary is also affiliated with Fidac, an association of women's
auxiliaries of veterans' organizations in the nations allied during the World
War, which was organized in Rome in 1925. See *Unit Handbook of the
American Legion Auxiliary,* prepared at national headquarters, Indianapolis,
1936. The Legion and the Auxiliary interest themselves also in the work of
the Sons of the American Legion, Junior Auxiliaries, and boy and girl scout
groups.

[42] In addition, in 1935, the department auxiliary paid $6,707.43 to the na-
tional auxiliary. The bulk of the Auxiliary's funds is derived from annual
dues of from $2 to $5 per member. *Proceedings of the American Legion
Auxiliary, Department of New York,* 1935, p. 11.

tors and addresses delivered to other women's organizations in the community.[43]

The legislative program of the Legion, based upon resolutions adopted at the annual department convention, is prepared, some time before the legislature convenes, by the Legislative Committee of the department, consisting of ten members.[44] When the bills have been introduced into the legislature, pressure for their enactment comes chiefly from the Veterans' Conference, a group organized in 1920, shortly after the founding of the Legion itself. This Conference is composed of legislators who served in the World War and the Spanish American War.[45] Each year early in the legislative session the Veterans' Conference meets and selects officers and a steering committee of six legislators. To the Veterans' Conference and its steering committee, as well as to the Governor, the legislative program of the American Legion is presented. The steering committee, working in close cooperation with the Legislative Committee of the Legion and such other veteran organizations as may be interested in the measures, studies the program, often holding hearings before it decides what stand it will take. The members of the steering committee, especially assisted by other members of the Veterans' Conference, play an active part in introducing and in maneuvering through the legislature the bills which have been approved. As a testimonial to their work, a dinner is held at Albany in honor of the members of the Veterans' Conference in January of each year, under the auspices of the Legion's Legislative Committee. The dinner is frequently attended by the Governor, leg-

---

[43] Interview, Mrs. Ida N. Ashby, Secretary-Treasurer, Feb. 19, 1936. *Cf. Unit Handbook,* 1936, p. 32, and *Proceedings,* 1935, p. 57.

[44] Although the vote on legislation at the convention is theoretically binding on all members, occasionally individual Posts or Legionnaires appear in Albany in opposition to the stand taken at the annual convention. *Proceedings,* 1935, pp. 31, 135, 175–182. The convention may authorize the appointment of a special committee to study, prepare, and take the necessary steps for the introduction into the legislature of a particularly important but controversial bill, such as the bill to amend the Public Welfare law in connection with the administration of veteran relief. See *supra,* p. 205, note 31.

[45] In 1935 there were 54 World War veterans in the legislature, though in 1920 there were only 9. *Proceedings,* 1935, p. 116. In 1936 there were 56 World War veterans of whom two served also in the Spanish American War. Letter, Assemblyman John P. Hayes, Mar. 17, 1936.

islative leaders who are not veterans, and other high state officials.[46]

When there is opposition, the Legion usually attempts to overwhelm the legislature with letters and telegrams from veterans and their wives back home. And in addition, the leaders attempt to see that large delegations of veterans attend all hearings. Bulletins sent by the chairman of the Legislative Committee to the 840 Posts in the Legion and the 600 units in the Auxiliary stimulate immediate action. For example, when an important amendment to the Public Welfare law was pending in 1935, the chairman of the department Legislative Committee dispatched two bulletins to the various Posts and Auxiliary units throughout the state, requesting both the men and the women to communicate with their legislators. The effectiveness of this response was amply demonstrated when the units of the Auxiliary alone received 178 letters of acknowledgment from the legislators.[47] In 1935, moreover, the department was actively interested in 22 bills introduced into the New York State Legislature. In the case of 14 the action of the Legislature coincided with the Legion's stand: 12 bills that were endorsed by the American Legion passed the Legislature, but four were vetoed by the Governor; and two disapproved by the American Legion were defeated in the Legislature.[48]

Some idea of the large number of laws affecting war veterans that have been passed in New York State may be gained from an examination of these statutes which were compiled in one volume by the state in 1930 and revised and brought up to date in 1932 and 1935 at a cost of $3,500.[49] These compila-

---

[46] *Proceedings*, 1935, pp. 117, 136.

[47] *Proceedings of the Auxiliary*, 1935, p. 57.

[48] In addition, the usual annual appropriation of $1,500 for the printing of the Legion's convention proceedings was approved. *Proceedings of the American Legion, Department of New York*, 1935, p. 113, and *Proceedings of the American Legion Auxiliary, Department of New York*, 1935, p. 57.

[49] *The New York State Veterans Laws* (revised edition), 1932, and the supplement, 1935, sell for 25¢ per set. Prior to the appearance of these volumes, compilations of veteran laws affecting their own veterans appeared in the *Proceedings of the New York Department of the Grand Army of the Republic* and in that of the *United Spanish War Veterans*. In 1929, the American Legion published in book form the laws of New York affecting all veterans of the wars of the United States.

tions of veteran laws in New York State give a detailed account of the benefits won for veterans by their organizations. These preferences and advantages reach into many varied fields, including pensions, bonus, civil service, exemptions, licenses, quarters, and relief.

For such a record of accomplishments in the interests of veterans by veteran organizations, particularly by the American Legion and its Auxiliary, there are three reasons. In the first place, the demands are made by veterans of the wars of the United States primarily on patriotic grounds. In the second place, the American Legion, working through a regularly constituted agency of over 50 veteran legislators, the Veterans' Conference, is represented, though not officially, on almost all the committees to which bills affecting veteran interests are referred. The dinner in honor of the veteran legislators, early in the legislative session, creates an atmosphere of goodwill. Furthermore, the department commander and the chairman of the Legislative Committee of the Legion who contact the legislature are selected with care. They know and are known by a large number of legislators; some of them have themselves served in the legislature.[50]

Finally, the American Legion and its Auxiliary alone, exclusive of the other veterans' organizations and their auxiliaries, represent a combined membership of 100,000 individuals throughout the entire state, substantial numbers of them living in all legislative districts. While the constitution of the American Legion, Department of New York, expressly states that it is "absolutely non-political and shall not be used for the dissemination of partisan principles nor for the promotion of the candidacy of any person seeking public office or preferment," [51] legislators do not wish to encourage the ill feeling of so large a number of voters.[52] Thus, the veterans join the list

---

[50] Edward J. Neary, for example, was a member of the State Legislature before he held the positions of department commander, chairman of the Legislative Committee, and national committeeman in the American Legion, Department of New York. Interview with Mr. Neary, Apr. 27, 1933.

[51] Art. II.

[52] Legislators friendly to the Legion's program are prominently mentioned in the Legion's *Proceedings,* 1935, p. 117. At the annual convention in 1936, the department commander stated: "The Legion should not be tailed to any political party's kite. It should, however, show its appreciation to friends of the Legion regardless of political affiliation. There is no reason, when we go

of pressure groups whose chief strength lies in their numerical following, such as those of labor, the farmers, the teachers, and the parents.

Women's and Civic Groups

A sixth minor stream of legislative pressure in New York State proceeds from civic organizations that exist primarily to promote social and political progress. Some of the most influential of these are groups composed entirely of politically-minded women, such as the New York League of Women Voters. Organized in 1920 as an affiliate of the newly-formed National League of Women Voters,[53] this organization is concerned with the political education of women. Its membership of some 12,000 women is composed of local leagues in the state,[54] while its organization is modeled on that of the National League. Its officers consist of a chairman, five vice-chairmen, a treasurer, a secretary, and 14 directors, one for each of the regions into which the state is divided. These directors are elected for a term of two years. The eight officers and 14 regional directors constitute the Board of Directors. The Board of Management of the League consists of the officers and the regional directors, the five borough chairmen of the City of New York, and the chairmen of the standing committees. In general, the Board of Management develops and recommends ways and means for more efficient and enlarged activities.

The structural organization of the League is decentralized, since it is organized on the basis of counties and boroughs,

---

to the polls, why we should not show our recognition of friends who have aided us." *New York Times,* Sept. 4, 1936.

[53] In 1920, when the National American Woman Suffrage Association was dissolved as a result of the successful achievement of its purpose, Mrs. Carrie Chapman Catt instigated the organization of this League as a permanent group devoted to the political education of the newly enfranchised women.

[54] The New York League functioned in 1933, a depression year, with a $28,000 budget, of which $13,000 was derived from the counties in quotas. The sum of $9,600 was raised by the Finance Committee from contributions, the remainder from dues and contributions for the *Weekly News* and other publications. Fifty cents of the $1.00 dues paid by each member of the local leagues is turned over to the state treasurer to defray expenses connected with the *Weekly News*. The state and local leagues cooperate with the national organization in all matters, including legislation. See *Program of Work for the National League of Women Voters, 1932–1934,* Apr., 1932.

each with a leader and such other officers as may be needed. Counties may be divided into local league units, provided there are at least 25 active members for the purpose. The elected officers of the county and of the local league units and the members of the standing committees of the state League form the County Board, which is responsible for the development of a study program for the county. The state League suggests the subjects for such study, though local units are not required to follow these suggestions. For this purpose, the state League, like its national prototype, maintains the following seven committees:

Government and Child Welfare.
Government and Education.
Government and Its Operation.
Government and International Cooperation.
Government and Legal Status of Women.
Government and Economic Welfare—Labor Section.
Government and Economic Welfare—Consumer Section.

Each committee is composed of one representative of a similar study committee in each of the local leagues, acting under the supervision of a chairman selected by the Board of Directors. These committees select items for study which are voted upon at the state convention.[55] Some of the topics may be taken from the national program of work.

The results of these studies are remarkably fruitful. Kits are prepared by each committee, outlining the program for study, with references which may be purchased at the League's headquarters listed under each topic. A large number of the references listed are studies that have been made by the League itself through these committees. The committee on Government and Its Operation, for example, will prepare a detailed pamphlet on how to conduct a round table discussion on Proportional Representation for the use of the committees on Government and Its Operation of the local leagues.

Out of the studies made by these groups usually arises a legislative program. The state legislative program is tenta-

---

[55] The annual convention is held between election day and Dec. 15. Each county is entitled to one delegate to the convention for every 25 members. Chairmen of county, borough, and local league units are delegates ex officio.

tively prepared by the New York League's Legislative Committee—composed of one member from each local league unit, the chairmen of the state committees, and the chairman of the state League—at its bi-weekly meetings.[56] The tentative program is then sent to the county and local league chairmen for their criticism. When the tentative program has been revised, it is published in the *Weekly News* and sent to all members in the state two weeks before the state convention. This allows time for discussion by the local leagues. The program is then submitted to the state Board of Management, which presents it to the annual convention for its approval, item by item. The legislative program as finally adopted by the convention appears in the *Weekly News,* usually in December. The form is simple:

THE LEGISLATIVE PROGRAM—1933

1. Women jurors.
2. Reorganization of county government.
3. Maintenance of essential governmental services and improved standards for education, health, child welfare, labor.
4. Readjustment of the local tax burden.
5. Unemployment insurance, state regulation of private employment agencies and increase of public employment agencies.[57]

Legislative pressure at Albany must first be authorized by the Legislative Committee. This restriction applies even to state legislation affecting a particular locality, which was requested by a local league but which was not included in the state legislative program. The League is represented at

---

[56] The chairman of the Legislative Committee is appointed by the state chairman with the approval of the Board of Management. Minutes of the meetings are dispatched to every local member of the Legislative Committee. Many local members of the committee, particularly those from upstate, do not attend the meetings because of their frequency. They are, therefore, urged to read the minutes carefully and to send suggestions from local members to the chairman of the Legislative Committee. Recommendations for the inclusion of topics in this legislative program come usually from the chairmen of the standing committees.

[57] *Weekly News,* Dec. 9, 1932. Although the local leagues are not required to support every item in either this or the national program, they may not oppose any proposal adopted at the state or national conventions.

Albany by a legislative secretary [58] who receives her instructions from the chairman of the Legislative Committee. She, in turn, reports to the Legislative Committee the status of bills and what action is necessary.

The chief pressure methods employed by the League, to supplement the work of its study groups, have been (1) seeing and informing the local legislator, (2) seeking the active cooperation of other organizations, (3) interrogating candidates for public office and informing the electorate accordingly, and (4) seeking the assistance of public opinion by publicity.

The organization of the League in small local units has proved to be a convenient way of reaching individual members in the state Assembly and Senate. Local members of the state Legislative Committee are urged to see their assemblyman or senator before the January session opens, and to discuss the entire legislative program with them. Brief reports, sent to the chairman of the Legislative Committee by these local members, indicate the attitude of the legislators on each measure, and are put to good use when the legislative representative appears in Albany during the session. Requests for telegrams and letters to legislators, moreover, are relayed to the members of the League through the local representative of the state Legislative Committee.

The New York League of Women Voters was among the active organizations represented in the New York Women's Joint Legislative Conference, which determined to put a forty-eight-hour bill for women on the statute books in New York. In the course of this campaign the League published the significant pamphlet on the *Daly Lobby*.[59] The League, furthermore, was a very active member of the Marriage Law Committee, created in 1925, in which 25 organizations cooperated in order to place greater restrictions on child marriages.[60] The files of the League's office are replete with messages to legislators unfriendly to the child marriage legislation, and to such women as those on the Republican State Com-

---

[58] In 1933 this practice was temporarily abandoned as an economy measure.
[59] See *supra*, pp. 35, 52.
[60] Eveline W. Brainerd, editor of *Weekly News,* served as secretary of this committee.

mittee urging pressure upon the Republican leader in the Senate. "Word from Republican women all over the state is the only thing that will move him." [61] Even the New York Council of Jewish Women was asked to exert its influence upon a Jewish member of the legislature who was known to be opposed to the child marriage bill.[62]

The League has also followed the practice of preparing questionnaires on current public questions in which it is interested, and of submitting these to candidates for public office. Their replies are carefully compiled and are distributed, with biographical sketches of the candidates, as circulars through the local leagues. These are accompanied by a statement that "the League does not recommend or condemn candidates. It seeks only to give unbiased information to the voter."

The League secures publicity through its publications, especially the *Weekly News,* which reaches all its members throughout the state. The first issue in January contains the names and districts of the members of the new legislature and of the newly elected state executive officers. Throughout the session the membership is kept informed of bills of interest to the members, with an explanation and comment, such as "approved" or "disapproved." In the case of specific bills, additional publicity is requested of local leaders. The following, for example, is a typical request:

> The Child Marriage Bill has reached its third reading in the Senate. There is a chance of its passing, so we must do our utmost for it. It is felt that a campaign of newspaper publicity will help. To that end will you not see the editors of your local newspapers at once and try to get them to publish special articles on the subject, and if possible some favorable editorial comment. In order to be effective, this should be done as quickly as possible. I am sending herewith a copy of the survey made by the Women's City Club of New York. As you will see, this furnished information which might be the basis for interesting and useful articles. Show it to the editors.[63]

---

[61] Letter, dated Mar. 16, 1928, from Dorothy Kenyon, chairman of the Legislative Committee.

[62] Letter, Mar. 21, 1929, signed by Eveline W. Brainerd.

[63] Letter from Mrs. Leslie J. Tompkins, chairman of the Legislative Committee, Mar. 11, 1929.

The interest of women in state legislation, as seen in the activities of the New York League of Women Voters, is further exemplified in the seriousness with which bills introduced into the State Legislature are studied by the New York State Women's Joint Legislative Forum. Plans for the organization of this group were adopted at a luncheon conference meeting of representatives of state women's organizations at the invitation of the New York State Federation of Women's Clubs. The Forum held its first meeting in a specially assigned room in the state Capitol at Albany on January 12, 1932, and it has held weekly meetings at this place during the legislative session since that date. The group is strictly non-partisan and is organized for the sole purpose of studying current state legislation. None of its members is bound to support any conclusions which it may reach, while member groups may take any action they wish as individual organizations, but not as members of the Forum. Membership is open to state organizations of women interested in legislation, to national groups having no state organization, and to local organizations. Each member organization is represented in the Forum by its president, two representatives, and one alternate.[64] In 1935 fourteen state and 20 local women's organizations were members of the Forum.[65]

The Forum elects a chairman, a vice-chairman, and a secretary at its first meeting each year. For the study of bills the chairman appoints five sub-chairmen, each of whom studies the bills in one of five classes, according to the Senate committee to which they have been referred:

1. **Finance:** Banks, Taxation, Insurance.
2. **Judiciary:** Codes, General Laws, Revision of Laws.
3. **Public Service:** Education, Elections, Civil Service, Pensions.
4. **Public Welfare:** Health, Penal Institutions, Labor (unemployment).
5. **Internal Affairs:** Agriculture, Conservation, Cities, Towns and Villages.

---

[64] *By-Laws* as amended, Dec., 1934.

[65] The meetings of the Forum are well attended. On Mar. 3, 1936, 174 women were present, of which 124 were visitors, and 50 represented state and local organizations.

Each sub-chairman is responsible for obtaining copies of the bills in her group, selecting those worthy of discussion, and allotting these bills to members who are willing and qualified to report upon them.[66] This study, supplemented by discussions with members of the legislature, is calculated to produce specialists on particular bills. In addition, members of the Forum are assigned to attend public hearings before committees of the legislature and to report back to the Forum.

The secretary of the Forum prepares a weekly report, known as a "clipsheet," in which a brief summary is given of the bills introduced into the legislature during the previous week, and the dates of scheduled public hearings. The concluding sheet of the series of clipsheets for the legislative session gives a summary, under the five headings, of the important bills passed and killed. These clipsheets are sent to 1,200 clubs and individuals, the annual subscription charge being only fifty cents to cover the cost of mailing and mimeographing.

The Forum lists among its members several important statewide women's organizations that regard the study of bills in this informal manner as the first important step to be taken before pressure is brought to bear upon the legislature.

One of the most enthusiastic supporters of the Women's Joint Legislative Forum is the New York State Federation of Women's Clubs, organized in 1894. The membership of this organization consists of 479 women's clubs throughout the state, representing between 40,000 and 50,000 individuals.[67] The affairs of the Federation are managed by its officers and

---

[66] The Forum attempts to keep abreast with thousands of bills by discussing those bills introduced in the legislature during the previous week at its meetings held each Tuesday.

[67] *Annual Report,* 1934–1935, p. 52. It is difficult to determine exactly the number of individual members represented because of the overlapping membership in many of the clubs and district federations affiliated with the State Federation. Replies to a questionnaire distributed to all the clubs in 1931 and answered by 68 per cent of them reveal: (1) that meetings are attended by an average of 60 per cent of the members; (2) that 187 have "civic interests"; (3) that 212 engage in "communal activities"; (4) that 65 per cent of them are "more or less" interested in legislation but have difficulty in finding people willing to assume the responsibilities of leadership; and (5) that the greatest problem encountered has been that of securing funds. To be eligible for membership in the State Federation, organizations must have been in existence at least one year and must have a minimum of 10 active members. *By-Laws,* Art. 3.

by district directors for each of the nine judicial districts of the state, with chairmen for each county in each district. The officers and district directors together constitute the Board of Directors of 17 members, elected for a two-year term. When the president retires, she becomes the director to the General Federation of Women's Clubs, the national organization of which the State Federation is an affiliate, and acts as the official link between the two groups. Annual conventions of the State Federation, held in November, are attended by a large percentage of the affiliated clubs.[68]

Of the eight departments which conduct the detailed business of the Federation,[69] the Department of Legislation has been very active. One of the five women on the Legislative Committee is the secretary of the Women's Joint Legislative Forum. Through the informational clipsheets that she prepares for the Forum, attempts have been made to stimulate interest and activity in legislation among the constituent clubs of the Federation.

While the Federation has rendered valuable service in the field of legislation when it has cooperated with other women's organizations, it has seldom assumed leadership. The chief reasons for this are its decentralized organization and the diversified, rather than unified, interests of its huge membership.[70]

The training and experience derived by women in their historic struggle for the enfranchisement of their sex have been carried over and on in subsequent campaigns before Congress and State Legislatures. Slowly women are beginning to realize their greater potential strength in government, now substantially enhanced with the ballot. Because of their deep concern in the three Wilhelminic K's—*Kinder, Kirche, Küche*

---

[68] The expenditures of the Federation of some $8,500 annually are defrayed chiefly from dues of 10¢ per capita. *Annual Report,* 1934–1935, p. 54. Minimum dues for clubs are $2 annually. For special scales see *By-Laws,* Art. 4. *The Clubwoman,* its official publication, is supported by annual subscriptions of 50¢. Five issues appeared in 1935. *Annual Report,* 1934–1935, pp. 43, 93.

[69] These are the departments of American Home; Arts; Civics, Citizenship and Conservation; Education; International Cooperation; Juniors; Legislation; Welfare and Health.

[70] Many of the clubs have neither interest in nor liking for "politics." See summary of analysis of replies to questionnaire in 1931 by Marion W. MacCoy. Recently the clubs could not agree on a position even on the Child Labor Amendment. *New York Times,* Feb. 8, 1936.

—American women leaders are more and more calling women's attention to the direct and indirect interest that they have in legislation. Among the organized women in New York State, especially among those whose programs are diversified or call for only incidental and occasional contacts with legislation, much remains to be done to awaken women to their great political strength along these lines. In New York State, organized women who have immediate, direct material gains to secure for themselves through legislation, as teachers, for instance, are aware of their strength and have developed the most effective pressure techniques.[71] It is undoubtedly accurate to say that they are both feared and respected. Acting independently of one another, they would make little impression upon the legislature. But, significantly, women in New York have worked well cooperatively with one another. For the most part they appear before the legislature as the organized women of the state. Women in industry, teachers, and women primarily interested in temperance and the church, in the farm, in social community and philanthropic work, in training for more effective work through political parties, have time and time again stood together in their legislative activities. The outstanding issues upon which organized women's groups of the state are not in agreement are temperance, equal rights for men and women in all fields, and the ratification of the child labor amendment to the Constitution of the United States.[72]

However, taken by and large, the organized women in New York wield greater influence in legislation than is usually credited to them. Their methods are clean and honest, free for the most part from coercion. They rank among the first exemplars of the "front door" lobby. They exemplify the happy faculty of studying problems before acting. This has been characteristic of the women's organized movements from their inception.[73] Those organizations whose interest in legislation is incidental to their other activities have had this

---

[71] *Supra,* pp. 26, 177.

[72] For a contrary impression of the unity among organized women in Washington, see E. P. Herring, *Group Representation Before Congress,* Baltimore, Johns Hopkins Press, 1929, p. 188. See also *New York Times,* Feb. 8, 1936.

[73] Inez H. Irwin, *Angels and Amazons—A Hundred Years of American Women,* Garden City, N. Y., Doubleday, Doran, 1933, p. 414.

interest whetted by the Women's Joint Legislative Forum. More and better trained leaders are needed among the organized women of the state. It is very probable that in time the Forum will emerge as a training school for such leaders. Women's organizations in New York, with few exceptions, have not yet learned the tremendous power that goes with united action at the ballot box. This power stands as a constant threat before political leaders and elected officials, and on occasions the women have not hesitated to remind political leaders of this fact to thus strike a better bargain. However, many political leaders still count on women's aversion to active politics, and on their failure in the past to deliver a united women's vote. The New York League of Women Voters, with its non-partisan policy and all-partisan membership, encourages more active participation by women in their respective parties.

The program that will make of organized women in the State of New York an unrivaled pressure group with generally salutary results is (1) greater interest and action in state legislation among existing women's associations and clubs and (2) the exercise of the ballot with definite legislative demands in mind.[74]

Among the prominent organizations which exist to promote efficiency in government is the Civil Service Reform Association, a statewide organization interested in developing the merit principle in the civil service. Organized in May, 1877, as the first civil service reform association in the United States, this Association played a prominent part in the establishment of other associations of a similar kind. Such great civil service reformers as Dorman B. Eaton, George William Curtis, and Carl Schurz were connected with its early history.[75] As a reform association of interested citizens, rather than an employees' group, it functions with an annual budget varying

---

[74] At recent annual sessions of the New York League of Women Voters and the New York State Federation of Women's Clubs, serious consideration was given to the recommendation that these organizations narrow their fields of activities so that greater progress may be made on fewer fronts. *New York Times,* Nov. 21, 1935.

[75] F. M. Stewart, *The National Civil Service Reform League—History, Activities and Problems,* Austin, The University of Texas Press, 1929, pp. 23–30. Because of limited facilities, the Association has concentrated its attention upon the civil service in New York City.

from approximately $6,000 to $10,000, much of which is voluntarily contributed. A large portion of its legal work, too, is voluntarily conducted by members of the Association's Law Committee.[76]

The Association drafted the first state civil service act in 1883, shortly after the passage of the federal civil service law. Through its investigation of the maladministration of the state law, moreover, it caused the adoption, in 1894, of the constitutional provision for the competitive system in the selection of public officials.[77]

The Association has encountered many difficulties in securing constructive state legislation to extend the principle of the competitive system and in opposing exemptions for specific individuals and groups, such as the veterans. These campaigns, in fact, have constituted a frontal attack upon political machines of both Democrats and Republicans and upon powerful minorities. It has thus been necessary for the Association constantly to appeal to the courts, securing interpretations of the existing civil service laws and compelling their enforcement upon civil service commissions and administrative officers.[78] It is claimed by the Association that in this way political machines are deprived of thousands of dollars of patronage. "It is easier for John Jones to get a bill through the legislature that would reinstate him in the civil service than for sixty civic organizations to get a bill in the interest of public good. That is because the civic organizations do not have the votes that will aid the legislator in his election, while John Jones lives in his district, is a member of the legislator's club, and will make trouble for the legislator if he does not help him. Thus what we accomplish is that perhaps in five years we will get through one constructive bill and stop one hundred bad ones, the latter frequently through the Governor's veto." [79]

The chief pressure medium used by the Association, accord-

---

[76] See recent *Annual Reports of the Civil Service Reform Association.*

[77] Stewart, *op. cit.,* pp. 34–36. *Cf. Report of the Executive Committee of the Civil Service Reform Association,* 1933, p. 4.

[78] This legal procedure has been simplified by what appeared at the time to be an innocuous bill sponsored by the Association, which was passed in 1914. This law permits a citizen or taxpayer to bring an action to prevent payment of the salary of a person illegally employed.

[79] Interview, H. E. Kaplan, Counsel and Secretary of the Association, May 9, 1933.

ingly, is the newspaper, which publishes a large number of news releases prepared by the Association in addition to favorable editorials that appear from time to time. Frequent personal appeals for cooperation are also made by letter to interested civic and women's organizations. Pamphlets, too, are occasionally published by the Civil Service Reform Association. Such publications, however, including a little monthly pamphlet called *Good Government,* appear, for the most part, under the auspices of the National Civil Service Reform League, of which the Civil Service Reform Association is a constituent member, and with whose history and activities it is closely identified.

Dry Forces

The seventh minor stream of pressure on the New York State Legislature flows chiefly from the Anti-Saloon League of New York and the Women's Christian Temperance Union of the State of New York, two organizations whose ultimate aim is the prohibition of the manufacture and sale of intoxicating beverages. Although these organizations were most active before the repeal of the Eighteenth Amendment in 1933, they still exert pressure and wield influence upon legislators at Albany.

The Anti-Saloon League of New York is a unit of the national organization, the Anti-Saloon League of America, and employs in its work the same methods as the national body, but on a statewide scale. In addition to its officers and Board of Directors, there is a Board of Trustees of 35 members, on which are represented the evangelical churches of the state. The number of such delegates, selected by the churches themselves, is proportionate to their church membership.[80] The executive head of the League is the salaried state superintendent, who is elected by the Board of Directors upon the nomination of the Board itself and of the superintendent of the Anti-Saloon League of America. The members of the latter body are in turn selected by the Board of Trustees.

The League is not a membership organization, but, rather,

---

[80] The number of non-church members elected to the Board is restricted by the League's constitution in order to insure a majority representation for the religious bodies.

an agency of the church. For administrative purposes, the League divides the state into three districts, each in the charge of a district superintendent: the Metropolitan district, with headquarters in New York City; the Central district, with headquarters in Syracuse; and the Western district, centering in Buffalo. Voluntary contributions secured by "pledge-cards and sawed-off pencils" circulated among church congregations in these districts, after appeals from the pulpit, are the chief source of the League's finances.[81]

The greatest strides in the temperance movement in the state were made by the Anti-Saloon League of New York between 1914 and 1923, under the superintendency of William H. Anderson.[82] With the repeal of the Eighteenth Amendment, its activities were, of course, curtailed. Since 1933 it has been concerned chiefly with pointing out the "destructive" results of the repeal of Prohibition, and the "lax" enforcement of the liquor laws in New York. Each year, alone or in cooperation with other dry organizations, recommendations are submitted to the Governor and the Legislature for the restriction of the traffic of intoxicating liquors. Such proposals sometimes take the form of additional taxes on the sale of beer, the prohibition of the issuance of driver's licenses to persons who drink, or the restriction of liquor advertising. The repeal or weakening of the state Scientific Temperance Instruction law

---

[81] *The Christian Advocate*, May 25, 1933, p. 484. Though these have been substantially decreased since repeal, the Anti-Saloon League of New York has been the best financed of the state Leagues. Its income in 1914, when W. H. Anderson became state superintendent, was $30,000. This was more than quadrupled in 1918. *Cf.* Peter Odegard, *Pressure Politics*, New York, Columbia University Press, 1928, p. 239. The average annual income between 1920–1925 was $308,471. For annual apportionment of expenditures of the Anti-Saloon League of New York, see Odegard, *op. cit.*, p. 201.

[82] For a complete account of these activities see Odegard, *op. cit., passim.* Anderson, a colorful and dynamic personality, led the dramatic fight for the ratification of the Eighteenth Amendment by the New York Legislature in 1919, and for the enactment of the Mullan-Gage Enforcement law in 1921. With the repeal of the Mullan-Gage law in 1923, for the first time since 1664, no liquor legislation of any kind which restricted or regulated the liquor traffic existed on the statute books of the State of New York. See Frances W. Graham, *Sixty Years of Action, 1874–1934*, p. 133, published by the WCTU, State of New York (no date). Prior to Anderson's administration the New York Civic League under the direction of Rev. O. R. Miller with headquarters in Albany was regarded as the official spokesman of the Allied Temperance Organizations in New York State.

has thus far been blocked by concerted drives from dry sources. The privilege of local option in the control of liquor consumption has been one of its chief goals.

The phenomenal influence of the Anti-Saloon League in the nation and state was built upon its ability to elect and defeat candidates for public office. This the League was able to accomplish not by forming a party of its own and nominating a ticket, but by the support of the mighty constituency of the church. Through speakers who were and are permitted to address the congregations of cooperating churches, the League has built up dry sentiment and gathered votes for candidates for public office friendly to the "drys." Its support in this direction has come especially from the following evangelical denominations: Methodists, Baptists, Presbyterians, and Congregationalists. A recent annual report of the state superintendent of the Anti-Saloon League says:

> Not a single cooperating church has lowered its flag—total abstinence for the individual and prohibition for the state and nation is the declared purpose and program of these bodies. And the Anti-Saloon League of New York is still their officially approved and endorsed agency for the attaining of their declared purpose and program.

> During the year every Methodist Conference, the Conferences of the Evangelical and United Brethren, the Congregational State Convention, the Seventh Day Baptist Convention, the Synod of the United Presbyterian, the Baptist State Convention,—all took official action to this end. . . .[83]

The number of churches that actively cooperate with the League varies from year to year, though dry sentiment is

---

[83] However, not all local churches accept the advice or follow the leadership of their denominational convention, conference, or synod in supporting the League. In one year, however, speakers representing the League appeared in the pulpits of 362 churches. This does not represent the total number of cooperating churches, however, since at times as many as ten churches join together to hear the League speaker. *Report of State Superintendent to the Board of Trustees,* Feb. 26, 1935. In addition, community meetings are held, and special youth and adult groups reached. In the six-months' period from Nov., 1933 to Apr., 1934, shortly after the repeal of the Eighteenth Amendment, some 20,000 people were reached by League speakers. This number has since increased. The League distributes annually many thousands of pamphlets to directors of youth education, ministers, writers, and members of church schools.

strong in all the evangelical churches, whether they give active support to the League or not. The aggregate church membership of the evangelical churches in New York State, about three-quarters of a million, is strategically concentrated in upstate rural sections.

With this potential voting power, the League is able to approach candidates for public office and, in return for temperance pledges, to work for their election. This support the League has usually given to the Republican party, since the Democratic party has been avowedly and solidly wet. The wet delegation from New York City in particular, constituting 42 per cent of the members of the State Legislature, has always been one of the League's most harassing problems. So long, however, as the rural sections of the state continue to hold disproportionate representation in the legislature, a dry nucleus is assured.[84]

The second temperance group whose influence is felt at Albany, the Women's Christian Temperance Union of the State of New York, was founded in Fredonia, N. Y., in 1873. It is composed of 35,000 women found in over 700 local county unions throughout the state.[85] The WCTU has been the most active woman's organization to champion the cause of the "drys" in New York State, having always favored total abstinence. To many of its members this crusade has been iden-

---

[84] Dry sentiment is particularly strong in such rural counties as Chemung, Yates, Tioga, Delaware, Schoharie, and Schuyler. It should be noted that even before repeal, when the League thought the cause of temperance would be better served by endorsing an independent candidate, this procedure was followed. In 1926, for example, it succeeded in defeating the Republican U. S. Senator James W. Wadsworth for reelection by naming an independent Republican candidate, F. W. Cristman, an ardent dry, in whose behalf the dry leaders waged a vigorous campaign. Robert F. Wagner, the victorious Democratic candidate, defeated Senator Wadsworth by a plurality considerably smaller than the vote polled by the dry candidate, Cristman. The dry leaders knew well that this procedure would result in the election of another wet candidate, but they were anxious to remove Senator Wadsworth, with an unequivocal wet record, from his position of leadership in state and national Republican party councils. Odegard, *op. cit.*, pp. 100–103.

[85] A peak membership of 46,000 was reached in 1925. The activities of the state Union are distributed among 15 departments. Its expenses, totalling $60,000 in 1934, are defrayed chiefly by contributions and the dues paid by the individual members to the local unions. Half of this amount is retained by the local union, the remaining half being shared equally by the county and state unions. In financing its activities, the state Union has followed a "pay-as-you-go" policy.

226   Other Groups

tical with Christianity itself, so that alone or in cooperation
with the Anti-Saloon League of New York, the New York
State Grange, the New York Civic League, and the New York
Women's Committee for Law Enforcement,[86] the Union has
unceasingly registered protests against the legalization of all
"distilled, fermented, and malt liquors" for more than sixty
years.[87]

Although the Union was most active in the cause of temperance before repeal,[88] it still exerts pressure upon the legislature through the action of its local units under the direction
of the county and the state presidents. The latter regularly
follows the activities of the State Legislature by frequent
appearances in Albany, where signed petitions are submitted
with dramatic ceremony. Since the beginning of the century
the women have emphasized personal contacts with legislators
through letters and interviews, particularly in the case of local
representatives. The cooperation of churches in the community has also been effectively enlisted by the Women's Christian Temperance Union in its temperance campaigns. Some
of the most dramatic public hearings ever held in Albany have
been those of the dry forces in which the women loomed large.[89]

In addition to this, the WCTU has exploited the voting

---

[86] The New York Women's Committee for Law Enforcement, Inc., was
founded in 1923 as a branch of the Woman's National Committee for Law
Enforcement, "to arouse and create interest in law enforcement and law
observance throughout the state and its political subdivisions." This was to
be done by the political education of its members and pressure for the enactment of temperance legislation. The Committee came into existence when
Alfred E. Smith, pledged to the repeal of the Mullan-Gage Dry law, was re-
elected as Governor of New York. The Committee drew the bulk of its
membership from women residing outside of New York City, but never
approached in membership its rival organization, The New York State Division of the Women's Organization for National Prohibition Reform. Through
publications and meetings, the Committee unsuccessfully tried to arouse public sentiment in favor of the dry delegates to the state convention for the
repeal of the Eighteenth Amendment. In all its dry activities, however, this
Committee has since its establishment been overshadowed by the better organized and financed WCTU.

[87] See *Sixty Years of Action, 1874-1934,* by Frances W. Graham, published
by the WCTU. A pledge of abstinence is a condition for membership in the
WCTU.

[88] Mrs. Ella S. Boole, President of the WCTU in New York, unsuccessfully
sought the Republican nomination for U. S. Senator against Senator James W.
Wadsworth, an avowed wet, in 1920. She then ran against him as the Prohibition party candidate, and polled almost 160,000 votes.

[89] Attention should be called in this connection to the public hearings held
at Albany, Feb. 26, 1918 and Mar. 23, 1933.

power of women. For many years its members sought and secured places on the committees of the political parties, often winning the incorporation of dry planks in party platforms and the selection of dry candidates by the major parties. The influence of the women in nominating and electing dry candidates for the State Legislature has been of considerable force in many districts in upstate New York. When the cause seemed lost, the women concentrated with greater vigor upon piling up a large dry vote by supporting candidates in the Prohibition party when this party presented a slate of candidates to the voters of New York State. More recently, "after the betrayal of the moral forces of the country by the two large political parties," the WCTU has favored the organization of a new national political party committed to prohibition of the liquor traffic.[90]

In furtherance of its "Do Everything" policy, the WCTU has not confined its activities to the temperance cause alone, but has joined with other groups in urging social welfare laws affecting women and children.[91] However, it optimistically looks upon repeal as a "temporary" setback, maintaining its effective organization throughout the state for future campaigns:

> We have a marvellous response from our membership. There is no other organization which on such short notice can get in direct communication with its members as can ours. We have 35,000 stencils, representing 35,000 members and if we wanted to we could circularize each of those within a short time. We also work through our county presidents, one for each county. The president can com-

[90] Graham, *op. cit.*, p. 142. It should be noted, however, that most of the members in the local unions are still either Republicans or Democrats. In upstate rural counties, where such members are openly affiliated with these parties, the political organizations would generally ascertain what qualifications successful candidates for the State Legislature should possess. Interview, Miss H. G. H. Estelle, Treasurer, Feb. 25, 1936.

[91] The WCTU was a member of the New York State Women's Joint Legislative Conference, organized to campaign for a 48-hour and minimum wage law for women. It has also aided the New York League of Women Voters and the New York Branch of the National Woman's Party in their campaign for a Woman Juror bill, and has joined with other organizations in urging a uniform marriage and divorce law. One of its recent campaigns was waged for a Woman Juror bill, members being urged as "home women" to write to their legislators informally, "on plain paper, even with a lead pencil." Instructions from Mrs. D. L. Colvin, President, Feb. 24, 1936.

municate without any loss of time with the presidents of
local units in her county. So that a communication sent
out from this office can be in the hands of each local president within twenty-four hours. Our women are church
women and have church connections, so as soon as an
appeal is sent to them, they start action among our own
membership and many Christian people in the churches.
They take petitions to churches on Sunday morning and
so cover every church. The WCTU has the best machinery
to aid local work.[92]

The dry forces fight on despite tremendous pressure from
those interested in the extension of the lucrative liquor traffic:
newspaper publishers who benefit from liquor advertisements;
the liquor interests themselves, such as the National Distillers'
Association and the United States Brewers' Association; [93] and
the political leaders in the urban centers particularly, whose
machines are reputed to be well-lubricated by contributions
from alcoholic sources.

Thus, in the face of this great counter-pressure, the dry
organizations have resorted to modern publicity methods used
by their opponents, such as newspaper and radio advertising—
on a much more restricted scale, to be sure, largely because of
limited funds. For example, the Women's Christian Temperance Union has tried to curb social drinking by direct public
appeals through newspaper and radio advertising.[94] Furthermore, the Union has been responsible since December, 1935
for 66 road signs on the main highway between New York City
and Buffalo, each containing some pithy statement, such as:
"A Friendly Glass May Cause an Unfriendly Crash."

---

[92] Interview, Miss Helen G. H. Estelle, Treasurer, May 31, 1933, and Oct. 3,
1935. In 1935, on short notice, such prompt response from its members helped
to block the repeal of the Scientific Temperance Instruction law, known as
the Ainsworth law, which has been on the statute books in New York since
1884. The repeal of the Ainsworth law as a rider to an education bill passed
the Senate unnoticed by the WCTU. When detected, word went forth from
the president of the WCTU to the county presidents of the Union, and the
flood of telegrams and letters that followed effectively blocked further action.

[93] The New York State Hotel Association has been among the active "wet"
pressure groups in the state. The New York State Brewers' Association is
little more than a paper organization completely overshadowed by the United
States Brewers' Association.

[94] See such advertisements in *New York Times, New York Herald Tribune,*
and *New York American,* Dec. 5, 1935. For this same purpose, a four-reel
cinema was released by the Union in Nov., 1936.

CHAPTER VIII

Summary of Techniques

OUR study of the organization and procedures of typical pressure groups in New York State has revealed the extent and the general nature of their lobbies. It remains for us to examine in retrospect the significant elements in the pressure techniques that they employ, so that our view of these groups may be complete.

Without question, the outstanding feature of modern pressure group technique is the widespread use of propaganda channels for the purpose of building and corralling support both within and without the pressure organization itself. These channels are frequently utilized to influence public opinion long before the direct attack on the legislature begins, and resort to them is not abandoned but is, rather, intensified during the legislative drive.

Pressure propaganda usually begins within the group as a process of building up and rallying its membership. Because of the frequent charge that lobby groups are not really representative,[1] one of the first aims of such a body is the development of a large and, perhaps, diversified membership. To secure members and maintain their support, all organizations are compelled to offer a protective program of some kind.[2] In order to justify their existence, groups commonly point to exaggerated achievements won in the face of equally exaggerated dangers from legislative bodies. This, in turn, forms the basis for more or less systematically planned membership campaigns.[3] It is pointed out to prospective members that, since they have benefited by the organization's achievements, it is unfair of them not to join the organization.

---

[1] *Infra,* p. 262.

[2] Associated Industries, Inc., for example, was formed in 1914 for protection against the "riot of social legislation" enacted in the New York Legislature during 1913 and 1914.

[3] For instance, in 1930, Associated Industries employed a professional agency to conduct a campaign for new members. See *Monitor,* May, 1931, p. 271.

For example, if the numerous veteran associations in the State of New York have been instrumental in securing veteran civil service exemptions, much is made of the benefits accruing to the veterans who are not members, just as Associated Industries will assert that manufacturers and merchants who are not affiliated with the association benefit from its successful attempts to retard further extensions of the Workmen's Compensation Law.

Pressure bodies are not merely concerned in building up and widening the membership within their own groups; they are also interested in rallying other groups into cooperative attempts to further a legislative program of mutual benefit to all. In this way, a much enlarged combined membership is secured, as in the case of the Joint Committee of Teachers' Organizations and the Conference Board of Farm Organizations. Furthermore, through the Women's Joint Legislative Conference, the combined efforts of sixteen organizations were utilized in a campaign to provide progressive social legislation for women. Similarly, in 1930, cooperation among leading business men led to the formation of the New York State Economic Council. In order to rally such combinations, it is not unusual for some groups to make concessions to others for the purpose of securing their cooperation. As an instance, the State Charities Aid Association, in its campaign to revise the Public Welfare Law, made important concessions and compromises as the basis of winning the support of the influential New York State Association of Public Welfare Officials.[4]

Although much of this propaganda is face to face in character, a great deal of reliance is placed on mail. Letters, bulletins, and periodicals regularly sent to members contain reports of the progress of legislative activities and, frequently, instructions for further action. In some cases, at its annual meeting the group submits a report of the number of such communications distributed during a year, actually pointing to this as one of its achievements.[5]

Mail propaganda, beginning within the group, is often directed also at certain elements of the general public. The

[4] See *supra*, pp. 32, 56, 123, 148, 167. Earlier known as the County Superintendents of the Poor.

[5] See *Proceedings of the New York State Bankers Association*, 1932, p. 16.

State Charities Aid Association, for example, made appeals to prominent persons in various stations of life to communicate with the legislators in support of a bill. Furthermore, studies and investigations are conducted by groups on particular phases of a bill, and the results are transmitted to members and to the general public both by direct mail and by the holding of public meetings.[6]

Externally, the most effective way of influencing public opinion, however, is through such means of mass communication as the newspaper,[7] the radio,[8] and the school.[9] Through these channels attempts are made to cultivate a friendly attitude on the part of what is vaguely known as the general public, which can be differentiated to a greater or less degree from those who have a direct material interest in the work of the group. Pressure groups leaning heavily upon these channels consider it tantamount to victory if they can keep large numbers from becoming active in the enemy's camp. The privately-owned public utilities, for example, would undoubtedly consider their efforts to influence public opinion entirely successful if they staved off a public of protesting consumers.

In directing propaganda through the newspaper, news items, special correspondents' articles, and editorials have been the most productive forms of publicity. When such forms have not been available to a group, newspaper propaganda has been utilized more expensively and less effectively through paid advertisements. The Women's Christian Temperance Union, for example, inserted paid advertisements in newspapers in its campaign against "social drinking." In this way, many people

---

[6] In this connection, the organization of the Pomona Lecturers' Association and the Mid-Atlantic Lecturers' Association should be noted. See *supra*, p. 96. Cornell University offers a brief annual course in contemporary agricultural problems to the lecturers of the New York State Grange. See *supra*, p. 96.

[7] In New York State there are 140 English daily and Sunday newspapers with a total net paid circulation of 13,324,503. This represents 21 per cent of the total circulation of all such newspapers in the United States. These figures are for Oct., 1934. See *Editor and Publisher*, Jan. 26, 1935, p. 118, published by James W. Brown, 1475 Broadway, N. Y. C.

[8] In Apr., 1930, 57.9 per cent of the private families in the state owned radio sets (*U. S. Census Abstract*, 1930, p. 431). By Jan., 1935, it was estimated that the number of radio sets had increased by more than a million, reaching a new peak of 2,928,870 for the state. *Cf. World Almanac*, 1936, p. 323.

[9] In 1930 the total school attendance in New York State was 2,637,172. *Cf. U. S. Census Abstract*, 1930, p. 264.

who were not "drys" were reached.　The ardent "drys" were easily influenced through the "regular" channels of the WCTU and other similar organizations.[10]

Goodwill advertising, moreover, has been recognized by some pressure groups as a valuable means of winning newspaper support.　In fact, the privately-owned utilities in New York attached so much importance to this aspect of their publicity work that they actually established an industry advertising service for this purpose.[11]　It is, of course, not surprising to find that newspaper publishers are well disposed toward their advertisers, since they form the chief source of income for the newspapers.　Most newspapers, nevertheless, find it necessary to observe some restraint in their editorial policies [12] for fear of offending a conflicting pressure interest or a large bloc of readers.　For the publishers are well aware that the volume of newspaper advertising depends upon circulation and that the purchasers of consumers' goods far outnumber as newspaper readers the followers of any organized minority's point of view.

In the event that the influential newspapers just will not "see your side" but give wide publicity to your adversary's point of view, plans for influencing the legislature must, of necessity, center about overcoming and answering such adverse publicity as effectively as possible.　After the *New York Herald Tribune* launched a campaign for the reduction of teachers' salaries in 1932, and the other newspapers were no more than passive, the teachers found it necessary to purchase space in a weekly magazine, *School,* for the purpose of answering the unfriendly press comments.

Pressure groups, like other space seekers, may be reasonably certain of wide publicity when they can present news of a "dramatic" character.　In 1911, Frances Perkins, legislative agent of the Consumers' League of New York, sponsored in the New York Legislature a bill providing for greater sanitation in bakeries.　The bakery interests objected and the battle of opposing assertions bewildered the legislature.　Just before

---

[10] *New York Times,* Dec. 5, 1935.
[11] See *supra,* p. 68.
[12] The verbatim reprint of the public utility material to the contrary, notwithstanding, see *supra,* p. 67.

the bill came up for its third reading, however, a newspaper item "leaked" from Miss Perkins' office to the effect that on one of her tours of the bakeries she had seen kittens "born on a bread board." Newspapers from New York to California carried this revolting story of the lack of bakery sanitation, and the bill passed.[13]

Another way in which pressure groups secure favorable newspaper publicity is through friendly contacts with the various Albany correspondents. Some 36 of these reporters, representing individual newspapers in the ten largest cities of the state, and three press associations, are organized in the Legislative Correspondents Association.[14] This Association gains some prestige through the fact that it is the oldest one of its kind in the United States, outdating even the national association in Washington. The majority leaders in the Senate and Assembly designate the persons entitled to admission to the chambers as representatives of the public press. Such designation, however, is purely perfunctory, for the authorized representatives of the daily papers and the press associations are always acceptable to the legislative leaders.[15] The Association elects officers annually and holds business meetings during the legislative session. Official Albany looks forward annually to the banquet and entertainment of the Legislative Correspondents Association, which are similar to those of the Gridiron Club at Washington.

The extent of favorable newspaper publicity given to certain interest groups is, of course, conditioned by the fact that the newspaper itself is a commercial enterprise and frequently, therefore, has a stake in legislation. While the rules of the legislature require that the Albany press representatives must not be actively interested in pending or contemplated legislation,[16] newspaper publishers, either through their Albany correspondents or their associations, have, on occasions, been most active in opposing bills considered inimical to the inter-

---

[13] *New York World,* Nov. 9, 1913.

[14] The Legislative Correspondents Association maintains headquarters in the state Capitol building.

[15] Interviews, W. O. Trapp, Albany representative of the *New York World Telegram,* May 2, 1933, and Lee W. O'Brien of the *Albany Times-Union,* Feb. 2, 1933, Sept. 4, 1935.

[16] Senate Rule 3, Assembly Rule 26. *Cf. New York Clerk's Manual,* 1936.

ests of the press. In 1935, the bill to abolish county sales tax advertising was speedily killed in the Senate committee, and in 1936 a bill that would have assigned to the New York Law Journal official status for foreclosure advertisements in the second Judicial Department of New York State was defeated after vigorous opposition was voiced by newspaper interests. Furthermore, newspaper publishers encountered little difficulty in winning the assurance of both the State Industrial Commissioner and the legislature that the recently enacted legislation raising the school-leaving age of children and reducing the weekly hours of work for boys would not in any way affect newsboys or other minors employed by newspapers.[17] Mayor La Guardia of New York City has scored newspaper reporters in the role of lobbyists: "It is not the job of a newspaper man, simply because his employer is in the real estate business, to get reductions in assessments and, similarly, it is not the job of a newspaper man to 'fix' violations of the tenement house laws or the fire department regulations. In the army we had a term for it. It was 'dog-robber'." [18]

The radio has not been utilized by pressure groups so much as one might expect in a state whose Governors have used so effectively this means of bringing public pressure to bear upon the legislature.[19] The chief reason for this lies in the great expense involved where the regulations of the broadcasting companies do not actually interfere with such programs.[20] The privately-owned public utilities have made greater use

---

[17] At the public hearing on these bills the newspapers were represented by the New York State Publishers Association and Associated Dailies, rather than by the correspondents stationed at Albany. *Cf. New York Times*, Feb. 6, 1935. The New York State Publishers Association was established in 1921 and represents publishers of the daily newspapers of the state outside of New York City. Its membership in 1935 was composed of 55 such daily newspapers. Members are kept informed of legislative matters through a monthly bulletin. *Cf.* letter of the secretary, Karl H. Thiesing, Jan. 4, 1936. The publishers of newspapers in New York City are organized in the Publishers Association of New York City, which was founded in 1897 and whose membership in 1936 covered 16 newspapers. Interview, C. B. Palmer, Secretary, July 28, 1936.

[18] *New York Times*, May 30, 1936.

[19] This has been particularly true of Governors Smith, F. D. Roosevelt, and Lehman.

[20] See Merrill Denison, "Editorial Policies of Broadcasting Companies," *The Public Opinion Quarterly*, Jan., 1937; and *The Annals of the American Academy of Political and Social Science*, Jan., 1935, pp. 15, 179.

of the radio than any other organized pressure interest. This is not surprising when it is realized that such expenses are charged to operating costs, which are ultimately met by the consumer. The absence of challenging and compelling programs presented by absorbing speakers, and the desire of some broadcasting companies to avoid an unfavorable public reaction, probably explain why more time is not contributed by the privately-owned broadcasting companies during the "sustaining" periods. It is possible, nevertheless, to look forward to a more extensive use of the radio by organized minorities as the depression lifts and funds become more readily available. Until that time these groups will undoubtedly continue to feel that more successful results can be achieved through other media.

The effective use of the third channel of mass propaganda, the schools, may be most strikingly observed in the systematically planned program of the public utilities.[21] As we have seen, their campaign in the schools "to disparage all forms of public ownership and to preach the economy, sufficiency, and general excellence of the privately-owned utilities" included sending speakers into the schools and showing specially-prepared cinemas. More than 100,000 copies of pamphlets distributed in the schools of New York were used as texts or for reference purposes. Textbooks for school use were specially prepared under the auspices of utility officials, while books already in use were examined for the purpose of correcting their "deficiencies." Attempts were even made by the utilities to "sell the idea" to college professors, but, apparently, not with so much success in New York State as elsewhere in the country.[22]

Such well organized groups as teachers and parents, who are primarily interested in the schools, have exerted little cooperative effort to resist propaganda of this sort.[23] Furthermore,

---

[21] See Robert Bruce Raup, *Education and Organized Interests in America*, New York, Putnam, 1936, for a study of the relations between schools and pressure groups, including the utilities.

[22] *Supra*, p. 70. See *Summary Report of the Federal Trade Commission on Efforts by Associations and Agencies of Electric and Gas Utilities to Influence Public Opinion*, 1934, pp. 139–221.

[23] The recent decision of the Board of Education to install radios in the schools of New York City may be wrought with great dangers if unwisely

there has not been much cooperative action from students in the past. However, the recent unprecedented political activities of students organized on a national scale indicate, perhaps, that organized student movements will grow in the United States. If this be so, greater organized pressure from student groups, alone or in cooperation with teacher and parent organizations, in the interests of legislation will follow.[24] In this connection, it might be well to recall that the presence of a delegation of 500 students from 13 colleges in the state, armed with a petition containing the signatures of 7,500 students, at a hearing in Albany played no small part in the defeat of a student-oath bill.[25]

Without overlooking the importance of securing a favorable public opinion through these channels of mass communication, pressure groups realize that their fortunes are closely linked with the American party system. The two-party system in the United States has encouraged the establishment of pressure groups and has added to their prestige and influence. It would be interesting to observe what effect a new party alignment or a strong third party would have upon the strength, activity, and control of interest groups. Although remote and foreign to the present American setting, a multiple party system with or without proportional representation at its base, in which the political groups present platforms aimed to attract specific social classes, may be a direct step toward an official basis of functional or occupational representation.[26]

---

administered. *Cf. New York Herald Tribune,* June 25, 1936. See also H. L. Childs, ed., *Propaganda and Dictatorship,* Princeton, Princeton University Press, 1936, p. 29.

[24] The establishment since Dec., 1935 of chapters of the new militant student organization, the *American Student Union,* in colleges throughout the country appears to be a step in this direction. The Union states that it, "in cooperation with labor and other progressive groups, is dedicated to the realization of a society of peace and plenty." In June, 1936, this organization estimated that approximately 20,000 American students were enrolled. See *The Student Advocate,* monthly publication of the American Student Union. Student-teacher cooperation is open to serious dangers when student support inside or outside of the classroom is enlisted for such "selfish" purposes as teacher salary increases.

[25] *New York Times,* Mar. 8, 1935. For an account of a successful strike with parental approval of elementary school children in New York City to secure better school quarters, see *New York Times,* Mar. 19, 1935. For additional references to student strikes, see *New York Times,* Sept. 29, 1936.

[26] In Germany under the Second Reich, the system of proportional repre-

Certain interest groups in New York have become identified with particular parties, for in the sharp clash of interests so typical of organized minorities today, it has not been possible effectively to ally each interest with both of the major parties. Labor groups in New York have always secured greater assistance from Democratic than from Republican administrations, while industrial groups have found the reverse situation to exist.[27] However, not all pressure groups can be so closely identified with either of the major parties in New York State, since the constituencies of such groups cut across party lines. Pressure groups do not divorce themselves from the proceedings of political parties in their conventions and primaries, particularly if there is a contest between various factions and candidates.[28] However, for the most part, such activity is not open and is conducted in the names of particular individuals rather than that of the group itself. Occasionally, though, pressure groups will actually prepare planks for inclusion in party platforms. In the case of the New York State Federation of Labor it is a regular practice.[29]

Furthermore, it is a common practice for pressure groups to question candidates before election with reference to their views on matters of interest to these groups, their replies serving as guides to the members in voting for public officers. These pre-election pledges are becoming more important, as attested by their increased number, the promptness with which legislators respond to them, and the wider publicity which they attract. Although some organizations maintain an attitude

---

sentation tended to increase the influence and direct representation of interest groups in the Reichstag. See H. Finer, *Representative Government and a Parliament of Industry,* London, G. Allen and Unwin, 1923, and *The Theory and Practice of Modern Government,* New York, Dial Press, 1932, Vol. II, pp. 775, 918.

[27] Many legislators assign more credit to Alfred E. Smith for the repeal of the 65 per cent surtax on motor trucks in 1933 than to the pressure exerted by the motor truck associations and the farmers. There are not many at Albany, however, who, "by virtue of their prestige and strategic situation, may be considered virtually as interest groups in themselves." *Cf.* A. G. Dewey, *Political Science Quarterly,* Dec., 1923, p. 640.

[28] Reverberations, in Republican councils and conventions in 1934, of the charge by W. Kingsland Macy that the legislature was controlled by the public utilities resulted in his replacement by an "Old Guard" Republican State Chairman. *New York Times,* Dec. 9, 1933, and Sept. 29, 1934. *Cf. supra,* p. 79.

[29] *Supra,* pp. 18, 128.

of disinterestedness in influencing the votes of their members, more and more groups are recognizing this as a fundamentally valuable means of reaching their ends. The New York State Federation of Labor openly declares that it will support those members of the legislature for reelection who by their records have proven themselves the friends of labor. To this end, it has established a Non-Partisan Campaign Committee to conduct its political activities.[30] The teachers' organizations are openly following in the footsteps of labor in this respect. There are other organizations with large membership rolls, such as those of the farmers and veterans, who do not openly engage in political activities of this kind, but whose large membership of potential voters, of itself, exerts a strong influence upon public officials. Certain small powerful groups, such as the industrialists, restricted as direct vote givers, are still in a position to offer the wherewithal that keeps the political machine operating. But even such groups do not overlook the value of mass action at the polls, which they attempt to obtain by influencing their employees, small stockholders, and the general public.

Few organized groups are so ignorant of practical politics as to fail to appreciate the role and influence of that "invisible" yet all too visible agency of government: the American political boss. Exceptional indeed is the pressure group which would hesitate to approach the political leaders responsible for the nomination and election of the men and women who sit in our State Legislature. This has been universally recognized as one of the most practical and realistic ways of obtaining results. The "boss" in American politics is thus widely courted by individuals and groups with the noblest, as well as the most ignoble, purposes. However, one must not overlook the fact that in recent years political leadership in New York has not been concentrated in one person or in one party. Party control in both legislative and executive branches has been divided between the Republican and Democratic organizations, while within each party there have been serious factional divisions that have prevented unified control.

Although pressure group activity before the legislature is not wholly free from corruption, there has been less of it since

[30] See *supra,* p. 18.

the investigation of the Armstrong Committee in 1905 disclosed the shocking lobbying practices of the insurance companies.[31] Isolated instances of malpractice, such as that of Senator Warren T. Thayer, have received public attention from time to time,[32] as a result of which legislative investigations have been ordered. These investigations have not for the most part unearthed widespread official misconduct.[33]

Nevertheless, while the outright bribing of legislators is perhaps no longer common, it has been shown that legislators are ambitious and poorly paid, and have much to gain from wealthy groups in a material way through favors, retainers, and contributions to campaign funds. We know enough about the contents and the enforcement of corrupt practices legislation to realize that it is no difficult task for a legislator to defeat the purposes of such laws without being detected. Thus, as an example, while it may be true that money less openly changes hands, strike bills continue to be introduced, amid the usual clouds of suspicion. The feeling still persists at the state Capitol that the introduction of these strike bills, which openly aim to do damage to the interests of certain groups, is just another way of "shaking down" these groups. Ex-Governor Alfred E. Smith is reputed to have stated humorously to a member of the legislature, on the occasion of his admission to the bar, "Now you can take a bribe and call it a fee."

At times, pressure groups influence the selection of officers

---

[31] *Proceedings of the Joint Committee of the Senate and Assembly of the State of New York—Appointed to Investigate the Affairs of Life Insurance Companies,* 10 vols., Albany, 1906.

[32] See *supra,* p. 78. For another such case in New York, see *Proceedings of the Senate in the Matter of the Investigation Demanded by Senator Jotham P. Allds,* Albany, 1910. See also H. C. Tanner, *"The Lobby", and Public Men,* Albany, G. MacDonald, 1888.

[33] The Joint Legislative Committee to Investigate Public Utilities was created in 1934 after responsible public officers charged that Senator Thayer was not the only paid agent of the utilities in the legislature. After a somewhat superficial investigation of this aspect of the problem, the committee found no further examples of official misconduct. *Cf. State of New York, Final Report of the Joint Legislative Committee to Investigate Public Utilities,* Legislative Document, no. 78, 1936, p. 33. See also statements by W. Kingsland Macy, chairman of the Republican State Committee, *New York Times,* Dec. 9, 1933, and Governor Lehman's statements on lobbying activities in connection with his vigorous public utility program, particularly during legislative session, 1934, *supra,* pp. 79–81.

in the legislature.   The extent of this influence depends upon which party controls the legislature, how closely the pressure group is identified with that particular party, and, to a lesser extent, upon such legislative rules as that of seniority.   It is considered politically unwise to assign to legislative committees persons unfriendly to certain organized minorities that are interested in the bills coming before these committees.

Normally, pressure groups in the legislature concentrate on the chairman of the committee in charge of the bill and on the majority leaders: the Speaker in the Assembly and the Temporary President in the Senate.   If there is any possibility that party ranks will not stand firm inside or outside of the committee, a special point is made to contact and win over leading members of the minority.

More and more, however, the pressure groups with large active memberships and great voting strength have been presenting their cases to the rank and file of the legislature.   This practice serves the purpose of flattering the so-called unimportant legislator who likes to feel that he has not been completely overlooked in the legislative process.   At the same time, it acquaints the legislator with the sources in his local district from which he may expect support or opposition at the next election.   Such an approach has not only been of much value in securing the passage of local bills, but it has also acquainted party leaders both in and out of the legislature with the special local electoral dangers to which individual legislators are exposed.   For this reason, legislative leaders have, at times, excused individual members from adhering to party lines in voting on a measure to which strong organized opposition comes from their particular districts.[34]

In addition to their contacts with members of the legislature, pressure groups strive to maintain intimate relations with the chief executive and the various administrative departments.   The executive and administrative departments in both state and nation have steadily played a larger and more important role in the initiation and execution of legislative programs.   Governors of New York have in recent years been very active in lawmaking.   This is partially evidenced by the

---

[34] See *supra*, pp. 25, 179.

executive budget system, the frequent and forceful messages to the legislature, the radio appeals to the public to exert pressure upon recalcitrant legislative members, and the energetic use of the executive veto.[35]

Because of the Governor's potential legislative influence and his power of the veto, certain pressure groups have come to depend more and more upon the executive than upon the legislature for the success of their movements. For example, organized minorities, such as the Association of State Civil Service Employees of the State of New York and the Civil Service Reform Association, that strike at the political machine, or more specifically at the system of patronage, have on several occasions prevented the authorization of exemptions to the civil service laws by the legislature through the threat or actual exercise of the executive veto. Furthermore, pressure groups know that legislative majorities, even those of the Governor's own party, often pass on bills that the legislators themselves trust the Governor will veto.[36] Nor has the legislature hesitated to pass rival and conflicting bills, and left it to the Governor to choose between them. All of this makes the Governor important as a target of pressure activities.

Similarly, the officials of administrative departments have at their disposal information on pending legislation that is often of inestimable value to the legislature. In consequence, pressure groups inevitably strive to remove administrative opposition to their bills before bringing pressure upon the legislature, since the opposition of an administrative department is often sufficient to cause the defeat of any bill, no matter how vigorous is the pressure of the lobbyist.[37] In fact, at certain critical periods it is customary for very important legislation to originate with the administrative departments. Such was the case in both the banking and milk crises of 1933. One consequence of this is that pressure groups even strive to influ-

---

[35] Perhaps presidential aspirations have influenced such activity by New York Governors. Since the Civil War, six New York Governors won the Republican or Democratic presidential nominations: Tilden, Cleveland, Hughes, Smith, and the two Roosevelts.

[36] In 1935 and 1936 the legislature *unanimously* passed bills rescinding the emergency pay cut for teachers of New York City, and they were vetoed by Governor Lehman.

[37] See *supra*, pp. 14, 32, 46, 148.

ence the appointment of the administrative personnel and to seek and encourage the appointment of their own members to administrative investigatory commissions.[38]

The judicial branch of the government increasingly becomes the deep concern of organized minorities because of the courts' great power to interpret the laws. By this authority the state courts and the United States Supreme Court may declare state legislation unconstitutional and, hence, inoperative. Moreover, they may at times place upon laws an interpretation not intended by either the Legislature or the Governor. In such cases, of course, especially when the acts in question have been sponsored by their representatives, organized minorities become militant pressure groups in an attempt to dilute the effects of the judicial decisions. Under these circumstances, pressure groups may seek new legislation or a constitutional amendment. They may even become parties to a movement to curb the power of the courts or may play a direct role in the selection of judges.[39]

Even the pressure groups whose relations with the political leaders and the executive branch of the government are both close and fruitful, find it advisable to resort to mass pressure. This pressure is most commonly applied through letters, telegrams, petitions, and large attendance at public hearings. It is a mistake to underestimate the legislators' reaction to this form of pressure. The arrival of hundreds of letters and telegrams within a short period of time may have a decisive effect upon the fate of a bill.[40] Legislators, while very suspicious of the ultimate source of popular interest, have nevertheless admitted that the arrival of "basketfuls" of letters and telegrams at the opportune time has helped them out of many a "tight spot." The receipt of a large number of letters and telegrams may give legislators some idea of the potential voting strength of a particular group. When, however, the

---

[38] See *supra*, pp. 44, 56, 98, 165n.

[39] For example, after the passage of the multiple dwelling law by the New York Legislature in 1929, the real estate interests immediately turned their attention to the courts and sought an early decision concerning the constitutionality of this law. The New York Court of Appeals held the law constitutional in its decision on Aug. 8, 1929 in Adler vs. Deegan (251 N. Y. 467). See *supra*, p. 45. For another example, see *supra*, p. 40, note 102.

[40] See *infra*, pp. 279, 288, for the discussion of public hearings.

suspicion prevails that unfair pressure or threats have been used in securing such wide responses, more harm than good can then be done. When employees of particular companies, for example, unanimously sign petitions or telegrams in opposition to legislation which would obviously benefit them, legislators are apt to be wary.[41] All organized groups, the public utilities and labor, as well as church and civic organizations, recognize the influence of "voluntarily" secured popular responses.

A very significant recent trend in pressure techniques in New York has been the practice of widening and variegating the popular base to influence the legislature. Where the actual membership in a reasonably well organized body is large, as in labor, teacher, farm, veteran, and automobile associations, it is not difficult to secure such a wide popular response. But the groups that are by their very nature small in membership attempt to secure wide popular responses by actively cooperating with other organizations whose programs are more or less similar.[42] At the same time, these groups attempt to make a wider public appeal by emphasizing the public's interest in their programs. The Medical Society of the State of New York, for example, has attributed its support of health insurance and its opposition to chiropractors, osteopaths, and antivivisectionists to its interest in the welfare of the general public as well as in that of physicians.[43] Industrial associations likewise depict in glowing terms how with a reduction in taxes and public expenditures there will be a return of prosperity, with higher wages and better working conditions. Certain industrial groups, especially the public utilities, have encouraged a wide public reaction from their employees and small stockholders. In this way do the industrial groups strive to overcome the advantage such opposing pressure bodies as labor, the teachers, and the veterans possess at the ballot box.

---

[41] *Monitor*, June, 1935, p. 25 published by Associated Industries, Inc. *Cf.* The New York League of Women Voters' pamphlet, *The Daly Lobby*, 1920, *op. cit.*, pp. 11–14. Note, also, the extremes to which the Power Lobby resorted in the attempt to defeat the federal Wheeler-Rayburn bill, in the evidence submitted to the United States Senate Lobby Investigation Committee, *New York Times*, July, 1935.

[42] See *supra*, p. 41.

[43] Interview, Dr. Joseph S. Lawrence, Jan. 27, 1933.

On the other hand, there are some groups whose programs are so specialized and restricted that it is almost impossible for them to arouse any real public interest. In such cases the campaign must be won on its merits [44] or by resort to "back alley" tactics. The first of these is often difficult, while the latter is always accompanied by the danger that an opposition will become articulate if the program is inimical to the general welfare.

Campaigns of extensive letter-writing, telegraphing, assembling large delegations to march on the Capitol for public hearings, and issuing bulletins to members and special releases to the press often constitute specialized work in the group and are classified as part of its "educational" activity. A large number of the associations actually maintain "educational" departments, though it is unusual to find permanently employed "publicity" men in charge of such departments.[45]

In addition to these common pressure techniques, there are some that deserve special notice because of their novelty or rarity. The New York Department of the American Legion, for example, possesses a strikingly novel feature in pressure organization. This group of World War veterans was responsible, in 1920, for the organization of the Joint Veterans' Conference, composed of veterans of the World and Spanish American Wars serving in the State Legislature. At an annual meeting, these ex-service legislators elect officers and examine the legislative programs prepared and presented by the veterans' organizations in the state. The Joint Veterans' Conference works through its steering committee for the enactment of those bills in the veterans' programs of which it approves. In particular, it introduces bills, presents the veterans' point of view in the numerous committees in which these legislators sit, and assists in the establishment of contacts with the legislative leaders.[46]

----

[44] The New York State Highway Chapter of the General Contractors of America, concerned primarily with problems of highway construction, has won legislative enactments in this way.

[45] However, the legislative agent is sometimes selected because of his training and experience in publicity work. For example, John M. O'Hanlon and Mark A. Daly, two of the best known of Albany lobbyists, had training of this sort. See *supra*, pp. 13, 52n.

[46] See *supra*, p. 208. Interviews, Samuel E. Aronowitz and Edward J. Neary, chairmen of the Legislative Committee of the New York Department of the

Another interesting variation of pressure politics is the resort to a strike. It was used in what was perhaps its most spectacular form in the independent farmers' milk war against the Dairymen's League Cooperative Association in 1933. A milk strike had been called by over one thousand farmers organized in the Western New York Milk Producers Association, causing much violence and resulting in the failure of milk to reach its sources of distribution. The legislature met the demands of this association by hurriedly passing the important Milk Control Board bill, which contained price-fixing features opposed by the powerful Dairymen's League Cooperative Association, and the strike was called off.[47]

A still more novel demonstration was recently witnessed in Albany when one hundred air pilots swooped down over the state Capitol in protest against a bill providing for state regulation of airways. The later appearance of the pilots in their picturesque flying suits presented an unusual scene at a public hearing.[48] As a prelude to a public hearing on bills alleged to be inimical to the interests of taxicab drivers and owners, a three-hour protest strike was staged by Albany taxicab drivers.[49] Again, only the threat that marchers would be met by police clubs is believed to have prevented a delegation of over one hundred demonstrators for relief legislation from marching on the state Capitol.[50]

Women demonstrated their skill in devising spectacular ways of attracting public attention in their legislative activities when Mme. Anna Pavlowa, the dancer, appeared at a winter hearing on the woman's juror bill dressed from head to toe in an ensemble of white.[51]

American Legion, Jan. 30 and Apr. 27, 1933 and Assemblyman John P. Hayes, Mar. 12, 1936.

[47] A truce had been agreed upon by the striking farmers as the milk bill started through the legislature. After passage in the Assembly, it was temporarily blocked in the Senate. The striking farmers immediately called off the truce, which had lasted just one week, and violence broke out anew. Within 24 hours after the announcement was made that the truce was void, the bill went through the Senate. *New York Times,* Mar. 30, Apr. 8, Apr. 9, 1933.

[48] *New York Times,* Feb. 21, 1935.

[49] *New York Times,* Feb. 21, 1935.

[50] *New York Times,* Aug. 1, 1934.

[51] At a public presentation of a play in New York City, in which a jury was to be chosen from the audience, Dorothy Kenyon, a representative of the New York League of Women Voters, rose from her seat and demanded and

The "social lobby" in Albany is not particularly active and has never achieved the reputed influence of its counterpart in Washington.[52] Unlike the situation in Congress, the sessions of the State Legislature are short; they open in January and seldom run beyond the middle of April. Sessions open Monday night, and by Thursday are usually lightly attended, many of the legislators having returned home for the week-end. Since very few legislators establish permanent residences in the capital city, very few bring with them their wives and daughters, the reputed "social climbers." However, informal social functions are arranged by lobbyists for legislators during the legislative sessions. Wives and daughters are not usually invited to these affairs.

The increased number of women as lobbyists, however, has undoubtedly raised the tone of lobbying activity in Albany, despite the negligible part which they now play in the social lobby. Even before the passage of the women's suffrage amendment to the United States Constitution—in the days of the Black Horse Cavalry, when there was much talk of the employment of women for the purpose of influencing legislators—there were some women legitimately employed as lobbyists. Today, however, the state Capitol swarms with women legislative agents energetically and openly persuading legislators to particular points of view. They are seen in large numbers during public hearings on bills, at times outnumbering the men.[53] They are to be found in the corridors during the session, in conversation with legislators, and in the outer offices of members, awaiting their turns to speak with

---

received the right to sit on the stage jury. Shortly thereafter newspaper advertisements of this play carried the announcements that "women jurors may serve at all matinees." Later these advertisements were developed dramatically, a typical one reading: "First all-woman jury in the State of New York finds Karen Andre (a character in the play) Not Guilty of Murder." In addition to increasing the box office receipts, this advertisement provided the women of the state with a medium of influencing the public between legislative sessions. Thus, the groundwork was laid for the convening of the legislature in January, 1936, when the women for the sixteenth consecutive year made their plea for a woman juror law for New York State. *Cf. New York Sun*, Oct. 3, 1935, and *New York Times*, Oct. 8, Oct. 29, 1935. The play referred to was *The Night of January 16th*.

[52] The "social lobby in Washington is the most dangerous of all," said Representative William L. Nelson of Missouri. *Cf. New York Times*, July 30, 1935.

[53] In 1933, at a beer bill hearing more than half of those present and those who addressed legislators were women.

them. Their names, too, are found among those who register
with the Secretary of State under the lobbying law. But the
majority of those who appear at Albany are not required so
to register, since they are not "paid" agents or counsel.

This redoubtable influence of women in legislation is not
surprising when it is realized that two million women are part
of the active electorate in New York State,[54] and that in 1935,
132 women held governmental appointive and elective offices
in the state.[55] New York women also occupy positions of
importance in party councils, and are represented in equal
numbers with the men on the national and state party committees.[56] The influence of women in legislation, however,
has been directed not through the positions that they occupy
in the government service or in political party councils, but,
rather, through their unofficial organized groups. This influence has been enhanced, of course, by the fact that women
in governmental and political positions have frequently been
called upon for assistance.[57]

Only recently have many pressure groups learned the importance of maintaining at Albany legislative agents who are
equipped by personality and experience to win and hold the
confidence of legislators, particularly the leaders. Many organizations continue to send "new faces" to Albany, often in

---

[54] Registration figures computed on a sex basis for the entire state are not
available. Such figures are, however, available for New York City. In 1932,
38.3 per cent of those who registered in the city were women. If this proportion of women to men is maintained throughout the state, over 2,000,000
women registered in the state in 1932. On this same basis over 1,750,000
women registered in 1934. (37.1 per cent of those who registered in New York
City in 1934 were women.)

[55] Of these, 105 were appointive and 27 elective posts. Three of the latter
were in the State Legislature. *Report of the National Federation of Business
and Professional Women's Clubs. Cf. New York Times,* July 16, 1935. In
1931, 146 women served as legislators in 39 states. *Cf.* S. P. Breckinridge,
Women in the Twentieth Century, 1933, p. 324.

[56] In the Republican National Convention of 1932, nine of the 88 women
delegates and 25 of the 307 women alternates were from New York. At the
Democratic National Convention of the same year, seven of the 208 women
delegates and 26 of the 270 alternates were New York women. At the state
conventions the proportion of women to men was much greater. *Social
Trends,* New York, McGraw-Hill, 1933, Vol. I, p. 741, and S. P. Breckinridge,
op. cit., p. 287; Inez H. Irwin, *Angels and Amazons—A Hundred Years of
American Women,* 1933, and *Proceedings of the Democratic and Republican
National Conventions,* 1932.

[57] Many examples of such contacts can be found in the campaigns for the
48-hour and minimum wage laws for women and the woman juror bill.

the person of the newly-selected chairman of the organization's legislative committee. The loss of time in learning one's way about Albany and the lengthy introductions and explanations necessary to get past the legislative leader's secretary are serious obstacles to the novices. Knowledge of the legislative process or of the personal eccentricities of individual members of the legislature cannot be learned overnight by agents who devote part of their time to their legislative work and who are replaced at frequent intervals. Undoubtedly the most tangible results have been achieved by the rapidly increasing number of pressure groups who year after year have stationed the same representatives at Albany throughout the session, and whose names have become inextricably connected with the interests they represent.[58]

[58] Among these lobbyists should be mentioned John M. O'Hanlon and George Meany, New York State Federation of Labor; Mark A. Daly, Associated Industries, Inc.; Edward P. Doyle, Real Estate Board of New York, Inc.; Ray Hofford, Real Estate Association of the State of New York; Merwin K. Hart, New York State Economic Council, Inc.; Paul W. Albright, Savings Bank Association of the State of New York; J. Henry Walters, Trust Companies Association of the State of New York; Gerald F. Dunne, Retail Liquor Dealers Association of New York City; Frank Boland, New York State Hotel Association; J. H. Griswold, New York Telephone Co.; Frank A. McNamee, Jr., New York Central R. R. and the Associated Railways of New York; Ross M. Lovell until his death in 1935 represented about half a dozen railroads; L. G. Stapley and T. D. Pratt, New York State Motor Truck Association; David J. Henderson, New York Petroleum Industries Co.; Warner Bates and Melvin T. Bender, New York State Automobile Association; Bert W. Miller, New York State Farm Bureau Federation and the New York State Conference Board of Farm Organizations; Elsie M. Bond, the State Charities Aid Association; Lawrence Veiller, Charity Organization Society; George A. Hall, New York Child Labor Committee; N. J. Walker, the Convention of Societies for the Prevention of Cruelty to Children and Animals of New York State, Inc.; Charles J. Tobin, New York State Catholic Welfare Committee; Dr. Arvie Eldred, New York State Teachers' Association; May A. Healy, Anna R. Pettebone, Lillian A. Hatch, Grace H. Miller, Dr. Abraham Lefkowitz, the Joint Committee of Teachers' Organizations of New York City; Dr. Bella V. Dodd, the Teachers' Union of the City of New York; Dr. Joseph S. Lawrence, Medical Society of the State of New York; Burton D. Esmond, New York State Chiropractic Society; Emily J. Hicks, New York State Nurses' Association; Charles W. Walton, New York State Bar Association; William F. McDonough, Association of State Civil Service Employees; William P. Capes, New York State Conference of Mayors; Reuben A. Lazarus, City of New York; Andrew Ronan, City of Buffalo; Seth T. Cole, Firemen's Association of the State of New York; Vincent K. Kane, Uniformed Firemen's Association of Greater New York; Thomas P. Cummings and Peter Keresman, State Police Conference; George A. Hallett, Jr., Citizens Union of the City of New York; Isidor Begun, Communist Party; Fred A. Victor, Anti-Saloon League of New York; Mrs. D. L. Colvin, Women's Christian Temperance Union of the State of New York; Rev. O. R. Miller, New York Civic League.

At the public hearings, on the other hand, a better impression is produced and a wider demand for the enactment of the legislation under discussion is conveyed if "new faces" appear and present the arguments. The "old timers" on such "public" occasions are content with an inconspicuous role.[59]

Although former legislators reappear at the state Capitol from time to time to oppose or promote legislation, perhaps not more than a half dozen appear regularly year after year in behalf of the same interests.[60] Such persons are thoroughly at home in Albany. They are familiar with the legislative process, and their political contacts inside and outside the legislature are of value. Over a period of time, scores of such former legislators may reappear at Albany in one capacity or another, but unlike the situation in Washington, the hiring of ex-legislators as lobbyists has not been indulged in to such an extent as to result in excesses peculiar to this practice. It must be remembered that the prestige of a state legislator is not so great as that of a member of Congress. Furthermore, an influential ex-legislator does not usually end his political career in the State Legislature. Those who hold higher political posts, on the other hand, do not usually appear publicly as the agents of organized minorities, unless it is for legislation that can be defended in the public interest. It must be remembered that the State Legislature itself is composed, for the most part, of lawyers and business men who are actively engaged in their own private enterprises while performing their duties as public servants.[61] For this reason it is not always necessary for organized minorities to employ ex-legislators, for at times the interests of some members of the legislature and the pressure groups themselves are the same.

It is not always true that pressure groups utilizing the most effective techniques are the most successful. Special circumstances surrounding pending legislation are often of greater importance, particularly during abnormal economic periods. Forces behind public opinion, for example, are at times so

---

[59] In such states as Wisconsin and Massachusetts, where a distinction is drawn between legislative agent and counsel, the legislative agent is not permitted to appear before committees. This, however, is not true in New York.

[60] Prominent among these are Edward P. Doyle, Merwin K. Hart, J. Henry Walters, Gerald F. Dunne, L. G. Stapley, Charles W. Walton, Burton D. Esmond. *Supra,* note 58.

[61] See *Appendix A.*

strong that the most powerful opposition cannot prevent the passage of a particular type of legislation. Such were the recent bills in New York providing for increased and new taxes and for a mortgage moratorium. Similarly, welfare groups find a depression an opportune time to win such types of welfare legislation as minimum wage laws for women, old age pensions, and unemployment insurance. Organizations opposed to such legislation, though at a disadvantage at such times, are, nevertheless, alert to suggest compromises and to preach the doctrine of gradualness.[62] The public temper during crises, moreover, is such that scapegoats are sought after, and bankers and public utilities can play the role effectively. Thus, public officials find such times opportune for the enactment of their programs, since legislators do not dare to block them. Such was the case, for example, of Governor Lehman's utility program in 1934.

The bicameral legislature in New York, especially when each of the two dominant parties is in control of one chamber, further complicates the results of propaganda techniques. In long drawn out campaigns a milestone is reached when the legislation passes one house, for this frequently means that the final goal is within sight. Such has been the history of much legislation in New York, particularly social legislation. Nevertheless, the work of the lobbyist, who must make the most of the political setting by planning carefully his strategic moves, is doubled. For he must somewhere include a defense of the legislation on its merits, because the opposition, by the setup, is given a second point of vantage from which to work at blocking the normal progress of the bill.[63]

The outstanding characteristic of modern pressure techniques centers about the ballot. Universal suffrage has assumed a new and deeper significance. It is for this reason that the emphasis in legislative pressure has come to be placed more and more on building favorable public opinion through channels of mass propaganda, without, however, abandoning the old and tried methods.

---

[62] See *Monitor,* Apr. and May, 1935, published by Associated Industries, Inc. for notes on the unemployment insurance bill campaign. See the July, 1935 issue, p. 47, for objection to the thirty-hour week.

[63] See discussion of bicameralism and pressure groups, *infra,* pp. 274, 281.

CHAPTER IX

Governmental Control of the Lobby

BECAUSE of our federal system of government and despite legislative restrictions in the long, detailed state constitutions, the state lawmaking bodies in the United States enjoy extensive powers.[1] The broad and varied scope of the legislative function in New York may well be imagined when it is realized that in recent sessions of the legislature more than four thousand bills are introduced annually, of which more than one thousand are passed.[2]

It is, therefore, not surprising to learn that the activities of pressure groups before the New York Legislature give rise to certain problems.   These problems fall into five categories. The first relates to the use of what might be termed unethical practices on the part of the lobbyists, ranging from outright bribery of legislators to the securing of legislative favors through innuendo and indirection.   The second is concerned with the representative character of the groups that appear and pretend to represent various interests.   The third deals with the lack of balance among the various groups, owing to the inertness of those whose interests do not appear to be so directly or so immediately affected (for example, the consumers).   The fourth pertains to the advantage that the lobbyist, with his greater knowledge, has over the amateur legislator. The fifth relates to the advantages some groups have over others under the existing structure of the legislature, with its

---

[1] Pressure groups are as much interested in state constitutional amendments as in ordinary statutes. The special procedure required for state constitutional changes will, of course, be borne in mind when these groups exert their influence. See *New York State Constitution*, Art. XIV. For an example of pressure group interest in state constitutional amendments, see *supra*, p. 17, for interest in bond issues, see p. 142.

[2] During a 20-year period (1917–1936), the average number of bills introduced annually was 3,641, whereas the annual average of bills passed was 1,009. The Governor vetoed 21.6 per cent of these. Thus, an average of 795 laws were enacted annually during this period. *Cf. New York Legislative Manual,* 1935, pp. 743, 744, and *New York Times,* June 12, 1936.

two houses, its unfair district system, its cumbersome committee system, and its ineffective and haphazard public hearings.

In so far as there has been any cognizance of these various and sundry problems, only the first has received recognition. It represents the oldest attempt at control.

✓ In 1906 a lobbying law was passed.[3] This law provides that "every person retained or employed for compensation as counsel or agent by any person, firm, corporation or association to promote or oppose directly or indirectly the passage of bills or resolutions by either house or to promote or oppose executive approval of such bills or resolutions, shall, in each and every year, before any service is entered upon in promoting or opposing such legislation, file in the office of the Secretary of State

---

[3] Cahill's Consolidated Laws of New York, 1930, ch. 33, sec. 66. This law was passed after the Armstrong Joint Legislative Committee investigation disclosed that the country was divided into three districts, each covered by a large insurance company. Legislation was closely watched by a representative of the insurance companies stationed in each state Capitol. Huge sums of money were spent in promoting or opposing legislation that affected the interests of insurance companies and in securing the nomination and election of friendly legislators. See *Proceedings of the Joint Committee of the Senate and Assembly of the State of New York—Appointed to Investigate the Affairs of Life Insurance Companies*, 10 vols., Albany, 1906. See Vol. 10 of these *Proceedings* for the bill prepared by the committee, for the summary of the legislative activities of the insurance companies, and the committee's recommendations in this connection. The testimony gathered by this committee in New York and Governor LaFollette's message to the Wisconsin Legislature in May, 1905, were largely responsible for the movement that led to the enactment of state lobbying laws at that time. However, a law on lobbying was originally passed in New York in 1892. New York was thus among the first states to pass such legislation. Lobbying legislation in some form can be found today in 32 states. See E. B. Logan, "Lobbying"—*Supplement to the Annals of the American Academy of Political and Social Science*, July, 1929. See also Library of Congress—Legislative Reference Service, *State Laws Regulating Lobbying* compiled by Jennie Welland, Nov. 28, 1932 and Dec. 20, 1934. Beginning with 1907, many congressional bills were introduced, passing the Senate in 1928 (Senate no. 1095, 70th Cong. 1st Session), and in 1935 (Senate no. 2512, 74th Cong. 1st Session). In 1936 another bill passed the House of Representatives (H. R. 11663, Report no. 2214) and the Senate in amended form, but the House rejected the report of the conference committee. Much testimony has been gathered in lengthy congressional hearings. See H. D. Lasswell, *Propaganda and Promotional Activities—An Annotated Bibliography*, Minneapolis, University of Minnesota Press, 1935, pp. 278, 279; United States Senate, hearing before a subcommittee of the Committee on the Judiciary, 74th Congress, 1st Session on Senate 2512, Apr. 16; 1935; and United States House of Representatives, hearing before the Committee on the Judiciary, 74th Congress, 1st Session on Senate 2512 and House of Representatives 5725, July 16 and 26, 1935.

a writing subscribed by such counsel or agent stating" by whom he was retained or employed, "together with a brief description of the legislation in reference to which such service is to be rendered." The Secretary of State is required to provide a "docket of legislative appearances," setting forth this information, to be open to public inspection. The notice filed is valid for only thirty days following the adjournment of the session of the legislature held in that year.[4] No person may be so employed whose compensation is contingent in whole or in part upon the passage or defeat of any legislative measure.

The law further provides that within two months after the adjournment of the legislature there shall be filed with the Secretary of State a sworn itemized statement showing in detail all expenses paid or promised, including disbursements paid or promised to counsel or agents, directly or indirectly, in connection with legislation pending at the previous session. Payees and amounts are to be specified, and also the nature of the legislation and the payer's interest in it.

The provision of the law "requiring docket entries" does not apply to the "accredited counsel or agents of counties, cities, towns, villages, public boards and public institutions." The provisions of the law are not to be "construed as affecting professional services in drafting bills or in advising clients and in rendering opinions as to the construction and effect of proposed or pending legislation where such professional service is not otherwise connected with legislative action." A violation of this law is classified as a misdemeanor and penalties are provided.[5] Such, in brief, is the lobbying law of New York State.

Between the years 1908 and 1935 an average of 134 legislative appearance statements were filed with the Secretary of

[4] It is, therefore, necessary to file such notices for all sessions of the legislature, including special sessions, if they convene more than thirty days after the close of the regular session.

[5] The punishment provided for an individual is imprisonment not to exceed one year or a fine of not more than one thousand dollars or both. In the case of a corporation or association, a fine of not more than one thousand dollars is provided. In addition to these penalties, any corporation or association failing to file the statement of legislative expenses within the time required forfeits one hundred dollars a day for each day after the expiration of the two-month period allowed.

State at Albany yearly.[6]   The following table shows the actual number filed each year.

Year	No. of Legis- lative Appearance Docket Statements	Year	No. of Legis- lative Appearance Docket Statements
1908	208	1922	101
1909	163	1923	123
1910	196	1924	114
1911	240	1925	75
1912	113	1926	76
1913	203	1927	61
1914	154	1928	121
1915	167	1929	110
1916	149	1930	129
1917	179	1931	100
1918	110	1932	86
1919	130	1933	123
1920	141	1934	145
1921	106	1935	131

Although most of these declarations are those of the representatives of business and economic groups,[7] large expenditures are not indicated in the expense statements filed.   The largest items cover payments for legal services.   The total expenditures recorded in the expense statements filed in 1935 aggregated $103,796.39.[8]

On the one hand, the New York State Federation of Labor records with its expenses, the salary paid to its secretary-treasurer, who devotes most of his time to legislative duties

[6] An examination of these statements indicates that in a few instances several persons who appeared for the same corporation or association, or for the same legislation, filed joint statements.

[7] For example, in 1931, the agents or counsel of the public utilities alone filed approximately one-third of the statements.   In 1926, 51 firms representing industrial, commercial, and financial interests were registered.   Cf. Evelyn E. Smith, The Third House of the State Legislature—A Study of the Diverse Interests Which Sought by Various Means to Influence the Passage of Legislation During the 1926 Session of the New York Legislature, Columbia University Master's Essay, May, 1936.

[8] Too much emphasis should not be placed upon this figure in estimating the amount of money spent in influencing legislation by agents or counsel in any one year, because many agents and counsel who filed appearance statements neglected to file expense statements.   In a few cases the figure recorded covered the full annual salary of the agent or counsel.   Furthermore, it may be assumed that many who came within the purview of the law filed neither the appearance nor the expense statements.   Others active in influencing legislation—for example, the teachers—are not subject to the lobbying law.

while the legislature is in session.[9]   On the other hand, it is customary for the New York Telephone Company to record only the expenses incurred during the legislative sessions by the three or four men who usually appear for the Telephone Company and who are otherwise employed and retained by this corporation.[10]

Two typical expense statements read as follows:

Name of Payee [11]	Purpose	Amount Paid, Incurred or Promised
Melvin T. Bender	Yearly salary as counsel. Professional services rendered in drafting bills, clients, and rendering opinions as to the proposed or pending legislation relating to automobiles..................	$1,500.00
Disbursements	Postage, stationery, telephone, telegraph, etc.............................	39.73
Legislative Index	Legislative Index Service for 1931.....	225.00
		$1,764.73

The foregoing expenditures were not paid in connection with any legislation.

Dated	Notarized	Signed
May 28, 1931		Warner Bates

Name of Payee [12]	Purpose	Amount Paid, Incurred or Promised
Charles J. Tobin	Legal Services	$1,000.00
George C. Cutler	Travelling Expenses, Legislative Committee	25.50
George C. Cutler	Travelling Expenses, Legislative Committee (second trip).................	29.87
J. Henry Walters	Legal Services.......................	7,500.00
		$8,555.37

From a study of the legislative appearance and expense statements one may justly conclude that the law is broken

---

[9] *Supra,* p. 13.   *Cf.* Statements filed by John M. O'Hanlon with the Secretary of State.

[10] *Supra,* p. 63n.

[11] Legislative expense statement filed with the Secretary of State by counsel for the New York State Automobile Association in 1931.

[12] Legislative expense statement filed with the Secretary of State by the legislative agent and counsel who appeared for the Trust Companies Association of New York State in 1932.

with impunity.   In 1931 exactly one hundred legislative appearance docket statements were filed.   Thirty-three persons
or corporations who filed these appearance statements failed
to file the expense statements required by the law.[13]   There
were further infractions of the law in eight cases in 1931, when
expense statements were filed after the expiration of the legal
two-month period following adjournment of the legislature.

Similarly, during the regular session of the legislature in
1932, 86 appearance statements were filed, but accompanying
statements of expense were not filed for 32 of these.   Significantly, among those who did file expense accounts, five had
not filed legislative appearance statements during the session,
and five filed their expense statements after the legal two-
month interval.[14]

The cardinal weakness of the law is that no one is specifically charged with its enforcement.   There is nothing in the
law, for example, that requires the Secretary of State to check
the records or to call violations of the law to the attention of
the Attorney General.   The Secretary of State is simply required to provide the docket for the filing of such statements.[15]

Undoubtedly, if some interest were shown and the matter
were publicly aired, the Attorney General might act.   But
even then he would act only in the case of an overt violation of
the law, for unfortunately the New York law suffers from the
weakness characteristic of lobbying legislation generally: no

---

[13] This figure is conservative, because if more than one agent or counsel representing the same corporation filed separate appearance statements, and if the
name of only one of these agents or counsel was given in the expense statement, both were credited with having filed expense statements.   Besides, if
an agent or counsel indicated in the legislative appearance statement that he
was representing more than one corporation, but in the expense statement
mentioned the name of only one corporation, it was assumed that the expense
statement covered all the corporations listed in the appearance statement.

[14] Twenty-six known interests represented in the 1926 session of the New
York Legislature failed to register.   Although most of these were welfare and
reform organizations, they were required by law to register.   Cf. Evelyn E.
Smith, op. cit.   There is no double entry or numbering system for the filing
of expense statements such as is now used for the appearance statements.
Moreover, since these files are open to public inspection, expense statements
can be removed or added without detection.

[15] The Secretary of State keeps a supply of legislative appearance and
expense blanks which are forwarded to those who request them.   It is not
compulsory, however, to use these blanks in filing the information required.

satisfactory definition of what constitutes legitimate lobbying practices is given in the statute.[16]

Under the existing law, consequently, there may be a reasonable doubt as to whether a person who files neither a legislative appearance nor an expense statement falls within the purview of the law. Nevertheless, the law was and is clearly and overtly violated by many who file appearance statements but neglect to record a statement of the expenses incurred by such appearances. The enforcement of the law is occasionally directed against those who have openly violated the law and who have unwisely offended those who are in a strategic position to retaliate. For example, the Anti-Saloon League of New York was the subject of an abortive move in this direction in 1920, when the Albany County Grand Jury and the Attorney General of the state investigated charges that the legislative agent and counsel of the League had failed to file appearance and expense statements. While no further action was taken, even such slight activity in connection with the New York lobbying law has been unusual.[17]

The law does serve the purpose, on occasion, of frightening lobbyists who, by their persistence, have exasperated legislators. An irate legislator may threaten on such occasions to take action against those lobbyists who have not registered.[18] A rapid exit from the chambers, for the purpose of registering with the Secretary of State, may then occur, to be followed in turn by an equally prompt return to the chambers. Such a dramatic incident is often necessary to remind legislative agents of the registration requirement. The writer, too, served as a reminder while moving about interviewing agents

---

[16] This difficulty has been undoubtedly a strong reason for the failure of Congress to enact a lobbying law.

[17] The Assembly had failed to pass the resolution of Assemblyman Louis E. Cuvillier to investigate the activities of the Anti-Saloon League after its Superintendent, W. H. Anderson, had made severe attacks upon legislators. Cf. New York Times, Apr. 21, 1920. Assemblyman Cuvillier then stated that the legislative counsel and agent of the Anti-Saloon League had failed to file appearance and expense statements. He charged that the expense statements were overdue for close to two years, and that on the basis of $100 a day for each day of delinquency as provided in the law, the Anti-Saloon League owed the state about $70,000. Cf. New York Times, Apr. 29 and May 20, 1920.

[18] There are occasional requests that an offending lobbyist be cited for contempt, New York Herald Tribune, Apr. 7, 1933.

and counsel during sessions of the legislature. When this happened, the usual comment was: "Silly law, isn't it?"

In its application only to those who are *compensated* for their legislative activity, many who are very much in evidence in Albany during legislative sessions are excluded from its compass. Moreover, some doubt has been expressed as to whether the law really covers those who receive regular salaries from the persons, corporations, or associations they represent at Albany when only one of their functions deals with promoting or opposing legislation. While the law does cover persons employed for compensation who promote or oppose directly or indirectly the passage of laws *inside* or *outside* the City of Albany, it is possible to envisage the fruitful results that could be achieved by contacting, for example, political leaders outside of the City of Albany. The subsequent difficulty of applying the law to those who participate in influencing state legislation from outside of the capital city is very obvious, indeed.[19]

If lobbying activity in the State of New York has been conducted more honestly and more openly since the enactment of the law in 1906 than it was before—and it undoubtedly has—little credit, perhaps, should be given to the law itself. Nevertheless, despite the apparent weaknesses of the statute, somewhat better results might be achieved if the disposition and desire on the part of public officials were present to invoke the law more frequently and to prosecute more vigorously under it. But do most legislators want the lobbyists harassed in this fashion? Or are not the legislators too frequently the recipients of material considerations from lobbyists, ranging all the way from entertainment to contributions to campaign funds and to employment? Although the New York lawmakers are the highest paid state legislators in the United States, they receive only $2,500 annually,[20] and practically no

---

[19] See Logan, *op. cit.*, p. 72, for analysis of additional difficulties surrounding a regulative lobbying law.

[20] See H. W. Toll, "Should We Pay Law-Makers," *State Government,* Feb., 1931. See also *State Government,* Jan., 1935, or *The Book of the States,* published in Chicago by the Council of State Governments and the American Legislators' Association, 1935, Vol. I, p. 67, for summary of salaries and allowances of state legislators in the U. S. A. F. Macdonald states: "The miserable stipends . . . have served chiefly to attract miserable men [to the state legislatures], to whom the prospect of even a small wage, coupled with oppor-

additional allowance is made for traveling expenses.[21] The
legislators spend a considerable portion of their salaries in
attending to their legislative duties at Albany. They must,
therefore, depend for their support upon income from private
sources. A survey of the private occupations of members of a
recent (1935) legislature indicates that 47 per cent were lawyers, 35 per cent were engaged in commercial enterprises, and
9 per cent were farmers.[22] Is it not inevitable, therefore, that
some legislators will be retained in private capacity by the
very interests that seek legislative protection at Albany? Did
not several legislators ask to be excused from voting on the
utility bills in 1934 because they were serving as counsel, officers, or directors of utility companies?[23] Do not legislators
consistently block legislation that adversely affects their private professions and occupations? Quite recently Governor
Lehman called public attention to the fact that several lawyer-
legislators were blocking his anti-crime program: "One per-
ceives in them a still more sinister conspiracy than that of
politics—the conspiracy of lawyer-legislators to perpetuate
for their profession the obstructions to justice by which it
prospers."[24] This close connection between certain legislators
and organized minorities may be a reason not merely for the

---

tunities for illicit gain, has proved alluring. Most honest men in moderate
circumstances have felt that they could not afford the financial sacrifices
entailed by service in the legislature, and most honest men of independent
means have hesitated to brave the unpleasantness of a political campaign in
competition with second-rate politicians interested solely in private profit.
Mediocre salaries have begotten mediocre legislators; no other result could
reasonably have been expected. The payment of adequate compensation
would not in itself guarantee a higher standard of legislative efficiency, but it
would remove one of the major causes of inefficiency." *American State Government and Administration*, New York, Thomas Y. Crowell, 1934, p. 185.

[21] A meager mileage allowance of one dollar for every ten miles traveled
going to or coming from a meeting once a session, is permitted. *Cf. Constitution of the State of New York*, Art. III, Sec. 6.

[22] See *Appendix A.*

[23] *Supra*, p. 80.

[24] *New York Times*, Feb. 24, 1936, p. 8. For example, lawyer-legislators
frown upon legislation extending guardianship privileges to trust companies.
Lawyer-legislators were believed responsible for blocking in 1935 the hospital
lien bill which required reimbursement for medical services in hospital accident cases where compensation was won by the accident victim. Interview
with Dr. Jos. S. Lawrence, legislative agent of the Medical Society of the
State of New York, Sept. 3, 1935. Legislators with insurance company connections are believed responsible for blocking since 1920 a woman juror's bill.

weak provisions in the lobbying law itself but, more particularly, for the laxity in its enforcement.

Although it is difficult, if not impossible, to "legislate" bad lobbying practices out of existence, it is perhaps better to retain the New York law, poor as it is, than to repeal it completely.[25] It does afford an opportunity for some degree of publicity, and can be used to expose flagrant cases to the glare of even greater publicity.

The law might, perhaps, be strengthened as follows: [26]

1. A very specific definition of lobbying might be included in the statute to cover paid professional lobbyists, stating clearly the practices that are permissible and those that are not. Legislators and enforcement agencies could thus invoke specific sections of the law when bringing charges against those who improperly influence the course of legislation.[27]

2. Employers as well as their legislative agents or counsel might be compelled to register within a short stated period of time after their legislative activities begin.[28]

3. In addition to the information now requested, a written authorization to act as counsel or agent, signed by the employer and filed with the Secretary of State when the employee registers, outlining the nature and purpose of the employment, might be required.

---

[25] As state lobbying laws go, the New York law is considered "good." See J. K. Pollock, *American Political Science Review*, May, 1927, p. 339. The provisions of the Wisconsin law and the record achieved under it rank highest in the country. See Logan, *op. cit.*, p. 7.

[26] Parenthetically, it might be added that the problem of the regulation of the "third house" has not been without its humorous aspects. It was the former Senator Reed of Missouri who proposed to exterminate lobbyists by putting them "into a uniform, or livery of as striking a pattern as possible." *Cf. New York Telegram*, May 26, 1928. A New York legislator vexed at lobbyists said he had been thinking of having the New York law amended to compel lobbyists to file their photographs, apparently with the hope that some would give up their professions upon the realization that a reproduction of themselves would become part of the records of the great State of New York. Another legislator waggishly suggested that lobbyists might all be fingerprinted, so that people would know what bills they were handling. *Cf. New York World*, Feb. 27, 1929.

[27] For the provision in the Wisconsin law that aims at discouraging personal solicitation, see *Wisconsin Statutes*, 1931, ch. 346, p. 2332.

[28] The law now provides vaguely that legislative counsel or agent register "before" their activities begin.

4. The period for filing expense accounts might be cut from within two months to within thirty days, in order that the Governor, in considering thirty-day bills, might know what expenses were incurred by lobbyists.[29]

5. Where agent or counsel receives an annual salary and performs other duties in addition to legislative work, some indication of the proportion of time devoted to legislative work and the expenses incurred in connection therewith might be required. This would not only give a more accurate picture of expenses incurred in influencing legislation but would tend to bring within the purview of the law many professional lobbyists who claim exemption because they are not compensated specifically for legislative work.[30]

6. Employees of the state and of localities who are actively engaged in promoting or opposing legislation and whose expenses are not defrayed—aside from their salaries —through the public treasury might also be included within the compass of the legislation. Thus, representatives of the Association of State Civil Service Employees and of the many teachers' associations who are stationed at Albany for most of the legislative session would be forced to register.

7. Those who serve on the following political committees might be restricted from service as legislative counsel or agent: county executive committees (this would cover all county and assembly district ward leaders), state central and executive committees, and the New York members on the national committees.

8. Those found guilty of violating the law might be disbarred from service as a legislative agent or counsel for at least a three-year period.

9. Finally, the enforcement of the law might well be placed in the hands of a responsible agency. It seems almost superfluous to add that, no matter how stringent are the regulative provisions of the law, it will soon become

---

[29] Although this would place an additional great burden upon the Governor during this exacting thirty-day period, the executive veto might be used in those exceptional cases that aroused suspicion or unfavorable publicity.

[30] This legislative work might include not only the direct contacts of agent or counsel with legislators, but also such matters as the drafting of bills or the preparation of briefs.

a dead letter unless an enforcement agency is set up. Such an agency might be a legislative committee, the Governor, the Attorney General, or some other administrative officer with authority to conduct such investigations as may be necessary for the purpose of learning whether or not the law has been violated. A formal report might be submitted to the legislature at the opening of each annual session, to become part of the official record of that body. In addition, the list of lobbyists might be read once a month during the session and printed in the Journal of the legislature. Chairmen of the various legislative committees might cooperate in the enforcement of the law by interrogating those who appear before their committees as to their status—both questions and answers to be placed in the official records of the committees. Violations might be prosecuted immediately, since the general criminal statute of limitations undoubtedly would apply.[31]

Obviously, however, no regulative lobbying law nor any revision of the present one can solve the five problems indicated, especially the newer ones among those that have emerged, for the very nature of our legislative process itself makes it impossible for what Schattschneider [32] has called the "laissez-faire of pressure group activities" to operate fairly.

No attempt is made under our existing committee procedure to determine the character of the representation claimed by those appearing. It is, consequently, very probable that the representatives of the various groups claim for both themselves and their groups much more than is actually true. For example, when the New York State Federation of Labor claims that it speaks for close to one million workers in the state, what attempt is made to ascertain the truth or falsity of the claim? What attempt is made to ascertain the nature and composition of the Federation membership — to determine whether the Federation has the right to speak for the unskilled workers as well as the skilled? Nor is any effort made to discover whether or not all classes of membership were given a

---

[31] The three-year limitation is applicable to the lobbying law. Interview with Mr. Harold Greenstein of the Department of Law in Albany, Feb. 2, 1933. Several of the above suggestions can be found somewhat modified perhaps, among existing lobbying statutes.

[32] E. E. Schattschneider, *Politics, Pressures and the Tariff*, New York, Prentice-Hall, 1935.

fair opportunity to participate in drafting the legislative program or whether it is essentially the work of an inside clique.
Similarly the question can be raised, for whom do the Real
Estate Association of the State of New York and the Real
Estate Board of New York, speak? Do they represent the big
fellows or the little fellows among the real estate interests?
Does the New York State Teachers' Association represent the
views of its 45,000 classroom teacher members or its 400 members in the administrative and supervisory division? Why do
some groups, such as the chiropractors, withhold information
concerning the size and composition of their membership?

Greater publicity might be given to this very fundamental
and vital aspect of pressure group activity during the consideration of legislation. A step might be made toward checking
this frequent and flagrant abuse of pressure group politics
through strengthening the lobbying law. Much more effective, however, would be a requirement that all who appear
before a legislative committee shall present not only the name
of the organization or association for whom they are speaking
but also data on the character, objectives, and membership of
that organization or association. Similar information might
be required of those who file briefs with the committees.

If data of this kind were consistently collected, it would undoubtedly indicate that the consumer, a group admittedly
difficult to classify, is underrepresented before the legislature.

Under our existing constitutional and economic system,
pressure groups are indispensable, despite the fact that many
New York State legislators tend to minimize and underestimate the constructive part played by these groups. These
legislators realize that to assign to them a larger constructive
role may possibly be interpreted as a reflection upon their own
inadequacy, inefficiency, or lack of concern for the public welfare. These legislators are willing to admit that in the enactment of laws, the practical experience and knowledge of
interest groups can well be and is utilized in making legislation
workable—in pointing out the application of the law to stated
cases. Valuable as this is, pressure group activity does not
begin and end here. The origin of programs of social progress
and retrogression are undoubtedly more the responsibility of
organized minorities than of any other agency in our whole

political, economic, and social structure. It has been rightly said that "it is an illuminating fact that almost no great social reform has ever begun in a legislative body," [33] and that "the nature of public policy is the result of effective demands upon the government" by organized minorities.[34] It is undoubtedly true that most organized minorities are not interested in "great social reform," but rather in protecting the interest groups that they represent. The demands of these groups may or may not be in keeping with the best interests of the general public. Before the legislature, this mighty array of pressure groups clashes; for it is, by and large, a clash of interests considerably sharpened by the recent economic crisis. Labor demands are resisted by industrial groups.[35] Railroad interests urge greater governmental supervision and control of their competitors: motored vehicles. Or examine, for instance, the line-up of pressure groups when suggestions to balance the state budget are offered: [36] on one side are generally found welfare, civic, women's, labor, church, professional, and public employee groups resisting the demands for the curtailment of expenditures of social welfare services. These demands are usually made by chambers of commerce, trade associations, bankers' groups, real estate associations, public utilities, economic coun-

---

[33] *Pathfinding in Health and Welfare,* pamphlet published by the State Charities Aid Association, New York, May, 1930, p. 29.

[34] E. E. Schattschneider, *op. cit.,* p. 4. See also C. E. Merriam, *Social Trends,* 1933, Vol. II, pp. 1511–1515 and J. P. Chamberlain, *Legislative Processes—National and State,* New York, D. Appleton-Century, 1936, p. 64.

[35] This clash of interests can best be indicated in the conflicting opinions, expressed by Associated Industries on one hand and the New York State Federation of Labor on the other, concerning the social legislation passed by the New York State Legislature in 1935. Associated Industries: "No legislature since 1913 did as much damage to business as did the 1935 session." *Cf. Monitor,* organ of Associated Industries, May, 1935, p. 227. New York State Federation of Labor: The session of the New York Legislature in 1935 "will take its place in history as the most constructive and liberal annual session of the state Legislature ever held." *Cf. Bulletin of the New York State Federation of Labor,* Apr. 22, 1935.

[36] The deficit in New York on June 30, 1935 was $97,048,752.52. The chief sources of revenue from taxation for the state in recent years have been taxes on personal income, corporations, motor vehicles and motor fuel, inheritance and stock transfers, sales, alcoholic beverages and licenses. See *New York Times,* Jan. 14, 1936, also the reports issued since 1931 of the New York State Commission for the Revision of the Tax Laws, and the annual reports of the State Tax Commission of the New York State Department of Taxation and Finance.

cils, and economy and "liberty" leagues bent either upon reductions or upon no increases in taxes.   Lines are not always
so sharply drawn.   Real estate groups and merchant associations do not see eye to eye when the demand for increased
taxes is inevitable.   The sales tax is then as vigorously supported by the real estate interests, in the hope of reducing the
burden on real estate, as it is resisted by the merchants.   It is
again the old story of "Knock hell out of mutton, but don't
touch rice."   Even such uncompromising adversaries as the
New York State Federation of Labor and Associated Industries stand together in order to check the competition of
prison-made labor goods.   One thing only is obvious—the
consumer is nowhere adequately represented.

Just what should be the role of the legislature while all this
is going on?   The legislature should serve as impartial referee
in seeing that these opposing groups do not take unfair advantage of one another.   But it should do more than that.   It
should protect the interests of the general public.   Admittedly,
the public interest is not always an easy thing to determine.
In this clash of interests, the good of society in general may
be on one side or the other; or it may be on neither side.

Nevertheless, by and large, the interests of the general public
can be said to be the interests of the great mass of consumers.
Consumers' leagues and "People's" lobbies have failed generally.   For the most part they have been diverted from their
original noble purposes because of inherent difficulties in
building an organization necessary for the effective carrying
out of a consumer program.[37]   In consequence, until the consumer can be organized effectively, the legislature must constitute itself the protector of this diffused, inarticulate interest.[38]

It must be remembered that our state legislators are, for the
most part, amateurs who are annually concerned with the disposition of over 4,000 bills.[39]

---

[37] See discussion of the Consumers' League of New York, p. 29.   For a
brief description of purposes and early activities of the People's Lobby under
the chairmanship of Professor John Dewey, see Logan, op. cit.

[38] E. P. Herring, Public Administration and the Public Interest, New York,
McGraw-Hill, 1936, p. 244.

[39] More experienced men are found in the New York Legislature at present
than half a century ago, since the personnel does not now renew itself so
rapidly.   In 1882, almost 60 per cent of the legislative members had had no
previous experience in either house of the legislature, and the average length

Fortunately, the administrative departments are ever present as indispensable sources of information for the legislature. The executive agencies have served effectively in offsetting the specious pleading of the special interests on many occasions.   Nevertheless, it might be well to supplement the administrative departments in this capacity by extending the services of the legislative reference and bill drafting divisions and by making greater use of legislative interim committees and special commissions of inquiry.[40]

There is at present in Albany a state legislative reference service, a legislative library, and a bill drafting commission. The state legislative reference service was established by Dr. Melvil Dewey in 1890 as a section of the New York State Library, for the purpose of supplying lawmakers with information on legislative proposals before them.   It is, therefore,

---

of service for all members of the legislature was 1.1 years.   In 1935, only 18.4 per cent were without experience in the State Legislature, and the average length of service was 4.69 years.   See *Appendix A,* which indicates even better statistics for 1933.   For early records in other states, see R. Luce, *Legislative Assemblies,* Boston, Houghton Mifflin, 1924, p. 356.   Furthermore, more than 70 per cent of the members in the New York Legislature of 1935 received a college or professional school education as compared with less than 50 per cent who were so educated among its members in 1892.   *Cf. Appendix A.*

[40] It is highly advisable that official research agencies maintain close contacts with such unofficial and nonpolitical agencies as the American Legislators' Association and the National Conference of Commissioners on Uniform State Laws.   The former was organized in 1925 and is composed ex officio of 7,600 members in the state legislative bodies of the United States.   It is supported in part from state appropriations and in part from foundation grants.   The association "investigates methods of improved organization and procedure of state legislatures; provides inquiry and information service to state legislators and state legislative reference bureaus; conducts research directed to the improvement of legislative personnel."   The Association publishes the monthly magazine *State Government* and many special bulletins.   See *A Directory of Organizations in the Field of Public Administration,* published by Public Administration Clearing House, Chicago, 1936, p. 21. See also *The Book of the States,* 1935, Vol. I, published by the Council of State Governments and the American Legislators' Association.

The National Conference of Commissioners on Uniform State Laws, organized in 1892, is composed of 158 uniform law commissioners, three or more being appointed by each of the Governors of the states and territories. It is financed by funds appropriated by states, the American and State Bar Associations.   The conference formulates and approves uniform laws which are recommended for adoption by the states, and publishes an annual handbook containing proceedings, committee reports, and acts approved and recommended for adoption.   *Cf. A Directory of Organizations in the Field of Public Administration, op.cit.,* p. 89.

not only the oldest legislative reference service in America but also ranks among the finest state legislative research aids. Attached to the service is a full time staff of eight members who are appointed through the civil service.[41] In 1915, the Legislative Library was established in the state Capitol. The librarian and the three assistants in charge are appointed by the majority leader of the Senate and the Speaker of the Assembly. It supplies the legislature and the offices housed in the Capitol with such information as it has in its files or can be secured on short notice.[42]

The bill drafting service in New York State is supplied by the Legislative Bill Drafting Commission, which is independent of the legislative reference section. The majority leader of the Senate and the Speaker of the Assembly appoint the two bill drafting commissioners, who in turn select a deputy, all three of whom must qualify as attorneys who have practiced in the state for at least five years. With the assistance of a counsel, a secretary, and a clerical staff, totalling 25, the commission devotes itself chiefly to drafting and assisting legislators, administrators, and the representatives of pressure groups in the preparation of bills and to advising on their constitutionality.[43] The commission drafts or inspects from 80 to 90 per cent of the bills introduced into the legislature.[44]

In order that the services rendered by these agencies may be improved, the following suggestions are offered:

---

[41] The annual budget of this division is estimated at $14,000 (1933–1934), which does not include maintenance. This division received a severe setback in 1915, when the director of the State Library was drawn into a serious controversy with legislative leaders over the establishment of an independent library in the Capitol. In 1911, a fire destroyed the preparation of indexes of state legislation which was then in preparation, and thus put an end to this valuable service. *Cf.* Interviews with W. E. Hannan, librarian of the Legislative Reference Section of the New York State Library at Albany, Sept. 4–6, 1935, and May 5, 1936. *The Book of the States*, 1935, Vol. I, pp. 207, 254–258.

[42] Its budget for 1933–1934 was $19,600. *New York Legislative Manual*, 1935, p. 742.

[43] Although directed by law to make examinations and researches on subjects of proposed legislation, the commission devotes little time to this task. *Cf.* ch. 37 of the laws of 1909.

[44] The annual budget of the commission in 1933–1934, covering personnel service, maintenance, and operation, totalled $71,600. Interview with Don Holbrook, Secretary to the Bill Drafting Commission at Albany, Sept. 5, 1935. *The New York Clerk's Manual*, 1936, p. 141. *The Book of the States*, 1935, Vol. I, pp. 207, 254–258.

The task of consolidating and revising the statutes in broad related fields might be turned over to the Bill Drafting Commission. This agency would then be kept busy on cognate work throughout the year and not merely during the legislative session.[45]   The Bill Drafting Commission might be charged with the responsibility of publishing the consolidated statutes of the state in one volume, at frequent, stated intervals,[46] and in this way provide a speedy and less confusing access to the statutes.[47]

The Legislative Library might be abolished and the Legislative Reference Section might take over the present functions of the library.[48]   The latter agency should be housed in the Capitol.[49]   All employees in the Legislative Reference Section and in the Bill Drafting Commission might be placed under the classified service, and their salaries fixed by law.[50]

---

[45] Another suggestion would be to place this work in a newly-established office, such as the Revisor of the Statutes. See *The Book of the States,* 1935, Vol. I, p. 283. The Bill Drafting Commission or the office of the Revisor of the Statutes might assist special commissions, like the New York Law Revision Commission, in its gigantic assignment of examining the common law, the statutes, and current decisions for the purpose of discovering defects and recommending reforms. See first report of this commission, Legislative Document, 1935, no. 60. *Cf.* Chamberlain, *op.cit.,* p. 257 and the *New York Legislative Manual,* 1935, p. 513.

[46] Between these intervals the task of indexing the annual sessional laws might fall to the Drafting Commission or to the Revisor of the Statutes.

[47] It would thus no longer be necessary in New York to resort to special commissions to do this technical work.

[48] The library has neither the trained personnel nor the equipment to perform any extensive research for legislators, despite the fact that its annual budget is higher than that of the Legislative Reference Section.

[49] The Legislative Reference Section is at present housed in the Education building, across the street from the state Capitol, and easily accessible to the volumes and material in the other parts of the well equipped State Library, particularly the Law Library division. While much can be said for this arrangement, it is advisable that quarters for this division be found in the Capitol, since the primary purpose of the Legislative Reference Section is to serve the legislature.

[50] Just now, there is no apparent disadvantage in continuing the appointment of the bill drafting commissioners by the legislative leaders, since the present two commissioners have served without interruption, one since 1928, the other since 1929, despite changes in the political control of the legislature. *Cf. New York Legislative Manual,* 1935, p. 741. The salaries of the employees who assist the bill drafting commissioners are fixed by the majority leader of the Senate and the Speaker of the Assembly. *Cf. The New York Clerk's Manual,* 1936, p. 141. It seems unnecessary, although much can be said for it, to combine under one control the bill drafting commission and the legislative reference service, as was done in the state of Wisconsin, where

Efficient and impartial agencies performing research and reference work for the legislature, drafting bills and revising the statutes, as outlined above, could in time compel the confidence of the legislators and become indispensable to them in supplying information on legislative proposals—at least sharing, and perhaps, in time, overshadowing pressure groups in this role.

Legislative interim committees and commissions of inquiry are used frequently in New York State.[51]   Professor Chamberlain [52] has described the circumstances under which these agencies are often created: "Frequently a matter which comes before the legislature is so important and so contentious, the investigations necessary to clear it up so complicated, and public opinion so hard to estimate or so uninformed, that the legislature does not feel safe in dealing with it in the usual way."

These devices for aiding legislators afford a means of gathering data on which to base legislation, away from the turmoil, confusion, and haste of legislative sessions.   As official bodies, members are concerned particularly with the attitude of the *public* on the subject under investigation, and are therefore

---

the director was peculiarly well qualified for both jobs.   The office of the Revisor of the Statutes in Wisconsin is an independent agency, however. *Cf. The Book of the States*, 1935, Vol. I, p. 281.   In 1925 a Joint Legislative Committee was appointed in New York to investigate the advisability of consolidating the Legislative Library, the Legislative Reference Section and the Legislative Bill Drafting Commission.   No action was taken in this direction.   *Cf.* New York Legislative Document, 1926, no. 52.

[51] The legislative committee is usually composed wholly of legislators (see *New York Legislative Manual*, 1935, p. 735, for exception), while the commission is composed partly of legislators and partly of non-official persons appointed by the Governor or wholly of lay persons appointed by the Governor.   In 1935 the legislature appropriated $1,310,188 for the work of 28 temporary interim committees and commissions.   Seventeen of these commissions were in existence for from one to eight years.   See *New York Legislative Manual*, 1935, pp. 504–522, 734–740, and *Laws of New York*, 1935, Vol. 2, ch. 975, p. 1889, for an incomplete list of these commissions. At times the sincerity of the legislature in creating commissions and in voting funds for their use may be justly questioned.   Governor Lehman in 1936 vetoed appropriations totalling $98,600 for 12 commissions.   *Cf. Clipsheet of Women's Joint Legislative Forum*, June 20, 1936.   By joint resolution adopted Apr. 15, 1935 the majority and minority leaders of the legislature are members of all joint legislative committees and ex officio members of all statutory commissions unless specifically exempted.

[52] *Op.cit.*, p. 96.

less likely to submit recommendations based on partisan considerations or to yield as easily to the requests of pressure groups that are incompatible with the public interest. For these reasons the findings of the commissions do as a general rule carry more weight with the legislators. For it must be remembered that the representatives of organized minorities themselves frequently serve on these advisory and investigatory commissions and are therefore brought into more intimate contact with the views of the public. In turn, "the avowed presence of organized interests in the membership of advisory boards is doubtless a frequent aid to their vitality." [53]   Since these commissions have for the most part been effective in both normal and stressful periods, their use should not be curtailed, nor should they be hampered by lack of funds.[54]

Should advisory administrative commissions continue to be used on a wide scale in the United States, it might not be unreasonable to expect a modification of pressure techniques, which in turn might affect the problem of lobby control.[55]

Increased powers of initiative and leadership for the execu-

---

[53] A. W. Macmahon, "Advisory Boards," *Encyclopaedia of the Social Sciences,* New York, Macmillan, 1930, Vol. II, p. 611.

[54] See Chamberlain, *op.cit.,* ch. 7; H. F. Gosnell, "British Royal Commissions of Inquiry," *Political Science Quarterly,* Mar., 1934; M. E. Dimock, *Congressional Investigating Committees,* Baltimore, Johns Hopkins University Press, 1929; "Interim Committees and Commissions," 1929–1930, *State Government,* May, 1930; "Interim Committees and Commissions," 1931–1932, *State Government,* Feb., 1932; G. B. Galloway, "The Investigative Function of Congress," *American Political Science Review,* Feb., 1927.

[55] The overlapping personnel on the Governor's Agricultural Advisory Commission and the New York State Conference Board of Farm Organizations aided materially in the legislative accomplishments of the farm groups. See *supra,* p. 129. Furthermore, in this connection, it might be well to examine the principle of occupational representation and the role of organized minorities applied so extensively in Europe after the close of the World War. The principle of occupational representation at least permeates the Russian, Italian, and German systems of government and receives official recognition in the large number of economic councils created in many nations. E. P. Herring, *op.cit.,* p. 381. See also the splendid summary of economic councils in the brochure prepared by the Economic Committee of the League of Nations by Elli Lindner, *Review of the Economic Councils in the Different Countries of the World,* 1932. See also *Final Report of the National Planning Board,* 1934, Sec. IV. See references on economic councils and economic planning prepared by the Division of Bibliography of the United States Library of Congress; Lewis L. Lorwin, *Advisory Economic Councils,* Washington, Brookings Institution, 1931; and A. J. Zurcher, *The Experiment with Democracy in Central Europe,* New York, Oxford University Press, 1933, ch. 14.

tive and administrative branch of the government in its contacts with the legislature would further aid in reducing the
advantage that the professional lobbyist has over the amateur
legislator. It has been noted that New York governors, assisted by the personnel in the administrative departments
are influencing to an increasing extent the course of state legislation. The governor's relations with the legislature would
probably be improved by a term longer than two years.[56] The
longer term would tend to focus attention upon the executive
as the leader of his party, to make him more independent of
local "bosses," which might produce a solidifying effect upon
factional party disputes, inside and outside of the legislature.
A chief executive, so strengthened in his relations with the
legislature, is bound to attract greater attention from organized minorities who concentrate upon centers of power and
influence. This, in turn, might well affect the methods, status,
and efficacy of pressure groups, and thus simplify the problem
of lobby control. In Great Britain, where the corridors of
Whitehall rather than Westminster echo with the footsteps
and voices of lobbyists, where the initiation of and the responsibility for legislation lie with the executive and administrative
agencies, the activity and influence of pressure groups are
more restricted and their methods are less obnoxious. British
lobbies resemble those in the United States in number, character, composition, and purpose, but not in the power and influence they wield in the process of government. In Great
Britain the lobby does its most effective work through deputa-
tions to administrative departments, where ministers and permanent officials are reached, and by giving evidence to Royal
commissions of inquiry and departmental committees. In the
electoral field, the lobby's influence over individual members
of Parliament is weaker because of strong party control.[57]

For even now it can be said of the Governor of New York in

---

[56] A constitutional amendment to increase the term of the governor from
two to four years is pending. If repassed by the legislature in 1937, and
approved by the voters in Nov., 1937, it will become part of the constitution
Jan. 1, 1938.

[57] See H. Finer, *The Theory and Practice of Modern Government*, 1932,
Vol. II, p. 774; E. P. Herring, "Great Britain Has Lobbies Too," *Virginia
Quarterly Review*, July, 1930; J. K. Pollock, "Auxiliary and Non-Party
Organizations in England," *Southwestern Political and Social Science
Quarterly*, Mar., 1931.

his relations with the legislature, as it has been said of the President and Congress: "The President has time and time again been better able to uphold the public interest than a Congress controlled by blocs and organized minorities. While the increased power of the chief executive is open to abuse, it seems an almost inescapable result of congressional weakness in coping with pressure groups." [58] With greater responsibility concentrated in the executive acting under a glare of publicity, even organized minorities can be made to realize that beyond certain limits the executive, unlike the more decentralized legislature, cannot yield. Under such circumstances, is not the lobbyist forced more into the open; are not facts, rather than threats and hearsay, the order of the day?

Proper preliminary planning of the work of the legislature would further decrease the advantage which the professional lobbyist has over the amateur legislator. Toward this end, it is suggested that a legislative council be established, small in number, reflecting in its composition the political setup in the legislature.[59] The council would function chiefly during the periods when the legislature is not in session, and its chief task would be to *prepare* the legislative *program* for the ensuing session of the legislature. As an interim body, it would afford recognition of the fact that legislation-making is an all-year task. With such planning before the session opens, there would be less likelihood of pressure groups reaping advantages from a hurried, overtaxed legislature. Any agency that makes provision for advance planning resulting in greater orderliness in our legislative bodies should serve as a check upon those interests that benefit from confusion and from unexpected moves in the introduction of bills that take their rivals by surprise.

---

[58] E. P. Herring, *op.cit.*, p. 383.

[59] Whether the Governor is a member of the council or not is not so important as that very close contacts and cooperation be maintained between the council and the Governor. In the establishment of the legislative council with minority party representation, the principle that both majority and minority parties have a legitimate and important part to play in the formulation of a legislative program is recognized. In New York the legislative council would work more smoothly perhaps if the same party controlled majorities in both houses and the Governorship. Such a result could be achieved more regularly if a fairer legislative districting system were provided See *infra*, p. 282.

In the preparation of the legislative program, the council would participate in directing research on special problems and in placing the information so gathered, along with its recommendations for legislative action, before the legislature when it again convened. It is not intended that the council should usurp the authority that rightly belongs to the legislative body itself, but rather that it should guide the legislature in considering what it believes to be the most important subjects.[60] With adoption of the recommendations suggested in this chapter for the improvement of our legislative bodies generally, it would seem that the danger of usurping power by the council would be greatly minimized.[61]

To prevent duplication of work and to sustain progress in a definite direction, it would be most important to have the council maintain close contacts with the state administrative departments and with the legislative reference and bill drafting divisions. Many of the problems under study by the legislative interim committees and the special commissions of inquiry would be shaped by the guidance of the legislative council. It is not intended to have the legislative council perform the tasks that rightly fall to these research and investigatory agencies.[62]

---

[60] Chamberlain, op.cit., p. 254.

[61] However, it should here be reiterated that a longer term for legislators is essential. The work of a legislative council acting chiefly as an ad interim body would be greatly impaired if new political majorities were possible as each session of the legislature opened. Kansas, Wisconsin, Michigan, Colorado, Virginia, and Kentucky have established legislative councils. See Chamberlain, op.cit., pp. 254–259; W. F. Willoughby, Principles of Legislative Organization and Administration, Washington, Brookings Institution, 1934, pp. 587–594; H. M. Dorr, "A Legislative Council for Michigan," American Political Science Review, Apr., 1934; F. H. Guild, "Achievements of the Kansas Legislative Council," American Political Science Review, Aug., 1935; F. H. Guild, Kansas' Experiment with a Legislative Council, Kansas Legislative Council, Topeka, Kansas, 1936.

[62] Professor Chamberlain suggests that law revision should be one of the legislative jobs that falls to the legislative council. See Legislative Processes, p. 257. It has been suggested by the writer that this might well be done by the Bill Drafting Commission or the Revisor of the Statutes. Supra, p. 268. In the State of Kansas, where a legislative council was recently established, a major part of the tasks performed by the Research Department of the Council might have been done more appropriately perhaps by a Legislative Reference Section. See F. H. Guild, op.cit., American Political Science Review, Aug., 1935; and State Government, Nov., 1934, p. 250. In Kansas, the Revisor of the Statutes is charged with the duties of bill

Defects in the structure and procedure of the State Legislature vitiate the possibility of equality among pressure groups. For example, the bicameral system admirably serves special and predatory interests who are more interested in preventing legislation than in promoting it. To accomplish their ends, the control of one house is all that is necessary. Evidence in the New York insurance investigation of 1905 "indicated that a large share of the bills with which insurance companies and other corporations [had] to deal [were] those bills which they [were] endeavoring to prevent the passage of rather than those which they [were] promoting." [63] It will be recalled that Senator Thayer, in his indiscreet letter to an officer of the Associated Gas and Electric Company, stated that he hoped his services as chairman of the Senate Public Service Committee were satisfactory, not so much for the new legislation enacted as for his part in killing many detrimental bills in his committee.[64] Special minority groups concerned with preventing legislation inimical to their interests can intentionally encourage deadlocks between the two chambers. In the long struggle waged by the women for a 48-hour law, the spark of hope was ignited at times by the passage of the legislation in one house, only to have it die out again when the bills were throttled in the other.[65] The pamphlet published by the New York State League of Women Voters in 1920 contains illustrations of how the representative of Associated Industries allegedly played off one house against the other in his campaign to prevent the extension of social industrial legislation.[66]

Moreover, the bicameral legislature necessitates some special procedure to adjust inevitable differences between the two chambers, with the attendant evils of concentrating power in the hands of a few who operate in secret, who keep no record of their proceedings and votes, and whose reports or failure to

drafting, statutory revision and research. The Revisor of the Statutes is also ex officio Secretary of the Council, which is a logical and sensible tie-up of the two bodies. Cf. The Book of the States, 1935, Vol. I, p. 230.

[63] D. L. Colvin, The Bicameral Principle in the New York Legislature, New York, Columbia University Press, 1913, pp. 123, 130.

[64] Supra, p. 78.

[65] Similarly, woman juror bills were passed by the Assembly in 1935 and 1936 but each time the bills died in committee in the Senate. Cf. New York Times, Feb. 2, 1937.

[66] Report and Protest to the Governor, the Legislature and the People of the State of New York: The Daly Lobby and Propaganda as a Danger Confronting Popular Government, op.cit., p. 8; also supra, p. 52.

report are usually accepted by the houses without debate or change.

In the Congress of the United States, this task devolves upon the conference committee.[67]   In New York, however, the conference committee is rarely used.[68]   When differences between the chambers do arise, they are usually settled through informal conferences of the party leaders in both houses. The adjustment of minor bills is left to the individual senators and assemblymen sponsoring these bills.   But whether it is the more formal, rigid conference committee or the less formal procedure of New York, interest groups are offered another opportunity to exert their pressure and influence when differences between the chambers are adjusted.   "The interest groups backing a particular measure exert a strong influence towards bringing about an agreement.   Their object is to secure action, and they will be active in working in both houses to secure consent to whatever amendment may be necessary to bring them together, provided the changes are not sufficiently important to destroy the purpose of the bill." [69]   Such practices are susceptible to underhand influences of self-seeking special interests.

Thus, the bicameral system enhances the influence and enlarges the activity of pressure groups in enabling them to block legislation in one of the chambers and to play an important role in adjusting the inevitable differences between the two chambers.

In addition, the very district system of the state results in still further advantages for certain interests by perpetuating

---

[67] The conference committee does not hear witnesses, yet E. E. Schattschneider, in *Politics, Pressures and the Tariff*, 1935, p. 211, cites the case of a most unusual practice when persons interested in tariff rates were permitted to appear and argue their case before the conference committee. See G. W. Norris, "The One-House Legislature," *The Annals of the American Academy of Political and Social Science*, Sept., 1935, and the radio address by Senator G. W. Norris on Feb. 5, 1935 in series entitled *The 44 State Legislatures of 1935*, published by the National Municipal League; J. P. Senning, *The One-House Legislature*, New York, McGraw-Hill, 1937.

[68] Although recognized in the rules of at least 31 states, including New York, conference committees are rarely resorted to in State Legislatures. Chamberlain, *op.cit.*, p. 252; C. I. Winslow, *State Legislative Committees: A Study in Procedure*, Baltimore, Johns Hopkins Press, 1931, pp. 26–28; *The New York Clerk's Manual*, 1936, pp. 97–98.

[69] Chamberlain, *op.cit.*, p. 253.

in office representatives of a party that would actually stand repudiated at the polls under a more equitable apportionment of the seats. It has already been indicated that certain pressure groups, although they work with both major parties, expect and do receive more fruitful results from one or the other. Organized labor, for example, has fared better at the hands of Democrats, while certain economic groups, Associated Industries for example, have been the recipients of favors from the Republican party.[70]

Moreover, certain pressure groups have made unfair claims to prominence because they have succeeded in decisively influencing the nomination and election of candidates in districts unfairly represented in the State Legislature. For example, dry support in New York, after the overwhelming vote registered for the repeal of the Eighteenth Amendment, is derived chiefly from rural districts that are for the most part overrepresented in the State Legislature.[71] It is not unreasonable to assume that pressure groups which benefit from an unfair district system would discourage the correction of this situation.

In addition, the standing committee system in general, and the assembly rules committee in particular, afford special advantages to those members of the majority party who serve on the limited number of committees that decide the fate of most of the bills. The consequence is that "special interests" with the right contacts have a tremendous advantage.

The 4,600 bills, some of a general nature, others private and local, that were introduced into the legislature in 1935 were referred to thirty standing committees in the Senate and to thirty-seven in the Assembly. Although the average assignment in the Senate was one member to 6.82 committees, the senators of the majority party actually served on 8.38 committees, while the members of the minority party served on 4.77 committees.[72] In the Assembly, where the average

---

[70] Supra, pp. 24, 54.

[71] Supra, p. 225.

[72] The 348 posts on Senate committees were distributed among 51 senators. The Senate majority and minority leaders are members of the Rules Committee and ex officio members of Finance, Judiciary, Public Service, Internal Affairs, Public Education, Affairs of the City of New York, and Affairs of Cities.

assignment was 3.28, members of the majority party served, however, on 4.32 committees and the minority on 2.19.[73]   A study of the standing committees in 1935 disclosed that a majority of the bills introduced were referred to six committees in the Senate and to five committees in the Assembly.[74]

In the Senate, 43 different persons manned the 86 posts on the Rules Committee and the six committees to which a majority of the bills were referred.   While the average is exactly one person to two of these seven important committees, the assignments disclose that eleven senators served on three of these committees, two served on four, and one served on as many as five.[75]

In the Assembly, where only three members served on as many as three of the six most important committees, the distribution of places is not of great significance.   This is due to the enormous power of the Rules Committee.   An Assembly rule provides that bills not reported out of committee ten days prior to the date set by concurrent resolution for adjournment be turned over to the Rules Committee for action.   Actually this committee acts on bills for more than the ten days set in the rule, because the adjournment of the legislature is invariably postponed beyond the first date set.[76]   For the Assembly

---

[73] The 493 posts were distributed among 150 members.   The Speaker and the minority leader are members of Rules only.

[74] In the Senate 53.1 per cent of the bills were referred to 6 committees, 68.4 per cent to 10 committees.   In the Assembly 52.1 per cent of the bills were referred to 5 committees, 70.6 per cent to 10 committees.   See *Appendix B*.

[75] Senators Feld and Mandelbaum served on the four committees, and Senator Berg on the five.   *Cf. New York Legislative Manual*, 1935, and *Appendix B*.

[76] "During the last ten days of the session a notice may be given, requesting that any matter be made a special order, or that the rules be suspended for the purpose of reading a bill out of its order, which shall be referred, without debate, to the Committee on Rules.   The member making the motion or giving the notice shall submit in writing the reasons for making such special order or suspension, and attach thereto a copy of the bill.   The committee may report at any time, and such report shall stand as the determination of the House, unless otherwise ordered by a vote of a majority of the members elected . . ." (Assembly Rule 21, 1936).   In the Senate, the standing committees have charge of all bills up to the close of the session.   The Senate Committee on Rules has the power to take a bill from a committee and place it immediately upon the order of final passage.   It may also amend a bill in any particular.

to be in "Rules" for a full month is not unusual.[77]   Thus, during a substantial period of the three- or four-month legislative session, the Rules Committee is the only committee in the Assembly that is functioning.   The Rules Committee has not relieved congestion during the closing days of the session, when a large number of the total bills passed in the Assembly and the Senate are reported by Rules.[78]   The activity of the Rules Committee appears to indicate an appalling waste of time on the part of the Assembly standing committees generally—that the assemblymen have been drifting aimlessly and tarrying needlessly—although the leaders may be at work conducting negotiations before adjustments are made.   Moreover, it does seem to indicate that the rank and file of the Assembly membership scattered among more than thirty committees have abdicated and have permitted a handful of fifteen members— the leading members of the majority and minority parties—to decide the fate of a substantial number of the bills introduced into the legislature.[79]   A study of the New York Assembly Rules Committee in 1918 led Professor H. W. Dodds to remark: "It would be hard to imagine a method by which a house could more completely subject itself to the control of three members and the Speaker, who is ex officio chairman of 'Rules,' and still retain the form of a freely deliberating body." [80]

Moreover, the smothering of bills in the Rules Committee has been resorted to at times in order to save the rank and file of the membership in the Assembly the embarrassment of putting themselves on record.   For example, in 1936 the New York State Federation of Labor was unable to compile its customary roll call of votes in the Assembly on important labor bills because "the majority members (Republican) of

[77] In 1911, a record was established when Rules was in control of bills from May 8 to Oct. 6.   *Cf.* H. W. Dodds, "Procedure in State Legislatures," *The Annals of the American Academy of Political and Social Science,* supplement no. 1, May, 1918, p. 60.

[78] For example, it has been estimated that one-third of the bills passed by the legislature in 1936 were reported by the Assembly Rules Committee.

[79] The rules provide that a request must be submitted to the Rules Committee to report a bill.   If no request is received, the bill is usually not considered.

[80] "Procedures in State Legislatures," *The Annals of the American Academy of Political and Social Science,* supplement no. 1, May, 1918, p. 61.

the Assembly Rules Committee buried all of these labor bills as fast as they came from the Senate by refusing to report them to the Assembly for a vote." [81]

Picture the great confusion and the burning activity of the lobbyist during abnormally long sessions on the closing days, often without the legal quorum present, as he mingles freely with members of the legislature on the floor of the chamber, on the rostrum, in the corridors, all the while keeping a close watch in the Assembly on the Speaker and the other members of the Rules Committee,[82] despite the rules that:

> No lobbyist shall be permitted on the floor of the Assembly advocating, opposing or influencing, requesting, soliciting or demanding any member of the Assembly to vote for or against any measure that is pending in the Assembly during the last two days of the session of the legislature.[83]
>
> No person shall be entitled to the privileges of the floor, who is employed by or receives compensation from any corporation for influencing legislation.[84]
>
> During the sessions no person other than a member shall occupy the chair of a member.[85]

The rules notwithstanding, only a trained eye can distinguish the members of the "Third House" from those of the official houses at this juncture. The Black Horse Cavalry invades both Senate and Assembly and holds the fort as at no other time during the session.

Public hearings before legislative committees have not been utilized to the extent they might well be. They have not for the most part served as a sober painstaking instrument of inquiry through which legislative decisions are reached after interested parties have presented their evidence. Both legislators and lobbyists alike frankly admit that public hearings before the New York Legislature seldom alter the decisions reached by committee members before the hearings take place.[86]

---

[81] *Bulletin of the New York State Federation of Labor,* June 15, 1936.

[82] Chamberlain, *op.cit.,* p. 147.

[83] Assembly Rule 2, sec. 10 (1934).

[84] Senate Rule 3, Assembly Rule 31 (1934).

[85] Senate Rule 47, sec. 8, Assembly Rule 37 (1934).

[86] They do, however, sometimes serve to bolster up legislators and give them greater moral strength in making decisions they would like to. Hear-

Chairmen of committees grant requests for public hearings to those opposed to the pending legislation rather freely in order to convey the impression that the committee is impartial and not subject to orders from any self-seeking interest groups.[87]

With the date of the hearing set about a week in advance,[88] the interested groups set about to make as big and fine a showing as possible. The impression must be conveyed that there is great public demand for or against the legislation under discussion.[89] Dramatic situations may arise when the adversaries confront each other. Spectacular devices are resorted to: jamming the legislative chamber [90] with the women victims of a 54-hour law; [91] the wearing of brightly-colored labels bearing pithy messages for the legislators to read; or calling upon a potential beneficiary of a pending mortgage moratorium bill

---

ings before congressional committees, in contradistinction, are "of real importance in building up a mass of information for the benefit of the committee and in bringing to light mistakes which it may be making." *Cf.* Chamberlain, *op.cit.*, p. 93.

[87] Professor Chamberlain has stated that requests for hearings "are sometimes refused where the chairman or party leaders do not want a matter aired in public and do not believe that there is sufficient strength behind it to make their refusal politically unwise." *Cf. Legislative Processes*, p. 91.

[88] Frequently there are last minute changes. Assembly Rule 18 (1934) provides for only a one-day notice. See the *New York Legislative Record and Index,* which is indispensable to all interested in following legislation at Albany. In addition to giving advance notices of committee hearings, it gives accurately a complete cumulative record of every bill and resolution introduced in the Senate and Assembly. It is compiled and published weekly by The Legislative Index Publishing Company of Albany, a private company, and compares admirably to similar services in the national and state Capitols, whether prepared and published under public or private auspices. By the close of the legislative session the completed record is recorded in a volume of about 600 pages. *Cf. The New York Red Book,* 1935, p. 433. A less comprehensive service is offered by the *New York Legislative Service,* established in 1935 with offices in New York City, under the auspices of the National Municipal League but now independent. This agency furnishes a weekly digest, analyzing all important bills.

[89] It is customary at important hearings for those who plan to be present to meet an hour or so in advance for the purpose of deciding on the speakers and the points to be stressed before the committee.

[90] Large hearings are held in either the Assembly or Senate chamber, usually in the afternoon, when the legislature is not in session, while public hearings at which a large turnout is not expected are held in committee rooms.

[91] This was done by the women's organizations in their campaign for a 48-hour law for women. *Supra,* p. 38.

to tell in his own homely way what the passage or failure to enact such a law would mean to him and his family.

However, very little important information is secured through these hearings that could not be obtained through other means. It is an effective device for registering an emotional appeal with reference to its effect upon the general public rather than its effect upon the legislators.

It is apparent, consequently, that any attempt to solve the problem of the lobby and to create a system in which the various pressure groups will exert an influence in proportion to their social usefulness necessitates not merely a better-drawn and more vigorously-enforced lobby law, and the extension and improvement of official research agencies, but also a thoroughgoing reorganization of both the legislative structure and the procedure itself.

It has not been within the scope of this study to make a detailed analysis of reforms of this sweeping nature, but upon the basis of studies already made, one may venture tentative suggestions.

The establishment of a small unicameral chamber of from forty to sixty members, elected for at least a two-year term, would make it impossible for one house to "pass the buck" to the other. It would concentrate responsibility for the passage or defeat of legislation and thus would tend to bring legislative activities into the open, especially if it were possible for one or two legislators to secure a roll call on every measure. The whole legislative process could and would be simplified. In consequence, the voters could more easily follow the records of the members and vote for or against them accordingly. A unicameral body might, moreover, facilitate the problem of responsible legislative leadership and aid in its promotion.[92]

---

[92] The single chamber legislature is not foreign to American legislative experience. The Articles of Confederation provided for a unicameral Congress and some of the colonies operated under one-chambered bodies. Three of our states began with single chambers: Georgia, Pennsylvania, and Vermont. Although short-lived in Georgia and Pennsylvania, it was not abandoned in Vermont until 1836. See R. Luce, *Legislative Assemblies*, ch. 2. The people of Nebraska in Nov., 1934 accepted the constitutional amendment providing for a unicameral legislature selected on a non-partisan ballot. The advocates of the non-partisan principle, chief among them Senator Norris, feel that it will make legislators less dependent on political parties stressing national issues and candidates, and that the non-partisan ballot will free legis-

Moreover, in a small unicameral legislature it would be possible without additional budgetary burden to increase the salaries of our underpaid state legislators and to make them less dependent upon their private occupations and connections for additional income. There would be fewer patronage positions to hand out and, in consequence, less delay in getting legislative sessions under way.[93]

Whether the bicameral legislature is abolished or not, the flagrantly unfair districting should be changed. The New York constitution provides for single-member Senate and Assembly districts. In the case of the Assembly, it also provides that every county, with the exception of Hamilton, is entitled to at least one representative, regardless of how small the population. Furthermore, any county having the quota plus a major fraction thereof is entitled to a second member. This permits Schuyler county, with less than 13,000 population, to be represented in the Assembly by one member, as is Jefferson county, with more than 83,000, whereas the county of Queens, with more than one million people, has only six Assemblymen. It is apparent that the basic principle of reapportionment must be unsound when built upon such an arbitrary county system. Moreover, a district system, even if only partially based on such a county arrangement, is bound to present a sadly gerrymandered pattern.

Although the problem of adjusting senatorial districts would not be so difficult as with the Assembly, because the constitution provides for some degree of flexibility in the size of the Senate and permits the combination of counties to form a district,[94] there are, nevertheless, striking examples of unequal Senate districts.[95]

---

lators from their obligations to irresponsible local bodies and machines— sources to which interest groups have not always turned in vain. By act of the Nebraska Legislature, the number of members in the new unicameral body to take effect with the session of 1937 was fixed at 43.

[93] In 1933, when the Democrats gained control of the New York Senate after a lapse of ten years, there was close to a month's delay in organizing the Senate because of factional squabbles among the Democrats in the distribution of petty patronage positions. For a list of the offices in the Senate and Assembly filled by the legislative leaders, see The New York Red Book, 1935, pp. 25, 79.

[94] The minimum is set at 50 members in the Senate, but an increase is permitted under certain conditions. However, the constitution does provide that senatorial districts "shall be in as compact form as practicable, and

Difficulties in reapportionment in New York State have centered around the unique situation [96] in which 52 per cent of the citizen population of the state is found in the City of New York, while the representation from the city in the Assembly is 41.3 per cent and in the Senate 45.1 per cent.[97]

There seems to be general agreement among Republicans as well as Democrats that Greater New York is underrepresented in the State Legislature. However, it has not been seriously suggested that Greater New York be given representation absolutely proportional to its citizen population, for this would mean that this single dominant urban center would have a clear majority of the state's representation in the legislature. This situation is further aggravated by the fact that New York City is Democratic, whereas the Republican party draws its strength chiefly from upstate New York.[98]

The recent futile attempts at reapportionment in New York and adverse court decisions in apportionment disputes [99]

. . . shall at all times consist of contiguous territory, and no county shall be divided in the formation of a senate district except to make two or more senate districts wholly in such county." See *New York State Constitution,* Art. III, Sec. 2, 3, 4, 5.

[95] For example, Rockland and Richmond counties, the latter an island, were combined into one district originally for the purpose apparently of assuring a Republican majority in this district.

[96] The nearest comparable example, perhaps, is Cook County, Illinois, comprising the City of Chicago.

[97] The City of New York is represented in the State Legislature by 62 assemblymen and 23 senators (one of these senators represents Richmond and Rockland counties). The greatest population shifts in New York State since the last reapportionment in 1917 are found in the counties comprising the City of New York. Although the Democrats controlled both houses of the legislature in 1935, and the Governor was a Democrat, redistricting was blocked by the Tammany organization of New York County. See Exhibit I, p. 58 in *Counsel's Report in the Matter of the Reapportionment of the State of New York,* Legislative Document no. 85, Mar. 13, 1935.

[98] Apportionment computations in New York State are based on the number of inhabitants, excluding aliens. This as a general procedure is unwise, although it is defended in New York on the ground that to include aliens would result in an even greater representation for New York City, resulting in a greater lack of balance between New York City and the rest of the state. New York City has 68 per cent of the alien population of the state.

[99] Reapportionment bills were passed by the Republican-controlled legislatures of 1926, 1929, and 1930, but were vetoed by Democratic Governors or declared unconstitutional by the courts. In opposing an additional expenditure of $10,000 during 1936 for the Joint Legislative Committee on Reapportionment, created at the extraordinary session of the legislature in Aug., 1934, Governor Lehman stated that $160,500 had already been appro-

prompts one to suggest that New York might place the power of reapportionment in a nonlegislative agency, such as the Court of Appeals [100] or a constitutional convention.[101]

Furthermore, the committee system might advantageously be reorganized.[102] Such a reorganization might look toward a drastic reduction in the number of committees and a redefining of their jurisdictional activities. It might be well in this connection to consider seriously the suggestion of W. F. Willoughby that in reducing the number of committees and in redefining their jurisdiction by broad fields rather than specific topics, "the committee system be made to conform as nearly as may be to a logical setup of the administrative branch of the government." [103]   It might be feasible, therefore, to create some 16 committees: Rules, Judiciary, Finance, Education, Health, Welfare, Labor and Industry, Public Works, Public Service, Banking and Insurance, Agriculture, Commerce, Gen-

priated for this committee with "absolutely no definite results achieved." *Cf. New York Times,* June 8, 1936.

[100] This was suggested by Governor Herbert H. Lehman. *Cf. New York Times,* Jan. 2, 1936.

[101] It is, of course, impossible to suggest a procedure wholly free of criticism or objection. See V. O. Key, Jr., "Procedures in State Legislative Apportionment," *American Political Science Review,* Dec., 1932. There are precedents for the direct participation of voters in apportionment procedure. *Cf.* F. W. Hastings, "Voters Initiate Reapportionment," *State Government,* Feb., 1931.

[102] The number of committees in New York during the past 50 years has fluctuated only slightly, and then with occasional and slight reorganization only, as the size of the Senate increased since 1885 from 32 to 51 members and the Assembly from 128 to 150, while the number of bills handled by these committees more than quadrupled during this period.

1835—	S.	21 committees	A.	25	committees
1885—	"	33 "	"	38	"
1895—	"	34 "	"	36	"
1905—	"	26 "	"	36	"
1915—	"	25 "	"	32	"
1925—	"	26 "	"	31	"
1935—	"	30 "	"	37	"

There are a large number of states whose standing committees exceed, in number and in size, those of the State of New York. Seventeen lower houses and 12 senates have each 40 or more standing committees. Furthermore, it is not unusual to find committees with more than 40 members. *Cf.* C. I. Winslow, *op.cit.,* pp. 36–37; *State Government,* Aug., 1931, reprinted in *The Book of the States,* 1935, Vol. I, p. 65. See also A. E. Buck, *Modernizing Our State Legislatures,* Philadelphia, The American Academy of Political and Social Science, 1936.

[103] *Principles of Legislative Organization and Administration,* 1934, p. 608.

eral Laws (as a catchall, miscellaneous committee), Internal
Affairs, Cities, Natural Resources and Conservation.[104]   There
is no justification for retaining as standing committees in the
legislative process such committees of a technical, nonsubstan-
tive nature as Revision, or Printed and Engrossed Bills, whose
functions are performed by employees and not by members of
the legislature.[105]

In defining the jurisdiction of these committees, it would
be well to consider the character and the number of bills introduced in recent sessions of the New York Legislature,[106] and,
without stretching the point too far, to keep in mind the setup
of the New York administrative system.   The problem at
hand is the more equitable distribution of bills among the
committees in order to make possible the more intelligent
study and disposition of these bills.

In the interests of greater efficiency and as an effective time-
saving device, a joint committee system might be developed
in the bicameral legislature.   In three states of the union the
joint committee system now predominates.[107]   In this way
some of the advantages of a unicameral system might be
secured.[108]

The appointment of members to the committees might well
remain in the hands of the Speaker in the Assembly and of the
majority leader in the Senate,[109] although much could be said
for vesting the appointment of committees with a more repre-

---

[104] Greater need for a committee on Natural Resources and Conservation
may be anticipated with the recent establishment of the State Planning
Council. See *Report of the New York State Planning Board,* Jan. 14, 1935;
Report of the National Resources Board on State Planning, 1935, p. 67. Also
C. E. Merriam, "Planning Agencies in America," *American Political Science
Review,* Apr., 1935.

[105] The Senate in New York recently consolidated the committees on
Revision, and Printed and Engrossed Bills.

[106] See *Appendix B.*

[107] These states are Massachusetts, Connecticut, and Maine. *Cf.* Winslow,
op.cit., p. 32. In New York the joint committees that are established are,
for the most part, investigatory in character. See *New York Legislative
Manual,* 1935, p. 734. However, in New York, joint hearings of committees
of both houses of the legislature are frequently used.

[108] Difficulties might arise where the two houses are controlled by different
parties, but these do not appear insurmountable. The joint committee system
would minimize perhaps the need for the settlement of differences between
the two houses by the legislative leaders or through the conference committee.

[109] Senate Rule 3, Assembly Rule 1, Sec. 3, 1936.

sentative committee on committees. Whichever procedure is
followed, the rules of seniority and greater attention to the
training and experience of legislators might be observed more
closely.[110] The rapidly changing committee personnels and
multiplicity of committee assignments should be discouraged,
and, equally important, the legislative term could and should
be increased.[111]

These suggestions, if they are adopted, should improve the
committee system and tend to weaken the dictatorial and arbitrary control now existing in both houses. In addition, members might be more reluctant to bind themselves in caucus
agreements. A more liberal discharge rule in the Assembly,
especially, might operate against the indiscriminate and arbitrary smothering of bills by committees.[112] The systematic
recording of proceedings in the committees and legislative
chambers, so palpably neglected in New York and in most
other states, might better enable both the legislators and the
general public to know what is going on.[113]

It would be a physical impossibility for the legislature, as
at present organized, to give proper attention to as many as
4,500 bills, even if the sessions were substantially lengthened.
In the New York Legislature there is no serious limitation
placed upon the number of bills that may be introduced,

---

[110] Chamberlain, op.cit., p. 88.

[111] A four-year term is found in four states for the lower house and in
31 states for the upper house. Cf. State Government, Jan., 1933 and Jan.,
1935. New York and New Jersey are the only states that still retain the
one-year term for members of the lower house. There is an amendment
pending to the New York State constitution to raise the term of Assemblymen
to two years, corresponding to the term of New York Senators.

[112] In the Assembly, motions to discharge a committee from consideration
of a bill must be passed by a majority of all the members elected to that
body, whereas in the Senate a majority of a quorum is sufficient. Cf. Senate
Rule 25, Assembly Rule 11, New York Clerk's Manual, 1936.

[113] An assembly rule provides that stenographic notes be taken of debates,
to be filed with the clerk of the Assembly. Such notes are written out only
upon request by members and the stenographer is compensated by the
member. Cf. Assembly Rule 3, 1936. See Phillips Bradley, "Legislative
Recording in the United States," American Political Science Review, Feb.,
1935. Much time can be saved and some confusion avoided by an electrically
operated voting system and page call system. It was recently estimated
that approximately one-third of the legislature's time in New York is consumed in taking roll calls orally. Cf. Pamphlet: Modernize the Legislature,
published by the City Club of New York, 1932; Willoughby, op.cit.,
pp. 614–617.

although an Assembly rule requires that no bill may be introduced after the fifth of April, except by message from the Senate or with the unanimous consent of members of the Assembly.[114]

As a device that may discourage the introduction of so many unnecessary bills [115] and provide for a more systematic and logical sequence in the legislative process, it is suggested that the split or trifurcated session might be adopted in New York.[116] During the first period of the split session, bills would be introduced. Then the legislature would adjourn to permit study of bills and to provide for necessary hearings. Each of these first two periods would continue about a month. Upon reconvening for the third and final period, unlimited as to time, the business of the legislature would be concerned with bills reported for debate, revision, and vote. During this last period no bill would be allowed to be introduced, except with the approval of a large majority in each house.[117] It is hoped that with the split session, the legislature might get off to a prompt start and avoid the confusion and lack of discussion that characterizes the enactment of bills during the closing days of the session.[118] The second period would be in many respects the most important. It is hoped that during this period the opportunity would be afforded the gen-

---

[114] Assembly Rule 20, 1936.

[115] In general, state legislatures should be discouraged from handling local and private bills. Such legislation should be delegated to claims courts, administrative departments or commissions, or specially created local administrative agencies. See Chamberlain, *op. cit.*, pp. 238–242; Senate Rule 16 and Assembly Rule 7, 1936. Where retained by legislative bodies, it might be well to examine the judicial, non-partisan procedure provided for private bills in the British House of Commons. See in this connection, G. F. M. Campion, *An Introduction to the Procedure of the House of Commons*, London, P. Allan, 1929, ch. 9.

[116] For a summary of restrictions on the time for the introduction of bills in the 48 state legislatures, see *State Government*, Jan., 1933, reprinted in *The Book of the States*, 1935, Vol. I, p. 64.

[117] The same results may be accomplished through legislative rules, as in New Jersey.

[118] The split session is now in use in California. It has been authorized but not used in Massachusetts and Georgia. It was tried but abandoned in West Virginia in 1928. For the experience of these states with the split session, see Chamberlain, *op.cit.*, pp. 208–209; V. J. West, "Our Legislative Mills: California—the Home of the Split Session," *National Municipal Review*, July, 1923; M. L. Faust, "Results of the Split Session System of the West Virginia Legislature," *American Political Science Review*, Feb., 1928.

eral public to learn what bills were introduced and to give expression to their views on these bills. It would be neither a "loafing period" nor a "cooling off" recess.

It is during the second period that public hearings on bills would be held. The public hearing is a unique feature in the American legislative process and should be developed until it plays an important part in the process of popular government.[119] The public hearing affords an opportunity for the legislature to maintain the balance necessary if democratic government is to be preserved in the battle of opposing interest groups. It should be made an integral part of the legislative process, an inseparable adjunct of the committee system, with which it should share the honors in the orderly enactment of legislation. To this end, the customary procedure should call for a public hearing with reasonable advance notice on all important bills of a general nature. The presence of all members of the committee should be required unless they are specially excused. Important public hearing proceedings should be stenographically reported and printed, and should be part of the official records of the legislature. Sufficient time should be allowed, depending upon the importance of the legislation, to permit full opportunity for the presentation of information and for discussion between committee members and those supplying the information. The presentation of briefs should be encouraged, and they should be filed in time for members of committees to acquaint themselves with the evidence contained therein. Such procedure would force into the open those wishing to exert influence upon the legislature. They would be given their day in court before an impartial judge (it is hoped) who had not reached a decision before all the facts were in and all the witnesses heard from. Some of the information secured in this way might be incorporated in committee reports when bills were carried back to the legislative body for discussion and vote.[120] Information thus submitted could become the property of all members of the legislature, not merely of an individual member of the committee, and could be used effectively in debate in the legislative

---

[119] Willoughby, *op.cit.*, pp. 34, 368.

[120] The occasions are now rare indeed when committee reports accompany bills carried back to the chambers.

chamber. This would tend to check any arbitrary or unfair action by the committee. Furthermore, such information, if given the proper publicity, would tend to crystallize the public's views on the pending legislation.

If more importance were attached to the work of our public hearings in our state legislative bodies, it might serve as an incentive to the more poorly-organized groups with socially useful programs. It might serve as an incentive, for example, to the consumers, who have been out of the running in the highly competitive race of pressure politics. In addition, the institutionalization of the public hearing, in keeping with recent trends, would provide a modified functional representation in our legislative bodies.

It seems superfluous to add that the hearing, unless conducted in an honest, aboveboard manner with fair opportunity for all, can become an effective instrument through which groups with predatory interests can get their own way.[121]

In so far as one can see on the basis of a priori reasoning, these suggestions for reorganizing our legislative structure and procedure should go a long way toward redirecting the activity of pressure groups, now recognized as a serious menace to democratic governmental processes, into channels that would vitalize the representative character of governments.

---

[121] See Schattschneider, *op.cit.*, for intensive examination of the tariff in 1929–1930, wherein tactics employed in public hearings are discussed, some of which indicate unfair advantages accruing to interest groups.

APPENDICES

APPENDIX A

Personnel Study of the New York State Legislature

Year	Political Affiliations		Average Number of Years of Experience in the Legislature[1]	Legislators with no Previous Experience in Either House		Legislators With or Without College and/or Professional School Education			Principal Occupations of Legislators		
	Party	No.		No.	%		No.	%	Occupation	No.	%
1882[e]	Republican	76	1.106	95	59.3	Information not available			Lawyers	51	31.8
	Democrat	84							Farmers	30	18.7
									Other Professions	6	3.7
									Business	68	42.5
									Retired	2	1.2
									No information	3	1.8
1885[d]	Republican	91	1.200	78	48.7	Information not available			Lawyers	55	34.3
	Democrat	66							Farmers	22	13.7
	Labor and Republican	1							Other Professions	6	3.7
	Labor and Democrat	2							Business	76	47.5
									Retired	1	.6
1892[b]	Republican	75	1.575	72	45.0	With	78	48.7	Lawyers	46	28.7
	Democrat	84				Without	73	45.6	Farmers	27	16.8
	Independent Republican	1				No information	9	5.6	Other Professions	10	6.2
									Business	74	46.2
									Retired	2	1.2
									No information	1	.6

1900[c]											
Republican	120	1.960	66	33.0	With	100	50.0	Lawyers	66	33.0
Democrat	79				Without	81	40.5	Farmers	14	7.0
Independent Democrat	1				No information	19	9.5	Other Professions	7	3.5
								Business	111	55.5
								Retired	2	1.0

1907[b]											
Republican	131	2.109	84	41.7	With	126	62.6	Lawyers	79	39.3
Democrat	67				Without	63	31.3	Farmers	17	8.4
Independent	2				No information	12	5.9	Other Professions	9	4.4
Independence League	1							Business	89	44.2
								Retired	5	2.4
								No information	2	1.0

1909[a]											
Republican	133	2.355	69	34.5	With	128	64.0	Lawyers	86	43.0
Democrat	67				Without	62	31.0	Farmers	20	10.0
Vacancy	1				No information	10	5.0	Other Professions	11	5.5
								Business	81	40.5
								No information	2	1.0

1910[c]											
Republican	129	2.154	74	36.8	With	115	57.2	Lawyers	77	38.3
Democrat	70				Without	65	32.3	Farmers	20	10.0
Independence League	1				No information	21	10.4	Other Professions	11	5.4
United Citizens	1							Business	91	45.2
								No information	2	1.0

1913[a]											
Republican	59	1.786	97	48.2	With	114	56.7	Lawyers	76	37.8
Democrat	136				Without	70	34.8	Farmers	19	9.4
Independent Democrat	1				No information	17	8.4	Other Professions	15	7.4
National Progressive	5							Business	88	43.7
								Retired	3	1.4

1915[b]											
Republican	132	1.885	77	38.3	With	119	59.2	Lawyers	80	39.8
Democrat	66				Without	64	31.8	Farmers	26	12.9
Progressive	3				No information	18	8.9	Other Professions	6	2.9
								Business	86	42.7
								Retired	2	1.0
								No information	1	.5

Personnel Study of the New York State Legislature

Year	Political Affiliations		Average Number of Years of Experience in the Legislature[1]	Legislators with no Previous Experience in Either House		Legislators With or Without College and/or Professional School Education			Principal Occupations of Legislators		
	Party	No.		No.	%		No.	%	Occupation	No.	%
1921a	Republican	159	2.776	55	27.3	With	131	65.1	Lawyers	81	40.3
	Democrat	38				Without	46	22.8	Farmers	32	15.9
	Socialist	4				No information	24	11.9	Other Professions	10	4.9
									Business	75	37.3
									Retired	2	1.0
									No information	1	.5
1923b	Republican	106	2.751	62	30.8	With	133	66.1	Lawyers	82	40.7
	Democrat	95				Without	49	24.3	Farmers	24	11.9
						No information	19	9.4	Other Professions	13	6.4
									Business	77	38.3
									Retired	3	1.4
									No information	2	1.0
1928c	Republican	115	4.318	21	10.4	With	137	68.1	Lawyers	93	46.2
	Democrat	86				Without	52	25.8	Farmers	24	11.9
						No information	12	5.9	Other Professions	11	5.4
									Business	64	31.8
									Retired	8	3.9
									No information	1	.5

Year	Party										
1933[a]	Republican	102	5.437	28	13.9	With	139	69.1	Lawyers	94	46.7
	Democrat	99				Without	50	24.8	Farmers	22	10.9
						No information	12	5.9	Other Professions	11	5.4
									Business	68	33.8
									Retired	6	2.9
1934[e]	Republican	104	4.721	50	24.8	With	147	73.1	Lawyers	95	47.2
	Democrat	91				Without	41	20.4	Farmers	19	9.4
	Republican-Fusion[2]	5				No information	13	6.4	Other Professions	9	4.4
	Independent	1							Business	71	35.3
									Retired	6	2.9
									No information	1	.5
1935[b]	Republican	95	4.696	37	18.4	With	146	72.6	Lawyers	95	47.2
	Democrat	106				Without	41	20.4	Farmers	18	8.9
						No information	14	6.9	Other Professions	7	3.4
									Business	71	35.3
									Retired	10	4.9

[a] Both houses of the Legislature elected at same time as President of the United States and the Governor of New York.
[b] Both houses of the Legislature elected at same time as the Governor of New York.
[c] Election of Assembly only (without state Senate or President or Governor).
[d] Assembly elected at same time as President of the United States.
[e] Both houses of the Legislature elected without the President or the Governor.

[1] Senate for previous year excluded from computation in 1885, 1900, 1910, 1928, 1934.
[2] In the Legislature of 1934 a larger number of Republican assemblymen were returned from New York City than usual because of Mayor La Guardia's Republican-Fusion victory.

APPENDIX B

Standing Committees of the New York State Legislature (1935)

SENATE

29 Democrats....56.8 per cent
22 Republicans...43.1 per cent

Name of Committee	No. of Members	Party Representation		No. of Bills Referred	% of Bills Referred
		Dem.	Rep.		
Judiciary	14	9	5	359	16.8
Internal Affairs of Towns, Counties and Public Highways	16	12	4	193	9.0
Codes	13	9	4	187	8.7
Finance	20	16	4	182	8.5
Taxation and Retrenchment	9	6	3	120	5.6
Affairs of the City of New York	9	6	3	93	4.3
Affairs of Cities	13	9	4	91	4.2
Public Education	11	7	4	89	4.1
Labor and Industry	10	7	3	75	3.5
Conservation	11	8	3	71	3.3
Motor Transportation and Traffic Regulation	10	7	3	71	3.3
General Laws	10	7	3	62	2.9
Insurance	16	10	6	58	2.7
Banks	9	6	3	57	2.6
Pensions	12	8	4	55	2.5
Affairs of Villages	9	6	3	54	2.5
Public Service	11	8	3	48	2.2

ASSEMBLY

77 Democrats.....51.3 per cent
73 Republicans...48.6 per cent

Name of Committee	No. of Members	Party Representation		No. of Bills Referred	% of Bills Referred
		Dem.	Rep.		
Judiciary	15	10	5	484	19.2
Codes	15	10	5	281	11.1
Ways and Means	15	12	3	209	8.2
Internal Affairs	15	13	2	201	7.9
Mortgage and Real Estate	13	9	4	137	5.4
Taxation and Retrenchment	15	11	4	125	4.9
Insurance	13	10	3	91	3.6
Labor and Industries	13	9	4	91	3.6
Conservation	15	11	4	80	3.1
Motor Vehicles	13	9	4	79	3.1
Public Education	13	10	3	78	3.0
Claims	13	7	6	77	3.0
Public Service	13	9	4	77	3.0
Pensions	13	8	5	76	3.0
Affairs of the City of New York	13	9	4	68	2.7
Banks	15	12	3	59	2.3
Public Relief and Welfare	13	9	4	59	2.3
Affairs of Villages	13	10	3	57	2.2
Affairs of Cities	13	9	4	55	2.1
Agriculture	15	12	3	34	1.3

Committee					
Public Relief and Welfare	13	9	4	36	1.6
Agriculture	15	11	4	34	1.5
Public Health	10	7	3	25	1.1
Civil Service	12	8	4	23	1.0
Excise	14	10	4	22	
Mortgages and Real Estate	16	12	4	17	
Penal Institutions	8	5	3	16	
Military Affairs	9	6	3	3	
Commerce and Navigation	9	6	3	2	
Public Printing, Revision and Engrossed Bills	11	8	3	1	
Reapportionment	15	10	5	1	
Privileges and Elections	8	6	2	0	
Rules	5	4	1	0	
No Committee				87	
Totals	348	243 (69.8 per cent)	105 (30.1 per cent)	2,132	

Committee					
Excise	13	9	4	29	1.1
Penal Institutions	13	8	5	22	
Public Health	13	8	5	19	
General Laws	13	8	5	14	
Reapportionment	13	9	4	4	
Canals	13	9	4	2	
Aviation	13	9	4	1	
Military Affairs	13	8	5	1	
Charitable and Religious Societies	13	7	6	0	
Commerce and Navigation	13	7	6	0	
Public Institutions	13	7	6	0	
Public Printing	13	7	6	0	
Printed and Engrossed Bills	7	5	2	0	
Revision	13	8	5	0	
Social Welfare	13	7	6	0	
Soldiers' Home	13	7	6	0	
Rules	15	11	4	0	
No Committee				9	
Totals	493	333 (67.5 per cent)	160 (32.4 per cent)	2,519	

[a] The Senate majority and minority leaders serve as ex officio members on these committees.
[b] The Assembly Rules Committee is very powerful because all bills not reported by standing committees within ten days of adjournment are referred to Rules. See supra, p. 277.

Index

Colvin, D. L., 274

Colvin, Mrs. D. L., 227

Commission on Interstate Compacts, 56

Committees (*see* Standing committees of New York State Legislature)

Communist Party, 248

Condon, W. F., 11

Conference Board of Farm Organizations (*see* New York State Conference Board of Farm Organizations)

Conference committee, 274–275

Conference of Mayors (*see* New York State Conference of Mayors)

Congress of Parents and Teachers (*see* New York State Congress of Parents and Teachers)

Congressional Union, 36

Consolidated Edison Company of New York, 65, 74–76

Construction Council (*see* New York State Construction Council)

Consumers, 76, 83, 251, 263–265

Consumers' League of New York:
campaign for forty-eight hour week and minimum wage legislation, 31–40
organization and activities of, 8, 29–40

Control of the lobby, 251–289

Convention of Societies for the Prevention of Cruelty to Children and Animals of New York State, 248

Cooper, R. D., 124

Cooperative Grange League Federation Exchange, Inc., 117–119

Cornell University:
Agricultural Experiment Station, 86
Colleges of Agriculture and Home Economics, 85–86, 104, 107–109, 120
Geneva Agricultural Experiment Station, 86
Morrill Act, 85
(*See also* Agricultural setup in New York State)

Cortelyou, G. D., 80

Corwin, E. H. L., 188

Cosby, A. F., 59

Council of City and Village Superintendents, 158, 163–164

Council of State Governments, 258, 266

County Farm and Home Bureau Associations, 88–91

County Superintendents of the Poor (*see* New York State Association of Public Welfare Officials)

Crisfman, F. W., 225

Crone, F. W., 67, 68, 71

Cummings, T. P., 204, 248

Curry, H. I., 136, 137, 149

Curtis, G. W., 220

Cutler, G. C., 255

Cuvillier, L. E., 257

D

Dairymen's League Cooperative Association, 110–117, 119, 245

Daly, M. A., 36, 52–56, 244, 248

Delegations to State Capitol, 38, 242, 244, 245, 280

Democratic Party, relations of labor groups with, 21–26, 237, 276

Denison, M., 234

Depression, effect of, on demands of pressure groups, 249–250

Dewey, A. G., 237

Dewey, John, 265

Dewey, Melvil, 266

Dewson, Mary, 40

Diamond, H. M., 72

Dimock, M. E., 270

Disabled American Veterans of World War, 204

Dodd, B. V., 175, 248

Dodds, H. W., 278

Doody, L. M., 152

Dorr, H. M., 273

Doyle, E. P., 43, 248, 249

Drier, M. E., 36

Dry forces, legislative pressure by, 222–228

Dunne, G. F., 248, 249

Dunnigan, J. J., 16

E

Eaton, D. B., 220

Eaton, M. C., 22, 23

Ecob, K. C., 141

Economic Council (*see* New York State Economic Council)

Edison Electric Institute, 66, 76

Educational group pressure in New York State, 156–180

Ehrlich, H. B., 22

Eighteenth Amendment, repeal of, 223–224, 226, 276